"The most factual writing by any author on the Shoshone Nation."

Raymond D. Yowell
Western Shoshone Citizen

"I wholeheartedly support the truth as written in Mr. Gale Ontko's series, *Thunder Over the Ochoco*. This writing is most exciting, factual and represents the Shoshone oral history as close as could be expected. He represents our heroes as no other could—dog soldiers such as Red Wolf, Wolf Dog and Has No Horse, men who played such important roles in our history and culture.

Jack C. Orr (Dogowa)
Citizen of the Western Shoshone Nation

Also by Gale Ontko:

Thunder Over the Ochoco, Volume I: The Gathering Storm

Thunder Over the Ochoco, Volume II: Distant Thunder

Thunder Over the Ochoco, Volume III: Lightning Strikes!

To be published:

Thunder Over the Ochoco, Volume V: And the Juniper Trees Bore Fruit

THUNDER OVER THE OCHOCO

RAIN OF TEARS

Volume IV

GALE ONTKO

Illustrations by Gale Ontko

— A Maverick Publication —

ISBN 0-89288-275-1

Library of Congress Catalog Card Number: 93-18698

On the cover:
Moving Camp by John Clymer
Courtesy of Mrs. Doris S. Clymer
and the Clymer Museum of Ellensburg, Washington

For additional copies of Gale Ontko's books, contact:
Maverick Publications
(541) 382-6978
1-800-800-4831

Published and printed by Maverick Publications, Inc.
P.O. Box 5007
Bend, Oregon 97708

DEDICATION

To my grandchildren,
the sixth generation to live and play
in the Upper Ochoco Valley.

Top row, left to right: Jason, Rachel, Jerad.
Middle row, left to right: Erin, Kyle, Celee.
Bottom row, left to right: McKenna, Tamera, Necole.

IN MEMORY OF

Andrew Gale Ontko

Born: August 18, 1927
Died: July 2, 1998

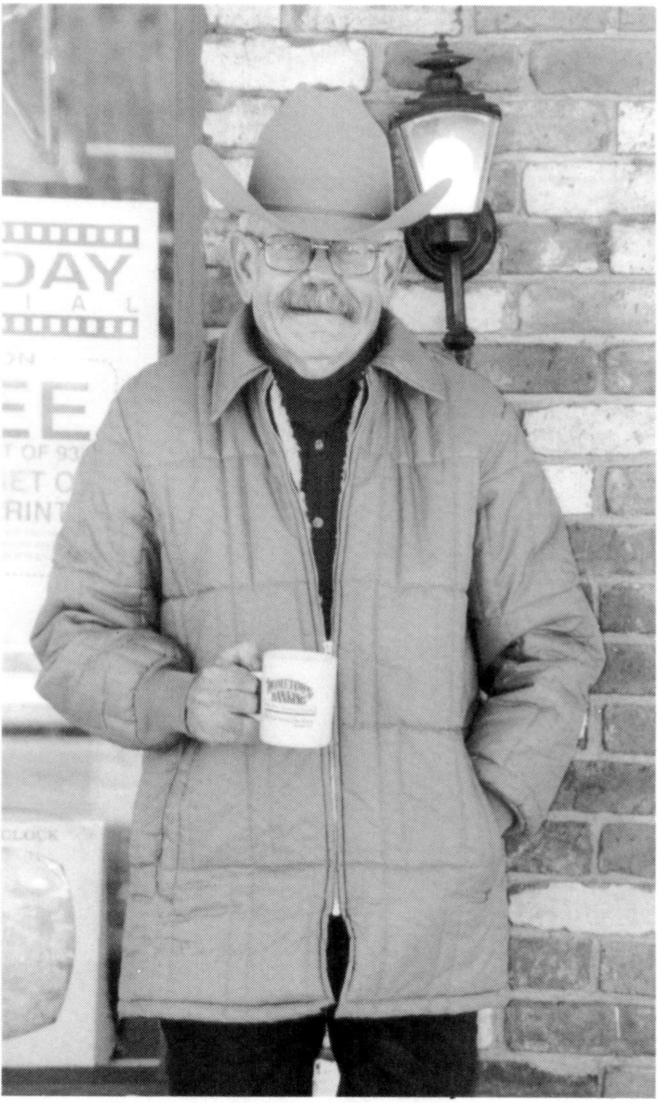

TABLE OF CONTENTS

PART VI
Rain of Tears

APPENDICES

FOREWORD

By Jim and Peggy Iler
Richland, Oregon

History is always written by the conquerors. The vanquished rarely have a voice. In the softening and wearing of old father time, however, their story might be told, but only by a great and exhaustive undertaking by dedicated historian-authors.

Our real interest in history is our own backyard, the Ochoco country. For many years we have studied old journals, pioneer stories, government records and a few isolated regional books, but the whole picture was never there. This is a big country, and we always knew a lot happened here, but had no way of putting it all together. Over time, there was a gnawing empty void. We would see the remnants of earlier days, a rusted wagon rim in the desert, a depressed wickiup ring beside a dry lake bed. We felt the ghosts of interesting people and yearned to know their stories. One eventful day in 1994, we were rummaging through the fabulous "Oregon Room" at Eastern Oregon State University in La-Grande, Oregon, and happened to find a new book called *Thunder Over the Ochoco, Volume I, The Gathering Storm*. We could not believe our good fortune! We argued over "reading rights" until we bought our own copy. That copy is now so ragged, dog-eared, and notated that it looks like a survivor of the Lost Wagon Train of '45! We had finally found information and truth bound up in a fabulous living story.

The author, Gale Ontko, we soon found, spoke his mind and spared no traditional conceptions. He had wrestled and tackled this local history for decades, a life-work unknown to most of his friends and associates. The task of compiling, cataloging and organizing a library full of material, packing in liberal footnotes and whopping bibliography and then transforming it into a highly readable, interesting story line which fills FIVE volumes is indeed a marvel! In our own personal research of old records we found that Mr. Ontko had not only reported the collaborated facts (many never before in public print), but had splendidly interpreted the emotion and gist of the times. And what times they were!

If not for Mr. Ontko's work, we would never have known of the incredible exploits and accomplishments of Shoshoni chiefs such as Wolf Dog, Has No Horse, Winnemucca, and Paulina. These never-before chronicled stories portray them to be more skilled as warriors, more formidable as foes, more ingenious, and more tenacious survivalists than other well-known chiefs whose stories were not covered up for pure political purposes. The flight of Chief Joseph, the saga of Geronimo, the victory of Sitting Bull all pale in comparison to our unheralded local freedom fighters.

Our lives have changed since we discovered this literary legacy. Our hobby has been expanded to higher levels of interest as we discover within its pages obscure characters and places that intrigue us. We spend a great deal of time exploring the back country from Astoria, Oregon, to South Pass, Wyoming, just to experience standing on sites where so much has happened. We enjoy talking to the local ranchers and to the local Indian people about events of significance in their area that we have read about. We always visit local historical societies and add their material to our private library. We have met the relatives of several *Thunder* characters and have developed some valued friendships. We have sat and talked with the oldest local Shoshoni/Paiute alive (age 96) who, as a boy, remembers old Chief Has No Horse in his final exciting assault (with his cane) against a white teacher who was abusing the Indian school children.

Gale Ontko is giving us the exciting story of our region in these volumes. Of significance is the support and great interest of the Western Shoshoni Nation, who have seen much of their rich oral history in writing for the first time. Mr. Ontko has no interest whatever in politics or agendas or political correctness (as Volumes IV and V will more vividly demonstrate), and to him, history is purely a story of humanity and what truly happened. He has overcome many obstacles and has successfully defended his work against twisted traditional concepts, prejudices, and attitudes. Gale Ontko is a paradox, for in this case it can truly be said that the true history of the Ochoco country is written by the conqueror.

ACKNOWLEDGMENTS

By writing man has been able to put something of himself beyond death. . . a row of black marks on a page can move a person to tears though the bones of him that wrote it are long ago crumbled to dust.

Julian Huxley

I found the above citation to be especially true when pouring over the journals, diaries and random notes of those who recorded their private thoughts accompanied by personal observations which contributed in large measure to the writing of *Rain of Tears*. Their recognition of what was happening during this period provides the glue which binds the other information into a meaningful work. In preparing this volume I am indebted to many people for putting me on the right track. Although I gained valuable firsthand testimony from early settlers of Crook, Grant, Baker and Harney counties I still had to rely heavily on other sources of information. Included in this group are U.S. House and Senate Executive documents, U.S. War Department Reports, U.S. Bureau of Indian Affairs Reports, U.S. Bureau of Commerce Records, Oregon Legislative Documents and eastern Oregon county records. I am also grateful for all the help received from staff members of the National Archives, Washington, D.C.; the Library of Congress; the Oregon Archives, Salem, Oregon; the Bancroft Library, Berkeley, California; and the many central libraries I visited throughout the western states.

Many people helped not only in providing data but in finding and sharing photographs which appear in this volume. Among those are Lois Wocken (Grant County Chamber of Commerce), Ellen Stull and Grace Williams (information on old photos, Canyon City Museum), Hugh Forrell (information on old photos, Canyon City and Whiskey Gulch), Greg Hodges and Larry Purchase (research team on the Bannock War),

Mabel Wilson Binns and Norma Macy Smith (descendants of James Macy, Army scout in the Bannock War), Maxine Stocks (Sunshine Mine, Crook County), Sara Gooch and Paula Murphy (Modoc County Historical Society and Museum), Jo Anne Cordis (Central Oregon Community College), Melissa Minthorn (Tamustalik Cultural Institute, Umatilla Reservation, Pendleton, Oregon), Tom Black (Bannock War information), Gene Luckey (Harney County Historical Society), Raymond Yowell (Western Shoshoni National Council, Indian Springs, Nevada), Steve Lent (central Oregon historic photos, Crook County Historical Society), and Gordon Gillespe (historic photos, Bowman Museum, Prineville, Oregon).

And last but not least, my heartfelt thanks to Bridget Wise who went far beyond the call of duty to make certain that all volumes of *Thunder Over the Ochoco* were correctly presented.

Gale Ontko

INTRODUCTION

Disregarding Western Shoshoni traditional land use the United States immediately encouraged its citizens to enter our territory and claim up all lands. We have faced every form of adversity, degradation and misery known to mankind.

Western Shoshoni National Council
How to Kill a Nation

The thirteen year interval between 1866 and 1879 would witness monumental changes in the Ochoco. Following the U.S. Army's 1868 victory over a starving foe lacking in military power and strength, hundreds of American homesteaders whooped and jostled over the Lost Emigrant Trail leading from The Dalles City to the Ochoco Valley where a brawling settlement had mushroomed on the sullen banks of the Ochoco River. Known throughout the Pacific Northwest as "The Bucket of Blood, U.S.A." this frontier trading post—named for a saloon keeper—was destined to go down in history as Prineville. . . county seat of Crook; oldest town in central Oregon; and the spawning ground for Oregon's bloodiest war! But for the moment the major concern of the newcomers was to hold the Indians at bay while confiscating their tribal lands.

Four years after the Shoshoni setback, Modoc rebels—skirting the southwest boundary of the Shoshoni Ochoco—made a last-ditch effort to sever relations with the U.S. government. They were successful in holding the enemy at a standstill for several months during which time peace commissioners sent into the Modoc stronghold to negotiate a cease-fire were slaughtered. This action caused the newly arrived citizens in the Ochoco Valley to panic, believing that the Shoshoni had joined with the Modoc dissidents. There is little doubt that Shoshoni dog soldiers were lending their covert support to this worthwhile cause.

During the period of insurrection, gold—from the grassroots down as one enthusiastic prospector would put it—was discovered on Scissors Creek, a tributary of the upper Ochoco River. This wasn't the type of publicity that the new residents of the Ochoco desired. If word of a gold strike got out it could lure undesirables into the area—such as gamblers, prostitutes and thieves. It might even—heaven forbid—encourage the immigration of "heathen Chinese" laborers which Oregon officials were doing their utmost to discourage. Therefore, another information blackout was in progress. Meantime, Has No Horse and his weary followers continued to roam their old haunts, discreetly avoiding any contact with the invaders and their destructive herds of sheep and cattle. It wasn't easy, as the stockmen offered the Shoshoni the same consideration they would have extended to a sheep-killing coyote. But the day was fast approaching when the old White Knife dog soldier would refuse to turn the other cheek and eastern Oregon would be saturated with the blood of men and livestock alike. In keeping with the times, his patience snapped when a herd of Idaho hogs rooted out a Shoshoni camas patch.

THUNDER OVER THE OCHOCO

RAIN OF TEARS

Volume IV

Part VI

RAIN OF TEARS

RAIN OF TEARS

1866-1879
THE SETTLEMENT OF CENTRAL OREGON

I do not believe there was another spot in the whole nation so near to the first principle of human society as ours. We had neither law, gospel nor medicine.

George Barnes, Prineville Attorney

The Civil War had split the Union in half. The Shoshoni war had split Oregon not into halves but into thirds—with the western one-third of the state showing interest in the eastern two-thirds only to the extent of what it could reap economically from lands it had wrenched from the native population. Now, with the surrender of Has No Horse's battered army, western Oregon had free rein to exploit the Ochoco as it saw fit. Eager opportunists would breach the Cascades before the final shots of war were fired and they would find that the land itself was a cruel adversary. In a blind daze, the Shoshoni would witness frontier towns spring up where once their lodges stood. The unwelcome guests of two hostile reservations, they chose to roam their old haunts—no longer rulers of the land, but scavengers finding whatever they could to survive. As thousands upon thousands of bawling cattle and sheep trampled their ancestral hunting grounds to dust, the proud warriors of a by-gone year again rebelled. And, for a fleeting moment, shook the state of Oregon to its very foundations. Then it was over. Stripped even of reservation rights, the few survivors drifted between the four winds on their final journey into the bitter rain of tears.

If the Indian cried "Rape!" the whites would tell him it was not rape, but love, and its child would be progress.

Wallace Stegner, Western Critic

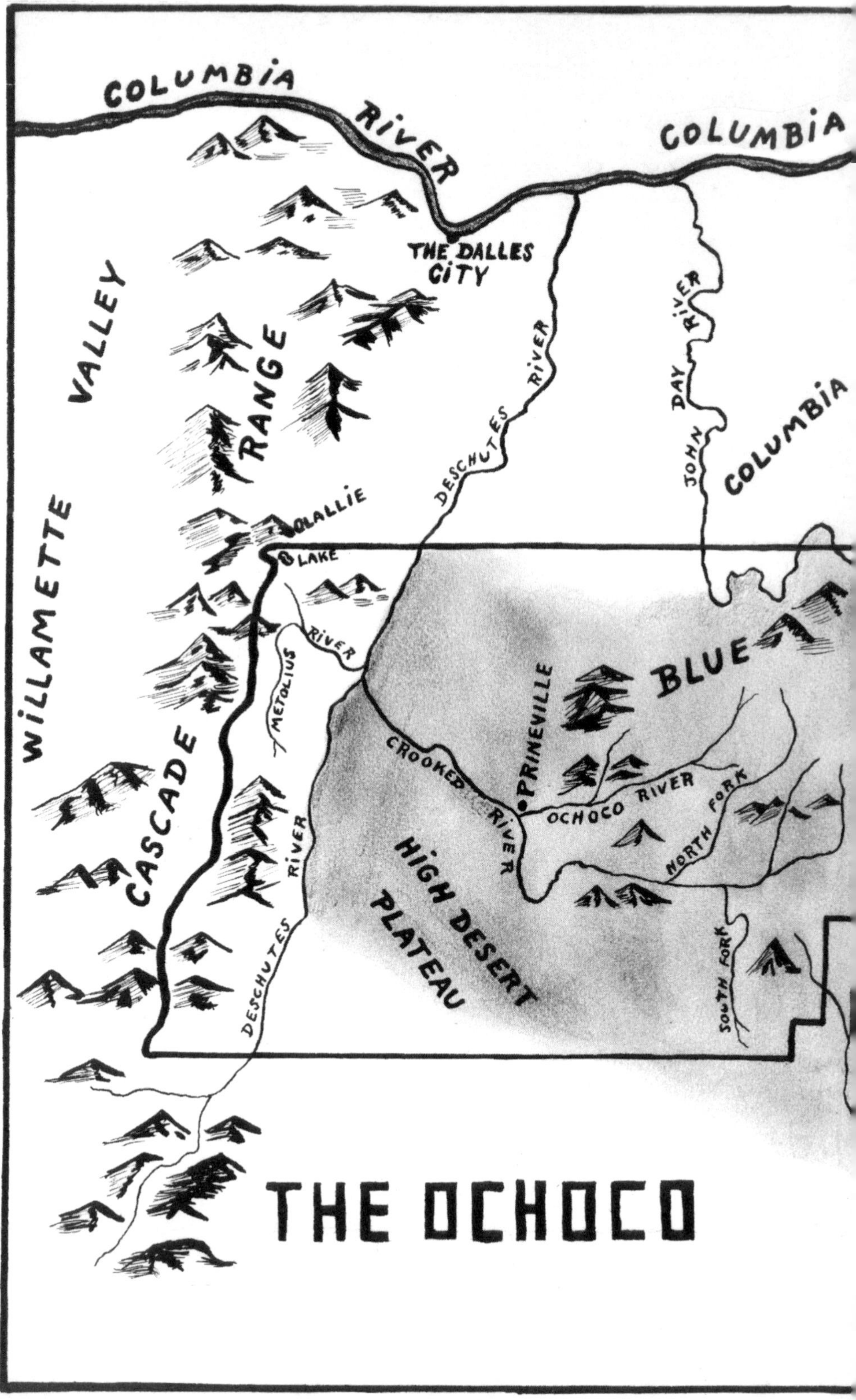
COLUMBIA
RIVER
COLUMBIA
THE DALLES CITY
VALLEY
RANGE
DESCHUTES RIVER
JOHN DAY RIVER
COLUMBIA
WILLAMETTE
OLALLIE LAKE
METOLIUS RIVER
BLUE
PRINEVILLE
CROOKED RIVER
OCHOCO RIVER
NORTH FORK
CASCADE
HIGH DESERT PLATEAU
DESCHUTES RIVER
SOUTH FORK
THE OCHOCO

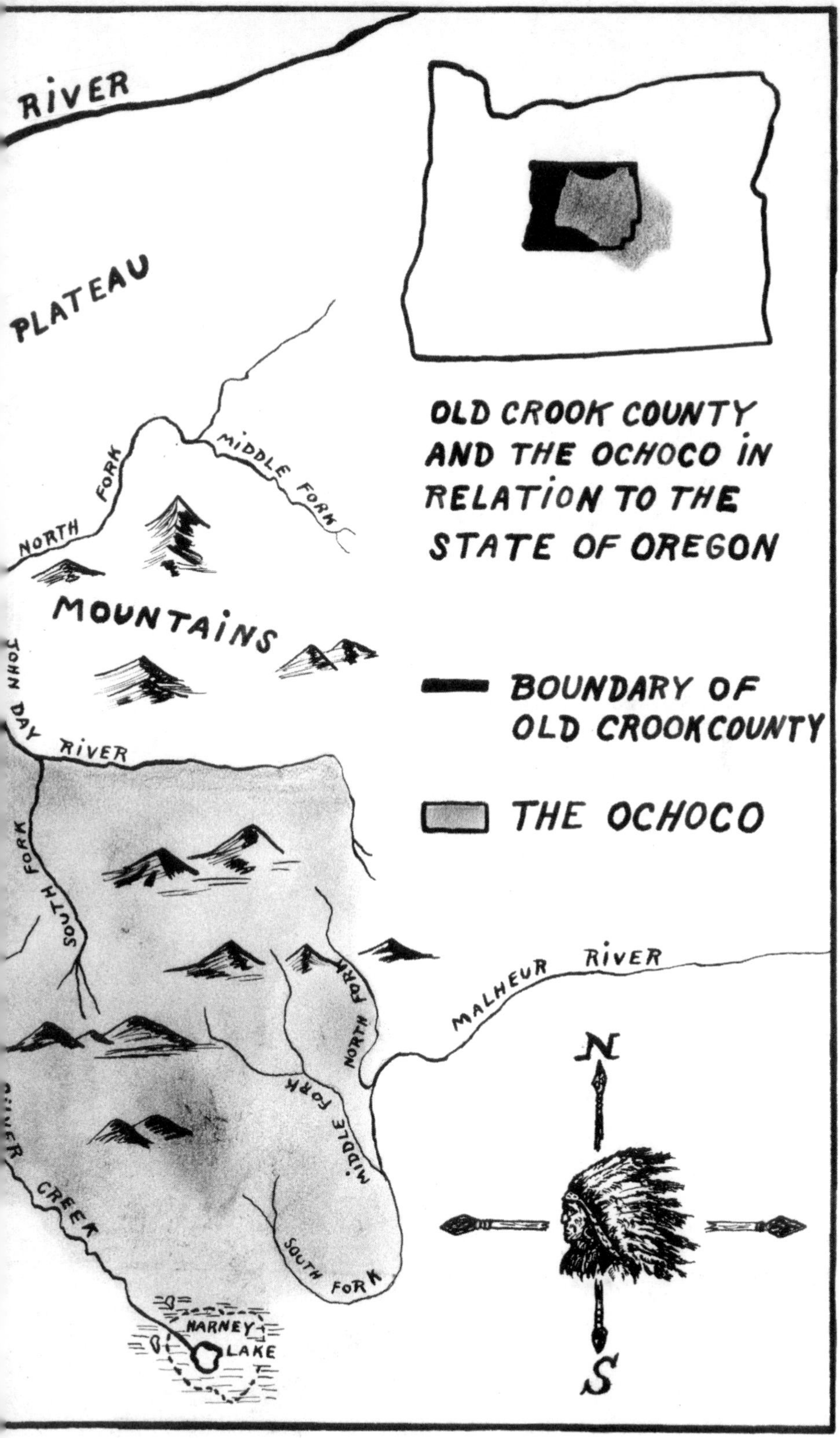
RIVER
PLATEAU
NORTH FORK
MIDDLE FORK
MOUNTAINS
JOHN DAY RIVER
SOUTH FORK
NORTH FORK
MIDDLE FORK
SOUTH FORK
MALHEUR RIVER
CREEK
HARNEY LAKE
OLD CROOK COUNTY AND THE OCHOCO IN RELATION TO THE STATE OF OREGON
BOUNDARY OF OLD CROOK COUNTY
THE OCHOCO
N
S

CHAPTER 150

INTO THE OCHOCO

Not a drum was heard, not a bugle note, as our course down stream we worried. But like boys caught in a melon patch, we whooped, and humped, and hurried.

George Barnes
Ochoco Homestead Party, 1866

Deep in the rimrock country of central Oregon, Capt. Charles LaFollette in command of Co. A, 1st Oregon Volunteer Infantry, moved cautiously into the lower Crooked River Valley. It was late September 1865. Near the mouth of McKay Creek, he found his brother, Lt. Jerome LaFollette and Sgt. George Moore who, with a platoon of Co. H, had been missing for two days. Because of this delay, Capt. LaFollette had lost precious time.

Some sixty miles to the west, Capt. Edward Newton White, commander of Co. B, 1st Oregon Infantry and Sgt. George Conn, with a detachment of Oregon Cavalry, had been assigned escort duty for the newly formed Willamette Valley and Cascade Mountain Military Road Company now hacking a crude trail up the western slope of the Cascades to provide a supply line from the upper Willamette Valley to the army posts in eastern Oregon and western Idaho. LaFollette and Capt. Berryman Jennings—White's brother-in-law—were supposed to rendezvous with White at the eastern base of the Cascade Mountains.[1]

Rumor was running rampant that all volunteers were to be mustered out of the service immediately and replaced by regular army

1 Both White and Jennings were members of the lost wagon train which traversed the Ochoco in 1845. See *Thunder Over the Ochoco*, Vol. II, pp. 36, 44, 54. Capt. Berryman Jennings was married to Lucinda White, Capt. White's sister.

personnel—veterans of the Civil War. At this time all terms of enlistment had expired, yet LaFollette was marching on orders to establish winter headquarters in central Oregon in an effort to block the Snakes from escaping Lt. Col. Drake's advance from the east. During his march across eastern Oregon, Capt. LaFollette had been recording and marking elevations with an aneroid barometer. On his return to the Cascades, he crossed the Deschutes River just below the present Tumalo Avenue bridge, long before Mirror Pond took shape. At this crossing, the soldiers established a bench mark. Data on that marker was used in the early 1900s in mapping irrigation ditch intakes and for establishing street lines in the city of Bend.

Some forty miles west of the confluence of the Ochoco and Crooked rivers, LaFollette pulled his troops to a halt and established winter quarters on Squaw Creek, naming the barren outpost Camp Polk in honor of his home county. Meanwhile, White moved over the Cascades with the road company equipment—which consisted of a one-horse fresno (an earth mover) and nothing more. Scouting for him was William Smith, an ex-Hudson's Bay employee and currently agent for the road company.

Smith had been unable to locate LaFollette, so upon reaching the Metolius River, White set up camp some twelve miles northwest of LaFollette's camp, naming his headquarters Camp Sherman for the famed Civil War hero, William Tecumseh Sherman. Both waited patiently for the other to arrive. Finally, in late November, Sgt. William Moulder, wagon master for the Oregon command, moved into White's camp and let it be known that there were two military detachments in the area and they best get together as there was a large Shoshoni encampment in the lower Ochoco Valley. After much discussion over defensible positions, White abandoned his outpost and moved in with LaFollette.

In this camp was born the nucleus of a settling party that would enter the Ochoco Valley. Chief instigators were the two captains and Lt. LaFollette. They were heartily joined by Sgt. Moore and Pvts. Albert Allen, James Allen, Charles Palmehn and Jerome Parsons of LaFollete's command; and Sgt. Wayne Claypool, Pvt. Raymond Burkhart, and Pvt. Calvin Burkhart of White's command. It just so happened that White was also a brother-in-law to the Burkharts, having married their sister, Catherine, who had recently passed away.

During the long winter months to follow, talk ran high. The soldiers believed they had the inside track. By spring of '66, word drifted in that the Scott brothers—who had tried settlement in 1862—had sneaked into the Trout Creek area again this winter and once more had been chased out by Has No Horse's warriors. George Masterson and James Clark had also been run out of the Bridge Creek country. To date, the only white men who claimed any part of the Ochoco as their own—and only because they were under the protective wing of Fort Watson—were Chris Meyer and Frank Hewot on Alkali Flat; George Jones in Spanish Gulch; Ed Allen (brother to Albert and James) on Mountain Creek; and Howard Maupin up on the head of Trout Creek who had little good to say about the country. In short, the Ochoco was wide open for the taking if you could dodge the Indians.

In late spring, the volunteers marched over the Cascades to be mustered out of the service at Eugene City, turning over the Indian fighting to Lt. Col. George Crook's professionals. On arrival at Eugene City, LaFollette and White started talking up a homestead party. However, news from the Shoshoni front brought on very few takers. In fact, some of the original avid promoters, namely Charles LaFollette, the Allen boys, Palmehn and Cal Burkhart decided to pass and others were weakening. Perhaps one thing that finally convinced a few hardy souls to take the challenge was a devil-may-care Irishman, John O'Neil, an ex-49er who had just pulled into Eugene City from the Kootenai goldfields in British Columbia.

O'Neil and his partner, Ed Freeland, not only volunteered to take the risk but O'Neil enticed weaker souls with the offer to take along his girlfriend, Rhesa Kraus, a Bavarian beauty he had picked up in the rowdy settlement at the mouth of the Willamette River. This offer caused many eyebrows to raise and no doubt explains why the various accounts of the first homestead party into the Ochoco Valley list an "unnamed person" in the group.

For obvious reasons, Rhesa's presence in an all male stronghold has been a well-guarded secret. It is recorded that "Mrs. Reason Hamlin" was the first white woman in the Ochoco Valley.[2] Unless she arrived running ahead of the pack, this is not likely. Jane Hamlin arrived

2 "History of Prineville," *Oregon Journal*, March 31, 1927, p. 4.

arm-in-arm with Nancy Johnson, Harriett Veazie, and Suzanna Barnes to name just a few. As for single girls, there were Clara and Elizabeth Claypool; Della and Clara Clark; Celestine and Margaret Johnson; and Etta and Ginevra Marks.

Whatever, Miss Kraus' presence caused problems. Maybe she accompanied the gentlemen colonizers going on the old adage that it took a woman's touch to make the frontier cabin a home. Probably the men agreed but others such as Suzanna Barnes, Louisa Claypool and Anna White didn't quite see it in that light. About the only one who could be trusted on this excursion was Billy Smith, a confirmed bachelor.

While the battle of the sexes was going on, George Jones and Ed Allen had arrived from the interior and were also organizing a homestead party. Unhampered by petticoats, they struck out in the late summer of 1866 with Jerry Parsons, Sam Coleman, Cal McCracken, Joe Huntley and Andy Clarno headed for the John Day Valley. These men holed up for the winter on Rock Creek within gunshot of Fort Watson.

Three weeks after their departure, Capt. White moved out and headed for Crooked River followed by Billy Smith, ex-Sgt. Wayne Claypool, soldier of fortune Johnny O'Neil, Ray Burkhart and his new brother-in-law, Ed Freeland. At Lebanon in Linn County, White picked up Elisha Barnes, a tough privateer from Kentucky recently out of California. Left behind was an exceedingly irate Rhesa Kraus.

Moving over ten-foot snow drifts, they crossed over into no-man's land and arrived at the mouth of the Ochoco River in October, 1866. The first item on the agenda was to locate a proper shelter. White, wise in the way of Indians, knew that the junction of the two rivers was a mighty poor place to go into a winter encampment. Moving some ten miles up the Ochoco, the pioneers found a sheltered basin at the mouth of a tributary which they later named Mill Creek. At the mouth of this feeder stream, Claypool staked his claim. Billy Smith moved up stream a couple of miles and built a log cabin. He didn't like company.

There was little to do during the winter except survive. Deer hunting became the main pastime, causing some friction between Barnes and Burkhart. According to Barnes, "Burkhart owned a Henry rifle—one of the first made. It had a bad habit of scattering and was liable to hit anything but what it was aimed at. Its idiosyncrasy in this respect was apt to throw the shooter into a state of mind not altogether conducive to moral perfection." After nearly being shot a few times, Barnes was downright happy when "Indians stole the gun."[3] This vanguard of the Ochoco emigration came in the fall of the year mainly to test central Oregon weather to see if it would be safe to winter livestock in the area. Oddly, the winter of 1866-67—while devastating to the south—was one of the mildest winters recorded in the Crooked River basin. A hundred miles to the south, Crook's army was bogged down in drifting snow and facing sub-zero temperatures.

Elisha Barnes—writing to a friend—described that first winter on the Ochoco. Although exceptionally mild weather-wise, other aspects were not so pleasant. "There was not a white man living within one hundred miles of this place except at the Warm Springs Agency and they were 60 miles from us. This valley seemed to be the winter quarters of some of the worst renegade bands of the Snake Indians who was at war with all the other tribes in this country and was also exceedingly hostile to the whites. Unable to recross the Cascades, we was shut up here with about 300 of those Snake Indians all winter but being well armed and very causious [sic] succeeded in keeping them at bay until spring when they made a raid on us and captured all our stock."[4]

In April 1867, leaving O'Neil and Freeland to look after the claims, the rest of the men hiked over to Camp Polk for supplies only to find it abandoned. Crook had decided it was one of the poorer locations for an army outpost and never re-manned the depot. Leaving what personal property they had packed to Camp Polk under the care of White, the remainder of the group struggled over the Cascades for much needed provisions.

While Claypool's party was breaking trail over the mountains, more homesteaders followed the Canyon City Trail to Jones' settlement on Rock Creek.[5] By now, the Ochoco had lost its luster for the Burkharts and they decided to stay on the Willamette side of the Cascades. In the meantime, Ewen Johnson, a Kentuckian who arrived with the 1865 emigration; William Elkins, an official for the Willamette Valley and

3 George Barnes (Elisha's son) account in *The Prineville News*, June 1887.

4 Elisha Barnes' letter to R.V. Ankeny dated April 21, 1882. Found in the walls of the Barnes house at 136 S. Beaver Street, Prineville, Oregon in 1942.

5 This party included ex-Sgt. George Moore, William Saltman, Wick Cusick, Jim McNeil, Al Sutton, Jake Smith, Robert Seman, Henry Hal and Jim Marshall.

Cascades Mountain Military Road Company; and George Barnes, Elisha's teenage son, planned to join White's expedition on Mill Creek in the spring. When Rhesa Kraus found out about this, it didn't take long to persuade young George to include her in the group. Wallowing through snowdrifts ten to thirty feet deep, the new arrivals picked up White at Camp Polk in June and plowed into the Ochoco Valley only to find O'Neil and Freeland missing. When a couple of days passed and they didn't show up, speculation ran high that their hair was decorating some warrior's lodge. They were half right.

Thirteen years later in 1880, Freeland again made an appearance in the Ochoco Valley. He gave no reason for his long absence but did confirm that O'Neil had been killed by the Shoshoni a few days after the relief party had left for Camp Polk. Anyway, with Johnny missing, Rhesa was ready to abandon camp.

It is recorded that when young Barnes saw the Ochoco Valley, he jumped in the air, clapped his hands and yelled, "This is a country rich in everything!" Coming from an eighteen-year-old, one wonders if George didn't have at least one eye on his blonde traveling companion when he made this comment. Whatever joy may have transpired, it was shattered four days later when Bill Elkins and Rhesa Kraus skipped out with all the horses.

Although inconvenient, the three remaining men were not worried as they still had a yoke of oxen and they were certain Claypool would be arriving soon with supplies. Also, Crook's troops were hammering the Shoshoni from the Crooked River to the Nevada border so there was little fear of an Indian attack. With these pleasant thoughts in mind, young Barnes, Johnson and White proceeded to improve their claims.

The men kept busy with rail splitting, land-clearing, cooking, fishing and hunting. Each morning, with Barnes' "fierce soprano voice" ringing out in the crisp air, they "blithely took their way to the rail patch with an ox goad in one hand, a trusty U.S. gun on one shoulder and two Colt revolvers swung to their belts."[6] They were prepared to take on the Shoshoni nation, one at a time or all together, it made no difference.

Two days after Elkins made off with their horses, White was cooking dinner while Johnson and Barnes were loading the wagon with

6 All direct quotations taken from George Barnes' account in *The Prineville News*, June 1887.

rails. Johnson noticed a black column of smoke rising out of the valley, but as White was daily engaged in burning the heavy crops of wild rye that grew in the bottom lands, he paid little attention to it. Fifteen minutes later, Johnson and Barnes knew something was wrong when they saw White running toward them waving his hat. When he got closer, he yelled, "Boys! The Indians have broke out and killed every damn one of us!" Has No Horse had struck.[7]

That morning, the rail-splitters had neglected to take their rifles. Barnes had only a cap-and-ball revolver and this had been emptied at some sage hens. Without ammunition, it was about as deadly as a knot-hole. The remainder of the weapons were inconveniently stashed in Claypool's cabin. Scared witless, the trespassers held a war council and organized the first militia company in what would become Crook County. Each got a willow stick six feet long and marched back to the flaming cabin. It was totally destroyed. It appeared that the next bite to eat would be found somewhere west of the Cascade Mountains. Afoot, with some forty miles of snow to wade through over the grim Cascades, their prospects for survival were not good. So, they decided to head north for The Dalles-Canyon City road. Gathering a few traps, the refugees hitched up the oxen and headed for safety.

Two and a half days later, they blundered into the Warm Springs Agency by accident. Agent Smith's wife—according to young Barnes—furnished them with "enough provisions to run a small Methodist camp meeting for at least a week." Two days after arriving at Warm Springs, they borrowed some horses and rode toward the Santiam Pass. En route, they met Jim Blakely—headed for Fort Watson to negotiate a government beef contract—who assured them that the pass was open to travel.

Has No Horse won the first round but the initial break had been made. Within a year, the settlement of the Ochoco would be in full swing.

---

7 All accounts blame Paulina for burning the first settler's cabin in the Ochoco Valley. He was innocent of this charge. Before Barnes and Johnson crossed the Cascades from the Willamette Valley to unite with White at Camp Polk in early June 1867, Paulina was shot to death some four miles northwest of the present site of Ashwood, Oregon on April 26, 1867.

PRINGS
SALOON

CHAPTER 151

PRINE'S SALOON

One of the nice things about living east of the Cascades is that the state capitol and the inner workings of state government are out of sight and generally out of mind.

The Bulletin
March 27, 1991

Throughout the remainder of 1867 and well into 1868, Capt. White, Ewen Johnson, Elisha Barnes and Wayne Claypool organized for the big push into the Ochoco and the takers were many. Other prime movers in the bid for settlement were Abe Zell and Tom James, who were in Indian territory serving as scouts for Crook's winter campaign. Attached to Major Randall's command, they would begin clearing land in the upper Ochoco Valley when spring of '68 broke. Through them, White and Claypool received word of Randall's stockade, which would further help to promote their land scheme. Meantime, it would take the promoters the better part of six months to organize. Many families were eager to go but there was a problem of getting rid of the property they already owned. The emigration of 1867 would provide an answer to that dilemma.

Made up almost entirely of Scandinavian, German and French immigrants, the emigration of 1867 left St. Cloud, Minnesota on June 25 under the leadership of Capt. Peter Davey, wagon master. The crossing, recorded by Henry Lueg (a German immigrant), encountered the usual misfortunes in western travel. Their original destination was the Montana gold fields. Grinding across the Montana plains, they were surrounded by vast herds of buffalo which stripped the land of forage and left their livestock in starving condition. Unable to find gold and with their greenbacks worth only 75¢ on the dollar, they headed into Oregon and the war zone. A few days east of Canyon City, the train was stopped by 100 armed Snake warriors and forced to turn north to the Columbia. They abandoned their wagons at the river port of Wallula in Washington Territory and boarded the sternwheeler *Owyhee* for passage to Portland—accompanied by Lt. Rothermel and his red cavalry.[1] This leg of the journey—for those who could muster up the cash by selling wagons, livestock and personal belongings—cost $16 in gold per person, $12 per horse and meals were extra. This came as quite a shock for it had cost only $125—which covered all expenses—to make the trip from St. Cloud to Helena. Some—with names like Sturdivan, Brehem and Koch—who couldn't afford passage, settled in Washington Territory.

On board the *Owyhee*, the new arrivals got a preview of what lay ahead in Oregon. Parading the deck were Darragh's and McKay's Indian troops "carrying pikes from which dangled the rotting scalps" of their Shoshoni victims. The Warm Springs Cavalry parted with the emigrants at The Dalles to escort Oregon Indian Superintendent J.W. Perit Huntington into the interior. It is important to note that a young civilian named Prine—who would play a significant role in the settlement of the Ochoco—joined Huntington's military escort at The Dalles.

Arriving in the Willamette Valley in late October, the emigration of 1867 was in for more disappointment. They soon discovered that most of the fertile farm land had already been claimed. When they learned that a large number of settlers in the Eugene-Lebanon area were planning to locate east of the Cascades in Indian territory, they were more than willing to purchase their lands. And so, many prayers were answered.

By June 1868, with western Oregon going up in flames ignited by settlers clearing more land, the new Minnesota land owners were wondering if they had made a wise purchase. Likewise, the big Ochoco wagon train groping its way over the smoke-filled Cascades was due for some surprises. . . at least White, Johnson and Barnes were dumfounded. In their absence, George Millican had set up ranch headquarters on McKay Creek and was grazing hundreds of head of cattle in the lower Crooked River Valley. A surveyor for the Willamette Valley and Cascades Mountain Military Road Company, Millican had been at Camp Polk when

1 See *Thunder Over the Ochoco*, Vol. III, Chapter 144.

plans were made for settlement of the Ochoco and had beat White and LaFollette to the punch.[2]

Next, they would find the charred remains of the Ochoco Blockhouse constructed by Major Randall's 8th Cavalry a month after Barnes, White and Johnson had been burned out in 1867. It was still smoldering, having gone to the torch on July 11, less than three weeks before the caravan's arrival.

The final surprise would be more lasting. Pulling in on Major Randall's coattails—as White, Johnson and Barnes were floundering around trying to locate the Canyon City trail—was an enterprising gentleman in his 27th year by the name of Francis Bernard Prine. The eldest of nine children, 6'3" tall, broad-shouldered, and spare built with muscles like steel wire—Barney Prine slipped into the lower Crooked River Valley and liked what he saw. Soldiers, Indians and the promise of settlers to come, all needing supplies. Barney was the man to provide them.

Riding with Barney were his brothers, Dave, Frank and Bill, who would supply the labor. In his wagon was a 50 gallon barrel of Hostetter Bitters—some of the finest whiskey ever distilled—and in his pocket lay $80 in gold and a new deck of cards. However, the good whiskey was for private consumption only. Barney would concoct a more zestful brew for his paying customers—namely, U.S. Army troops and thirsty Snake dog soldiers. Most likely this nectar would be produced without any attempt at purification. Like most frontier whiskey peddlers who manufactured their own product, Barney knew nothing about the process of distillation. After filling a barrel to the halfway mark with water, these craftsmen would add various ingredients to achieve bite, tang and color until satisfied that they could sell their mixture as whiskey. Among things added to the half-barrel of water were a pint of creosote; one pound of burnt sugar; an ounce of sulfuric acid; liquid coffee until the desired shade of gold was achieved; then some red pepper and a plug of chewing tobacco to give extra bite. This mixture was then topped off with a half-barrel of new alcohol. It has been said that the drinking of these explosive liquors rarely led to addiction. . . death usually intervened

---

2 Southworth, Jo Smith, *Millican Memories*, pp. 1-2.

before any such distinction could be achieved.[3] Moving about a quarter mile upstream from where the Ochoco dumped into Crooked River, Barney discovered where the 1845 wagon train had been attacked by the Snakes. Metal from the wagons, pots and pans, furniture, stoves, trunks full of clothing, harness and other miscellaneous gear was scattered about the area. Although the items were badly weathered, Prine's fertile mind quickly grasped the significance of this valley flotsam and told him "this is the spot."

Some ten miles upstream, the axes of Co. F, 8th U.S. Cavalry, flashed in the morning sun as they fell trees for the new army supply depot at the mouth of Mill Creek. Within ten minutes, four axes joined their chorus as the Prine boys started dropping cottonwood and alder trees. By nightfall, a lonely little building squatted on the south bank of the Ochoco River. Over the front door, a jaunty rough board sign advertised "Prine's Saloon—Whiskey $1.00 a Cup." Daylight would reveal that Prine was also operating a livery stable, blacksmith shop and general merchandise store. A few feet to the rear of the saloon a large bubbling spring came in handy for producing some mighty potent trade whiskey and by 1869, he had added a poolroom to his saloon. Through no advance planning, Barney had located within twenty miles of the geographic center of the state of Oregon.[4]

The cavalry soon discovered that Barney was an excellent blacksmith but most of his business was conducted in the back room not the front. One of his first customers was Yellow Jacket, a Snake war chief. It was one thing to burn out some sod-buster but a damn fool mistake to chase out a man who sold whiskey, even if it did make a devotee's

3 See *Thunder Over the Ochoco*, Vol. II, p. 254.

4 Between August 17 and August 23, 1869, McLung and Meldrum (contract engineers) made a government survey of Townships 14 and 15 south, Range 16 east of the Willamette Meridian. Prine's blacksmith shop and saloon was located in the southwest quarter of the northwest quarter of Section 5, Township 15 south, Range 16 east, approximately one quarter mile south of the Ochoco River and three-quarter miles east of the Crooked River in what is now Davidson Field in Prineville, Oregon. It was south of the junction of Steen's military road and the Willamette Valley and Cascade Mountain Military Road. Prine would pick up four neighbors from the 1868 Ochoco emigration: William Hardman (single) south of the junction of Crooked River and Ochoco River near South Ewen Street; A.J. Norcross (family) on north Main, north of the Ochoco River;and William Bostwick (single) and Robert Smith, both south of Prine's in the Fairview area.

eyeballs bleed. In fact, during the summer of '67, Yellow Jacket and Major George Randall became Prine's best customers.

Barney was well-suited for a life such as this. He had learned the blacksmith trade from his step-father, William Ray, who operated a blacksmith shop, saloon and store on the Santa Fe Trail before coming to Oregon Territory in 1852. In 1850, Ray—a widower with seven children—married Alice Prine, a widow with nine children. Barney would recall: "When I was 12 years old, they brought me across the plains to Oregon. I drove a wagon to which was hitched two yokes of steers and a yoke of cows. They settled in the forks of the Santiam River."[5]

On the Santiam, young Barney was introduced to the three R's. His school teacher, William Bromlette, also taught him the fine art of survival in the boomtowns of the West. In 1862, Barney followed the gold fields into Idaho Territory. At the Florence Strike, he ran into his old teacher from Scio, Oregon and was given a tempting offer. It seemed that Bromlette was now in the counterfeiting business and he wanted to enlist Prine as a partner. Barney wisely turned the offer down and Bromlette left town that same day. Later, Barney ran into him again in Boise City and tipped off the authorities that Bromlette was not exactly a first-class citizen. Forewarned, Bromlette headed for Canyon City. It turned out he was not only a counterfeiter but a road agent as well. The law finally caught up with him in 1872 when he and two other men robbed the Prineville stage north of Grizzly Mountain and Bromlette was sentenced to serve ten years in the Oregon penitentiary.

Barney was only twenty one when he drifted into Canyon City, where he and his partner struck it rich. So rich, that Prine spent as much as $1,000 a day gambling, treating anybody and everyone to drinks at a dollar a toss. According to Barney, "I used to be pretty much of a plunger when it came to gambling. The fact of the matter was I was a lucky gambler. When I was a young chap three men combined against me and won all the money I had. I hunted up a card shark and he got those three fellows in a game, and we trimmed them out of over $5,000. I never used to drink when I was gambling. The biggest pot I ever won was $6,000. We were playing draw poker and everyone dropped out of the game but

5 "History of Prineville Founder's Family," *Central Oregonian*, October 23, 1969. Barney would also say that William Ray's oldest daughter married his brother, Dave Prine.

another fellow and myself. I kept a jack and an ace and I asked for three cards. I got two more aces in the draw. He had three kings but my three aces raked in the pot."[6]

With the reputation as a high-stake gambler, Barney soon made friends with the Shoshoni because of his racing ability. West of the Cascades, he had made most of his money foot racing.[7] Shortly after his arrival at the mouth of the Ochoco, Prine entered a mile foot race with nine Snake warriors. Only three men finished. Most of the dog soldiers were drunk but Bloody Antler (20-year-old son-in-law to the war lord Has No Horse) and Buffalo Horn, a young sub-chief, were not. Prine came in ten paces ahead of the other two and from then on was considered a good friend.

On another occasion, a race of a different sort took place involving Yellow Jacket—or "Poker Jack" as Prine called him. Yellow Jacket had just arrived at the saloon when McLung's government survey party drifted in. They were low on supplies (among other things, canned goods and axes) which Prine didn't have. McLung then asked Yellow Jacket how long it would take him to go to The Dalles City with some pack-horses and return. After a little thought, Yellow Jacket said it could be done in seven days if he went easy; six days if he went fast; five days if he went faster; and four days if he went damn fast. McLung didn't think so but he asked Yellow Jacket how much money would he want to make the trip in four days. Without hesitation, Yellow Jacket replied that it would take $40 and a gallon of Prine's best whiskey payable on his return. That sounded fair to McLung.

Given the proper papers and instructions, Yellow Jacket took off in a whirlwind of profanity, lashing blows, and swirling dust with pack animals in tow. Four days later the whirlwind (subdued as to noise but still vindictive as to the lashing of pack horses), blew into McLung's camp as promised. Yellow Jacket had crossed the Deschutes River two times, took time to pick up supplies and had traveled 300 miles in four days. . . 150 miles of that distance with heavily loaded pack horses. He had earned his pay.

---

6 Ibid, p. 5.

7 Fred Lockely, "Impressions and Observations of the Journal Man," *Oregon Journal*, March 31, 1927.

In the late fall of 1867, Dave, Bill and Frank Prine headed back over the mountains to the Willamette Valley but Barney—planning to winter in the Ochoco—headed for the Columbia River and more supplies. In fact, he was so excited about his new enterprise, he temporarily forgot about his young wife. Beth Prine, struggling for survival in a drafty log cabin on the Canadian Fork of the Santiam River was not as exuberant as Barney over his most recent adventure. Eventually, he would remember he had a wife and on December 8, 1869, Beth Prine gave birth to Frank Francis Prine. . . the first white child born within the present city limits of Prineville. In later years, Frank would recall that his father had built up a thriving trade with the Shoshoni guardians of the Ochoco.[8]

For the moment, however, Barney's only concern was to get to The Dalles and back to the Ochoco Valley before winter set in. Upon reaching The Dalles, he learned that the war was heating up on the Ochoco front. Nathan Olney—Army express rider between Fort Watson and Fort Dalles—had taken a Snake war arrow which nearly killed him.[9] After hearing this news, Prine—loaded down with barrels of liquor and a few trade articles—decided he best accompany Huntington's Klamath supply train back to Crooked River.

Protected by 70 U.S. cavalrymen, 20 Warm Springs Indian veterans and 15 Klamath scouts, this supply train blazed what was to become one of Oregon's most important thoroughfares, U.S. Highway 97—locally known as The Dalles-California highway. As Huntington's caravan plunged into the Crooked River canyon the morning of November 4, 1867, it was attacked by Has No Horse. In the ensuing confusion, Prine aimed his over-burdened wagon up stream and was ready and waiting when White's pilgrims entered the Ochoco Valley the following summer.

Other than a source of protection, the new arrivals from the Willamette Valley—in typical west-side manner—would view soldiers in the area in about the same light as Indians; the only difference being that the army was a necessary nuisance. . . the Indians were not.

---

8 Statement given by Frank Prine shortly before his death in 1930 to the California *Oroville News*.

9 Olney, who had been on Has No Horse's hit list for the past seven years, did survive and three years after being wounded by the Snakes, was adopted into the Yakima tribe. They thought he was "Big Medicine."

CHAPTER 152

WINTER SPORTS

With redskin maidens we romance,
We play their brothers games of chance;
For by this means, as can be shown;
Much that was their's became our own.

Owen Wister
Western Author

While the Ochoco migration toiled over the Cascade crest, a Kansas Pacific locomotive, inching along the tracks between Ellsworth and Sheridan, Wyoming—a distance of 120 miles—passed through an almost unbroken herd of buffalo. Something had to be done about this obstacle to progress and soon the plains were littered with rotting buffalo carcasses shot for their hides. Then as the wagons lumbered into the Crooked River basin, the commanding officer's quarters at Fort Dalles—said to have cost $100,000 when constructed in 1857—was engulfed in flames. Undisturbed by this conflagration or herds of buffalo, the Willamette caravan creaked into the lower Ochoco Valley just two days after Crook's bloody blitzkrieg of the upper valley had removed another hindrance to western expansion.[1] And, as the Sauk chief Black Hawk once put it, the wagon occupants were spreading out "like stains of raccoon grease on a new blanket." The one thing that did impress the newcomers was Billy Smith's mansion, described as "doing services as a dwelling or maybe more properly, as a bachelor's roost."

Has No Horse had not yet surrendered so it became urgent to rebuild a modified version of the army blockhouse. Before another year passed, this fortified structure—located some 300 yards west of the

1 For a list of known people in the 1868 emigration (taken from Wasco County files) see page 29.

original—would serve as the first schoolhouse between the Cascade Mountains and the Idaho frontier. For this purpose, Jim Marshall and Ike Swartz had hauled in a sawmill, setting it up on Mill Creek—thus giving it a name. The mill consisted of a saw, a sash to carry the saw and an eccentric on a flutter wheel to give it motion. It was a variation of the old whip-saw mill in which lumber was cut laboriously by cross-cut saws which were pulled up and down by hand and in the more modern communities, by steam driven machinery.

Unlike the severe winter of 1867-68 which hastened the downfall of the Shoshoni war tribes, the winter of '68-69 was exceptionally mild with no snow or rain. To the bachelors in the homestead party, this was a great adventure. George Barnes, with the optimism of youth, tells of that first busy winter when Oregonians laid claim to the Shoshoni's ancient homeland. Working sixteen hour shifts in the sashmill, Barnes and his companions "sawed lumber for the floors of our cabins at the rate of fifty board feet a day. Sundays we washed and patched our clothes, and right here I want to say that along toward spring our wardrobe got to be very thread-bare; we thought we had come with clothes enough for a year, but three months ranting around over rimrocks and through juniper trees after the mule deer had left us barefooted and naked."[2]

Barney Prine's specialty didn't cater to wearing apparel and toward spring Barnes and company "were the nakedest lot of white men in Oregon. The makeshifts we utilized were to hide our skins from the biting winds—we didn't care a cent for the public gaze. We even soled our moccasins with pieces of bacon rind. When we hired out in the spring for work to Bill Marks (who had brought in a band of sheep), we stipulated that we were to have beef once a day and each was to receive a yard and a half of the first cloth woven (from the wool) to patch our pantaloons."

There was good reason for this request and it wasn't for protection "from the biting winds." During the early part of the winter, it hadn't been all work and no play for the merry bachelors. They were not above visiting the Shoshoni refugee camps and bestowing their favors on those willing to accept. Neither did they show partiality for they managed to spend considerable time playing kissing games with the young white

2 Barnes' account, *Prineville News*, June 1887.

maidens. Barnes called them "bussing bees." Anyway, as spring approached, at least according to George, they "let up" on the snuggling bit. "In fact we got skittish of the girls. Not that we were naturally diffident or bashful, but because our trousers were more conspicuous by what was absent, than by what remained."

Apparently George's favorite bussing partner was Ginny Marks, for a year later when he reached the age of 21, Wasco County records revealed the wedding announcement of one George W. Barnes to Ginevra Marks. He then took up a homestead two and a half miles east of Prine's Saloon. Seven years later, Barnes—a strong Democrat who took a keen interest in political affairs—moved into town, studied law, and was admitted to the Oregon Bar in 1880.

During the winter of 1868-69, other sports beside kissing also occupied their time, not the least of which was racing—horses, dog or foot. Prine was reaping most of the young men's rewards for hard labor in foot races. He wasn't doing too bad in horse races either. One of his few losses was to James McDowell, described as "an odd genius" who went by the name of "the Governor of Canada."

McDowell came by the impressive title, according to those who claimed to know, for having been the laziest man on the Canadian Fork of the Santiam River. This honor did have some advantage for Bill McDowell—Jim's oldest son—married on the strength of his father being the governor of Canada. Always happy if he could get enough to eat and plenty of tobacco to chew, old Jim didn't care if he was ragged and dirty. He shaved once a week with a butcher knife and during the threadbare period, the governor was in his element. His sole means of support was racing and he stood ready to back his mare against any horse in the country for fifteen buck hides. Barney Prine and several Snake warriors contributed to his livelihood.

There was also some heavy betting in November 1868 as to who would become the next president of the United States. True to their peculiar preferences, the good citizens of Wasco County chose Horatio Seymour to run the country instead of Gen. Grant.[3]

As winter approached, Barney Prine's luck at cards had turned a little sour when it came to gambling with the Indians, notably the Snake

3 *The Illustrated History of Central Oregon*, p. 197.

high-rollers, Yellow Jacket and Beads. To liven things up, Prine decided it was about time for some of the younger members of the homestead party to learn the finer points of draw poker. One of the more eager students was George Barnes, who frankly confessed to his almost criminal ignorance in that useful branch of a boy's education. He used the excuse that his education was limited to a country grade school because his parents couldn't afford to send him to college—but he was willing to learn. That was good enough. After a few dedicated lessons on how to shuffle, cut and deal, including the important maneuver to always sit on Prine's right so George could cut the deck to Barney's advantage, the master and the apprentice were ready to take on the Shoshoni card sharks. According to Barney, they would "go through the Indians like a case of the itch in a country school."

Soon the game was in full blast with Barney and George secretly playing together against Yellow Jacket and Beads. Barney would run up the bet and George would cut using both hands to shield his clumsy action in getting the split correct. To Barnes dismay, "every time Barney and I would get a good shuffle and cut, those confounded heathens would pass paralyzing our hope of winning." Not only that, when it came the Indians' turn to deal, they always had the top hand. It wasn't long before they had all of Barney's money, which was probably all the hard cash in the Ochoco Valley.

Earlier in the fall, Prine had a load of apples hauled in from The Dalles. After the money was lost, the two bet apples at $4 a box. It wasn't long before the Indians had won the entire load of apples. The fruit was last seen disappearing into the foothills heaped on travois attached to Beads' and Yellow Jacket's war ponies.[4]

Abe Fry was another sporting man who had brought a thoroughbred greyhound into the valley and was picking up money matching his dog against anything that moved. His chief ambition was to get a race between the greyhound and a mule deer buck—a desire that would never be fulfilled. Fry made the mistake of turning his slim-waisted racer loose on a gaunt coyote. It was an exciting race for about a quarter of a mile. Then the long-legged greyhound overtook the coyote who proceeded to

---

4 Barnes account of this gambling episode appears in *The Illustrated History of Central Oregon*, p. 724.

give his city cousin the worse whipping a high-bred dog ever got. There followed another quarter of a mile race back to where Fry stood in open amazement. The greyhound was in the lead but the coyote, a good second, was nipping pieces out of the greyhound's hams. That race ruined the dog as a hunter. Fry couldn't even get it to chase a jack rabbit and the howl of a coyote drove it into hiding. The poor dog soon pined away and died.

Another source of income was a slight-built gentleman who spent most of his time in Prine's Saloon. He, himself, was not out to make profit but just to get a few drinks. When an unsuspecting stranger drifted in, he would bet—for the price of the drinks—that he could down more whiskey than they could and still stay on his feet. The local boys knew this was a sure thing and would place side bets with the stranger on the outcome. They never lost, for their entry in the contest was William Pickett.

Pickett, former editor of the *Albany Herald*, was a man of superior editorial and literary ability but he was also a drunkard. His friends in the Willamette Valley, hearing of White's plan to settle Indian country, loaded Pickett in a wagon and sent him to central Oregon where he would be remote from temptation. Little did they realize that Barney Prine was in the country. Pickett was not of the hardy build of western pioneers and could not emulate or even compete with the results of the strong muscles of his neighbors. He couldn't drive oxen, hew logs, cook or split rails. But he made friends with everyone, so when the fortified school-house was completed, they made him the first official school teacher in eastern Oregon.

A sure source of revenue was to bet on what length Newt White would take to stay clear of a nuisance named Charles Brotherhead. Son of a rich New York banker and Civil War veteran, Brotherhead had drifted into the Ochoco with the '68 wagon train. Why, no one knew. He didn't need the country nor it him. He wouldn't work and couldn't if he had wanted to but he could and did raise quarrels with Captain White. White, to avoid meeting Charlie, would cross over the mountains rather than travel the valley when he wished to go from one point to another. Brotherhead would lie about the captain and bluster about what he would do if he caught him out alone. On the frontier where settlers were mutually dependent upon one another for safety, Brotherhead was a fool.

Around the rest of the country, higher stakes were being gambled. By 1869, the government was riddled by corruption. Ben Holiday's Oregon Central Railroad bought legislators as if "they were maidens on an Arabian auction block." Jay Gould, Jim Fisk and sundry officials in the Treasury Department conspired to engineer the greenback swindle.[5] By the early 1870s a "whiskey ring" scandal reached into the oval office to touch President Grant's personal secretary, Gen. Orville Babcock. In the War Department, the secretary of war was discovered to have accepted a $25,000 kickback from an Indian trader he had appointed. Small wonder the Indians were starving on the reservation.

Back in the Ochoco, Jim Marks turned up missing. Knowing him to be an expert woodsman, the serious betting was that he had fallen victim to a Shoshoni bullet. Marks, a born hunter, was in pursuit of a mule deer when he slipped and fell over a cliff. Dropping about eight feet, his foot caught on a narrow rock ledge projecting from the rim wall. It was some two feet wide, just enough room for footing. Jim soon determined that it was impossible to climb back up and too dark to see how far it was to the bottom. He soon convinced himself that it was at least a hundred feet to the canyon floor where he would be dashed to pieces should he fall. He was doomed to hang there until starvation loosened his hold or an Indian wandered by and took mean advantage of his position. His thoughts turned to home, of neighbors looking for him and never finding his battered body—and thus passed an interminable night. Daylight found him two feet from the bottom of the cliff. Another bet was lost but the west-side emigrants, through no fault of their own, had survived their first winter in the Ochoco.

---

5 Adams, *The Epic of America*, p. 219.

Known people in the 1868 emigration (taken from Wasco County files)

Allen, Albert (single)
Allen, James (family)
Anderson, Billie (family)
Anderson, Hallie (single)
Baldwin, Dr. (family)
Barnes, Elisha (family)
Barnes, George (single)
Barnes, William (single)
Beamer, _____ (single)
Belieu, Anthony (single)
Belieu, Collet (single)
Bostwick, Issac (single)
Brotherhead, Charles (single)
Brown, W.W. (single)
Burkhart, George (single)
Burkhart, Raymond (single)
Calbreath, John (family)
Carey, E.R. (family)
Cartwright, Charles (family)
Chitwood, Pleas (family)
Clark, H. (family)
Clark, William (family)
Claypool, John (family)
Claypool, Wayne (family)
Colman, Henry (single)
Contrell, James (family)
Crabtree, John (single)
Davis, John (family)
Dougherty, Lou (family)
Fry, A.B. (family)
Gulliford, Jake (family)
Hamlin, Reason (family)
Hardman, William (single)
James T.B. (family)
Johnson, Ewen (family)
Judy, George (family)
Lawson, James (family)
Luckey, James (family)
Luckey, Jean (family)
Luckey, John (family)
Marshall, James (single)
Marks, William (family)
McDowell, George (single)
McDowell, James (single)
McDowell, William (single)
Miller, James (family)
Miller, Richard (family)
Millican, George (family)
Noble, John (family)
Pickett, William (single)
Prine, Barney (family)
Prine, Dave (single)
Prine, Frank (single)
Prine, William (single)
Riqua, Charles (single)
Robbins, Abner (family)
Rose, Jack (single)
Settle, I.M. (family)
Sickel, Moses (family)
Sites, Dr. J.B. (family)
Sizemore, John (family)
Slater, James (single)
Smith, Robert (family)
Smith, Sam (family)
Smith, William (single)
Solomon, C.L. (family)
Sommerville, John (single)
Sparks, Alija (family)
Sproul, Andy (family)
Statts, William (family)
Stewart, William (family)
Stewart, John (family)
Summer, Ann (family)
Swartz, Al (family)
Veazie, Edmond (family)
Vining, David (single)
Warren, Andy (family)
White, Newton (single)
Wichizer, James (single)
Wiley, Bob (single)
Wiley, George (single)
Wilhoit, W.M. (family)
Wood, S.S. (family)
Woods, Lin (family)
Zell, Abraham (family)
Zevely, John M. (family)

CHAPTER 153

THE ROAD TO RICHES

If the Indian had only known he was starving, being shotgunned off his hunting grounds and having his squaw debauched for his own good, he'd have tried harder to be like his white brother looting the treasury.

Will Rogers
Born in Indian Territory

By summer 1869, the Spanish Gulch miners—over on what would become the eastern frontier of Crook County—felt that they had created a stable community and were tampering with a new idea. On July 26, they appointed a three-man committee to locate and survey a town site five miles southeast of Fort Watson.[1] By this time, a number of stockmen had settled in the area. Although the teenagers of the new frontier settlement thought all was fun and frolic, their elders had more serious thoughts on their minds—not the least of which was Indian attack. The Shoshoni had submitted to force but it was a tedious task subjecting them to the will of the Indian Department. Has No Horse had made a bargain with Gen. Crook concerning the welfare of his tribesmen but bureaucratic interference was making it difficult to honor that agreement.

Crook, in effect, had told Has No Horse that he and his people could remain in the Ochoco so long as they kept the peace. Then Indian Superintendent John Webster Perit Huntington huffed into Fort Harney a few months after Crook's departure and insisted that "you signed a treaty in 1865 and by gawd, I intend to hold you to it." Neither Has No Horse nor Wolf Dog had signed anything in 1865. Huntington's stand on

1 Grant County records.

military enforcement of this treaty accomplished nothing but bad feelings on both sides.

Has No Horse could care less about losing benefits derived from a fraudulent treaty and Crook's reaction to army intervention was equally vehement. Addressing the civil authorities in strong words, Crook reminded them that "the Indian commands respect for his rights only so long as he inspires terror from his rifle. . . greed and avarice on the part of the white, in other words, the almighty dollar is at the bottom of nine-tenths of all our Indian troubles." He further admonished that "with all his faults, and he has many, the American Indian is not half so black as he has been painted. He is cruel in war, treacherous at times, and not overly cleanly. But so were our forefathers!" The citizens of Oregon were dumfounded by their military commander's outburst.

During this war of words, Huntington attempted to remove Wolf Dog to the Siletz Reservation in western Oregon.[2] Much to the westside's relief, he refused to go and with a keg of powder in the form of Has No Horse smoldering in the background, Huntington wisely backed down. Shortly thereafter, Huntington—one month shy of his 38th birthday—suddenly died.[3]

Bad as the Indian situation was, the Ochoco settlers had a worse problem facing them of which they were acutely aware. Once a week, they met at one cabin or another for a discussion of current events. Overshadowing the Shoshoni unrest, the main topic of debate was the Willamette Valley and Cascade Mountain Military Road Company's claim to public lands in the Ochoco and Crooked river valleys. It was one thing for whites to steal land from the Indians but an entirely different matter when road companies stole land from homesteaders.

Many eloquent charges were made against the company's tendency to stake old Indian trails and call them "wagon roads." Little did these critics realize that these same trails would become military roads by the action of two Oregon governors. Neither did they suspect that improvements on which some of the settlers were working so hard that winter would be taken from them and given to this company. Perhaps if

---

2 Bancroft, *History of Oregon*, Vol. II, pp. 551-51.

3 Huntington died of a heart attack in Salem, June 3, 1869. Corning, *Dictionary of Oregon History*, p. 121.

they had, the speeches would have run with more bitter accusations than they did. The blow would fall the coming summer.

It was late fall 1863, when Congress—disgusted with Oregon's inability to cope with the Shoshoni—came up with the idea of building military roads for easier access into the war zone. At this time, the proposal was quite basic. The federal government, in order to encourage construction of military roads, would grant the state three sections of public lands per mile for every mile of new road constructed. In turn the governor, acting as receiving agent for the state, could dispose of these lands to the road builders as work progressed. There were no specifications for the width and grade of the road. It was merely to be a road that could be traveled with team and wagon.

Some two and a half years later on July 5, 1866, Congress belatedly issued—along with the official land grant—specific instructions on the type of roads required. Among other provisions, the contractor would be required to construct necessary bridges, establish toll gates, provide ferry boats and be responsible for road maintenance. This was all well and good, except the damage had already been done.

Between 1864-1869, five land grants were received by the state for road purposes. All five were turned over to private companies for construction.[4] The Willamette Valley and Cascade Mountain Military Road Company got in on the ground floor. Conceived in 1864 by Abe Hackleman and Jason Wheeler, it was incorporated in 1865 with $30,000 in capital assets. The company consisted of Luther Elkins, president; James Richardson, vice president; James Elkins (Luther's son), a secretary; and seven board members.[5]

A land grant was not immediately in the minds of the men who organized the company. Its principal organizers were Linn County stockmen who wanted an access road across the Cascades to reach the grazing lands of eastern Oregon. Not until financial troubles beset them did the

---

4 Four of these road companies: Oregon Central Military Road, Corvallis and Yaquina Bay Military Road, The Dalles-Canyon City Military Road, and Coos Bay Military Road were basically reliable. Some fraud did occur but neither did they pick up as much land as the Willamette Valley and Cascade Mountain Military Road; not even the Oregon Central Military Road which was actually longer—or should have been—than the Willamette Valley and Cascade Mountain Military Road.

5 Members of the board of directors were: Isaac Congell, D.W. Ballard, Jack Suttle, John Powell, John Sette, Morgan Keyes and Jacob Keyes.

company turn to a land grant as a means of recovery. The actual construction costs were never determined but were estimated from $10,000 to $45,000. In total length, the Willamette Valley and Cascade Mountain Military Road traversed 448 miles, of which 330 miles were constructed in one season, entitling the company to a land grant of 861,000 acres.[6] In reality, road construction from the Deschutes River to the Idaho border was a farce.

At best, it was a rough trail and its steeper sections would tax the dexterity of a mountain goat. The builders had little concern for grade and the thoroughfare might be described as the shortest accessible distance between two given points—in this case, Albany, Oregon to Boise City, Idaho—and little less than a sheer cliff altered its beeline course. The obvious exception to this unwavering course was the Ochoco, which became Crook County in 1882.

After crossing the Santiam River nine times, the Willamette Valley and Cascade Mountain Military Road entered what would become Crook County two miles south and four miles west of Black Butte at the Santiam divide. From there to Buck Creek south of Snow Mountain—a distance of 160 miles—it wandered around like a drunken soldier in search of his horse. Crossing the Deschutes River, it headed northeast to the lower Crooked River Valley and followed the south side of the river to the mouth of the Ochoco. Jumping across stream at this point, it traced the approximate route of Prineville's East 7th Street into the lower Ochoco Valley. Upon reaching Veazie Creek, it angled southeast through Horse Heaven country and ended up on the North Fork of Crooked River. Plowing out of the canyon, it then dropped into Rabbit Valley, clawed its way over Sabre Ridge and plunged into Paulina Valley. Now, turning almost due south, it wandered up Grindstone Creek, took a straight course across Twelvemile Table, went up Long Hollow and then down Buck Creek. It was now apparent that the road company intended to acquire as much fertile land as possible.

Originally, the road was to go into Canyon City but it was so far off course by the time it zigzagged through the Ochoco, the builders headed directly into Fort Harney and down the Malheur River to the

6 Amundson, Carroll, *History of the Willamette Valley and Cascade Mountain Military Road Company*, p. 5; *Senate Executive Documents*, No. 124, p. 6, 50th Congress, 1st Session.

Snake. One early observer claimed the construction work "consisted of a party of men, most of them on horseback, accompanied by a wagon, going through the country at the rate of 10 to 15 miles a day, blazing trees when passing through open timber, doing a little grading at different spots, breaking sagebrush where it was too high and putting stakes in the ground one mile apart.[7]

The company constructed only two installations on the entire route and only one of these would be maintained. Two miles east of Sweet Home on the Santiam River (the road's actual point of origin), the company operated a toll gate. For the nominal sum of $3 for a team and wagon; $1.50 for a horse and rider; or 75¢ for a foot traveler, early day tourists could enjoy the wilderness route to the Ochoco settlements. The other installation, unmaintained, was a flimsy bridge across the Deschutes River at Tetherow's Crossing. One could guess that this bridge was constructed solely for publicity's sake.

Governor Addison Gibbs was invited to the dedication of the Deschutes Bridge with the assurance that he would be the first person in Oregon to cross over in a wagon. However the corporate heads—upon seeing the structure—had some misgivings about the safety of such a venture so they convinced Gibbs it would be much more spectacular to be packed over on the shoulders of the workmen. Gibbs consented and the Willamette Valley and Cascade Mountain Military Road Company board members were on their way to becoming millionaires.

On July 5, 1866, when Congress issued the state of Oregon a land grant, the company had to act fast for it was at this point the Act spelled out what was expected in the way of road construction. On the promise of road completion in 1867, the state legislature moved to transfer title to the contractors, although the company didn't carry out its agreement. Gov. Gibbs in 1866 and Gov. George Woods in 1867—whether through carelessness or willful neglect—accepted the road and the company received patents to 861,512 acres of public domain. . . 400,000 acres of which were in Crook County alone.[8]

---

7 Brogan, *East of the Cascades*, pp. 78-9.

8 *Oregon Historical Quarterly,* Vol. X, pp. 2-38; *Oregon Historical Quarterly*, Vol. L, pp. 2-29; *Illustrated History of Central Oregon*, pp 701-02; *Oregon State Archives*, RGC9-NPIP, Nos. 217-19.

Because there was no regular appropriation to check the lands claimed, the Governor's investigators had their expenses paid by the Willamette Valley and Cascade Mountain Military Road Company. Their report disappeared from the files. During later investigations—although the original land grant was for 860,000 acres upon location of the route—1,392,000 acres were withdrawn from settlement pending selection by the road company. This transaction is considered to be one of the most brilliant land frauds ever perpetrated on the American public.

The Ochoco settlers didn't have long to wait to see what their fate might be. On August 9, 1871, the Willamette Valley and Cascade Mountain Military Road Company board of directors sold all the land they had received from the state to T. Egerton Hogg—a railroad promoter with a vague past—for $75,000. Hogg immediately disposed of the land to Alexander Weill of San Francisco who claimed to have paid $375,000 to acquire control.[9] His main objective was to perfect company title by again working through the Oregon governor's office. Weill, working through two Portland lawyers—H.K.W. Clark and Col. E.S. Wood—sold out to Lazard Freres, a French banking house, for an undisclosed sum.[10] Shortly thereafter, Charles Alchul—agent for the Paris firm—moved into Prineville as the resident overseer of the Willamette Valley and Cascade Mountain Military Road Company lands and was supposed to see that the road was maintained in good repair. Most likely he was sent to see who was squatting on company lands, as the absentee owner refused to sell any parcel to the local settlers.

By 1909, Louis Hill and Watson P. Davidson had formed the Oregon and Western Colonization Company which purchased the huge land grant from the French company for five million dollars and another round of discontent would begin. The Oregon and Western Colonization Company, with close ties to James J. Hill's railroad interests, planned to promote an emigration of 100,000 people to eastern Oregon. This scheme would bring on a homestead rush to central Oregon's high desert.[11] But,

9 Amundson, *History of the Willamette Valley and Cascade Mountain Military Road Company*, pp. 23-26.

10 *Senate Committee Report*, No. 1088, pp. 3-4, 49th Congress, 1st Session.

11 Amundson, *History of the Willamette Valley and Cascade Mountain Military Road Company*, pp. 43-44; *Senate Committee Report*, p. 54, 86th Congress, 2nd Session.

this turmoil was hovering on a distant horizon and for the moment, the Ochoco argonauts had other things to occupy their collective minds.

CHAPTER 154

GROWING PAINS

Soap and education are not as sudden as a massacre, but they are certainly more deadly in the long run.

Mark Twain
Nevada News Reporter

Experiencing a very mild winter, things were booming in the Ochoco Valley settlement. Only one issue clouded an otherwise successful colonization. Thanks to the Indian Department, the Snake war tribes were getting restless. When the war chiefs first surrendered, they would have gone wherever Crook said they must go. Now they refused to go or stay on any reservation. Many of the ranking chiefs had drifted out of the country, especially those like Three Coyotes who had a price on his head from the Mountain Meadow massacre. Three Coyotes, whose mother was an Apache, rode south when the war ended. Ranging through Arizona and New Mexico, he once again ended up with Crook on his backtrail. But in 1872, he offered his services to peace commissioner Gen. Howard, as a scout to track down Cochise, which he did.[1]

Black Eagle, Paulina's brother, hid out in the Seven Devil Mountains on the Idaho-Oregon border and was later joined by Pony Blanket and Beads. Bad Face and Yellow Jacket took up residence in Nevada. Only Has No Horse and Wolf Dog—the two the settlers wished would vacate the area—remained dangerously close to the Ochoco settlements.

They had good reason for being nervous. During the start of the Shoshoni campaign, Warm Springs raiders under the leadership of Pipsher Simtustus had taken Wolf Dog's daughter, Sorrowful Woman,

1 Howard, O.O., *Hostile Indians*, chapters XII, XIII, XIV.

captive. Most likely under pressure from Indian Agent William Logan, Simtustus did send Wolf Dog 18 horses in payment for his reluctant bride. Shortly thereafter, the girl made a desperate attempt to find her family in the war-torn Ochoco. She was unsuccessful in this effort. On her third endeavor to escape from the reservation, Sorrowful Woman was again taken captive by Simtustus at Fort Maury in 1864. By now she had given birth to his son.[2] Although Sorrowful Woman enjoyed high status on the reservation as Simtustus' wife, she was not happy. She finally did escape with her son but the boy was apprehended by the newly arrived settlers and returned to Warm Springs where he spent the remainder of his life. This act of betrayal, committed by white intruders upon Wolf Dog's grandson, would make him a very dangerous neighbor.[3]

Determined to enforce the questionable 1865 treaty, Supt. Huntington forced Wolf Dog onto the Klamath Reservation. . . a move he would soon regret. Although Has No Horse had negotiated an arms agreement with Old Schonchin, there was no love lost between the Snakes and the Modocs. Placing them together was asking for trouble. Agent Ivan Applegate was aware of this and after Wolf Dog's arrival, he observed "signal fires on the mountains surrounding Silver Lake" conveying an idea that Has No Horse desired a conference with Wolf Dog.[4] In an effort to stall off trouble, Applegate set up a meeting with Old Schonchin and Wolf Dog at the northeast end of the Klamath Reserve known as Yainax Station. His purpose was two-fold; to commence farming operations and "to attempt to secure an interview with the wild Snakes." [5]Unfortunately for him, he was only half successful for Has No Horse arrived unexpectedly at the conference.

Has No Horse and Old Schonchin—who kept a war bonnet on hand in case he needed it—were of like opinion. If farming was to be their outlook for the remainder of their years, they wanted no part of it.

---

2 Prior to capture, Sorrowful Woman was the wife of the Walpapi dog soldier Lean Man. For more on Sorrowful Woman see: The Diary of Lt. John F. Noble, 1st Oregon Cavalry, entry for Sunday, June 4, 1864; also *Thunder Over the Ochoco*, Vol. III, p. 184.

3 It is interesting to note that this boy took the shortened name of Wewa for his maternal grandfather, Weahwewa (Wolf Dog) instead of that of Simtustus. His great grandson, Wilson Wewa, has become a religious and cultural leader among the Warm Springs Paiutes.

4 National Archives, Record Group No. 98, U.S. Army Commands, Department of the Columbia, 1868.

5 Voegelin, *Northern Paiute of Central Oregon*, Part 2, p. 253.

As this time, the Modoc war chief, John Schonchin, Old Schonchin's brother and Modicus (Captain Jack) were still at large. Old Schonchin, Has No Horse and Wolf Dog laid plans to join them. Before this could happen, Captain Jack and John Schonchin, deciding that reservation life was better than war, marched into the Klamath Agency in January 1869 and sued for peace.

Seething with rage over this sellout, Has No Horse and Wolf Dog began raiding Modoc camps. To avoid annihilation, the peace-seekers fled to the "land of the burnt out fires" where Little Rattlesnake had made his stand against Crook in 1867. The settlers in the area immediately complained so, on Applegate's request, Crook stepped in with the army, ordering Major John Jackson to contact the Modocs.

Jackson had barely arrived at the Modoc camp when Scarface Charlie came out of a tipi with a Colt revolver in his hand. Jackson ordered Lt. Boutelle, who also had a pistol in his hand, to arrest Scarface. Both men fired at the same instant and a soldier fell dead. In the next few minutes five soldiers were killed and as many Indians. The remaining Modocs escaped in the confusion but the seeds of the Modoc War had been planted.[6]

During this diversion, Wolf Dog and Has No Horse escaped from the reservation. Traveling with Has No Horse was his new wife Bessie, a Snake girl he had married in the final days of the Shoshoni war. Laying a swathe of destruction to the north, they killed eleven men and boys but spared all women and small children before taking separate routes.[7] Wolf Dog raided the Ochoco settlement and made off with three yoke of oxen and Billy Smith's only saddle horse. This attack was a rude reminder that the Snakes were not whipped yet. The settlers were not so foolish as to give pursuit but they did keep better surveillance thereafter and posted guards with all livestock.

It would later become obvious that Has No Horse had not broken his promise to keep the peace for he had not participated in the Ochoco Valley raid and in his mind, the agreement made with Crook was that he personally would not cause trouble in the Ochoco country. In short, Wolf Dog was raiding on his own initiative.

---

6 Brody, Cyrus Townsend, *Northeastern Fights and Fighters*, pp. 264-271.

7 Military Correspondence, Department of the Columbia, March 4 to May 8, 1869.

The Ochoco settlers, cut off from the rest of Oregon by lack of roads and threat of Shoshoni attack, lacked one service which was becoming serious and that was mail delivery. Newcomers to the valley were bringing in such interesting books as Alcott's *Little Women*; Collins' *The Moonstone*, both published in '68; and just hot off the press, Blackmore's *Lorna Doone*; Twain's *The Innocents Abroad*; and Bret Harte's widely popular *The Outcasts of Poker Flat*. But welcome as this reading material was, it didn't take the place of current news. In those days a newspaper or letter was an important event. The settlers soon were dependent upon the ex-army scouts, Jim and John Luckey to get mail to them one way or another. Shortly after Wolf Dog's raid, the Luckeys arrived at Prine's Saloon with some exciting news. One bit of information would be contained in a lost letter; the other was printed in glaring headlines.

When the Luckeys arrived at the frontier outpost, Jack Long, who was headed for Canyon City, volunteered to deliver the only letter addressed to the upper Ochoco Valley. On the way, he lost the letter intended for John Martin Zevely. Everyone turned out to hunt and the searched continued until the letter was found. Zevely probably wished it had remained lost for it contained the startling information that his wife, who had remained in the Willamette Valley while John improved their living quarters, was not about to join him in Indian country. "She ran off!" Zevely's granddaughter would exclaim, "Divorced him and married another man, an unheard of occurrence in those times!"[8]

The other piece of information which made just as lasting an impression, boasted of steel rails spanning the continent, wedding the Atlantic Coast with the Pacific. This union took place in the bleak Utah desert north of Great Salt Lake on May 10, 1869 and in so doing, put a slow-down on covered wagon traffic. Sluggish perhaps but not stopped. As late as 1919, the editor of the local paper would comment on Prineville's growing population, "A train of 12 immigrant wagons arrived in Prineville Saturday from eastern parts of the state and Idaho. This is the largest single immigration that has arrived here for some time."[9]

---

8 Letter from Mary Zevely Fraser to Vera Koch Ontko, dated Bend, Oregon, July 12, 1982.

9 Prineville *Central Oregonian*, September 1, 1919.

Another Ochoco inhabitant had received news of the transcontinental railroad quicker than the patrons of Prine's Saloon. After splitting from Wolf Dog, Has No Horse knifed into northern Utah where he made contact with Iron Crow, war chief of the Eastern Shoshoni. Curious to see an iron horse, they drifted down to Promontory Point and had their pictures taken by a Union Pacific photographer who even rode up into the mountains to photograph their lodges.[10] This photo session put Has No Horse in the clear concerning Wolf Dog's raid on the Ochoco settlements. While Iron Crow and Has No Horse posed for photographs, Gourd Rattler rode into Fort Brown, Wyoming Territory and offered his services as army scout against the hated Sioux.

During this interlude, Supt. Huntington gave up his effort to civilize Wolf Dog and died from pneumonia on June 3, 1869. Alfred Meacham, who had faced his share of problems with the Shoshoni, was appointed Oregon superintendent of Indian affairs. His first official act was to call for a council meeting with Has No Horse and Wolf Dog at Fort Harney. On Meacham's promise that he would release the Shoshoni prisoners of war held in the Fort Klamath guardhouse—among them Red Willow, Has No Horse's son—Has No Horse consented to be placed at Yainax Station on the Klamath Reserve. Elated over this prospect, Meacham would soon refer to Yainax as "the future home of a war chief who has cost the government much in blood and treasure."

At Fort Harney Meacham would finally meet Has No Horse, Big Man and Wolf Dog face to face. He was pleasantly surprised when Has No Horse rode into the council grounds. He would describe the White Knife dog soldier as being "mild-mannered, smooth-voiced and unassuming. . . a man of remarkable character." However, he got a much different impression of Wolf Dog. "There was in the face of this man a

---

10 The original picture of Has No Horse is now on file in the Union Pacific Railroad photos, American Heritage Center, University of Wyoming. This photo appears in *Thunder Over the Ochoco*, Vol. III, photo section two. There is also a picture of Has No Horse taken shortly before he was shot by the Izee Sheepshooters in 1898, a shooting he would survive only to die in prison in 1914. He is standing in front of his willow-woven big lodge photographed by DeLancy Gill and is now on file with the Bureau of American Ethnology entitled "Ochoco's Wickiup." This photo appears in Schmidt and Brown, *Fighting Indians of the West*, p. 280. The only other known picture of Has No Horse, entitled "Chief Ocheo circa 1900," was taken by C. Pederson and belongs to the Modoc County Museum in Alturas, California.

cunning, treacherous look that was anything but reassuring."[11] It was at this meeting of the Shoshoni high command that Meacham claimed to have seen Big Man outrun jackrabbits. Whatever, Big Man, who held no desire to live anywhere in his crippled condition, especially in a white man's holding pasture, refused to go to the Klamath Reserve.

Shortly after Has No Horse arrived at the Klamath Reservation, agency employees committed an unpardonable sin as seen through the eyes of a Shoshoni warrior. The touching of a dog soldier's hair by another person was considered to be the gravest of insults. In a misguided attempt to introduce the notorious war leader to the civilized ways of the white man, Has No Horse was taken to the fort barbershop and his hair cut American style. Never again would Has No Horse be lured onto a government reservation other than to visit tribal members. Overnight, Has No Horse, Wolf Dog, and the Shoshoni war prisoners disappeared into the landof the red willow.

Upon arrival, Has No Horse was told that a grim drama was unfolding in the high mountain prairies of the inner Ochoco. Big Man had been severely crippled in a shoot-out with the bounty hunter John Wheeler on July 27, 1868, nearly a year before Meacham's encounter with him at Fort Harney on August 24, 1869. After being taken to Pony Blanket's lodge at Fort Harney in 1868, Big Man had been transferred by litter to the comparative safety of Big Summit Prairie.[12] Buzzard Man, the medicine healer, was able to save his life but he couldn't repair bone shattered by .44 slugs. Big Man, a cripple forced to move about like a giant crawdad, was becoming more and more despondent. His distorted arms wouldn't allow him to hold his favorite weapon, a Sharps 38-55 buffalo rifle. . . a big gun for a big man. The will to live was fading, but the code of a dog soldier forbid self-termination of his life. Rumor now had it that the big warrior would circumvent that taboo.

Surprisingly, a short time before this while pursuing Shoshoni fugitives in the Salmon River country, Lt. Thomas Barker claimed he found footprints in a deserted camp measuring seventeen and one-half

11 All direct quotes taken from Meacham's *Wigwam and Warpath*, pp. 224-244.

12 Wheeler (a bounty hunter) had fired 16 bullets from a .44 Henry rifle into Big Man's body and then shattered both arms and legs with a .44 Colt revolver. For more on this gunfight, see *Thunder Over the Ochoco*, Vol. III, Chapter 148.

inches long. Perhaps he did, but most likely this startling discovery could be attributed to some Sheep Killer warriors wearing oversized moccasins stuffed with grass to protect their feet from the bitter cold—thus accounting for the large footprints. Whatever the reason, the press immediately took note of Lt. Barker's report and the legend of "Bigfoot" was rekindled overnight, causing mass hysteria on the Oregon-Idaho frontier.

After the Ochoco Valley raid in April, Wolf Dog and Black Buffalo (with their families) joined Big Man's camp in Big Summit Prairie. According to Dave Chocktote, Big Man talked his most trusted friend, Little Foot, into putting him out of his misery. There was a saying in the Old West that a gun which kills once will kill again. The Shoshoni believed that. What really transpired in some lonely glade, no one will ever know but in the later 1930's, Clarence Kemp—an employee of the Hay Creek Land and Livestock Company—was searching for strays in Gray's Prairie. He found a rifle leaning in the forks of a pine which apparently had been placed there many years in the past, for the tree had grown completely around the rifle, leaving only the stock and rifle barrel sticking out of the wood. For years, this oddity sat on display in Hugh Lakin's hardware store in Prineville. It was a Sharps Copper Bottom .38-55! One hundred years ago, a person just didn't lean their rifle against a tree and walk off without it.

Despite Indian scares, more people were drifting into the Ochoco.[13] By early spring, 15 more families and 18 single people had taken up residence, adding to the growing population. In the late fall of 1868, William Pickett had taken on the job of teaching school with sixteen students in attendance.[14] Now, his class was expanding. A meeting was held April 4, 1869 and a school district was formed, named Ochoco No. 11.[15] Forty-seven scholars were enrolled with an average attendance of twelve at any given time. Even that was too much for

13 For a list of those who emigrated in 1869, see page 56.

14 The first students enrolled in Pickett's school were: Ann Clark, Clara Clark, Della Clark, Clara Claypool, Elizabeth Claypool, Luther Claypool, Jay Davis, Celestine Johnson, Jacob Johnson, Margaret Johnson, Albert Judy, Arthur Judy, William Judy, Eta Marks, Ginevra Marks, and Virgil Marks.

15 First school board members for Ochoco District No. 11 were: William Clark, chairman; George Judy, secretary; Ewen Johnson, director; William Marks, director; Edmond Veazie, director.

Pickett and he resigned, turning over his schoolmaster duties to James Crawford.

Another old timer was also getting nervous. Prine's blacksmith shop-saloon was being joined by other business establishments and Barney was beginning to feel crowded. Used to the wild days of the mining camps, homesteaders were not exactly Barney's favorite customers—too tame. So he moved out in 1870 to Weston, a boomtown on the edge of the Umatilla Indian Reservation. Here, he was appointed city marshall. It wasn't long before an old acquaintance from Canyon City—Hank Vaughan, the gun artist—drifted into town and after a few drinks, Hank announced he was going to kill Marshall Prine just for the hell of it. Being good friends, Barney took Hank's gun away and told him to go home and sober up. No hard feelings on either side.

From Weston, Prine went to Fort Lapwai where he joined his step-brother, William Ray, Jr. in the operation of a blacksmith shop. He remained in Fort Lapwai for twenty years where, according to him, "I had lots of fights with men when they were drunk, but I always figured the best way to handle a drunken man was to wade right in and give him all you got before he can do any harm to you." After one of these brawls, Barney became a born-again Christian at a revival meeting. A few days later, temptation reared its ugly head when some men came to his blacksmith shop and wanted to play some stud poker. "They were fairly lousy with money and I knew from watching them that I could make a good cleanup. I tell you I had a pretty hard fight with the devil then, and I was certainly sorry they hadn't come before I was converted. It was a hard fight but I won out and wouldn't touch the cards."[16] And thus, passed another Ochoco warrior.

Adding to Prine's eagerness to get out of the Ochoco Valley, Abe Zell—his services no longer needed as an army scout—had built up a thriving trade as a coppersmith next to Barney's blacksmith shop. Within shouting distance of the saloon, a doctor's office was also under construction. However, most of its business would take place at the point of need—not at the office—so it would cause little disruption. Dr. Lark Vanderpool went to his patients, they didn't come to him. If necessary,

16 "History of Prineville Founder's Family," *Central Oregonian*, October 23, 1869, p. 5.

the doctor performed operations on the kitchen table, assisted by members of the household.[17]

Dr. and Mary Vanderpool arrived in the valley in the spring of '69. Traveling with them was their sixteen-year-old son, William and the doctor's sister, Martha Vanderpool. These two had a common purpose in mind. Young William immediately started courting Susanna Heisler and Martha set her eye on Jake Gulliford—veteran of the Rogue Indian War—who lost his wife in 1857. The elder Vanderpools decided Billy best reach the age of reason before he undertook such a serious step as matrimony and it took Martha awhile to convince Jake that was the right thing to do. During this period, Dr. Vanderpool was appointed justice of the peace and in June 1872, performed marriage ceremonies for his love-stricken kin.

Vanderpool never attended medical school but was considered to be the only doctor between The Dalles and Canyon City. Billy McKay (Warm Springs Agency physician) had a degree in medicine, but to white folks he was a half-breed, and therefore didn't count. Medicine man Vanderpool, who built and operated the first drug store in Prineville in 1876, concocted his own remedies which he peddled from a horse-drawn buggy. This colorful medicine wagon soon became a familiar sight, not only on the streets of Prineville and the Ochoco Valley, but throughout eastern Oregon. From this rolling pharmacy, Vanderpool dispensed remedies which promised to cure headaches, liver problems, coughs and consumption. All sold for 50¢ a bottle. He, like other doctors to follow, often traveled by horseback for days to reach a family in need of medical assistance, many times arriving back in Prineville only to head out again in another direction to answer a sick call.

A prime example of a doctor's hectic life occurred in 1886. Dr. Horace Belknap, who had graduated from the University of Michigan at Ann Arbor and finished his internship at Bellevue Medical Hospital in New York, came to Prineville to visit his parents. He was on his way to Chico, California to start practicing medicine. He barely arrived in town when a weary rider from Sisters reported the illness of a man badly in

---

17 McNeal, *Wasco County*, p. 327.

need of medical attention. Old Dr. Sites—Prineville's second doctor—not liking the long hard journey, prevailed upon the young Dr. Belknap to make the trip. This was his first case, and he started out not knowing until his arrival in Sisters whether the patient had died or was still living.

Upon returning to Prineville, another critical case was reported at Paulina and thus, the young physician's first two patients were 110 miles apart. But more was yet to come—as he wheeled his buggy back into Prineville from Paulina, hoping for some much needed rest, a sweaty horseman thundered down Second Street shouting that a man had been badly wounded in a shooting scrape south of Farewell Bend about where Sunriver is today. Again young Belknap was asked to make the journey. Leaving Prineville in the night, he rolled into Farewell Bend in the early morning, With such demand, he decided to stay in central Oregon.[18]

Along with the growing pains of medical ailments, new construction, Indian raids and match-making, the adverse effects of the Willamette Valley and Cascade Mountain Road Company land grants would be felt in 1869. Anthony Webdell bought John Crabtree's right to the swampland east of Prine's Saloon and thereby purchased a nineteen year legal battle with the road company owners. It seems that Charlie Alchul didn't subscribe to the idea that Crabtree had any constitutional rights to sell to Webdell. In fact, luck wasn't with Webdell on any transaction made that year.

Shortly after he bought the road company headache, Webdell talked to Ed Conant—big-time horse operator, a native Cuban and self-proclaimed "world adventurer"—into guarding his swampland property while he went to the Willamette Valley to buy horses.[19] In the process of looking for horses, Webdell met and married Nancy Wiley. Since he had no suitable living quarters, Anthony didn't bring his new bride into the Ochoco until the summer of 1870, but wedded bliss was not destined to last. Nancy came down with tuberculosis and Doc Vanderpool's "Alpha Pain Cure" didn't seem to work. She died May 6, 1871, making the third natural death in the Ochoco Valley.

---

18 "Years Ago in Crook County," *Central Oregonian*, March 16, 1959.

19 Portland *Sunday Oregonian*, September 18, 1927.

Ironically, Reuben Streithoff and Emily Powell had arrived with Nancy in August 1870.[20] Streithoff died December 6, 1870 and Emily Powell died two months before Nancy Webdell on March 9. 1871.[21]

After Webdell's clash with land agent Charlie Alchul, Elisha Barnes was the next target on the company's hit list. The land grant as defined by law amounted to every odd numbered section along the entire wagon route. The homesteaders who happened to locate their claims on even numbered sections were in good shape. Those who didn't were in for trouble and Barnes was one of them. He would later note in a letter to R.V. Ankeny, dated April 21, 1882 that Claypool and Johnson were lucky enough to locate on even sections and "now got good homes and is doing well, while I the leader and mover in the enterprise of settling this country have been thrown off my place and left without a home and this is not all. I had accumulated a little money and property by hard work and economy and had good reason to believe that I would have something to rely on in my old age to surport [sic] my family. The Road Company did not act fair with me as they never did make me any propisiton [sic] to let me have my place at any price or that they would allow anything for my improvements. . . . This country will never amount to anything unless the settlers can be pasified [sic] and be on good terms with the land owners [Paris Banking House]. This country is settled up with a class of men that is good friends but bad enimeys [sic]. . . . " And so it was.

One who would prove to be a good friend to those in need was young Jim Blakely. A trail boss by profession, Blakely rode into the Crooked River Valley in 1869, rounded up 500 head of beef cattle and drove them to Chico, California where he sold to Miller and Lux for shipment by rail to San Francisco. He then brought the horses and trail

---

20 For a list of the known emigrants of 1870, see page 56.

21 Reuben Streithoff had the unenviable distinction of being the first white settler to die and be buried in what is now Crook County. According to the records of probate filed in The Dalles City, Streithoff's estate was valued at about $4,300. That property was auctioned off in Prineville. It's interesting to note what some of his possessions sold for: 1 frying pan, 25¢, 1 chair 50¢, 1 horse $80, 1 ranch $20, 1 revolver $8, 1 gun 75¢, 1 wagon $51, 1 knife 25¢, 1 washboard 50¢, furs 50¢, 1 sheepskin 12¢—to name a few of the items sold. By 1997, Streithoff's original headstone had deteriorated beyond repair so the local genealogy society replaced the old marble stone with a new granite marker. (*The Central Oregonian*, Thursday, October 23, 1997, p.7)

outfit back to Prineville and settled on Willow Creek out of harm's way of the wagon road company.

One of Blakely's cowboys, Billy Tomlison, also added his contribution to the settlement of the Ochoco in 1869. . . or more correctly, the honor goes to his wife. According to George Barnes, "Billy Tomlison should not be forgotten, for his wife that summer gave birth to the first child born in the new settlement. Though this should be to this country what Virginia Dare is to America, [implying it was a girl] I have forgotten whether it was a boy or a girl."[22] If Barnes was correct this would cast doubt on Walter Millican's birth in 1872 as being the first white child born in what is now Crook County.

About the time Webdell made his land deal with Crabtree, Congress was out to gain more public domain and they were quite successful. In negotiations with Hudson's Bay Company, the federal government acquired all rights and titles to Company property in the United States for $650,000. Much of this land was located in the state of Oregon.

Merchants at The Dalles could also see a good source of revenue in the Ochoco settlement if it could be tapped. By late spring 1869, they had solved the problem. In a council meeting, the business men voted to foot the bill to build a toll road from Bakeoven on The Dalles-Canyon City road to Prine's Saloon on the Ochoco River. Lou Daugherty and Bill Clark got the contract and by the end of the summer a wagon road wandered down Cow Canyon, up Hay Creek and down McKay Creek to link Prineville with the rest of the world. In a distance of some 110 miles, the road passed only one house—the Coleman ranch on Trout Creek. This thoroughfare was known as the Grizzly Mountain Stage Road.

Something had to be done about the lack of comfort stations so, over a period of time, stage stops were established at the Circle Ranch on Lytle Creek; Henry Cleek's ranch on Willow Creek; Heisler's Stage Station at the mouth of Cow Canyon on Trout Creek; and August Schernickau's new establishment at Cross Hollows—the junction of the Grizzly Mountain Stage Road with The Dalles-Canyon City Road. Schernickau was the German baker who set up business at Bakeoven in

---

22 Article written by George Barnes appearing in *The Illustrated History of Central Oregon*, p. 708.

1862.[23] On March 31, 1900, Cross Hollows became officially known as Shaniko—the Shoshoni's way of pronouncing the German trader's name.

Under good conditions with changes of horses, the trip from The Dalles to Prineville could be made in 48 hours. . . or as much as a week for heavy freight wagons. Within a few years, daily stages left Prineville at 12 noon and were advertised to arrive at Cross Hollows at 12 midnight. One woman—writing to her sister—cast some doubt about the stage coaches maintaining that schedule. She wrote, "I managed to catch a day light [7 a.m.] special stage Sunday morning from Prineville and after walking half-way, in company with my fellow suffers, arrived at Shaniko at 2 a.m., only one hour ahead of the regular stage which started at noon, 5 hours behind us."[24]

But access to the trade center was not alleviating the Indian problem. Following Huntington's death in June, Alfred Meacham—a stage station operator on the Blue Mountain Trail—was appointed Oregon superintendent of Indian affairs by President Grant with the hope he could calm things down. It was not going to work. With the Shoshoni war officially at an end, the War Department lost little time dismantling the frontier military outposts. Fort Harney and Fort Warner would retain small detachments, while Fort Klamath—because of Snake hostilities on the reservation—would remain fully manned. Fort Watson, the nearest protection to the Ochoco settlers, was discontinued in mid-March 1869—some six weeks before Wolf Dog's raid in the Ochoco Valley—and the buildings turned over to the Holliday Stage Company.[25]

Almost simultaneously with the Snake revolt on the Klamath Reservation and eleven days before the War Department ordered closure of the military installations (thus turning over the Snake war tribes to civilian management), Crook had warned: "Among the bands are some as crafty and bad as any I have ever seen and if they are retained in the vicinity of their old haunts and the Indian Department manages them as

---

23 August Schernickau's original bakery was established on the Dalles-Canyon City Road when the Shoshoni attacked the pack train he was traveling with. This spot soon became known as Bakeoven. Later, Schernickau opened a stage station at what was called Cross Hollows. For more on the German trader, see *Thunder Over the Ochoco*, Vol. III, pp. 101-102 and 138.

24 Juris, *North From Prineville Over the Old Dalles Stage Road*, letter dated December 23, 1902.

25 *General Order No. 7*, Military Division of the Pacific, March 15, 1869.

they have other tribes, they will have trouble with them."[26] President Grant—having had first-hand experience with Oregon politics—agreed, but his cabinet did not.

By now, Motcunka Sket, known to the whites as Moses Brown, was showing a strong tendency to back Has No Horse. Instead of questioning why he found reservation policy distasteful, the Indian Department stripped him of rank and made Black Buffalo—a staunch supporter of Wolf Dog—leader of the reservation Snakes. This would prove to be a mistake.

On October 20, 1869, Meacham and Capt. Kelly (commander at Fort Harney) held council with Wolf Dog and Has No Horse. Again, they refused to go on the Klamath Reservation without Crook's direct order. Crook—certain that Meacham had promised more than he could deliver—declined to give it, sighting his reason for not doing so. "I did not order them to go with Mr. Meacham for the reason that I have their confidence that I will do or order only what is best and right both for themselves and the government.[27]

Undaunted, Meacham sent word to Has No Horse to meet with him at Fort Warner. Has No Horse arrived in November. Crook gave neither encouragement nor assistance to Meacham in this bid for confinement, although he was well aware that Has No Horse was "the worst of his race and dangerous to leave at large."[28]

Perhaps out of respect for Crook and the commitment they had agreed to the summer before, to everyone's astonishment Has No Horse agreed to go on the reservation but he didn't commit his warriors to any such foolish act. Upon arrival, he found Wolf Dog's tribesmen almost naked, living on crickets and some skimpy rations of flour given them by the army, not the Indian Department.[29] He then met with Archie McIntosh.

McIntosh had been working out of Fort Klamath as a scout. In so doing, he had observed that the Snakes were starving with no game to

26 *Military Correspondence*, Military Division of the Pacific, March 4, 1869.

27 *Military Correspondence*, Military Division of the Pacific, December 7, 1869.

28 *Military Correspondence*, Military Division of the Pacific, July 18, 1870.

29 *Annual Report of the Commissioner of Indian Affairs to the Secretary of Interior*, 1870, pp. 67-9.

hunt and short-changed on their government allotment of rations. Being a half-breed, the civilian authorities in charge branded him as a troublemaker. It's certain Crook believed Archie and that would account for his reluctance to cooperate with the Indian agents in forcing the Snakes onto a reservation.

Agent Ivan Applegate claimed the Indians were well fed and accused McIntosh of lying. The way he put it, Archie, in an effort to discourage the unstable Indian mind, "had been making mischief on the reservation by telling Ocheo [Has No Horse] that he was wanted and needed by his people." In the spring of 1870, having observed first hand that McIntosh was telling the truth, Has No Horse decided to leave the reservation mainly because Agency personnel could not be trusted.[30]

So as not to arouse suspicion, Has No Horse headed for Sprague River where he pitched his lodge in view of Yainax Station. To this day, the towering pine tree under which his lodge once sat is known as the Ochiho Tree.[31] While Applegate kept his eye on Has No Horse, his followers deserted in small detachments, with Has No Horse waiting to be the last. Knowing the search would be directed at him, Has No Horse headed for Fort Warner while Pony Blanket with the escapees rode north into the high desert. When Agent Applegate caught up with the war chief and demanded that he return to the Klamath Reserve, Has No Horse calmly replied that Col. Elmer Otis, commander at Fort Warner, "desired him to remain there." This was a true statement, at least in part, as Otis himself admitted in a letter to Applegate dated July 18, 1870.[32]

"I do not remember giving any Indian permission to stay here, but I have said that if they came I would not send them back. They can live better here." Otis did, however, persuade Has No Horse to return to the Klamath Reservation at least during the winter—which he agreed to do if allowed to roam during the summer.

---

30 Bancroft, *History of Oregon*, Vol. II, p. 553.

31 Wernie Foster, an old-timer on the Klamath Reservation, was rather droll when asked about the tree. "I don't know anything about this Chief Ochoco. But I do know Chief Ochiho. . . and not too much about him either." Wernie Foster to Gale Ontko, letter dated June 19, 1956, Beatty, Oregon. Burdette Ochiho, descendent of Has No Horse, had this to say in a letter dated August 4, 1956, Klamath Falls, Oregon. "There's a big pine tree between Sprague River and Beatty, Oregon that's named the Ochiho Tree."

32 *Military Correspondence*, Military Division of the Pacific, July 18, 1870.

On such a crumbling foundation, peace was being maintained in central Oregon. But, just to insure that life didn't become too serene on the east side of the mountains, LaFayette Grover, who assumed the duties of governor on September 14, 1870, began pushing for a public works program to be financed by the state. Since this would require some additional revenue, the state hand-out was soon followed by property taxes. This new levy was about as welcome to the citizens of the Ochoco as a Shoshoni raid on their livestock (which the military believed might be forthcoming).

Some five months before LaFayettte Grover was installed as governor, the Army contacted Sarah Winnemucca—an educated "Pah-Ute woman" as they called her—desiring full information in regard to the Indians in eastern Oregon and northern Nevada with the intent of "bettering their condition" by sending them to a reservation. Sarah's reply was not what they were expecting or wanted to hear. Following is one example from Sarah's letter to Major Henry Douglass.[33]

> Sir, . . . my father, whose name is Winnemucca, is the head chief [by proclamation of J.W. Huntington, Oregon superintendent of Indian affairs] of the whole tribe; but he is now getting too old and has not energy enough to command, nor to impress on their minds the necessity of their being sent on the reservation. In fact, I think he is entirely opposed to it.

Sarah then goes on to explain that many of the eastern Oregon and northern Nevada Indians had been on a reservation at one time:

> But if we had stayed there, it would be only to starve. . . . It is needless for me to enter into details as to how we were treated on the reservation while there. It is enough to say that we were confined to the reserve, and had to live on what fish we might be able to catch in the river. If this is the kind of civilization awaiting us on the reserve, God grant that we may never be compelled to go on one, as it is much preferable to live in the mountains and drag out an

33 Sarah Winnemucca to Major Henry Douglass, dated Camp McDermitt, Nevada, April 4, 1870, letters received, Office of Indian Affairs, Nevada Superintendency.

> existence in our native manner. . . . Remove all the Indians from the military posts and place them on reservations and it will require a greater military force stationed round to keep them within the limits than it now does to keep them in subjection.

Sarah then offers her opinion that if the Indians were treated as equals with their white neighbors the existing situation would change for the good of all concerned. "I warrant that the savage (as he is called today) will be a thrifty and law-abiding member of the community. . . "[34]

This peaceful integration of the two races would not come to pass. Within two fleeting years, the flames of war would again engulf the land on the Oregon-California border, as a new reservation for the exclusive use of Paiutes and Western Shoshoni was being established on the Malheur River in eastern Oregon.

34 For Sarah's letter in its entirety, see Jackson, *A Century of Dishonor*, pp. 395-96.

The emigration of 1869 would include:

Conant, Edward (single)
Foster, William (family)
Garret, Harlan (family)
Gates, William (family)
Glenn, Edward (single)
Hale, D.H. (single)
Hale, John (family)
Hindman, Samuel (single)
Holman, Hardy (single)
Holman, John (single)
Jinkens, Tom (family)
LaFollette, Jerome (single)
Leach, Marcy (single)
Lee, John (family)
Logan, Thomas (family)
Marks, Attwood (single)
Marks, Bluford (family)
Marks, James (single)
Monroe, Thomas (family)
Morgan, Orange (single)
Norcross, Jack (family)
Slaton, Samuel (family)
Smith, Harry (single)
Snedeker, Mary (single)
Snoderly, James (single)
Sumpter, Alex (family)
Thomas, David (single)
Toms, John (single)
Vanderpool, Larkin (family)
Webdell, Anthony (single)
Wells, W.C. (family)
Williams, Josiah (single)
Williamson, J.N. (family)

The known emigrants of 1870 were:

Bailey, Love (single)
Bailey, Zeke (single)
Beeker, Farrel (family)
Belcher, Milt (family)
Blakely, James (single)
Cannon, Tone (family)
Combs, James (family)
Cranston, Bill (single)
Darsey, Bob (single)
Daw, Frank (single)
Elkins, C.W. (family)
Elkins, James (family)
Ewell, Jim (single)
Ewell, Ples (single)
Heisler, Suzanna (single)
Heisler, William (family)
Hodges, Alexander (family)
Lister, Charles (single)
Lister, Thomas (family)
Logan, Lysander (family)
Logan, Lysander Jr. (single)
Nickolas, Larch (family)
Powell, Daniel (family)
Powell, David (single)
Powell, Emily (single)
Powell, John (family)
Powell, John Jr. (single)
Powell, Marcus (single)
Powell, Marion (family)
Powell, Oliver (family)
Powell, Thomas (family)
Smith, Henry (family)
Streithoff, R. (single)
Templeton, David (family)
Tomlison,William (family)
Webdell, Anthony (family)
Wiley, Nancy (single)
Zell, John (single)

CHAPTER 155

PRINE'S VILLAGE

Through the land where we for ages
Laid the bravest, dearest dead,
Grinds the savage white man's plow-share
Grinding sire's bones for bread.

Joaquin Miller
Grant County Judge, 1866-70

By 1870, the number of all Indians inhabiting the United States was estimated at about 300,000—35,000 of whom were of Shoshoni descent scattered across Oregon, California, Nevada, Idaho, Utah, Colorado and Wyoming with some 3,000 Comanches hiding out in Kansas Territory. In contrast, the U.S. white population was pushing 40 million and growing. Homestead lands were becoming increasingly scarce.

In an eight-month period between 1870-71, another 32 families and 28 single persons shoved into the Ochoco and there was no slow down in sight.[1] Crowded to the limit, a nervous Barney Prine sold out to Monroe Hodges and headed for the seclusion of the northern Blues, opening the way for his land claim to become the city of Prineville. Present Main Street marks the original dividing line between Hodges' and Prine's homestead claims. On April 13, 1871, Barney Prine's blacksmith shop and saloon became officially known as Prine, Wasco County, Oregon.

Having breached the barrier to the last unexplored region in the Pacific Northwest, the settlers were finding out that isolation from the trade centers had its price. There were only two shipping points, The Dalles and Eugene City. Although Eugene City was a little closer to the Ochoco Valley, it was only accessible four months out of the year due to

1 For a list of those arriving in 1871, see page 67.

heavy snows in the Cascade Range. First and foremost, all supplies had to come by stagecoach, freight wagon or pack train and shipping costs were not cheap. In a time when laborers were fortunate to earn $35 a month, packers, stage drivers and freighters demanded $35 a day paid for out of the items they transported. And the risks were great. If teamsters weren't fighting the weather, it was outlaws or marauding Shoshoni. All were artists with a twelve-foot whip, known in the trade as a "blacksnake," which they carried draped around their neck. These leather braided whips with buck-shot loaded butt and a silk or buckskin tip were used to guide the teams. The horses learned rather quickly to respond to the crack of a blacksnake and this precision of control also added to the worth of a good driver.

In the 1870's, delivery costs from The Dalles were expensive and, although the nation hadn't gone back to the gold standard, the West, plagued by wild-cat banks and the worthless paper money used after the Civil War, dictated you had best carry gold if you craved to buy anything. In order to make a run profitable, 60% of the price of goods delivered in Prineville were the transportation costs, due to the low volume of shipping. Freight for such luxuries as coffee and other like items ran high. For example: coffee (Java) 34¢ a lb.; eggs 50¢ a dozen; tea (in a paper bag from Japan) 75¢ to $1.00 a lb.; nails $11.00 a keg; kerosene $1.25 a gallon; flour, $5.00 to $8.00 per 100 lb.; or a hand sewing machine at $30.00 each. Because of this, the pioneers got by as best they could by doing without. It was even cheaper to haul wagon loads of wheat to the Warm Springs Agency to be ground into flour than to have it shipped in.

Hoping to capitalize on the freight trade, Joe Sherar spent over $7,000 for a bridge to be constructed over the Deschutes River and another $75,000 improving the roads leading to the bridge. About the same time, another event happened which would slow down supply shipments to Prineville and increase the costs. The Dalles shipping point—which had been swept by floods in the spring—was due for another set-back. On August 17, 1871, fire broke out in the Globe Hotel, destroying the eastern section of town and causing an estimated $100,000 in damage.

Another scarcity, due to the army's systematic depletion of the resource, was wild game. The only animal in abundance, and the Ochoco was overrun with them, was bear—both black and grizzly. These predators played havoc with livestock, so bear meat was a staple of the early diet. Also, bearskin coats and rugs became quite popular.

Besides people, livestock was flooding the land. While the Noble brothers—George and Andrew—herded sheep into the Beaver Creek area, others were in a frenzy to open more land. As they tore up the ground to plant crops and gardens, a new revelation came to light. The tillers of the soil were finding out what Has No Horse meant when he said, "You will have to plow deep to find the earth. . . the upper crust is dead Shoshoni." In disbelief, they were plowing up human bones. . . lots of them! These unpleasant discoveries would continue for nearly a century.

In 1956, the *Central Oregonian* would exclaim: "Prineville's mysterious skeleton has been identified as an Indian brave buried near Fort Watson." (The paper had to have meant Fort Maury.) Whatever, found in an attic on East Third Street and brought to public attention, the skeleton caused quite a clamor. According to Ron Raymond (a sophomore at Crook County High School) he was plowing on the Sharp Ranch west of Paulina near Fort Maury when his plow uncovered a grave and he brought the remains into town. However, the paper continued, "it is not known yet whether the skull found beneath a chicken house on South Main Street a week earlier belongs to the same skeleton."[2]

A few months later, the town was again jarred into excitement. "Two more skeletons have made their appearance in Crook County, the latest being unearthed last Friday by country road crews." It seems that Ralph Gilchrist while eating his lunch, discovered them in a rock slide on Little Bear Creek southeast of Prineville. They appeared to have been buried for a great many years.

One complete skeleton was dug out and brought into the sheriff's office along with the skull of another whose body had been buried in a sitting position. Sheriff Jesse Woolridge, expressing the belief that the remains "might be those of two Indians," sent the skulls to the state crime laboratory for identification. His guess was correct.[3]

---

2 The *Central Oregonian*, January 19, 1956. In the early 1960's, Ralph Heitman, who had a ranch in Rabbit Valley just south of the Watson battleground, plowed up several skulls and other human bones during farming operations.

3 The *Central Oregonian*, November 28, 1956.

This disturbance of Indian burial sites would not go unnoticed. Suzan Harjo, a Cheyenne, would denounce this practice. "Where we have buried our dead in peace, more often than not the sites have been desecrated. The total Indian body count in the Smithsonian Collection is more than 19,000, and it is not the largest in the country. It is not inconceivable that the 1.5 million of us living today are outnumbered by our dead stored in museums, educational institutions, federal agencies, state historical societies and private collections. The Indian people are further dehumanized by being exhibited alongside the mastodons and dinosaurs and other extinct creatures."[4] She was not happy with the plunder of Indian graves.

In 1870, Oregon Democrats again gained control of the state government and more skeletons would emerge in the form of racial discrimination. Touted by governor-elect LaFayette Grover as "the period of construction," state bureaucracy was to expand in many directions. Dr. William McKay was denied the right to vote because of Indian blood. He sued the election board and the case ultimately came before the august U.S. District Court Judge Mathew P. Deady, who decided in late November 1871 that McKay was either a British citizen or a member of the Indian community. In neither case was he legally eligible to vote. It took a special act of Congress signed by President Grant on May 20, 1872 to "naturalize" Billy McKay.[5]

Seven weeks and two days before McKay entered his legal battle over state election laws, the east-bound Prineville stage was held up by three men on August 6, 1870. Stage hold-ups were becoming quite common. In an effort to offset this high cost of individual shipping or perhaps to keep an eye on his daughter's courtship with young Vanderpool, Bill Heisler moved into town in 1871 and opened the first general store in Prineville at what is now the corner of West First and Main. Heisler, a native of Pennsylvania, had arrived in Wasco County by way of California. Arriving with Bill and Martha were their eight children:

---

4 In 1992 Suzan Shawn Harjo was executive director of the National Congress of American Indians, based in Washington, D.C.

5 *McKay versus Campbell*, Case No. 8839, District Court D, Oregon, September 26, 1870; *McKay versus Campbell*, Case No. 8840, District Court D, Oregon, November 7, 1871, Oregon Vertical File, Supreme Court Library, Oregon State Library, Salem; *Senate Bill 695*, 42nd Congress 2nd Session; McKay, *Papers*.

four girls and four boys. The boys—Monroe, Alexander, Jefferson and William—were a welcome addition to the community as they were considered to be some of the best rifle shots in eastern Oregon.

The green lumber used to build Heisler's general store didn't come cheap. Imported from Linn County, it cost 3¢ a pound for freighting it over the Cascade Mountains to the Ochoco Valley. On April 13, 1871, when the Prine post office was established, Heisler became the first postmaster. The name was changed to Prineville on December 23, 1872.

One block north of Heisler's general store, Monroe Hodges was building a hotel to accommodate the increased travel. Hodges, a native of Ohio, had come west at the age of fourteen with the emigration of 1848. He and his wife Rhoda rode into the Ochoco Valley in the spring of 1871 with a pack string of mules and saddle horses. They also arrived with two daughters and five sons. One of the boys, Lewis, became an importer of blooded horses, while daughter Sarah became the wife of ex-army scout John Luckey.[6]

Hodges, a staunch Baptist, soon decided that a church was in order instead of meeting at various homes for religious services. With that in mind, a Union Church was constructed in 1873 at the corner of West Third and Main, a block north of Hodges' hotel, meat market and livery stable. That same year, Elisha Barnes was elected town mayor.

About the time Hodges led his pack string into the Ochoco Valley in 1871, pint-sized Peter French—soon to become Elisha Barnes nephew by marriage—and a band of Mexican vaqueros rode out of California with a large herd of cattle and horses bound for Harney basin.[7] He established the P Ranch between Steens Mountain and Malheur Lake—a total of 150,000 acres. French was schooled to the ways of wresting large holdings from the public domain from his experience in California where he had been a vaquero and acquired the old Spanish land grant concept. From the time of his arrival in Harney Valley until he was killed in a gunfight with Ed Oliver, French kept adding to his empire.

---

6 Luckey's first wife was Ella Samantha Miller, sister of Joaquin and James Miller. In 1869, John Luckey joined his brother-in-law James Miller taking a homestead on Miller's Keystone Ranch. Shortly after, Samantha died. Luckey later married Sarah (Sally) Hodges, daughter of Monroe Hodges.

7 Elisha Barnes' wife, Suzanna Glenn, was the sister of Dr. Hugh Glenn, partner of Peter French. In 1883, French married Glenn's oldest daughter, Ella, a niece of Suzanna Glenn Barnes.

One of Hodges' first visitors at his new hotel was an army courier en route to Fort Harney and he had exciting news about a new weapon to use on the unrepentant Snakes. The townsfolk were equally enthusiastic. It seems that Ben Hotchkiss—an inventor who once worked for Sam Colt—had opened an arms factory in France where he developed a rapid-fire cannon with revolving barrels capable of slaughtering Indians even more efficiently than Dr. Gatling's machine gun. The only problem thus far with design was the Hotchkiss gun was more suited for battleships than artillery wagons. Nonetheless, the locals, along with the rest of Oregon, believed they could be adapted to Columbia River steamers. For what reason, is anyone's guess. Strange as it may seem, before another seven years had passed that would happen. The seeds for a grim harvest were now being planted.

In March 1871, while Charles Darwin was stirring up controversy with his philosophy on the descent of man and Phineas T. Barnum was holding the eastern seaboard spellbound with his greatest show on earth, President Grant—most likely on the recommendations of Gen. Crook—issued an executive order to set aside a reservation in eastern Oregon for exclusive use of the Snake war tribes. With the settlement of the Snakes on this reserve, their title to all Indian lands within the boundaries of the state of Oregon would be extinguished. However, this wouldn't happen overnight. It took a year and a half of wrangling before Congress and the citizens of Harney Valley (namely the big cattle barons, John Devine, Hugh Glenn, Pete French and Tom Overfelt) could agree on the establishment of boundaries. Containing 2,285 square miles between the Silvies River and the North Fork of the Malheur, it was officially designated as the Malheur Reservation on September 12, 1872 but more commonly known as "The Great Paiute Reserve." Title for all lands within this block were to be vested in the Snake tribes with the exception of the lands granted to the Willamette Valley and Cascade Mountain Military Road Company for military road purposes.[8]

This 1.8 million acre land grant was supposed to solve the Indian problem in eastern Oregon for all time, causing the historian Bancroft to

8 Report of T.B. Odeneal, Supt. Indian Affairs to Columbus Delano, Secretary of the Interior, September 4, 1872, House Executive Document 1, Serial 2100, 42nd Congress, 2nd Session, p. 346. More land was later added to the Malheur Reserve in May 1875.

comment: "Thus swiftly and mercilessly European civilization clears the forests of America of their lords aboriginal, of the people placed there by the Almighty for some purpose of His own, swiftly and mercilessly clearing them, whether done by Catholic, protestant or infidel, by Spaniard, Englishman or Russian, or whether done in the name of Christ, Joe Smith or the devil."[9] For whatever intent the Almighty had in mind, the Shoshoni who used to live on the newly created Malheur Reservation and should know, called the Malheur Valley the Source of Creation.

Encouraged by the prospect of a new reservation, Supt. Meacham attempted to negotiate another treaty with the Snakes. Has No Horse had already made up his mind that he was not going to be confined on any reservation and Meacham's proposal hinted of more treachery. No doubt the old dog soldier remembered that less than five summers had passed since the enlightened citizens of Idaho had voiced their opinion on how to rid the country of the Indian menace:

> This would be our plan of establishing friendship upon an eternal basis with our Indians: let all the hostile bands of Idaho Territory be called in (they will not be caught in any other manner) to attend a grand treaty; plenty of blankets and nice little trinkets distributed among them; plenty of grub on hand; have a real jolly time with them; then just before the big feast put strychnine in their meat and poison to death the last mother's son of them.[10]

Meacham was unsuccessful in his arbitration, which was just as well. Before he could agitate too much, Congress—with a stroke of the pen—discontinued negotiations and treaty-making with all Indian tribes in 1871. From 1780 to 1871, the U.S. government had arranged 370 treaties with Indian tribes and statistics reveal that every one of those agreements was broken either by the government or by individuals with full government support.[11] As French President de Gaulle once mused, "Treaties are like young women and races. They last as long as they last."

---

9 Bancroft, *History of Oregon*, Vol. II, p. 554.

10 U.S. Congress, Senate Executive Document No. 42, Series 1033, p. 137.

11 Jackson, Helen Hunt, *A Century of Dishonor*, Boston, 1901.

Meacham next tried to send Captain Jack's Modocs to the Malheur Reservation. That didn't work either. The Modocs refused to go and within weeks, in an attempt to force Captain Jack out of the southern Oregon lava beds, the Modoc War exploded into raw violence.[12]

During the shuffling of the Snakes, Gen. Crook had been temporarily relieved of command in August 1870 by Gen. Edward Canby so he could go to San Francisco to work on the so-called "Benzine Board," the soldier's name for the Army Appropriations Bill of 1869 which was aimed at the immediate reduction of army personnel.[13] The Benzine Board got its name for its tendency to clean matters up. While Crook was in San Francisco, the Apaches went on the rampage and Secretary of War Belknap requested Crook take command of the Military Department of Arizona. Crook had already made clear that he "was tired of Indian work" and besides that, Arizona had such a bad reputation that he "feared for his health." The outcome being that Secretary Belknap said he could remain in command of Oregon's Department of the Columbia.

But that was not going to happen. With a little political infighting, the governor of Arizona went over the secretary of war's head and had President Grant assign Crook there anyway. In June 1871, with Oregon ready to explode, Gen. Crook, Captain Nickerson, Andrew Peisen (Crook's personal servant) and Archie McIntosh, so drunk he had to be taken aboard ship under guard, set out to quell the Apache rebellion.

And so, Crook's tenure in Oregon was ended and for all practical purposes, so was Archie McIntosh's. By the time the Snakes re-opened hostilities, the army decided Archie was too old to be of any useful value. More likely, they were apprehensive he might join the enemy.

In a grouchy mood, Crook set out for Arizona to mend the Apache's errant ways while Felix Brunot, president of the Board of Indian Commissioners, eagerly headed west on June 1, 1871 to make a whirlwind tour of the Pacific Northwest reservations.[14] The main objective of his visit was to try and get the sullen Modocs, Klamaths and

12 Meacham, *Wigwam and Warpath*, pp. 351-54.

13 Ganoe, William A., *The History of the United States Army*, pp. 324-25.

14 The Board of Indian Commissioners was created by an act of Congress and approved by President Grant on April 10, 1869. Felix Brunot was its first and only president, a position he held until 1874 when it was abandoned. Brunot, like Gen. Crook, was a graduate of the Confederate Libby Prison. (Slattery, *Felix Reville Brunot*, pp. 69-81.)

Shoshoni now camped together on the Klamath Reservation into a more peaceful frame of mind. Brunot would never get the chance to see if he could smooth things over. However, en route from The Dalles City by stagecoach to the Warm Springs Reservation he did find out what he was up against when it came to cooperation from the white residents of Oregon. Later this same stage driver would tell Gen. Joseph Whittlesey about Brunot's trip from The Dalles.

> The last time I drove over this road I carried Mr. Felix Brunot. He was going up to the Warm Springs Agency and thought he was going to civilize the Indians. I told him I know how to tame Indians for I have an old well down on my place in the Deschutes Valley—a pretty deep well. It ain't got no water in it but if you look down you'll see seven tamed Indians in the bottom.[15]

This stage driver was speaking for the average American citizen insofar as his views on the treatment of Indians was concerned. Unfortunately Brunot, a deeply religious man, would never make it to the Klamath Agency to visit the Modocs and the Snakes. Forest fires raging out of control on the Paulina, Fremont and Klamath mountains made the journey impossible.[16] Brunot honestly believed he could have prevented the Modoc War, which would break out a year after his arrival at the Warm Springs Agency.

En route from Warm Springs to visit Western Shoshoni at the Fort Hall Reservation and Eastern Shoshoni at the Wind River Reservation, Brunot was traveling under heavy army escort across eastern Oregon. One day they met a Snake hunting party in the Blue Mountains under the leadership of Black Eagle, who still hadn't been confined on any reservation. During questioning, a small boy told how miserable life had been for the women and children in the recent Shoshoni war. His sorrowful talk of mistreatment so angered the young Army officer in charge of Brunot's escort that he quietly turned to Black Eagle and asked if the boy spoke the truth. Black Eagle looked at the officer in calm surprise and

15 As remembered by Gen. Whittlesey who was also a member of the peace commission. (Slattery, *Felix Brunot*, pp. 51, 147.)

16 Ibid, p. 181.

quietly replied: "Lieutenant, the boy never saw a white man before. He has not learned to lie."[17]

Following this push across the Ochoco and observing living conditions at Fort Hall, Brunot proposed the establishment of a reservation in eastern Oregon for the exclusive use of the Snake war tribes. This proposal would be vigorously endorsed by Alfred Meacham, superintendent of Oregon Indian Affairs. Both Superintendent Meacham and Commissioner Brunot would be greatly disappointed in the final outcome.

17 Ibid, pp. 176-177. Brunot would call Black Eagle "Eagle Feather." Black Eagle was also known as Eagle Eye by the Americans.

Those arriving in the 1871 migration were:

Adams, William (family)
Alchul, Charles (single)
Allen, Andrew (single)
Allen, B.F. (family)
Allen, William (single)
Blevins, Issac (family)
Booth, William (family)
Cecil, Logan (single)
Cecil, W.C. (family)
Hodges, Monroe (family)
LaFollette, Thomas (family)
Logan, Cecil (single)
McClure, James (single)
Miller, George (family)
Newsome, Sam (family)
Nicholas, B.F. (family)
Noble, Andrew (single)
Noble, George (single)
Nye, M.C. (single)
Polly, John (single)
Read, Perry (family)
Stephenson, Tom (family)

CHAPTER 156

SHELL FLOWER

Some say I am a half-breed. My father and mother were pure Indian. I would be ashamed to acknowledge there was white blood in me. . . .

Sarah Winnemucca
Paiute Activist

It was one thing to establish a new reservation but quite another to convince the Snakes to reside there. Finally in late 1872, on the promise that he would be recognized as head chief of the war tribes if he came onto the Malheur Reservation, Pony Blanket came out of hiding. It was difficult for Has No Horse to believe that the man who married his sister would now be the first to accept reservation life. Although Pony Blanket's followers were facing starvation, they were not enthusiastic about living on a government reserve. One of the main factors contributing to this reluctance was the name itself. Malheur—meaning a place of misfortune—unsettled the Shoshoni's peace of mind.

Even so, during the winter of '72-'73, a few Indians drifted onto the reservation, but they were mainly peaceful Paiutes.[1] The mountain warriors were with Has No Horse in the rugged plateaus of south-central Oregon and the plainsmen under the leadership of Iron Crow returned to Gourd Rattler's camp in western Wyoming. Bad Face, in defiance of his daughter, refused to go on the Malheur Reservation because he "was not going to farm for a living" and therefore, would be "in danger of starving!"

1 *Owyhee Avalanche*, October 11, 1873; *Indian Affairs Report 1873*, pp. 320-24, House Executive Document No. 99, 43rd Congress 2nd Session.

When he did consent to go, under heavy pressure from Sarah, Left Hand (the powerful Snake medicine man) chased him off.[2] About this time, the Shoshoni spiritual leaders were exercising tremendous influence on all the tribes. Coyote Droppings (Isa Tai, a Comanche prophet) convinced the Shoshoni he had ascended above the clouds and talked with the Great Spirit. As proof, he actually predicted a comet flaring over the southwest in 1873 would disappear in five days. He was urging the tribes to destroy all white men and promised to give them, by his magical powers, immunity from white men's bullets. To back up this promise, Coyote Droppings was said to have belched out a wagon load of cartridges and swallowed them again.[3] Now that was impressive!

Wovoka, The Cutter, now working as a Nevada ranch-hand under the name Jack Wilson, was prophesying the resurrection of all the Shoshoni dead.[4] In so doing, he sparked a religious movement that would sweep over all western tribes like a tidal wave and cause unprecedented fear in the white population. Lt. Col. Frank Wheaton reported that "Ocheho [Has No Horse], Egan [Pony Blanket], Weahwewa [Wolf Dog] and the renegade Modoc Jack are all firm believers in the Smoholla or new Indian religion which instructs them that the time is not far distant when all dead Indians will be restored to life and that through their aid and the magical efforts of their chief medicine men all white men will be spirited away and the country restored to its original Indian occupants."

He further stated that "Ocheho cannot be convinced today that a bullet shot at his chief medicine man [Buzzard Man] would harm or injure him in any way, and only a few weeks since, he kept a party of incredulous Klamaths waiting three days at his camp while his medicine man was arranging the Great Spirit to catch all bullets fired at him."[5]

It was against this hostile feeling that the great Malheur Reservation got off to a shaky start.

---

2 William M. Turner to the Honorable W.V. Rinehart, September 10, 1877, Letters Received, Office of Indian Affairs, Oregon Superintendency.

3 Russell, *Book of the American West*, p. 249.

4 The Cutter was the son of the Snake prophet, White Man, who had taken up permanent residence in the Spirit World in 1870. Baily, *Wovoka, The Indian Messiah*, p. 22.

5 Lt. Col. Frank Wheaton to Assist. Adj. Gen., Department of the Columbia, May 6, 1873, *Modoc War Official Correspondence*, Bancroft Library.

Probably by sheer chance, the Indian Department did appoint a good agent, Major Sam Parrish, to enforce reservation policy. Parrish, son of Josiah Parrish (an early Methodist missionary who served as one of the first treaty commissioners under Anson Dart in 1850[6]) believed the Snakes could become good citizens if the white man kept his word; treated them with respect; and cultivated their natural interests in learning. He himself was a hard, efficient worker and expected results from the work of the laboring Indians. Parrish also believed in paying the Indians for services rendered. "If you work for me," the agent said, "or any of my men, we are to pay you for it. If you cut or pile wood, we will pay you for it. If I send you to Canyon City for myself or my men, you shall be paid for it."[7]

With this kind of incentive, the Indians soon learned how to plow, harrow and plant. From this experiment, the settlers also gained some startling information. . . the Shoshoni were not lazy. One of their first major projects was the construction of a two and a half mile ditch ten feet wide to carry water from the Malheur River to their fertile croplands. This canal would soon cause jealousy among their white neighbors. Unfortunately for the Shoshoni, the Malheur Reservation boundary would encompass some of the best and most productive land in Harney Valley, including millions of board feet of virgin pine in the northern section.

Other distractions would take their toll on the new farmers. A sad turn of events split the house of Winnemucca into warring factions. Bad Face's second daughter, Shell Flower, married a white man, and thus placed Bad Face, Natchez and Leggins at the disadvantage of fighting against son-in-law, brother-in-law and uncle.

Shell Flower had been under the influence of whites most of her life. As a small child, her grandfather had taken her from Bad Face and placed her in the Catholic convent of Notre Dame in San Jose where she was raised by various white families and treated like a hard working servant. She and her sister Elma were enrolled in a Catholic school but

6 Hooper, Albon W., *Indian Affairs and Their Administration*, 1849-1860, University of Pennsylvania thesis, pp. 69-130.

7 Hopkins, Sarah Winnemucca, *Life Among the Piutes: Their Wrongs and Claims*, pp. 110-111.

quickly dismissed when wealthy parents complained about Indians being in school with their children.[8] Given the Christian name of Sarah Winnemucca, Shell Flower accepted European culture with the eagerness of youth—quite unaware of the prejudice that would befall her in adult life. Self-educated, fluent in several Indian languages, Sarah published one of the first works of literature by an American Indian in 1883.

By the time Sarah was born, Karl Marx was already criticizing contemporary political and social conditions. From 1852 to 1861, his theories of class equality were widely publicized by the *New York Tribune*. Young intellectuals of the time were quite impressed—not the least of whom was Sarah Winnemucca. Throughout her teens, she would attempt to persuade frontier society that Indians were their equals and she enlisted many influential citizens in her cause. Finding this to be a monumental and also discouraging task, Sarah scaled-down her efforts to concentrate on the peaceful Paiutes and specifically upon her own family. This too, would be extremely difficult in view of her father's and older brother's unrepentant social activities.

Sarah had just reached the age of twenty when the Shoshoni war burst into full bloom. It became an intense embarrassment that her father's best friend and confidant was the notorious war chief, Has No Horse. Neither did it help when her brother threatened to do bodily harm to an Indian agent and was sentenced to prison.

During one of Sarah's impassioned pleas for understanding, Natchez stalked into the Pyramid Lake Indian Agency, and cornering the cowering agent C.A. Bateman, told him if he ever refused his people food again, he would cut his heart out. That night a company of U.S. troops paid the lodge of Winnemucca a visit. They read Natchez the formal charge: threatening the life of a government employee and brewing trouble amongst the Paiutes. Put under military arrest, he was shackled in irons and taken to Fort Alcatraz in San Francisco Bay to spend the rest of his natural life.

This was a mistake, as the government soon found out. Sarah, wise to the white man's way of life, immediately took up the defense of her brother. She made personal appearances in San Francisco, speaking to large audiences telling them about the brutality suffered by her people.

8 Hopkins, *Life Among the Piutes*, p. 70.

She visited the press and soon California and Nevada newspapers were taking up her battle for the underdog. Public sentiment was on the side of Natchez and getting nasty. The army was faced with only one choice, for bad publicity was not what they needed with the Snake war tribes ripping eastern Oregon to shreds. It was only a matter of time before Natchez would gain his release from federal prison.

Sarah, desperately portraying Bad Face as the absolute leader of the Paiute tribes, vehemently denied his Snake heritage and established for all time her father's role as a Shoshoni statesman. She did everything in her power to assure the whites that Bad Face was a peace-loving man and only misbehaved under the sinful influence of Has No Horse. Much to her consternation, Bad Face refused to fit the mold, openly and proudly proclaiming that he and Has No Horse were inseparable. Undaunted, Sarah—in all her contacts with the American public, and they were many—would praise Bad Face as the redeemer of his race and Has No Horse as the destroyer.

As the Shoshoni war progressed, Sarah found it more and more difficult to be treated with respect as she fought with government agents over the treatment of tribesmen sentenced to the concentration camps. And so in 1869, torn between her youthful dream of Utopia and the harsh reality of the western frontier, she accepted a low-pay government interpreter position at Fort McDermit. Unfortunately, her boss—Capt. Henry Wagner, post commander—was the officer who had arrested Natchez and delivered him to Fort Alcatraz.[9] Wagner was less than sympathetic to Sarah's cause.

In 1868, Lt. Edward Bartlett saw "the little Princess" (as he called her) at Fort Harney where Sarah acted as interpreter for Gen. Crook. It made a lasting impression. When Fort Watson was discontinued in 1869, Bartlett was reassigned to Fort McDermit and the chase was on. Bartlett, a "hell for leather" Indian fighter was well-liked by his men but he was also an irresponsible drunkard who took advantage of people with his charming manners and handsome good looks. Undoubtedly, Shell Flower presented a challenge.

---

9 Sarah Winnemucca to Commissioner E.S. Parker, August 9, 1870, *Letters Received, Office of Indian Affairs, Nevada Superintendency*; *Daily Alta California*, January 30, 1874.

A reporter for the *Sacramento Record* claimed she was "the most handsome Paiute of her sex that I have ever seen," and supposedly, he had seen many.[10] Apparently Lt. Bartlett was of the same opinion and perhaps Sarah saw in Lt. Bartlett a way to be accepted by the whites. Whatever, she lost not only her heart but her good sense, too. Maybe she was becoming fearful of becoming an old maid for Sarah was now in her mid-twenties. Because it was against Nevada law for a white man to marry an Indian woman, Ed and Sarah eloped to the more lenient environs of Salt Lake City and were married by a justice of the peace on January 29, 1871, without the blessings of their commanding officer. Bartlett was absent without leave and Sarah neglected to tell Capt. Wagner where she was going.

Within a week, after the couple spent all of Sarah's hard-earned cash in the city's swankiest saloons, some of Sarah's romantic delusions were torn somewhat rudely from her. She would later testify in a Canyon City courtroom that her husband took all of her jewelry worth about $700 and pawned it for $200 which he spent gambling. "I never got a cent out of it."[11] But that wasn't the worst to come. Bad Face was so mad he nearly disowned Sarah and it was then that she realized she was of the warrior class and nothing could change that, but she had temporally lost the fire in her quest for recognition. . . recognition she no longer desired.[12]

The idyllic marriage lasted long enough to ruin Sarah's reputation and bring on family problems. On her return to Fort McDermit, she got into an argument with Capt. Wagner and quit her job. Eight months after vowing "til death do us part," Lt. Bartlett resigned his commission on November 15, 1871 and abandoned Sarah. This caused rumors to fly—with the blame falling on his Indian wife.

Later when questioned by the press about her marriage, Sarah replied, "My folks were very angry at my marriage, my father especially. He says he never will forgive me. They all knew the character of the man. He was nothing but a drunkard. He kept continually sending to me for money after my return home, and I supplied him as long as I could. . . ."

---

10 "Nevada Indians," *Bancroft Scrapbooks*, Vol. 93, p. 54.

11 Document of divorce proceedings of Sarah Winnemucca v. Edward C. Bartlett, September 21, 1876, Grant County Courthouse, Canyon City, Oregon.

12 Sarah's mother, Tubaitonie, had been killed in a cavalry raid in Harney Valley during the Shoshoni war.

This interview would continue along a different line of questioning. Bad Face had mysteriously disappeared from the reservation with a number of warriors and the report in circulation was that he had left to help the Modocs in Oregon. What did Sarah know about this? She knew very little. Sarah hadn't seen her father in two years. Although he had recently camped near Fort McDermit, he refused to see her. "Father was so angry at my marriage that, though living but a short distance from me, he would never send for me."

Sarah did recall, "During the late Indian fight in Oregon a cousin of ours, Jerry Long [a full blood Paiute named Angezah] was reported killed and my father immediately wrote to my uncles to send him some of the best young men to go over there with him. . . quite a number went. . . I think they went over to Oregon to join the Modocs. . . . " She couldn't bring herself to say that they may have united with Has No Horse.

The reporter would quickly ask, "Didn't you have no influence with your people in this matter?"

Miss Winnemucca sadly admitted, "Very little; when once they imagine an insult they seem to lose all reason. . . I cannot say that I know my father and his braves have gone to the Modocs, but that seems to be the general impression among us." In her own mind, Sarah could see the corruptive influence of Has No Horse in her father's latest escapade.

During this interview, the *Nevada State Journal* newshound went to great lengths in his description of Sarah whom he thought was pleasingly plump "but not too much so, and graceful in all her movements. Her jet-black hair hangs in heavy curls, and her sparkling black eyes forbid anything tending to too much familiarity. She dresses very tastefully, but not extravagantly—a la Americaine, upon this occasion, in a tight fitting suit of black Alpaca, very prettily trimmed with green fringe—in all making a very attractive appearance. When asked about the delicate question of her age and place of birth she laughed and said that was almost more than she knew herself."[13]

The stress of living in two worlds was taking its toll on Shell Flower. Not only shunned by her family, Paiute women were giving her a bad time. Because of her brief interlude with a white man, they

---

13 *Nevada State Journal* (Reno), February 12, 1873.

considered her a tainted woman and Sarah made headlines when she got into a brawl with one of "the gentler sex of the Paiute persuasion" as a reporter quaintly put it. According to him, Sarah was attending a dance when this woman began "slandering the virtue of Mrs. S.W. Bartlett." the outcome being that Sarah took to the warpath and after a lot of "scratching, biting and pulling of hair" threw her opponent to the ground and really worked her over. Sarah "sat upon her, bounced upon her and at every bounce gave her a lick in the face. Sarah warned her to never talk about her again in front of white folks."[14] Apparently, Sarah's fighting blood inherited from her father was coming to the fore.

Within two weeks, Sarah again made news at the Travelers Home Hotel in Winnemucca, Nevada. The fracas occurred in the hotel dining room when a waiter made a pass at Sarah. According to the reporter, "the young man got off with a black eye and Sally with a severe jolt in the mouth which split her lip badly." With blood gushing all over the place, the bartender interceded and stopped the fight. "Sally then rushed across the street to procure a warrant for the arrest of her adversary, but before the papers could be made out she went into spasms and soon was taken in charge by the Indians and carried off to camp." By now, the townsfolk feeling a little guilty about what happened, had her brought back to a room at the French Hotel where "she lay for two days in a stupor, apparently more dead than alive." The *Humboldt Register* speculated that Sarah may have been given a drugged drink. "Up to this time there have been no arrests," but it was expected that there would be as soon "as Sally goes marching around again."[15]

Disillusioned and out of a job, Sarah received word from the Malheur Reservation that Pony Blanket wanted to see her. By now, Bad Face was holed up in the Steens Mountains and in direct contact with Has No Horse. Dodging Pete French's cowboys for obvious reasons, Sally headed north but she had no intention of working for the government again. However, when Agent Sam Parrish offered her a $40 a month interpreter job, Sarah accepted.[16] She had nothing better to look forward to.

---

14 *Humboldt Register*, Winnemucca, Nevada, June 8. 1872.

15 *Humboldt Register*, June 22, 1872.

16 Hopkins, *Life Among the Piutes*, p. 105.

It's unknown if there was any connection, but shortly after Parrish hired Sarah he was replaced as agent of the Malheur Reservation by Henry Linville in the fall of 1873. Linville lasted only as long as it took Left Hand to run him off. The diplomatic explanation given was that "Agent H. Linville had a confrontation with the Indians that cost him his job."[17] In view of this little setback, Sam Parrish was reinstated as agent.

17 Account given by W.S. Linville (Henry Linville's son) and an agency employee in 1873-74. Young Linville would portray Left Hand as being "below medium height, stockily built with black, smoky-looking eyes giving an appearance of treachery about him." By contrast, Linville was favorably impressed with Pony Blanket whom he described as. . . "tall and muscular, straight as an arrow, his head well-poised, the eyes of an eagle and his hair was neatly made up in two braids that fell behind his shoulders. He looked every bit like an Indian chief." Linville would also note that Egan [Pony Blanket] was a Snake [Western Shoshoni] and not a Northern Paiute.

CHAPTER 157

FIND OCHIHO!

I ain't botherin' no body.
Just leave me alone!

Has No Horse
To Indian Agent Thomas Odeneal

The final days of 1872 would be chaotic not only for the Ochoco settlement but for Oregon as well. One Indian war was born and another one was brewing. Supt. Meacham, sensing that trouble lay ahead, left for Washington, D.C. in an attempt to straighten things out with the Interior Department. Instead, he lost his job.[1]

Thomas Odeneal—a professional bureaucrat—succeeded Meacham and quickly stirred the Indian problem east of the Cascades to a feverish pitch. It was Meacham's opinion that Odeneal, a prominent Portland lawyer, had "a limited knowledge of Indian character, and still less of the merits and demerits of this Modoc question."[2] Nevertheless, lending a sympathetic ear to the settler's complaints, Odeneal persuaded Interior Secretary Columbus Delano (who perhaps had a slight knowledge of the Modoc troubles) to issue an order confining all roving bands to the Klamath Reservation "peacefully if possible, forcibly if necessary."[3] Captain Jack, fearful of his life if imprisoned with the Snakes, was the first to react. His answer came the day after Thanksgiving. Charging into northern California, he killed eighteen ranchers and then dug-in within sight of the Oregon border and dared the whites to come after him.

1 Glassley, *Pacific Northwest Indian War*, p. 164.
2 Meacham, *Wigwam and Warpath*, p. 361.
3 Brady, *Northwestern Fighters and Fights*, p. 260.

Oregonians went into a state of panic, demanding the army stop this new threat at any cost. Everything from peace overtures to bribes were offered to lure Jack out of the lava beds. He refused to budge. In an effort to split the Modoc ranks, the military offered $100 to any Modoc who would defect. Four of Jack's warriors accepted the blood money—Steamboat Frank, Hooker Jim, Bogus Charley and Shacknasty Jim—the same men who accused Jack of "being a weakling and a coward" when he first considered accepting Odeneal's order to go on the reservation.

But the overriding fear was that Has No Horse would join Captain Jack in open warfare and in late December the order went out to forts Klamath, Bidwell, Warner, McDermit and Harney to bring Has No Horse in. The only information the army scouts had was that Has No Horse was hiding out somewhere between Hart Mountain and the Ochoco Valley but where, was anyone's guess. Special troops were assigned to the Malheur Reservation to observe Pony Blanket's every move while Wolf Dog was placed under arrest at the Klamath Agency to insure that neither war chief attempted a union with Has No Horse.

It was well known that the dog soldiers were ready and primed for battle. Lt. Col Frank Wheaton (commander of the District of the Lakes), in an effort to avert full-scale alarm, issued a statement to the press. "I cannot learn that any proposition has been made to Ocheho to join other Paiute chiefs in any projected outbreak, but I believe the young men of the different Paiute bands to be greatly excited and elated at the delay in exterminating Jack's renegade Modocs. . . . " He did warn, however, that "should Ocheho become disaffected and lead them a very expensive and bloody war will ensue."[4]

A cordon of soldiers was placed around Captain Jack's lava bed fortress to prevent Has No Horse from getting in with reinforcements while hundreds more scouted central Oregon trying to locate him. The army was certain that Bad Face (operating out of the Steens Mountains where he could observe troop movements from both Fort Warner and Fort McDermit), Pony Blanket watching Fort Harney, and Wolf Dog monitoring Fort Klamath, were in continuous contact with Has No Horse.

4 Wheaton to A.A.G. Department of the Columbia, May 6, 1873, *Modoc War Official Correspondence*, Bancroft Library.

Wheaton would later admit that Shoshoni runners had frequent communications with headmen of the various Snake war tribes and that he knew Has No Horse was "promptly advised of everything of interest to them that occurs at military posts in southern Oregon."[5] Wheaton also strongly advised that Fort Harney be heavily reinforced "as soon as was possible."[6]

In this manner, Has No Horse kept the army off balance, gaining valuable time for Captain Jack to prepare his defense, without actually breaking his agreement with Gen. Crook. Don't think for a moment that there was any great love between the Snake war chief and the embattled Modocs. There wasn't. Has No Horse was merely paying off a war debt to John Schonchin for supplying him with ammunition during the Snake war. His warriors were now returning the favor by smuggling arms and food into Captain Jack's stronghold.

Then, in a five day period encompassing Christmas 1872, the best laid plans of Salem and Washington, D.C. went completely astray. At 9:37 a.m. on December 22, a fire broke out in a Chinese laundry on the Portland waterfront. The *S.S. Oneatta* pulled up and turned a hose on the burning building, but withdrew hastily when flames leaped hungrily at its wooden decks. Before rain finally doused the inferno, three city blocks between Morrison and Alder Streets—mostly warehouses containing a half million dollars in war supplies for the coming battle east of the Cascades—went up in flames.

A brilliant military strategist, Has No Horse would cause further disruption without firing a shot. On December 23, while the Portland warehouses were still blazing, the Grizzly Mountain stage thundered into the lower Ochoco Valley bearing unexpected Christmas tidings. Wasco County commissioners had voted to bless the little settlement with recognition. Henceforth, it would be known throughout the Pacific Northwest as Prineville, Oregon. Unfortunately, the holiday joy would

5 In his youth, Raymond Yowell (citizen of the Shoshoni nation) knew an old Shoshoni runner who would run from his camp on the Oregon-Nevada line to visit tribal members in the Ruby Valley area some 100 miles to the southeast. He could cover this distance in one day while crossing several rivers. According to Yowell, the old man's feet were so callused you could strike a match on their toughened soles. This runner had never worn moccasins in his entire life. (Interview with Raymond Yowell, November 12, 1997.)

6 Wheaton to Lt. James A. Rockwell, April 16, 1873, *Modoc War Official Correspondence*.

be short-lived. As the happy city dwellers prepared for the celebration, a ghostly line of feathered horsemen, cloaked in a gently falling snow, appeared on the Crooked River rim. Laughter turned to shouts of fear as cabins were hastily barricaded for the expected onslaught. A frightened stage driver whipped his team towards The Dalles and word spread that the Modocs had Prineville under siege![7]

The fact that Captain Jack was hemmed in on the Oregon-California line and no attack was forthcoming had little bearing on what followed. Not only did it cause the army real concern but to this day, descendants of those first settlers swear that the town was under Modoc attack. It caused enough excitement to stampede Gov. Grover into calling for volunteers to protect the settlers of eastern Oregon.[8] Captain David Perry, who had been ordered out of Fort Warner on December 2 to the lava beds, got blessed with some of these volunteers. As he put it, "About one hundred Oregon militia, reinforced by a major and a brigadier-general from the same state, who looked upon the whole affair as sort of a picnic, arrived about the first of January 1873" to liberate eastern Oregon from the Modocs.[9]

Seventy-two hours after the Prineville uproar, a weary courier galloped into Fort Harney and informed the commanding officer that Gen. Canby was ordering all troops into the field. With a blizzard raging across the high desert, Major John Trimble was less than pleased with this directive. He would later write with a touch of sarcasm, "Should an officer stationed in Oregon receive an order about the 25th day of December to march his company 300 miles to take part in an Indian war, both he and his men, most likely, would consider the same a very cool proceeding. And they did. Now this [300 miles] is about the distance from Camp Harney to the Modoc country."

But march they did and the major was still complaining. Canby expected them to cross the desert in sub-zero weather without any of the luxuries of frontier warfare. Speed was of the essence and Trimble's instructions were "light marching order" which meant instead of travel-

---

7 Because of expected Indian attack only one family and two single men settled in the Ochoco-Crooked River valleys in 1872. They were: Joe Crooks (single), George Cline (family), and Ike Schwartz (single).

8 Glassley, *Pacific Northwest Indian Wars*, p. 197.

9 Brig. Gen. David Perry (retired) in Brady, *Northwestern Fights and Fighters*, p. 291.

ing in comfortable wagons loaded with tents, blankets, stoves and extra clothing, what supplies they took "were piled upon those unfortunate mules and off we went."[10]

With only a skeleton force left to man Fort Harney, everyone was nervous that Pony Blanket would take this opportunity to join forces with Has No Horse. There was no need to worry. His warriors were so weakened from starvation, they had neither the strength nor the desire to move out in the dead of winter. Things were now at a stalemate. Would Jack fight or sue for peace? Would Has No Horse join him in the lava beds or take the war to the settlements, thus opening a second front? Had Bad Face linked up with Has No Horse or was he just bidding his time? What mischief was the radical Paiute wench, Sally Winnemucca, up to now that she was hiding out on the Malheur Reservation? No one knew and for a period of three weeks, the winter of 1873 settled into a war of nerves as rumors swept rampant across the state.

On his forced march across the frozen desert, Major Trimble made no attempt to contact Has No Horse. From remarks made, it would appear that Trimble's sympathy was with the hunted. "We plodded on through the virgin wilderness never before disturbed by foot or hoof and at day's end dismounted to sleep in its fold. . . and for what? To drive a couple of hundred miserable aborigines from a desolate natural shelter in the wilderness so that a few thriving cattlemen might range their wild steers in a scope of isolated country." No, Major Trimble didn't feel sorry for the settlers.

In mid-January, he tied in with Lt. Col. Wheaton and to the enlisted men's utter joy, Wheaton decided to carry the fight to Captain Jack. On the morning of January 17, shouting they would have "Modoc steak for breakfast," the Army prepared for attack.

No doubt some of this enthusiasm was inspired by the arrival of Gov. Grover's celebrated Oregon militia, led by such stalwarts as Col. William (Bud) Thompson. At this point, the Army had the Modocs in a no-win situation—completely cut off from the outside world—and was patiently waiting for Captain Jack to either make a break and get gunned down; stay where he was and slowly starve to death; or sue for peace.

10 Reminiscence by Major J.G. Trimble, U.S. Army (retired) in Brady, *Northwestern Fights and Fighters*, pp. 280-85.

The military could care less which option he chose. Time was on their side. Gov. Grover thought differently. He believed the Army was stalling in a "needless waste of time and hints of graft were afloat." With this in mind, the governor called Thompson to Salem and requested that he go down to the southeastern Oregon front with State Militia General John F. Miller and put a stop to the Modoc uprising. Cocky as usual, and with an opinion on how the war should be fought, Thompson was eager to go.

Using Voltaire's description of Frenchmen, Thompson would portray the Modocs in general as being "half devil and half monkey," while he depicted Captain Jack as "a fiend dancing in the fire-light of hell." In a letter to the *Army and Navy Journal*, Thompson would also compare the Indians in the lava beds to "ants in a sponge." He claimed Lt. Col. Wheaton consulted him on how to attack and often admonished him for taking unnecessarily risks as bullets "sang over my head and hissed in my ears," all the while giving orders to the soldiers who apparently were at a complete loss without Col. Thompson's guidance. In short, without his help, the Modoc War would still be in progress. It was during this period of self-esteem that Harvey Scott, editor of *The Oregonian*, would label Thompson as "Gov. Grover's mad-cap colonel."[11] Just two days before Major Trimble arrived from Fort Harney, Lt. Col. Wheaton had written, "If the Modocs will only try to make good their boast to whip a thousand soldiers all will be satisfied." Now, he ordered Major Trimble and Major Mason with two infantry companies and a company of volunteers to hit Jack's fortress with intent to end the Modoc uprising for all time. In a day-long battle, the results were devastating. Trimble lost nine men, and thirty were wounded. The infantry company under Major E.C. Mason lost nearly one-fourth of its men. Capt. Perry, Lt. Kyle and Lt. Roberts were wounded. The volunteers, seeing that the battle wasn't going too well, skipped out with "only trifling losses." And, Lt. Col. Wheaton—no doubt having acted on Col. Thompson's advice—was relieved of his command.[12]

This was not exactly a banner day for the soldiers. Col. A.C. Gillem, 1st U.S. Cavalry was rushed in to replace Wheaton. His arrival placed the number of soldiers now engaged against Jack's Modocs at one

11 Thompson, *Reminiscence of a Pioneer*, pp. 74-75, 97, 114, 124.

12 Brady, *Northwestern Fights and Fighters*, p. 236-37.

thousand strong. Gen. Canby took command in person of the battle site and the search for Has No Horse was increased. To insure the Snake war chief would be limited on manpower, the word went out to get Bad Face as well.

To Sarah Winnemucca's dismay, her exaggerations of her father's influence within the Shoshoni tribes was coming back to haunt her. The citizens of Oregon were now blaming him for Has No Horse's noncooperation. Adding to the confusion, Sarah innocently commented to a Nevada reporter that she didn't know whether her father and his braves had joined the Modocs or not but "that seems to be the general impression."[13] This was in February. Two months later, her remark was taken up by a Portland paper and blatantly distorted. The article would begin with: "Mr. Jones, recently from Camp Warner, reports that Sally Winnemucca, an educated squaw, stated that her father's band was in constant communication with Jack and that it was agreed that if the soldiers did not whip Jack all the Indians (meaning Has No Horse's warriors) would join in a general war of extermination."[14] Jones was an Indian rancher whom Sarah was living with at the time.[15]

A different story emerged from one of the officers at Fort Warner. In late spring, Lt. Thomas Dunn made contact with Has No Horse south of the Maury Mountains. According to him, "Ocheo assured me that he was not friendly with the hostile Modocs." However, believing Sarah's publicity that Bad Face held great influence in the Snake war tribes, Dunn concluded, "We have thus far no occasion to doubt Ocheo's sincerity, but it is thought his future conduct may be governed in some degree by the attitude assumed by Winnemucca."[16]

In the meantime, all available resources were being mobilized, including the Oregon Militia, for an all-out offensive. Billy McKay was called upon to reassemble the Warm Springs Cavalry. He refused. At the close of the Snake campaign, McKay was appointed interpreter for the Snake prisoners held on the Klamath Reserve where he also served as

---

13 Reno, *Nevada State Journal*, February 12, 1873.

14 *Portland Daily Bulletin,* April 23, 1873.

15 Ltrs. Rec., Lt. Col. Wheaton to A.A.G., Department of the Columbia, May 6, 1873.

16 Thomas S. Dunn, Camp Warner, May 23, 1873, *Modoc War Official Correspondence.*

agency physician and chief of commissary.[17] The mistreatment of the prisoners and especially the lack of provisions did not meet with his approval so he returned to Warm Springs. At this point, he and Don McKay organized a search to recover captive Snake children now held as slaves throughout Oregon and Washington.[18]

For this humanitarian endeavor and his medical practice with the Indians, Dr. McKay received an honorary degree from the medical department at Willamette University.[19] A skilled surgeon, McKay held no desire to participate in another slaughter of his own race. The Snake offensive had pushed him to the brink of alcoholism.

Therefore, Billy referred the army recruiters to Don McKay who harbored no qualms about taking up the war-club. By virtue of his marriage to a Umatilla girl, Don was a chief in the Umatilla tribe. Educated by trail and campfire, veteran of two Indian wars, Donald McKay was a formidable opponent and because of his Cayuse (actually Paiute) blood was more sympathetic to the Snakes than his hereditary enemies, the Warm Springs Indians. This would cause problems. Although the army had extreme confidence in his abilities as a leader, the Warm Springs Cavalry—mainly out of fear—did not and therefore, they didn't perform too honorably during the Modoc battle. Nevertheless, by March 22, 1873 Don McKay and Louis Cozaire—army recruiting officer—had mustered seventy-five Warm Springs Indians into army service, including one Shoshoni.[20] Ironically, the Snake recruit was Buffalo Tail, the son of Paulina who, along with his mother, was taken prisoner by the Oregon Volunteers in 1865. Enrolled as Peter Paulina, his enlistment papers reveal the terrible effects of starvation and mistreatment on the Warm Springs Reservation. In a list of inductees ranging from 5' 9" to 6' 4" in height, Peter is described as "eighteen years of age, five feet

17 Oregon Superintendency, Indian Affairs, Letters Sent, National Archives, M-2, Roll 10, Meacham to Capt. O.C. Knapp, U.S. Army Sub-Agent, Fort Klamath, Oregon, April 19, 1870.

18 McKay Report to Meacham, December 20, 1871, *McKay Papers*, Umatilla County Library, Pendleton, Oregon.

19 Records, Department of Medicine, Willamette University, Salem, Oregon.

20 Louis V. Cozaire, Dispatcher to Headquarters, Department of the Columbia, April 4, 6, and 10, 1873.

tall."[21] Young Paulina was also denying that he was a Walpapi Snake, probably for safety's sake.[22]

It should be mentioned that all Indians sentenced to the reservation—generally under the administration of some religious organization—were given Christian names, the assumption being that this would civilize them. Has No Horse drew the inspired title of "Albert Ochiho." His grandsons were stuck with the names of Tom, Dick and Harry Ochiho.[23]

Another interesting recruit riding with the Warm Springs scouts was the tubby Wasco chief Schannawick, known to his tribesmen as Sharp Eyes. It was later claimed that his corpulence prohibited him from active participation in tribal functions. Anyway, when McKay was advancing on Capt. Jack's stronghold in the lava beds, Sharp Eyes spotted the Modoc chief. He carefully drew a bead on Jack's chest, touched off a round and. . . killed Jack's mother. That little mishap didn't serve to improve relations between the Modocs and Oregon's Warm Springs associates. Perhaps this is where Schannawick gained the name of "Sharp Eyes."[24]

Disregarding this unfortunate incident, there was already bad blood between the Modocs and the Warm Springs scouts. Jack's father—chief of the Lost River Modocs—was killed in battle with the Warm Springs Indians near the headwater of the Deschutes River when Jack was a small boy.[25]

---

21 Letter, Matthew Cullen to Gale Ontko, February 5, 1971, Oregon Historical Society, list of Warm Springs Scouts, Snake and Modoc Wars.

22 Peter Paulina, *The Yahuskin Band of Snake Indians v. The United States, U.S. Court of Claims E-344*, p. 997. In this document, it is stated that Pete Paulina was born at Silver Lake about 1866 or 1867. This statement would imply that young Paulina was only six years old when he enlisted in the Warm Springs scouts in March 1873, which is not likely. Actually, Young Paulina was about eleven or twelve years old in 1867 at the time of his father's death.

23 Burdette Ochiho to Gale Ontko, letter dated Klamath Falls, Oregon, August 4, 1956. The name Albert Ochiho is thought to be a misspelling of Alfred, A.B. Meacham's first name and the Oregon superintendent of Indian affairs who talked Has No Horse into going onto the Klamath Reservation. This would have been in keeping with the times to assign an Indian the name of a well-known white man.

24 In 1905 when Sharp Eyes was 72 years old, Benjamin A. Gifford—noted Oregon photographer—recorded Old Sharp Eyes' image for posterity in all his potbellied glory.

25 Meacham, *Wigwam and Warpath*, p. 295.

Now that the state was mobilized for action but unsure of how to proceed, the next step was diplomatic relations. One must remember that Oregon, unlike her bawdy western neighbors, was quite progressive for the times so a search for peace delegates was begun. However Salem's favorite warrior, Col Bud Thompson viewed this pursuit in a somewhat different light. According to him, "the churches succeeded in hypnotizing the grim soldier in the White House and the result was a peace commission."[26] After several delays and changes in representatives, the board consisted of Gen. Edward Canby, commander of the Military Department of the Columbia; Rev. Eleazor Thomas, a Methodist dignitary representing California; Mr. LeRoy Dyer, Klamath Indian agent; and Col. Alfred Meacham, ex-superintendent of Oregon Indian Affairs and currently an officer in the Oregon Militia. Official interpreters were Frank Riddle and his Modoc wife, Toby, a highly respected chief in the Modoc tribes known to the Indians as Strong Heart (Winema).

With a thousand soldiers surrounding Jack's stronghold of about one hundred and fifty Modocs, two-thirds of whom were women and children, settlement was near at hand. The only wild card was Has No Horse and no one knew for certain what path he would choose to follow.

During the scurry to find Has No Horse, Peace Commissioner Brunot rushed to the Wind River Reservation to make certain Gourd Rattler didn't have a change of heart and patch-up family relations with his western cousin. He intended to do this by offering to buy 500,000 acres of Shoshoni mining land already occupied by American settlers. To further complicate the peace-keeping effort, Brunot got momentarily sidetracked in Sweetwater, Wyoming when the word went out that the U.S. Infantry was engaged in a terrible battle with a large body of Indians which, in time, proved to be a volunteer company of settlers who also thought they were fighting Indians. Strangely, maybe due to poor marksmanship, no one was seriously injured but no doubt whatever casualties were suffered on either side would get blamed on the Indians.

The conference with Gourd Rattler and his head chiefs lasted for three days. Brunot assured the Shoshoni that the terms of the land sale were as fair to them as they were to the United States. From the signatures appended to the agreement, one could believe that they were titles

26 Thompson, *Reminiscences of a Pioneer*, p. 108.

bestowed with sarcasm by their Western Shoshoni brothers. Besides Gourd Rattler, among the dignitaries who signed the relinquishment document on the half million acres of Shoshoni land were: Dirty Back (Toopsepowots), Necktie (Konoka), Put His Finger in a Crack (Weawicke), and Horse's Grandfather (Teneandoka). Brunot was quite impressed with his success and he reminded the government in his report to Columbus Delano, secretary of the Interior, that this important treaty was effected without giving presents to the Shoshoni, which was contrary to the normal procedure.[27]

It was probably just as well that there was a lack of gifts, considering what the government foisted off on the Utes that same year. Among the goods bestowed upon these clansmen were hoop skirts and cases of sardines, which proved astonishingly expensive to the government, but not conducive to Indian bliss. It is certain that generosity of this nature would have had a tough time in luring Has No Horse from his mountain retreat.

In reality, the Modoc peace agreement should have been settled in 1870. At the Yainax Council, which was convened on December 29, 1869 in an effort to persuade the Modocs to come peacefully onto the Klamath Reserve, the important chiefs in attendance were Old Schonchin and Captain Jack of the Modocs; Allen David representing the Klamaths; and Ocheo—Has No Horse, who held little respect for either Klamaths or Modocs—acting as spokesman for the Western Shoshoni tribes. Because it ended on the night of December 31, 1869, this meeting was celebrated as "the death of 1869 and the birth of 1870." One of the principal speakers was Queen Mary, Captain Jack's sister and official mediator, said to have been a clever and intelligent negotiator. According to Meacham (who was at that time Oregon superintendent of Indian affairs) she was known as "Queen of the Modocs" because of her beauty and power over Jack. He also believed that Queen Mary had gained her considerable knowledge on how to deal with the white race because "she had been sold to five or six white men in the last ten years."

Meacham would further note, "While she had induced so many different men to buy her from her brother, she had made each one, in turn, anxious to return her to her people; but not until she had squandered all

27 Slattery, *Felix Reville Brunot*, pp. 184, 193-195.

the money she could command. It has been denied Captain Jack was ever a party to these several matrimonial speculations but [they] have been a great source of wealth to him."[28] Meacham, himself, believed Jack to be innocent in the bartering of his sister's honor and that it was more likely Mary's own doing. She was a headstrong woman to say the least.

The "Peace Tree" under which this council took place was on a sloping hillside overlooking the Sprague River valley. Allen David would give the most impassioned speech to welcome the Modocs onto the Klamath Reservation. It follows in part:[29]

> We have washed each others hands; they are not bloody now. . . . The sun is a witness between us; the mountains are looking on us. . . . This pine tree is a witness. . . when you see this tree, remember it is a witness that here we made friends with the Mo-a-doc-as. Never cut down that tree. Let the arm be broke that would hurt it; let the hand die that would break a twig from it. So long as snow shall fall on Yai-nax Mountain, let it stand. Long as the water runs in the river, let it stand. Long as the white rabbit shall live in the Man-za-ni-ta [groves], let it stand. Let our children play round it; let the young people dance under its leaves, and let the old men smoke together in its shade. Let this tree stand forever, as a witness. I have done.

It seems fitting that this majestic pine tree would become known as the Ochiho Tree. . . . named for a Shoshoni war chief whom present students of Oregon history claim never existed.

---

28 Meacham, *Wigwam and Warpath*, pp. 326-327.

29 For a full account of this peace council see Meacham, *Wigwam and Warpath*, pp. 329-341.

CHAPTER 158

SOLJERS A COMIN'

Damn ye! Maybe you believe next time what squaw tell you!

Boston Charley
Modoc Warrior to Rev. Thomas

When the old stage station operator, Al Meacham, was appointed superintendent of Oregon Indian affairs, one of his first official acts made Toby Riddle his friend for life. Meacham issued an order to all white men living with Indian women to either marry them or get off the reservation. This resulted in Frank Riddle making Toby a legal wife and she was always grateful to Meacham.[1]

Meacham—the delegate most trusted by the Modocs—and Frank Riddle began preliminary meetings with Jack in February of 1873. Although there was a free exchange of courtesies, it became apparent that Hooker Jim and his cohorts were against peaceful settlement. Riddle, regarded as "an unusually intelligent man," believed Hooker Jim was stalling in the hope of drawing Has No Horse and his dog soldiers into the fight. Meacham agreed and tried to warn the other peace commissioners that they were wasting time in fruitless negotiations which at best were merely camouflage for an unconditional surrender.

Throughout earlier meetings the Ben Wright affair—in which Wright killed 40 Modoc warriors under a flag of truce—kept coming up

1 Note by J.W. Redington, Brady, *Northwestern Fights and Fighters*, p. 246. As editor of *The Statesman* in Salem, Redington described some of the problems of newspapering in early Oregon: "I used to rustle ads for the four-page papers but it was worse than painful dentistry, and when I tried to collect bills, I invited getting shot, or at least half-shot. So I got scared. . . joined the army and went scouting through three Indian wars, thus getting into the safety zone."

but was dutifully ignored by the peace commissioners.[2] During another council soldiers (in direct violation of the existing truce) stole some Modoc horses, including Jack's favorite mount. It's small wonder that Jack and Scarface Charlie were having difficulty holding John Schonchin and his militant followers in check. It's even more challenging to explain how Jack kept Scarface Charlie on a tight rein. As a small boy, Scarface Charlie—now haunted by nightmares from the past—saw mounted white men run his father down, lasso him with a rawhide rope, drag him to a nearby tree and hang him without proof that he was guilty of any crime.[3] No, Scarface Charlie would harbor no tender feelings regarding his white brothers and it was he who fired the opening shot of the Modoc War.

Another round of negotiations was canceled when Captain Jack sent word that he couldn't attend because the Modocs were "burning their dead."[4] This admission would give substance to the rumor that Has No Horse had sent at least two Snake military advisors into Jack's lava bed hideout. The cremation of those killed in battle was unique to Shoshoni dog soldiers—a ritual not practiced by other western tribes.

When Jack was notified that soldiers were stealing Modoc horses under cover of the peace conference, he calmly replied that he would not fire the first shot but he wanted his horses returned. With this in mind a small group of Modoc women came in to the main Army camp and asked for their ponies. Placed under armed guard, they were permitted to go to a corral and see the stolen horses but they weren't allowed to take them. At this point, the women were then ordered out of camp and told not to return.[5] The reason being that several of these ponies had already been appropriated by the Oregon Volunteers for use at home when the war was over.

This horse rustling would generate some internal unrest. Arriving with Major John Trimble on his forced march from Fort Harney was Gray Fox (Letaiyo), a Pony Stealer Snake who would soon live up to his tribal name. Gray Fox had been given the Christian name of Louey Crook.

---

2 For more on Ben Wright, see *Thunder Over the Ochoco*, Vol. II, pp. 203, 267, 269, and 286; Meacham, *Wigwam and Warpath*, pp. 298-99.

3 Meacham, *Wigwam and Warpath*, pp. 369.

4 Ibid., p. 434.

5 Ibid., p. 437.

Has No Horse

Courtesy Modoc County Museum

Gen. Oliver Otis Howard

Dictionary of American Portraits
Engraving by Robert Whitechurch

Gen. Nelson A. Miles

Dictionary of American Portraits

Gen. Philip Sheridan

Dictionary of American Portraits
Courtesy New-York Historical Society

Gen. Lew Wallace

Dictionary of American Portraits
Photograph by Napoleon Sarony

Pres. Rutherford B. Hayes

Dictionary of American Portraits
Courtesy Library of Congress, Brady-Handy Collection

Lucy Hayes

Dictionary of American Portraits
Engraving by John Sartain

Gifford Pinchot

Dictionary of American Portraits
Courtesy Library of Congress

Sitting Bull

Dictionary of American Portraits
Courtesy Mercaldo Archives

Camp Warner near Klamath Falls, 1873.

Courtesy Steve Lent

Camp Harney near present Burns, 1872.

Courtesy Steve Lent

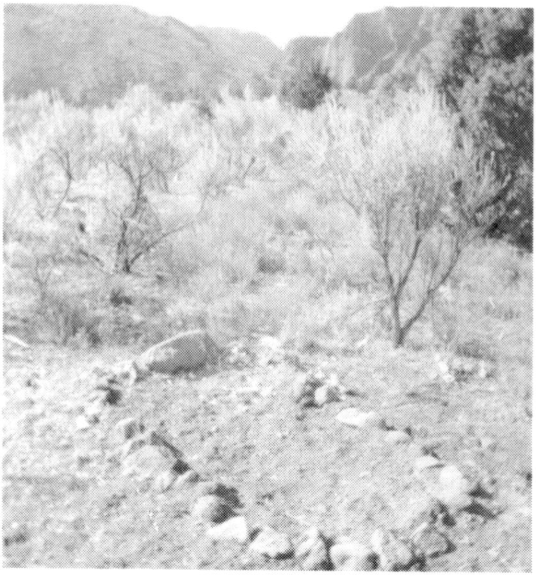

An unmarked soldier's grave on the South Fork of the John Day River. Killed in 1878 during the Bannock War.

Courtesy Gale Ontko

This fortress was bound on the north by West Third St., on the south by West 2nd St., on the east by North Claypool St., and on the west by North Deer St., Prineville.

Courtesy Gale Ontko

Wasco chief Sharp Eyes.
Photo taken in 1905
at the age of 72.

Gifford photo

Umapine

From Souvenir Album of
Noted Indian Photographs, 1906,
Lee Moorhouse

John Porter Langdon and his wife Caroline A. Simmons Langdon. John was killed by the Shoshoni on July 21, 1864. Lucius, George and Perry Langdon were cousins to John.

Courtesy Evelyn Brogi

Below:
Group photo of lieutenants featuring 2nd Lt. Guy Howard.

Front row, left to right (all 1st Lts.): Osgood or Pratt (3rd Art.), Samuel E. Mills (5th Art.), Greenough or Lundeen (4th Art.), Grugan or Harrison (2nd Art.), George F. Chase (3rd Cav.), unknown, Osgood or Pratt (3rd Art.), unknown. Back row, left to right (all 2nd Lts.): Guy Howard (12th Inf.), Price or White (1st Art.), unknown, Granger Adams (5th Art.), Herbert G. Squiers (7th Cav.), unknown, unknown, unknown.

Courtesy Massachusetts Commandery, Military Order of the Loyal Legion and the U.S. Army Military History Institute.

Capt. Reuben Bernard

Courtesy Massachusetts Commandery, Military Order of the Loyal Legion and the U.S. Army Military History Institute.

Gen. Jefferson Columbus Davis

Courtesy Massachusetts Commandery, Military Order of the Loyal Legion and the U.S. Army Military History Institute.

Gen. George Crook

Courtesy Massachusetts Commandery, Military Order of the Loyal Legion and the U.S. Army Military History Institute.

Gen. George Armstrong Custer

Courtesy Massachusetts Commandery, Military Order of the Loyal Legion and the U.S. Army Military History Institute.

Col. Evan Miles, commander of the 21st Infantry. He was the officer the Umatillas negotiated with to kill Pony Blanket.

Courtesy Massachusetts Commandery, Military Order of the Loyal Legion and the U.S. Army Military History Institute.

Brig. Gen. James William Forsyth, veteran of the Yakima War. He served as Gen. Sheridan's chief of staff during the Civil War and was commander of the troops at Wounded Knee in 1890.

Courtesy Massachusetts Commandery, Military Order of the Loyal Legion and the U.S. Army Military History Institute.

Lt. Edward S. Farrow
of the 21st Infantry.

Just out of West Point, he formed an elite group of Indian scouts—expert riflemen to hunt down any hostile Shoshoni not already captured, and with a fighting force of 28 men counting himself, he did just that.
He claimed to have captured 388 Indians in the campaign. If so, it was the largest number of Indians ever captured at one time by any U.S. troops.

Courtesy Massachusetts Commandery, Military Order of the Loyal Legion and the U.S. Army Military History Institute.

Col. Elmer Otis

Courtesy Massachusetts Commandery, Military Order of the Loyal Legion and the U.S. Army Military History Institute.

Gen. Edward Richard Sprigg Canby,
who was killed April 11, 1873
during a peace council with
Capt. Jack and his men.

Courtesy Massachusetts Commandery, Military Order of the Loyal Legion and the U.S. Army Military History Institute.

Gen. Frank Wheaton
was in overall command
of the Modoc campaign
until he was recalled.
Later he was the one who
notified the Modoc prisoners
of their death sentence.

Courtesy Massachusetts Commandery, Military Order of the Loyal Legion and the U.S. Army Military History Institute.

The old warriors last stand. Like the newly arrived settlers and the old dog soldiers, these Ochoco mule deer bucks locked horns and fought to the death.

Courtesy Gale Ontko

Fort Simcoe, Yakima Reservation. This is where the Shoshoni were taken on the death march after the Bannock War.

Courtesy Gale Ontko

Loa-kum Ar-nuk,
Warm Springs U.S.
scout during the
Modoc War.

Courtesy The Indian History of the Modoc War by Jeff C. Riddle

Donald McKay,
U.S. Army scout
and brother to Dr.
William McKay.

Courtesy California History Section, California State Library, Sacramento.

The traveling show of Alfred Meacham, circa 1875, which toured throughout the central and eastern United States. From left to right: Shacknasty Jim, Steamboat Frank, Frank Riddle, Jeff Riddle, Toby Riddle, and Scarface Charlie. *Courtesy Modoc County Museum*

Back row: Capt. Oliver C. Applegate, Toby Riddle, and Frank Riddle. Middle row: Lac-el-es (Long Jim's wife), and Martha Mainstake. Front row: Me-hu-no-lush (blind), and Sau-kaa-dush. The four Modoc women (not including Toby) were prisoners of Capt. Applegate. Taken at Gillem's camp in 1873.

Courtesy The Indian History of the Modoc War by Jeff C. Riddle

Capt. Jack's stronghold in the lava beds.

Courtesy Modoc County Museum
National Park Service photograph, R.C. Zinc photographer

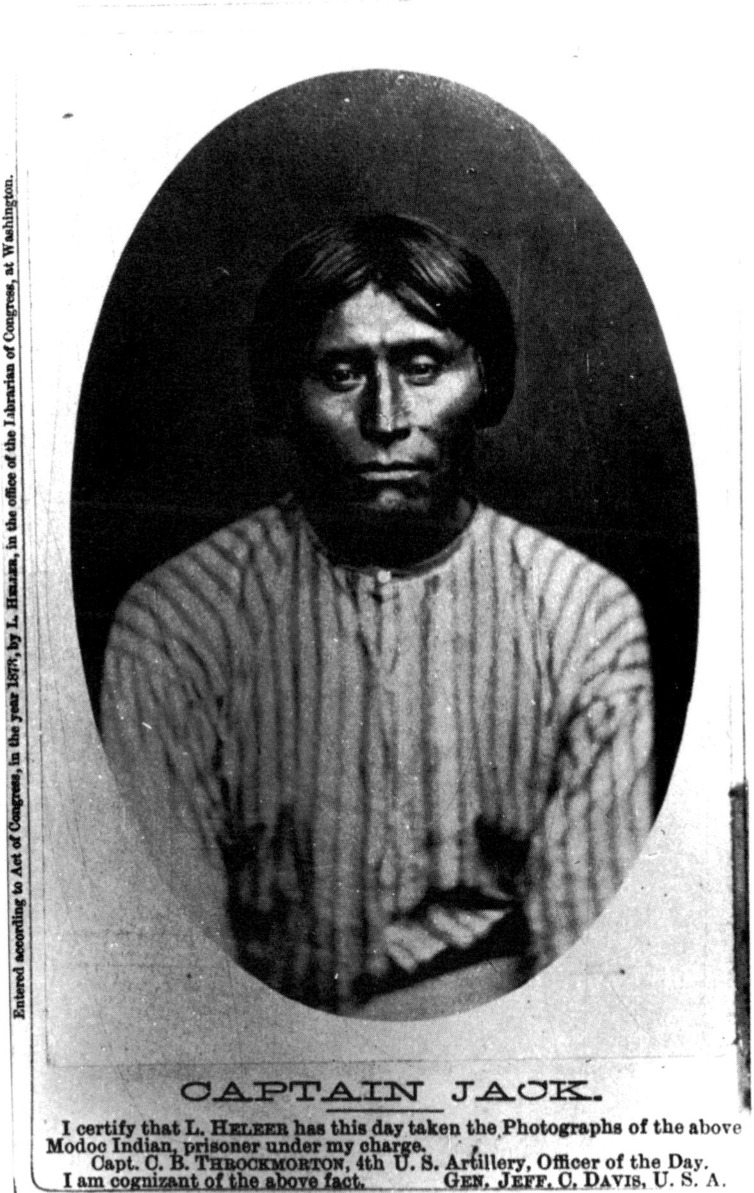
Entered according to Act of Congress, in the year 1873, by L. Heller, in the office of the Librarian of Congress, at Washington.
CAPTAIN JACK.
I certify that L. Heller has this day taken the Photographs of the above Modoc Indian, prisoner under my charge.
Capt. C. B. Throckmorton, 4th U. S. Artillery, Officer of the Day.
I am cognizant of the above fact. Gen. Jeff. C. Davis, U. S. A.

Capt. Jack,
leader of the Modoc insurrection.

Courtesy The Indian History of the Modoc War
by Jeff C. Riddle

Entered according to Act of Congress, in the year 1873, by L. Heller, in the office of the Librarian of Congress, Washington.
SCHONCHIN AND JACK.
I certify that L. Heller has this day taken the Photographs of the above Modoc Indians, prisoners under my charge.
Capt. C. B. Throckmorton, 4th U. S. Artillery, Officer of the Day.
I am cognizant of the above fact. Gen. Jeff. C. Davis, U. S. A.
Published by Watkins, Yosemite Art Gallery, 22 & 26 Montgomery St., opp. Lick House.

John Schonchin and Capt. Jack

Courtesy The Indian History of the Modoc War
by Jeff C. Riddle

Entered according to Act of Congress, in the year 1873, by L. Heller, in the office of the Librarian of Congress, Washington.
JACK'S FAMILY—Lizzy (young wife), Mary (his sister), Old Wife & Daughter.
I certify that L. HELLER has this day taken the Photographs of the above Modoc Indians, prisoners under my charge.
Capt. C. B. THROCKMORTON, 4th U. S. Artillery, Officer of the Day.
I am cognizant of the above fact. GEN. JEFF. C. DAVIS, U. S. A.
Published by WATKINS, Yosemite Art Gallery, 22 & 26 Montgomery St., opp. Lick House

Capt. Jack's family
Left to right: Lizzie (young wife), Queen Mary (sister),
Rebecca (old wife), and daughter Rose in front.

Courtesy The Indian History of the Modoc War
by Jeff C. Riddle

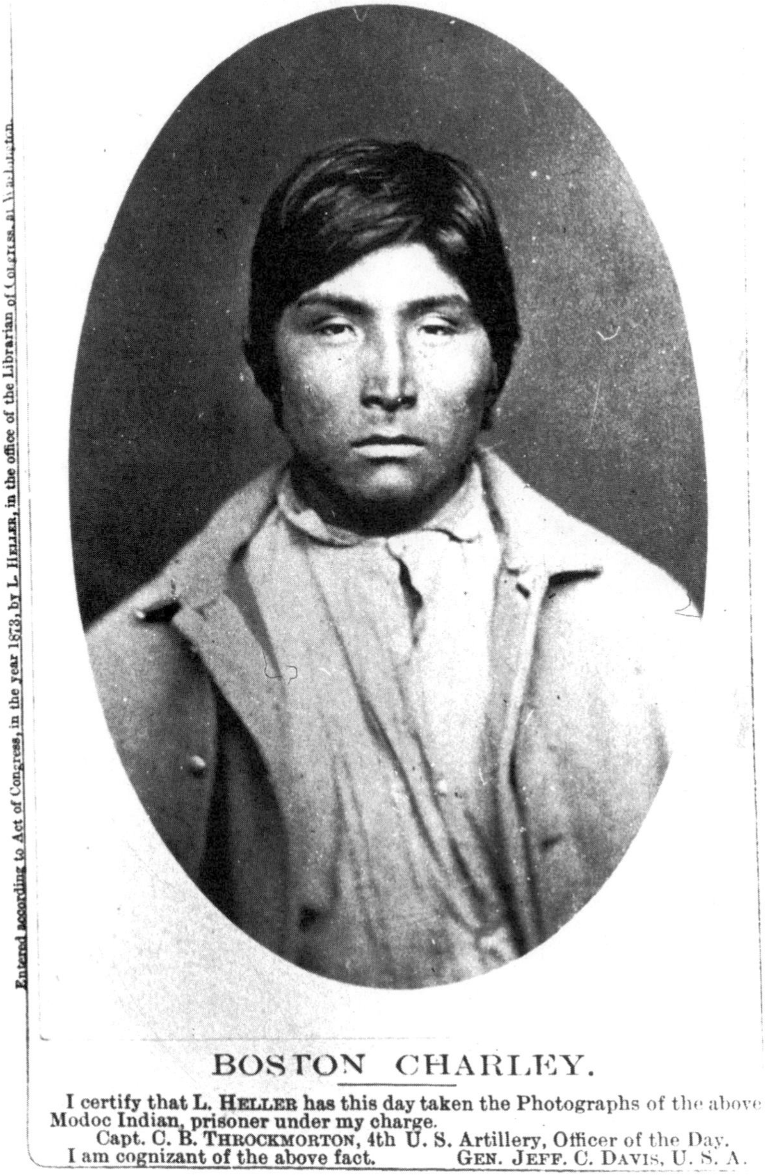
Entered according to Act of Congress, in the year 1873, by L. HELLER, in the office of the Librarian of Congress, at Washington
BOSTON CHARLEY.
I certify that L. HELLER has this day taken the Photographs of the above Modoc Indian, prisoner under my charge.
Capt. C. B. THROCKMORTON, 4th U. S. Artillery, Officer of the Day.
I am cognizant of the above fact. GEN. JEFF. C. DAVIS, U. S. A.

Boston Charley

Courtesy The Indian History of the Modoc War
by Jeff C. Riddle

BLACK JIM.
in the office of the Librarian of Congress, Washington.
I certify that L. HELLER has this day taken the Photographs of the above Modoc Indians, prisoners under my charge.
Capt. C. B. THROCKMORTON, 4th U. S. Artillery, Officer of the Day.
I am cognizant of the above fact. GEN. JEFF. C. DAVIS, U. S. A.

Black Jim

Courtesy The Indian History of the Modoc War
by Jeff C. Riddle

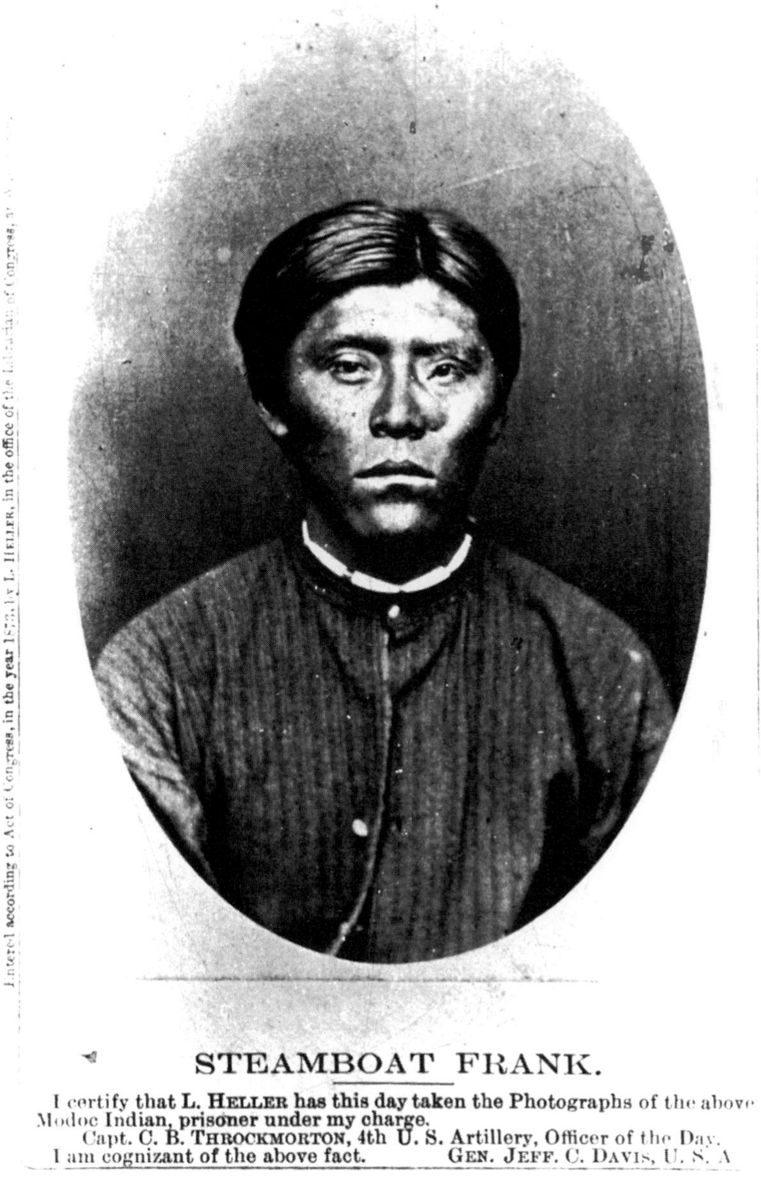
Entered according to Act of Congress, in the year
by L. Heller, in the office of the Librarian of Congress
STEAMBOAT FRANK.
I certify that L. Heller has this day taken the Photographs of the above Modoc Indian, prisoner under my charge.
Capt. C. B. Throckmorton, 4th U. S. Artillery, Officer of the Day.
I am cognizant of the above fact. Gen. Jeff. C. Davis, U. S. A

Steamboat Frank

Courtesy The Indian History of the Modoc War
by Jeff C. Riddle

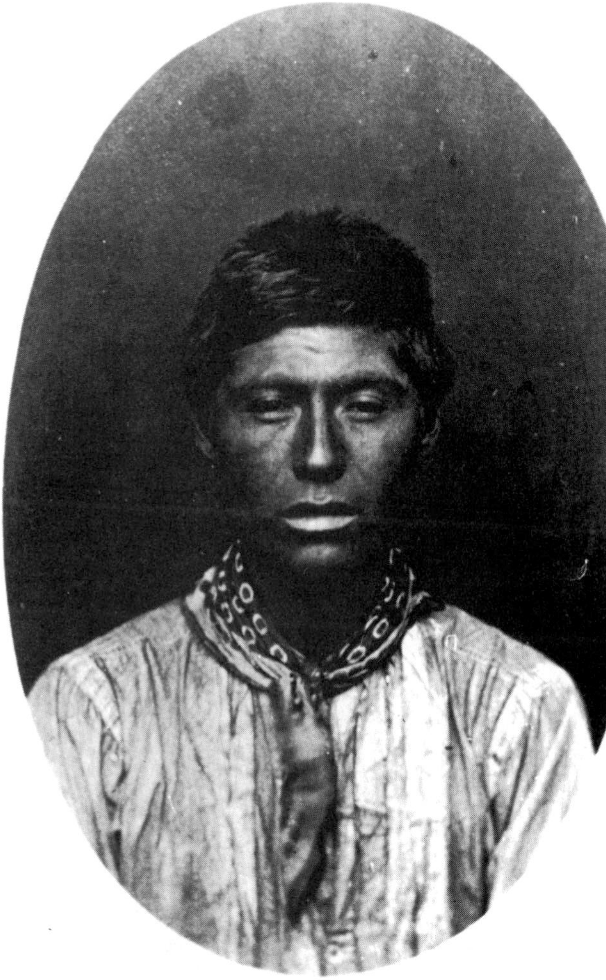

BOGUS CHARLEY.

I certify that L. HELLER has this day taken the Photographs of the above Modoc Indian, prisoner under my charge.
Capt. C. B. THROCKMORTON, 4th U. S. Artillery, Officer of the Day.
I am cognizant of the above fact. GEN. JEFF. C. DAVIS, U. S. A.

Bogus Charley

Courtesy The Indian History of the Modoc War
by Jeff C. Riddle

HOOKA JIM.
I certify that L. HELEER has this day taken the Photographs of the above Modoc Indian, prisoner under my charge.
Capt. C. B. THROCKMORTON, 4th U. S. Artillery, Officer of the Day.
I am cognizant of the above fact. GEN. JEFF. C. DAVIS, U. S. A.

Hooka (Hooker) Jim

Courtesy The Indian History of the Modoc War
by Jeff C. Riddle

Entered according to Act of Congress, in the year 1873, by L. HELLER, in the office of the Librarian of Congress, at Washington.
SCHONCHIN.
I certify that L. HELLER has this day taken the Photographs of the above Modoc Indian, prisoner under my charge.
Capt. C. B. THROCKMORTON, 4th U. S. Artillery, Officer of the Day.
I am cognizant of the above fact.
GEN. JEFF. C. DAVIS, U. S. A.

John Schonchin

Courtesy The Indian History of the Modoc War
by Jeff C. Riddle

Entered according to Act of Congress, in the year 1873, by L. Heller, in the office of the Librarian of Congress, at Washington.
LOST RIVER MURDERERS.
I certify that L. Heller has this day taken the Photographs of the above Modoc Indians, prisoners under my charge.
Capt. C. B. Throckmorton, 4th U. S. Artillery, Officer of the Day.
I am cognizant of the above fact. Gen. Jeff. C. Davis, U. S. A.

Curley Haired Jack (at left), others are unknown.

Courtesy The Indian History of the Modoc War
by Jeff C. Riddle

Entered according to Act of Congress, in the year 1873, by L. Heller, in the office of the Librarian of Congress, at W
CURLY-HEADED DOCTOR.
I certify that L. Heller has this day taken the Photographs of the above Modoc Indian, prisoner under my charge.
Capt. C. B. Throckmorton, 4th U. S. Artillery, Officer of the Day.
I am cognizant of the above fact. Gen. Jeff. C. Davis, U. S. A.

Curley-Headed Doctor

Courtesy The Indian History of the Modoc War
by Jeff C. Riddle

Ewen and Nancy Johnson,
members of the first homestead party into the Ochoco.
Ewen came in 1866 and Nancy in 1868;
they settled on Mill Creek.

Courtesy Crook County Historical Society

Captain John Smith,
Warm Springs Indian Agent
from 1865 to 1884,
when he died.

Courtesy Crook County Historical Society

Mrs. John Smith,
wife of Warm Springs Agent
John Smith. She did much to
help the first settlers to the
Ochoco Valley survive.

Courtesy Crook County Historical Society

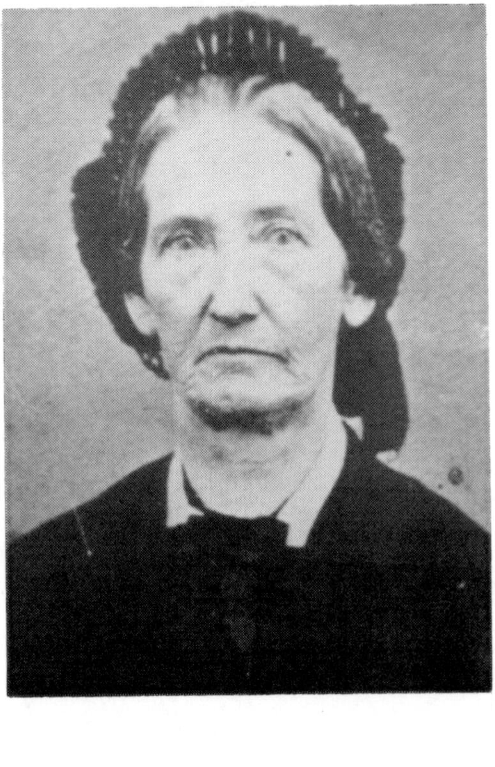

Shoshoni Indians. Photo taken at the Shoshoni camp on the eastern edge of Prineville in 1890.

Courtesy Crook County Historical Society

A Shoshoni tipi on the outskirts of Prineville near the Crooked River bridge, circa 1895.

Indian on horse, circa 1890.

Courtesy Steve Lent

During the horse raids, it seems that Louey took two of Jack's prized mares. A short time later, General Frank Wheaton took the mares away from Louey and gave them to Buck, chief of the Warm Springs scouts, as a present from the Oregon Volunteers. Gen. Wheaton was later recalled to Army headquarters because of his dependency on volunteer troops.[6] Louey got mad. Early the next morning he slipped into the Warm Springs' corral, liberated "some good" horses and was well on his way to Has No Horse's hideout before he and the ponies were discovered missing.[7]

While on the subject of deception, it's worth noting that the Modocs—although goaded into armed resistance on Oregon soil—would make their last stand in California just a few miles south of the Oregon-California state line. However, California was not eager to get involved in Oregon's war. As Oregon enthusiastically pumped volunteer units into the conflict, hampering U.S. regulars, California reluctantly sent but one company of the home guard to protect its citizens. At the start of the conflict California accused Oregon politicians of wanting another Indian uprising and darkly hinted that the Oregonians were "a little mercenary in their anxiety for war." After all, the Modoc War was a favorable thing for Oregon in more ways than one. To the office-holders and seekers it was a windfall. As one writer would put it, "No matter what the cause, it was the heroic thing to rush up to the recruiting office and volunteer to whip the Modocs." And that would go over big time in campaign speeches. Also the movement of the Army and its supplies over railroads, steamboat liner, freight wagons and toll roads was desirable monetary-wise.[8] Who knows, perhaps California was correct with its assessment that Oregon was trying to lure more federal dollars into its coffers. Now back to the real battle site where the ground was tinted with blood instead of greenbacks.

---

6 Glassley, *Pacific Northwest Indian Wars*, p. 172.

7 *The First Oregonians*, published by the Oregon Society for Humanities, pp. 75-76. Louey Crook (Gray Fox) would pronounce Has No Horse's name (Ochiho) as Hut-zi-hu. In Shoshoni many names are not pronounced as they are in English. An example is Tussawehee or Tosawi (White Knife) which in English is pronounced with a tee sound. In Shoshoni it is pronounced Dosawi with a dee sound. Louey Crook died in the 1920s at the Burns, Oregon Paiute colony. He was approximately 100 years old.

8 Meacham, *Wigwam and Warpath*, pp. 384-385.

Meacham suspected that the Modoc's delay in reaching an agreement with the U.S. government was deliberate in an effort to give the uncommitted hostiles—namely Bad Face and Has No Horse—time to supply Jack with food and ammunition. Riddle was so confident that treachery was intended, he personally alerted each member of the commission. Other than Agent Dyer—also wise in the way of Indian diplomacy—the commissioners and their advisors refused to listen to such nonsense. The Rev. Thomas snorted that this information was nothing more than propaganda. Meacham and Riddle were plagued by reporters, which helped to forestall any worthwhile action. According to Major Trimble, "everything that leaked out from their deliberations found its way to the eager newspapers and was then rehashed, recolored and fed to the community at large."[9] He also added that the telegraph wires were kept hot to Washington, D.C. conveying every word spoken and every movement undertaken in the war area.

In desperation, Meacham wired a message to Washington alerting Sec. Delano of the impending trouble—which turned out to be a poor decision. On March 5, Delano (who hated Meacham) replied that he didn't believe Meacham and further stated that he "could understand the unwillingness of the Modocs to place confidence in Meacham."[10] He then ordered the negotiations to proceed as planned. Frank and Toby Riddle again warned Gen. Canby, Rev. Thomas and Supt. Odeneal, who was acting as expert council to the peace commission, that if they continued one of two things would happen. Either Jack wouldn't show up or if he did it would be to kill the peace commissioners. Not only did they scoff at this, but Gen. Canby accused Toby of trying to block the peace effort until Has No Horse entered the fray.

Toby, of all people, was not making up stories about Jack, or his need for revenge. Only twenty-one years before when Jack was barely fourteen, Ben Wright, in a peace parley had violated a flag of truce, killing forty unarmed Modocs—only to receive reward and promotion from his fellow citizens for this act of deceit. Jack's war chief, John Schonchin, had escaped from the trap. It was unlikely that either one

---

9 Brady, *Northwest Fights and Fighters*, p. 286.

10 Glassley, *Pacific Northwest Indian Wars*, p. 176.

would be tricked again. Toby knew that someday Jack would avenge this slaughter—after all, she and Jack were first cousins.

And so, on Jack's terms, a date was set for final conference. The four commissioners, Frank and Toby Riddle and an equal number of Modocs would meet at the council tent in full view of the soldiers, government officials, curious civilians and the ever-present news reporters. Both parties were to come unarmed. On the return from Jack's strong hold with this long awaited message, a Modoc warrior hidden beside the trail whispered to Toby as she passed, "Tell old man Meacham and all the men not to come to the council tent. . . they get killed!"[11]

Again ridicule. Col. Redington would later write, "Toby Riddle warned them they were to be killed, and what I have learned from soldiers I should judge that Meacham did all he could to prevent the commission from going out."[12] Frank, Toby and Agent Dyer argued that if they were to be so foolish as to meet with Jack in defiance of this warning, they should at least go armed. Gen. Canby was tempted but Rev. Thomas insisted they go without arms. Meacham, reconciled to his fate, also declined a weapon. Silently, both Riddle and Dyer had already decided that they would pack concealed guns. . . Riddle a Colt .44 and Dyer a .41 Derringer.

The following morning as they rode toward the council tent, Toby grabbed Meacham's horse. She was crying and begged, "Meacham, you no go; you no go. You get kill! You get kill!"[13] During this halt, someone—perhaps Toby Riddle or maybe Lt. Col. Wheaton—dropped a derringer pistol into Meacham's pocket and he permitted it to remain. The meeting would be quick and to the point. Undoubtedly, the Rev. Thomas remembered that it was Good Friday, April 11, 1873.

When the assigned targets were gathered inside the tent, Jack stood up and Toby hit the ground. Gunshots shattered the morning calm. Gen. Canby staggered backward with a .44 slug in his head; Riddle—with Dyer in front of him—made a run for safety with bullets flying around them, but no one was trying to hit Frank for Scarface Charlie had warned all Modocs that he would kill anyone who hurt Toby in any way

---

11 Ibid., p. 181.

12 Note by J.W. Redington, Brady, *Northwestern Fights and Fighters*, p. 246.

13 Glassley, *Pacific Northwest Indian Wars*, p. 184.

and that included shooting Frank Riddle. Boston Charley blasted Rev. Thomas above the heart. Propping himself up on one arm, Thomas screamed, "Don't shoot again Charley! I am a dead man already!" Boston Charley emptied his revolver into Thomas' body shouting, "Damn ye! Maybe you believe next time what squaw tell you!" On this part of the tragedy, Col. Redington would remark, "Dr. Thomas, the Methodist preacher from Petaluma was butchered at the council tent."

John Schonchin drew down on Meacham as he leveled his Derringer on the war chief. Both fired. Meacham's gun misfired as he reeled backwards with a bullet in the face. With Toby clawing at him, screaming "Don't kill him! Don't kill Meacham!" Schonchin John drilled him four more times. Meacham was still twitching when Shacknasty Jim ran up to finish him off. In desperation, Toby grabbed Jim's rifle barrel deflecting the bullet. She then turned and saw Boston Charley calmly hacking away at Meacham's scalp. Like a wildcat, Toby sprang on Charley at the same time covering Meacham's head with her own body and screamed "Soljers comin'! Soljers comin'!"[14]

Jack and his warriors didn't pause to question. They took off. For some unknown reason, Meacham, with five bullets in his body, would live. Maybe the credit lies with what Col. Redington had to say after they packed Meacham from the blood spattered council tent. In his opinion, the army commissary whiskey had "sufficiently strong reviving qualities to set equestrian statues of General Jackson cavorting around single-footed on their pedestals." When Dr. Cabanis (contract surgeon who had replaced Dr. William McKay on the Klamath Reservation) and whom Redington considered to be a very brave man, tried to revive Meacham with whiskey. "The latter refused to take it, claiming he was a teetotaler and had taken the pledge." Cabanis replied, "Dammit, if that's the case, pry his teeth apart and pour canteen and all down him" which was done as nearly as possible.[15] It served its purpose and eventually Toby nursed

14 Ibid., pp. 185-86; Brady, *Northwestern Fights and Fighters*, p. 246.

15 J.W. Redington's account in Brady, *Northwestern Fights and Fighters*, p. 246. Incidentally, the initials "J.W." stand for John Watermelon. Col. Redington was an Indian fighter, prospector, humorist and eccentric. In 1883 when he was publishing in eastern Oregon, he promoted his paper by printing signs on rocks and fences all over the country side. A typical example: "The Heppner Gazette—Hell on Horse Thieves and Hypocrites." Karolevitz, *Newspapering in the Old West*, p. 137.

Meacham back to health. For her part in saving Meacham's life in the council tent, Toby was awarded a $25 a month government pension. . . and it only took seventeen years to receive the first payment.[16]

With the slaughter of the peace commissioners, confusion reigned. Col. Jefferson C. Davis was promoted to brigadier general and dispatched to Oregon to assume full command of the Modoc campaign. Col. Gillem took command of the immediate battlefront while Supt. Odeneal promoted himself to military strategist. He insisted that howitzers—which the army knew to be useless—were the key to sudden victory. On his order, the Oregon Artillery under Capt. Thomas Mountain began shelling the lava beds with about as much effect as hurling snowballs. The Oregon Artillery would be more successful seven years in the future when, on October 7, 1880, the battery fired its first presidential salute to honor Rutherford B. Hayes and leveled half the trees surrounding Jacksonville.

Meanwhile the new reinforcements, ignoring Wheaton's January attempt, wanted to rush Jack's stronghold in a frontal assault. Lt. Tom Wright—son of the late Gen. George Wright—was taking bets that two artillery companies, his own and Lt. Eagan's could whip the Modocs in fifteen minutes or less.[17] They soon got their chance.

When Odeneal's Oregon Artillery failed in its first attempt to dislodge the Modocs, he blamed it on poor firing location and demanded a detachment be sent out to secure a lava butte overlooking the stronghold. Col. Gillem listened and ordered a patrol sent out under the command of Major Evan Thomas, 4th U.S. Artillery, to give it a try. They didn't do too well.

In sight of the main military encampment, twenty-one warriors trapped Thomas' command in a lava pothole. The outcome was lethal. The Oregon Militia broke and ran, abandoning the U.S. regulars to their fate. McKay, attempting to come to the regular's aid with the Warm Springs scouts, was turned back by a hail of bullets. . . because the Oregon recruits though they were Modocs. Gen. Davis would charge the desert-

16 Riddle, Jefferson, *Indian History of the Modoc War*. Jeff Riddle was Toby's son. She and Frank had four boys, three of whom died in infancy. Jeff was named after General Jefferson C. Davis who took over General Canby's command in April 1873.

17 Glassley, *Pacific Northwest Indian Wars*, p. 183.

ers with "conspicuous cowardice" and go on to say that "many of the enlisted men here are utterly unfit for Indian fighting, being only cowardly beef-eaters. My recommendation is, however, that they be kept here and made to fight."[18]

When the smoke of battle subsided, Major Thomas was dead; Lt. Albion Howe, dead; Lt. George Harris, mortally wounded; Surgeon S.G. Semig, dangerously wounded. In all, fifty-three officers and enlisted men were killed or wounded. The Modocs didn't even suffer a wound. In fact, the battle was so one-sided that Scarface Charlie called out, "All you fellows that ain't dead had better go home. We don't want to kill you all in one day."[19]

Odeneal, in an effort to focus blame in some other direction, quickly pointed out that Major Thomas didn't know how to fight Indians. True enough. An officer twice brevetted for gallantry in the Civil War, this was Thomas' first encounter with Indian warfare. Lt. Boutelle would be just as quick to counterattack, "Experience in hell, even with the fire out, is rare. He died, as did many other brave fellows, sacrificed to the blunders of Odeneal!" Warming up to the subject, Boutelle blamed Odeneal for the trouble leading up to the Modoc War.

He would make public that in the first attempt to place Jack back on the Klamath Reservation after he had been chased out by Has No Horse, Odeneal refused to meet with Jack. "The greater sin lies at the door of Mr. Odeneal, who would not trust his precious skin to a council on Lost River; but preferred treacherously to send troops with guns in place of an agent of the Indian Department with an olive branch." Boutelle would also charge that the settlers instigated the attack on Lost River where eighteen white men were killed. "The citizens attacked an Indian camp without order or authority and had no more right for their attack than if it had been made on Broadway, New York. The Indians who repulsed them were called treacherous murderers and were indicted in the Oregon courts."

Other officers backed Lt. Boutelle and considered the disaster suffered by Major Thomas' command as being "one of the saddest in our military history... senseless and unnecessary... one of the most sickening

18 Brady, *Northwest Fighters and Fights*, p. 250.

19 Glassley, *Pacific Northwest Indian Wars*, p. 196.

errors of the whole Modoc fracas." And there were many.[20] Appropriately, Odeneal's superintendency of Oregon Indian affairs was abolished in 1874, less than a year after the Modoc War.

The Army wasn't perfect in its execution of the Modoc War, but neither was the state of Oregon. For whatever reasons, again Oregon administrators created their own Indian grievances, then unwilling or unable to cope with the situation, clamored for federal aid and refused to cooperate when assistance was given. But business was booming. With supplies in such great demand, a new mail order business was established bearing the title "The Original Grange Supply House." Within a few years it would become Montgomery Ward and Company.

With the newly discovered gold strike on the upper Ochoco River adding to its growth, Prineville, some 180 miles north of the war zone, became a boomtown overnight. Situated halfway between the port of The Dalles and Linkville (Klamath Falls) on the Modoc front, it became the major supply depot for army operations. Livestock production tripled and the lumber industry was born with a second sawmill operating on Mill Creek to provide lumber for the army camp. Heavily laden freight wagons, pack trains and express riders left town almost hourly and at times the going was rough.

Traversing the dry western fringe of the High Desert plateau, water for man and beast became a major problem. On one occasion, Marion Taylor, a freighter, watered his eight horse team with canned tomato juice destined for the soldiers.[21] Protected by media indifference, Snake dog soldiers were hampering shipping at will; shooting freighters and dispatch riders with total disregard while the Modocs garnered all the publicity. This suited the dog soldier's purpose quite well.

During the spring of 1873, Black Buffalo drifted up to Summer Lake to trade, and three of his people were killed as hostiles by the settlers. Black Buffalo retaliated by slaughtering a herd of cattle a short distance from the Klamath Reservation line and then fled north to join Has No Horse.[22] It seems the Oregonians were determined to drag the Snakes into the fray at whatever the cost.

---

20 Major Boutelle (retired) account in *Northwestern Fighters and Fights*, pp. 269-270, 305-308.

21 Biographical Sketches, *The Illustrated History of Central Oregon*, 1905.

22 National archives, Bureau of Indian Affairs, Oregon Superintendency, Letters Received, L.S.

After more infighting and blunders on the Modoc front, the Oregon militia and the U.S. Army settled in for the long haul. Unexpectedly in May, Bogus Charley, Hooker Jim, Steamboat Frank and Shacknasty Jim—taking half of Jack's fighting force with them—took the enemy's $100 bait payable to defectors and offered their services as army scouts.[23] When Hooker Jim slipped through the line of pickets and ran toward Gen Davis' tent holding his rifle over his head yelling, "I give up!" Davis couldn't believe his good luck. In speaking of the surrender, Davis would say, "Here was a man, an outlaw to every human being on earth, throwing down his rifle and saying I give up. He stood before me as stolid as a bronze. I have seen some grand sights, but taking everything into consideration, that was the grandest sight I have ever witnessed."[24] Hooker Jim's abandonment of Jack signaled the end of the Modoc War. And better yet for Gen. Davis, it saved his career as an army officer.

Following this division in their ranks, John Schonchin, Boston Charley and Captain Jack—taking his wife and infant daughter with him—left the lava beds and slipped north into Oregon in a desperate attempt to contact Has No Horse and patch up old enmities. They never made it. On June 1, Capt. Perry's cavalry caught up with the trio in Willow Creek Canyon. Jack had literally been run into the ground. As he stumbled out of Willow Creek Canyon, Jack asked to put on a clean shirt before he surrendered his rifle. When the request was granted, Jack sank to the ground exhausted and sadly remarked, "My legs gave out on me."

Gen. Davis prepared to hang the three on the spot but was stopped by a dispatch from Washington, D.C. ordering him to hold the Modocs in prison until the U.S. attorney general could review their case. The accused, shackled in chains, were taken to the Fort Klamath guardhouse and there they sat for four months while lengthy discussions took place as to the legality of the proceedings. During this political harangue over the legitimacy of prosecuting non-citizens of the United States, a curious thing happened. *The Congressional Globe*, a private publication which recorded congressional debates and speeches was replaced by the legis-

---

Dyer to H. Claywood, Klamath Agency Oregon, June 2, 1873.

23 Glassley, *Pacific Northwest Indian Wars*, p. 198.

24 Thompson, *Reminiscences of a Pioneer*, pp. 122-23.

lative-controlled *Congressional Record.* Apparently the politicians were reluctant to publicize their handling of the Modoc insurrection.

While the war criminals languished in the guard house, Oregonians suffered another setback. Flames exploded in Portland on August 3, 1873 and this time the blaze gutted twenty-two blocks and left two million dollars in devastation in its wake. The prisoners at Fort Klamath were unsympathetic to their white brothers moans of financial grief.

In late September, the Justice Department issued its decision. Captain Jack, John Schonchin, Barncho, Boston Charley, Slolux and Black Jim (Jack's half-brother) were ordered to stand trial charged with crimes in "violation of the laws of war." The turncoats Hooker Jim, Bogus Charley and Shacknasty Jim, who turned State's evidence, were never indicted. At this point, the State of Oregon wanted Jack tried in the circuit court of Jackson County, but the military refused.

Jack made one speech in his own behalf. . . pitiful in its futility. He couldn't even obtain a lawyer to defend him. The verdict was guilty and the four Modoc head-men and two warriors were sentenced to hang. Before the sentence could be carried out, President Grant—after reviewing the proceedings—concluded that Barncho and Slolux were merely tools of Jack and commuted their sentence to life in a federal prison.[25]

The prisoners, sitting on their own coffins, arrived at the place of execution in a wagon. At 10 a.m., Friday, October 3, 1873, Jack and his three war chiefs mounted the scaffold and were prayed over by Father Huegemborg, the post chaplain. Seconds later, they plunged to their death in full view of their wives and children who were forced to watch the hanging. The Modoc War had come to an end eleven months after its inception. They say it takes a ton of lead to kill one soldier in battle. Perhaps, in the case of the Modocs, it took more than that.

With the thousands of bullets, grapeshot and howitzer shells hurled at them, the Modoc losses—excluding the four executed and one suicide—were but twelve killed. Army Surgeon Cyrus Brady, who served both in the Army and Navy, would comment, "By contrast, to defeat fifty Modocs, about twelve hundred men were employed. Each Modoc ac-

---

25 For a full account of the condemned Modocs last words and the trial proceedings, see Meacham, *Wigwam and Warpath*, pp. 638-643 and Landrum, *Guardhouse, Gallows and Graves*, pp. 85-135.

counted for three men killed and cost the United States Government over ten thousand dollars before he was himself killed or captured. . . a fearful price indeed."[26] It was claimed that the Snakes (hiding out on Bear River) held a war dance in honor of the Modoc victory, prompting the editor of the Utah *Corinne Reporter* to fume, "They ought to be skinned alive for their insolence."[27]

The surviving Modocs who had joined Jack in the lava beds—39 men, 54 women and 60 children—were loaded into cattle cars and shipped to Kansas to be imprisoned on the Shawnee Reservation. But the indignities suffered by the Modocs were not over. A public relations man offered Gen. Wheaton $10,000 for Jack's body to use for advertising purposes. The general thoughtfully declined. However, a side-show promoter got hold of a corpse, had it made into a mummy and traveled the East Coast charging 10¢ admission to view Jack's body. It was also claimed that Jack's skull ended up in a Portland basement and was later sent to the University of Oregon for display and study.[28]

The story of the hanging of Captain Jack and the handling of the news by the *San Francisco Chronicle*—by relays of the best horses in the territory and telegraph—was unequaled until the advent of radio and wire photo service in the mid-twentieth century. The *Chronicle* spread the news to the nation in a matter of hours while silently in the background, the fuse to a Shoshoni powder keg was smoldering ever closer to detonation.

---

26 Brady, *Northwestern Fighters and Fights*, pp. 251-254.

27 *Corinne Reporter* (Utah), April 30, 1873.

28 Letter to Ray Glassley from N.H. Atchison dated Portland, Oregon, March 24, 1949; Meacham, *Wigwam and Warpath*, pp. 351-354; Longstreet, Stephen, *War Cries On Horseback*, p. 296.

CHAPTER 159

ENCORE! ENCORE!

Rub-a-dub, dub! Ho-daddy, hi-daddy;
Wo-hup, gee-kow!
Fetch water, fetch water, Manayunk!

Chief Bad Face
Metropolitan Theater, 1874

So it sounded to a news reporter who had come to cover the dramatic event of the year. Who knows, maybe Bad Face did want to "fetch some water" to extinguish the white flame. Whatever, Sarah Winnemucca would render the same message in perfect English. "My father says he is very glad to see you. He has heard a great deal about San Francisco and wanted very much to see it; so he has come to see it for himself!" Thus began the theatrical debut of the warring tribes of eastern Oregon.

The Metropolitan Theater would announce a unique attraction, the on stage appearance of "Winnemucca, the Chief of the Paiutes accompanied by his two daughters and eight braves in a series of tableaux vivants illustrative of Indian life—admission $1 for orchestra seats." What it lacked in drama, it made up for in tragi-comedy when Shell Flower fell on her backside by "pulling too hard on the tail of Coyote during the sacred Coyote Dance."[1] This performance may not have won critical acclaim but it gave Billy McKay an idea.

After the Modoc War, Don McKay's war experience made his name a household word throughout the United States so Billy turned to his half-brother for assistance in a new financial venture. Don was agreeable and in the summer of 1874 with twelve Warm Springs veterans

1 San Francisco *Daily Alta*, October 22-23, 1874

of the Modoc Campaign, the McKay boys embarked upon a "Grand Tour of the East." They tried to talk Sarah Winnemucca—a veteran of lecture tours—into going along as their press agent but Sally was occupied in political in-fighting on the Malheur Reservation and refused the offer. However, Dave Hill—Klamath leader of the Axe and Rifle Squad—got word of the McKay's new scheme and successfully got a Boston backer to organize a theatrical company to present American Indian frontier life on the stage. For actors in this production, Hill chose his old partner in crime, Rotten Belly—billed as Chief Tecumseh—and, of all people, Scarface Charlie, Steamboat Frank, Frank and Toby Riddle and Shacknasty Jim. By some quirk of fate, Hill's group met with the McKay thespians at St. Joseph, Missouri where they joined forces as "Redpaths Modoc Lecture Company." They, with their families, toured such cities as Terre Haute, Louisville, New York, Jersey City, Camden, Trenton, Philadelphia, Boston, Newark and Washington, D.C., where they appeared several times at the National Theater. Dave Hill, a natural ham, became very popular.

High living in the national capital soon placed McKay's group in financial straits. Only through the personal intervention of President Grant was enough money forthcoming to feed, clothe and transport the little troupe home.[2] Broke and disillusioned, Dr. Kay's company arrived back in Portland on the steamer *Oriflamme* on December 2, 1875. Oriflamme is the name for the Shoshoni war standard—a lance eight feet in length and decorated from tip to tip with eagle feathers.[3]

The Portland *Oregonian* would further report that Donald McKay didn't return with Billy but went on to bigger and better productions. He was now performing with a dramatic company in New York City and sailed with them for Germany. Before returning to the United States in 1876, the Umatilla chief would make a professional tour of Europe.[4]

Riding the crest of popularity, when Donald returned from Europe he was booked into "Texas Jack" Omohundro's patent medicine show (advertised as the Oregon Indian Medicine Company) where he helped

---

2 Lessie Moorehouse Schaefer, "President Grant Plays Samaritan when Wild West Show Goes Broke," in *WPA Oregon Historical Records Survey for Umatilla County, Oregon, State Archives*, Salem, Oregon; *Sunday Oregon Journal*, September 19, 1943.

3 Bourke, *On the Border With Crook*, p. 337.

4 Portland *Oregonian*, December 4, 1875.

promote such exotic remedies as Donald McKay's Indian Cough Syrup; Modoc Indian Oil; Wasco Cough Drops; Snake War Paint Ointment; Nez Perce Catarrh Snuff; Warm Springs Consumption Cure; and Donald McKay's Indian Worm Eradicator. *Daring Donald McKay*, a fictionalized account of the Modoc War, became the prime vehicle for the advertisement of these strange concoctions.[5] One can't help but think that William McKay, M.D. might have been more believable hawking such wares but Billy, the brains of the outfit, never did have much luck.

Above all, the most popular medicine was Don's special Ka-ton-ka elixir guaranteed by bank draft to cure most everything from abscessed teeth to zealous ulcers and it only cost a dollar a bottle. The medicine show was doing a booming business until the Pure Food and Drug Authorities stepped in and discovered that Ka-ton-ka "contained a significant percentage of alcohol, sugar, aloe and baking soda," none of which was known to cure much of anything.

Even though Texas Jack billed such dignitaries as Kit Carson—who had died back in 1868—he faced some tough competition. Pitted against such noted entertainers as Jenny Lind (the Madonna of her day) who put "The Last Rose of Summer" in the top ten list; and whose popular encore "Home, Sweet Home," brought down the house, the medicine show was doomed to failure.[6] At the end of his final curtain call, Donald McKay returned to the more prosaic job of interpreter on the Umatilla Reservation.[7]

A century later, Russell Means (Sioux leader of the American Indian Movement) would complain, "We're the only thing in the United States of America that's considered a tourist attraction, and we are human beings for Christ's sake!" And in 1874, both native and imported Oregonians were soon to be reminded of that fact when God's messenger arrived in Portland. . . dressed in an army uniform.

---

5 *Daring Donald McKay or, The Lost Trail of the Modocs*, pp. 30, 31, 50, 74, 80, 102, 108. "Texas Jack" Omohundro toured with Buffalo Bill's "Scouts of the Plains" and married the show's leading lady, the exotic Mademoiselle Morlaccki. McLaughlin, *Wild and Wooly: An Encyclopedia of the Old West*, p. 508.

6 Other songs made popular by Jenny Lind (the celebrated Swedish Nightingale whose American appearance was arranged at enormous cost by P.T. Barnum of circus fame), were "Comin' Thro the Rye" and the tear-jerker, "Oh Don't You Remember Sweet Alice Ben Bolt," *Heart Songs, Melodies of Days Gone By*, p. 14.

7 Portland *Oregonian*, April 21, 1899; Pendleton *East Oregonian*, April 19, 1899.

CHAPTER 160

THE INDIAN'S MOSES

Their criers go about the circular camp crying "God is coming" and all Indians must stop sinning against Him by swearing, lying, gambling, chewing tobacco, smoking or keeping dogs.

George Balcom
Baptist Minister

In 1874, with the Ochoco gold strike in full swing, the state legislature in an effort to gain better control over central Oregon, created Lake County, the fifth to be carved from the sprawling territory of Wasco. This act made Prineville the southernmost town in Wasco County and Scissorsville on the upper Ochoco River the second largest in population. At the same time, Fort Harney was established as a post office on August 10, 1874. Prior to this, if the people of Harney Valley wanted mail, they had to ride to Prineville to receive it. Now, with the endowment of postal service, Tom O'Keefe—veteran of the army post—would carry the mail by horseback and wagon between Prineville and Egan (Burns).

To show that Washington, D.C. held interest in local issues, Congress abolished the Oregon Office of Indian Affairs and Oliver Otis Howard (sixth ranking general in the Union Army) took command of the Military Department of the Columbia. His method of dealing with the Indians was diametrically opposed to that of Gen. Crook. Instead of firmness and honesty, Howard was conciliatory to the extreme—a trait that wouldn't sit well with either Oregonians or Shoshoni.[1]

1 It seems that Gen. Howard was plagued with bad luck no matter what he did. Shortly after the Bannock War, Joseph Pulitzer, publisher of the New York *World* and a brilliant journalist who was losing his eyesight, telegraphed his managing editor: "Please have on the front page of the magazine in next Sunday's *World*, the fine portrait of General O.O. Howard, head of the Army." Several days later the editor wired back: "Sorry we did not have that O.O. Howard

Howard had been a thorn in Crook's side during the Apache campaign of 1872-73. As head of the peace commission, Congress had granted him power to override Crook on any decision and to take command of the troops if he saw fit to do so. At Yuma, Crook would comment that "for some cause better known to himself, he did not take advantage of the power granted him."[2] Instead, Howard seemed content to undermine Crook on every occasion.

One of the first disruptions occurred when Howard sought out Three Coyotes, the Snake war chief who led the Mountain Meadow Massacre of 1857, as the man to contact Geronimo and Cochise for a peace settlement.[3] Crook—who had crossed battle-lances with Three Coyotes in the Ochoco—had little faith in his integrity. As it turned out, Three Coyotes, who had fled to the land of his Apache mother in 1869, had no qualms about changing sides and selling out his relatives to imprisonment.

In Crook's opinion, Howard's main stock in trade was religion and it was getting on his nerves. In one of their arguments which Crook found to be particularly funny, Howard confided that "he thought the Creator had placed him on earth to be the Moses to the Negro and having accomplished that mission he felt satisfied his next mission was the Indian."[4] In this ongoing battle, Howard would report to Washington that Crook disturbed him so badly that he could not sleep until he found relief in prayer.[5]

Crook's philosophy (which clashed with Howard's) was the same with the Apaches as it had been with the Snakes. Since they had brutally murdered white families, he refused to accept surrender. He promised he wouldn't harm them when Howard got them in for a peace conference but the Apaches had lied to him once and they could be lying again. In

---

picture. Instead, on the front page, I had a wonderful picture of Kate Swan in the electric chair and circulation is up 15,000." Pulitzer, an old Civil War veteran, took this news in good spirits. He wired in response: "You know perfectly well that I am blind, and must rely on you. Congratulations." ("Yellow Journalism," *Civilization*, May/June 1995, p. 36.)

2 Crook, *Autobiography*, p. 169.

3 Howard in his *Famous Indian Chiefs I Have Known*, refers to Three Coyotes as "Ponce." His full Shoshoni name was Ishaui Ponce.

4 Crook, *Autobiography*, p. 169.

5 *Secretary of the Interior Annual Report 1872*, Part I, pp. 533-59.

his own words, Crook told Howard if given the chance, "I would drive them all back into the mountains where I could kill them all."[6]

Howard had not always been a pacifist. He started his army career as a hell-for-leather pony soldier. At the Battle of Gettysburg, he received his baptism in fire and was given a vote of thanks from a grateful nation for outstanding bravery. Howard then received the Congressional Medal of Honor and $100 in gold for gallantry at the Battle of Fair Oaks where he lost his right arm. During his recovery from amputation, Howard "saw the light."

Perhaps because of Gen. Howard's influence, shortly after he arrived in Portland, ladies of the Women's Temperance Prayer League began invading the saloons with hymns and prayer. According to the *Oregonian*, a large crowd of men, boys and dogs followed the crusaders as they went from place to place collecting pledges to abstain from hard liquor. Whatever, Howard had his work cut out to convince the Snakes that the best place for them was the Christian-controlled reservation.

One of his first actions was to visit the Malheur Reservation in an effort to lure Has No Horse into willing captivity. He couldn't have picked a worse time. On February 9, 1874, Natchez was released from Alcatraz causing no little unrest among the white population. The Indian Department had lost face over his pardon and Natchez was now considered a hero by the Shoshoni. Even Has No Horse and his warriors had come down from the mountains to greet him. This prompted the local newspapers to advise Natchez to "bag his head and leave the country" which he did, heading for the Malheur Reservation.[7] In the interim, Has No Horse agreed to go on the Klamath Reservation, only to see twenty-five of his people die of starvation. Capt. Reuben Bernard, commander at Fort Bidwell, stirred up a hornet's next when he reported that it was because the Klamath Agency commissary refused to give Has No Horse any food.[8] It was not likely he would listen to any promises given by Howard.

---

6 Crook, *Autobiography*, p. 181.

7 Bancroft, *Scrapbooks*, Vol. 93, p. 43.

8 R.F. Bernard, 1st Cavalry Captain, Camp Bidwell to Assist. Adj. Gen., Department of California, May 17, 1874, Letters Received, Office of Indian Affairs, Nevada Superintendency.

On his visit to the Malheur Reserve, Howard was accompanied by his daughter, Grace, who had just graduated from Vassar College. They were met by Sally Winnemucca and the general was quite impressed with her perfect English, her attractive appearance and her "air of great self-respect."[9] He would also gain insight on what he was up against in trying to convince the settlers of eastern Oregon that Indians were also human beings.

His first lesson came on his stop in Prineville. As remembered by an old-time resident, the general visited the Baptist Church and gave an impassioned lecture on brotherly love. "Is there anything," he demanded, "that is stronger than love?" From the back of the congregation came the dour reply, "Yeah, garlic."[10]

This may seem humorous but the underlying feeling was grim. One of the best examples can be found in a comparison of the correspondence of an unschooled Shoshoni girl and those of an educated white maiden, both of whom expressed their thoughts on the impending prospect of another Shoshoni war. The pale-faced writer, a Prineville girl, had this to say about the Ochoco Indians: "The old stock will never change. The deep seated aboriginal ideas, the superstitions that rule their lives, the implanted customs and rights handed down to them since the first generation of their kind, all of these form a part of their lives of too much moment to be entirely removed in a few decades of years by their white-skinned guardians."

She continues, "Neither time nor schooling can bring about a change in their every-day life. The ground is never too warm or too cold to squat upon; their faces are never so attractive as when smeared with oil and paint; the heavy labor of camp is never done except by the hands of the squaws; the living still hire the howling, wailing mourners for the dead; the tiny papoose is better cared for strapped to a board than in the mother's lap—all these and a hundred more furnish food for the feeling that only with the total extinction of the race itself will there come an end to the primitive, and still barbarous methods and customs that have lived for centuries with these first inhabitants and are destined to exist as many

---

9 Howard, *My Life and Personal Experience Among Our Hostile Indians*, p. 377.

10 Elizabeth Miller Stanton, June 1936. Elizabeth was the daughter of R.P. Miller who arrived with the first Ochoco emigration in 1868 and related the story to her.

more if the life of this peculiar race shall endure to that end."[11] This, with few exceptions, was the attitude of most settlers in the 1870's.

In 1876, Mattie Shenkah wrote a letter to her school teacher, Annie Parrish, in which she expressed her thoughts on a possible Snake uprising.[12] Mattie, a refugee of the first campaign, was genuinely concerned. "When," she asked, "will my red brothers learn that it is more than foolish to rise up and go on the war-path against our white brothers? Even now we are hearing of war. We poor women and the innocent little children and the old and helpless are the ones who suffer most. But now I know that white men make war with their white brothers also! Why is this? Why do they make war and make us suffer? Oh, we suffer so much; not only our bodies by hunger, sickness, cold or heat, but our hearts bleed from the moment our dear ones go away under the sound of the song and the beat of the war drum. Then comes the terrible time of waiting—my breath stops when I remember it. Then there is the news of wounds and death to reach us at home. Very few can follow the cry of their hearts to run to the beloved ones because there are little ones to keep them at home."

Mattie saw her mother shot to death by Warm Springs scouts in 1864. Two years later, her father, Broken Knife, died in her arms from bullet wounds received in battle with the U.S. Cavalry. As an orphan, she lived with first one relative and then another. For a time, Mattie lived with her uncle, Pony Blanket, and near the end of the Snake conflict, she was with the shock troops of the terrible Big Man. It came as second nature for Mattie to work hard for the benefit of her people, for she possessed that rare quality of a kind manner and loving spirit—making everyone around her happy during her short tragic life.

Laying her soul bare to Annie Parrish, Mattie would continue: "I was again and again in war myself and it is horrid! I am no coward-girl, and I am not afraid even when the guns fire; but I do not want war. I am only a poor Indian girl and though I've been to school many days, yet I know but very little. Men who are so wise as to make so many wonderful

11 Letter of Miss Gertie Sharp, *Illustrated History of Central Oregon*, 1905, p. 702.

12 Annie Parrish was a sister-in-law to Sam Parrish, Malheur Indian agent. Hopkins, *Life Among the Piutes*, p. 109.

things should find a way to settle their trouble without causing so much wretchedness and sorrow and tears."

It is unfortunate that Miss Sharp didn't become friends with Miss Shenkah. Perhaps her thoughts on the unsavory character of the original Ochoco settlers would have changed. Then again, maybe not. Sarah Winnemucca, whose baby sister Siku Wita Tseah (One Little Girl) was badly wounded at the battle of Harney Lake, would bring these injustices to the attention of the American public in her lecture tours following the second Shoshoni war. They seemed to have but fleeting impact.

Gen. Howard was very much impressed with Sarah and made the statement that the name Tocmetone (Shell Flower) should have a place beside the name of Pocahontas in the history of our nation. If so, the name of Mattie Shenkah should blaze its way through the ages along side that of Sacajawea.

Howard would be equally impressed with Pony Blanket, whom he called Egan. "I noticed how superior Egan was to the others. He has on an ordinary farmer's suit of light linen duck with a leather belt around his waist. A sheath held a knife at his side. He wore a straw hat that he removed when he spoke to me. He had all the features of a full-blooded Indian but wore no braids or ornament. His hair, parted in the middle, was cut short at the neck. He had a pleasant face and resonant voice." It was difficult for Howard to imagine that only a few years before, Pony Blanket had an eagle feather in his braids, wore little more than a breech cloth, had a brace of pistols strapped to his side, a .50 calibre Sharps in the crook of his arm, and was one of the ranking war chiefs of the Western Shoshoni Nation.

That evening, Howard was stimulated in another way. The Paiutes—with Natchez in their midst—gathered for a religious dance which they called a "fandango" and kept up their singing, dancing and drumming so late, that the General spent many wakeful hours. He was particularly worried for Grace's safety and called Sarah to the Agency house to determine if the Indians were having a war dance. She laughed and replied that they were merely celebrating his presence on the reservation and were performing the ritual in his honor. Howard rested more soundly during the remainder of the night.[13]

---

13 Howard, *My Life and Personal Experience Among Our Hostile Indians*, p. 377.

Howard would return to Portland believing all was well on the eastern Oregon front. It wasn't. Rumblings were coming in from the settlers that they didn't think Parrish was the right man to serve as Indian Agent. Not only had Parrish chased all the whites off the Malheur Reservation but, heaven forbid, he refused to let them graze livestock on Indian lands. Something had to be done about this and damn quick. Anticipating the outcome of this complaint, Howard rushed a telegram to the War Department, "Think it very important that present agent be continued. Indians, whites and army officers commend Parrish for successful management of remote and difficult agency. Please inform Commissioner of Indian Affairs."[14] It was a good try but it wasn't going to work.

By now, the eastern Oregon Shoshoni were in bad need of a Moses to deliver them from trouble. George Balcom, a Baptist minister, unaware that The Cutter, a Paiute shaman, was prophesying the return of the Shoshoni dead, would puzzle over why they were so nervous. When he joined the Indian service in 1871 to lure Bad Face and Has No Horse onto the reservation—any reservation—Balcom noticed the Indians were fascinated with the idea that "God was coming" and they'd better clean up their act.[15]

The Snakes may have had good intentions; maybe even stopped swearing and keeping dogs, but the war paint was being mixed whether God was coming or not.

14 O.O. Howard, Department of the Columbia, telegram to Adjutant General, October 12, 1875, Letters Received, Office of Indian Affairs, Oregon Superintendency.

15 George Balcom to E.G. Parker, Commissioner of Indian Affairs, April 14, 1871, Letters Received, Office of Indian Affairs, Nevada Superintendency.

CHAPTER 161

WHISPERS OF WAR

So what can they do, these wards of the nation,
When White Brother moves on their reservation?
They can fold their white house like a shroud
Fold it, and fade away.

Owen Wister
Western Author

The Official Indian census for 1875 would reveal with the following disclaimer that "as the Indians are superstitiously opposed to being counted, the strength given is mostly estimations." This estimate concluded that 365 Snakes—Wolf Dog's followers—were held on the Klamath Reserve; 2,100 Snakes, 900 of whom were classified as Has No Horse's "Renegades" were roaming in Oregon; and another 160 of "Ochecholes" (Has No Horse's tribesmen) were held on the Yakima Reserve in Washington Territory. The vacillating Robber Snakes, officially known as Bannocks, were placed on the Fort Hall Reserve in Idaho and the Shoshoni Reserve in Wyoming. Little Rattlesnake's Pit River Snakes—64 in number—were herded onto the Round Valley Reserve in California.

The census also contains the interesting note that 1,100 Oregon Gros Ventres (the Arapaho allies of the Snake war tribes) were being held at the Milk River Agency in Montana. This information adds final proof to Gen. Crook's statement that the eastern Oregon Shoshoni were receiving outside help during the Shoshoni War. It also explains Gourd Rattler's reluctance to be associated with the Arapaho. Knowing that they were supplying the war tribes with arms, ammunition and manpower, it wouldn't help his stand of non-aggression to be on friendly terms with Has No Horse's allies.

Of equal interest, the only Indians known as "Piutes" or "Pahutes" were distributed as follows: 2,000 in Nevada; 4,000 in Wyoming; and 528 in Utah. None resided in Oregon, giving further proof that the Snakes were not considered to be Paiutes except in the mind of Sarah Winnemucca and a few civilian employees in the Indian service. The Western Shoshoni (Wolf Dog's followers) were always listed as Snakes while the Eastern Shoshoni (Gourd Rattler's followers) were called Shoshoni.[1]

By 1875, Oregon's white population was pushing the 100,000 mark and Prineville boasted enough people—or perhaps gunfights—to support a second doctor. In that year, Dr. James R. Sites set up practice in competition with the old medicine man Dr. Lark Vanderpool. Throughout the state there was a growing awareness that responsibilities increase with numbers of persons. Citizens saw the sprawling, brawling frontier tightening up and settling down so they turned their efforts more and more toward the needs of society as a whole—but this awakening would be slow in coming to eastern Oregon.

To encourage more rapid settlement, Congress decreed—with no strings attached, for neither a survey nor residence on the land was required—that a person could buy a section of land (640 acres) for $1.25 an acre if he would reclaim it within two years. This would become a road to wealth for many.

The California-based Miller and Lux Cattle Company, the largest ranch the West has ever known and operating under the "Bull's Head" brand, had their eyes on central and eastern Oregon. Henry Miller and Charlie Lux bought land to produce, not sell, and as soon as someone could gain title to a section of land, they had a willing buyer in Henry Miller who purchased land without abatement for thirty years. Heinrick Alfred Kreiser, a German butcher who preferred to be known as Henry Miller, was the brains of the outfit. His partner, Charles Lux, also a butcher and a native of Alsace-Lorraine (a disputed border region be-

1 In summary, by 1875 all the Shoshoni related tribes were placed on reservations with the exception of the Oregon Snakes, numbering, 2,689 men, women and children with only 589 held on three reservations. All of the eastern Shoshoni were on reservations in Idaho and Wyoming; all of the Paiutes on reservations in Nevada, Utah and Wyoming; all Utes were confined on reservations in Colorado, Utah and New Mexico; and all the Comanches were on reservations in Indian Territory (now Oklahoma). *Table of Indians, Census of Tribes Living in the United States of America Omitting Those Living in Alaska*, compiled and tabulated from the Latest Official Reports of the Commissioner of Indian Affairs, 1875, by Ado Hunnis.

tween France and Germany) was the politician preferring to mingle with the elite while Miller was the field man. Hank and Charlie would boast that they could drive cattle from the Mexican border to Canada and sleep every night on their own land.[2] They weren't lying.

About the time the Bull's Head brand was advancing on eastern Oregon, Gen. Crook was relieved from command of the Military Department of Arizona and ordered to take charge of the Department of the Platte, which was a part of General Sheridan's Missouri Division. On June 3, 1875, Crook and Gen. Alfred Terry (in command of the Department of the Dakotas) attended Sheridan's wedding which, according to Crook, was "rather a quiet affair."[3] Following the ceremony. Crook and Terry headed west where big trouble was brewing, spawned by cattle drives, discovery of gold and an influx of settlers.

The biggest problem, insofar as the Sioux were concerned, was the increasing loss of their food supply. By 1875, the buffalo had been reduced to two small areas: one in eastern Montana and the western Dakotas; the other in the Texas-Oklahoma panhandles and eastern New Mexico. Only three years before, the army on a scout between the Arkansas and Cimarron rivers—a distance of 100 miles—were never out of the sight of buffalo. In the period of 1872-75, 4.5 million buffalo were slaughtered. . . three million for their hides. Small wonder that the Sioux were entertaining thoughts of retaliation.

Trouble was also brewing in eastern Oregon. Henry Miller had his eye on the Malheur Reservation and Tom Overfelt would become his means to gain it. Keeping strictly in the background, Miller as "silent partner" told Overfelt to "buy Agency Valley at any price." The raising of cattle was big business.

Aside from roundup, a dozen cowboys—many of them Indians—could take care of 8,000 cattle. They received board and lodging plus $35 a month. Stage drivers made as much in one day. Escaped calves were called "slick ears" or "mavericks" and by local agreement slick ears belonged to the person who could get his brand on them. This could be a profitable sideline and many a cowboy got his ranching operation

2 Hanley, *Owyhee Trails*, pp. 106-10.

3 Crook, *Autobiography*, p. 187; *Army and Navy Journal*, Vol. XII, No. 44, June 12, 1875, p. 701.

started in this way. As one wit put it, all cowboys had several things in common: usually skin cancer, noses pitted like the craters of the moon and crippling arthritis in the hands and legs. He was probably right, but to a man, these afflictions were badges of honor.

Prior to the arrival of overland rail transportation in the middle 1880's, much of the eastern Oregon beef cattle, in both small and large herds, was moved to eastern markets on foot. Drives, sometimes numbering several thousand head, usually started in May and moved at a leisurely pace which allowed the stock to graze as they traveled. The trail out of the Ochoco country crossed the Malheur Reservation to reach the Snake River just above the mouth of the Owyhee and followed generally the route of the Oregon Trail. Crossing lower Idaho, the cattle drive pushed east, first to Cheyenne, Wyoming, but later when the bands of steel reached Laramie, this town became the terminus. Many tributary trails from the open range fed into this major artery. The 1,500 mile drive often took as much as five months to complete. A much-used secondary trail ran from the head of the Crooked River south past the Steens Mountains to Winnemucca, Nevada where it turned east to join the Oregon Trail route into Idaho near Green River. Both routes insured the destruction of any feed for the Shoshoni's horses.

The country was closing in on the Shoshoni. In La Grande (where only 54 years before, Pete Delore had been born on the frozen banks of a wilderness river 2,000 miles west of the nearest American settlement) the Blue Mountain University opened its doors under the auspices of the Methodist Episcopal Church and there was talk of opening a university in Eugene City.

Higher education wasn't the only topic causing a stir. The militant "Piute Princess"—as the news reporters of the day chose to call Sarah—was doing her share to tarnish the image of Shoshoni decorum in the eyes of their white critics. Early in the spring of 1875 she got into a free-for-all with another Indian woman and emerged as the undisputed champion. Soon after this fracas Sarah was strolling down the sidewalk in front of the Winnemucca Hotel when she was accused of carving on Julius Argasse (a prominent Nevada sheepman) with a scalp knife. It seems that Sally felt her dignity was threatened when Mr. Argasse touched her without permission. To his dismay, Julius soon found out that Sarah was very able to protect her honor. In a miscarriage of justice the Princess was thrown in jail overnight, charged with assault and the intent to do bodily harm. The case was dismissed before its merits could be evaluated because upon examination the "razor sharp scalp knife" was found to be nothing more than a fingernail file.[4] Sarah was not happy with the Nevada judicial system.

Of more interest to eastern Oregon miners, cowboys and loggers, Henry Weinhard, proprietor of a Portland brewery, advertised in the 1875 city directory that he would make Oregon famous with a number one lager beer.[5]

Monroe Hodges was busy surveying the town site of Prineville, advertising lots at $10 each, causing complaints among some of the local citizens about the high cost of real estate. The town site plat, consisting of 17 full blocks and 5 half blocks was officially filed at The Dalles City on March 28, 1877. During this period, John Darragh (melancholy ex-captain of the Warm Springs Regulars) was serving as deputy sheriff of Wasco County under the guidance of Sheriff James Baxter Crossen, a native of Ireland.

In April 1875, while riding from Nevada to Fort Harney to spend some time with her father, Sarah Winnemucca was thrown from her horse and dragged through the sagebrush—causing as much damage to her ego as it did to her body.[6] While recuperating at the army post, Sarah's half-brother Lee rode in from the Malheur Agency with an invitation from Agent Parrish to return to the reservation and serve as a paid government interpreter. Perhaps he was hoping to entice a few more Shoshoni onto the reservation through a spokesperson. Whatever the reason, to date, only Wolf Dog, Pony Blanket and Left Hand had taken up residence there. Bad Face came and left at leisure while Has No Horse, refusing to go on any reservation, came in only for supplies.

The more progressive Oregon became, the more they resented the Shoshoni having their own plot of land. Sam Parrish—introducing farming and setting up irrigation projects—was doing too good of a job rehabilitating the few stragglers who had come onto the Malheur and it

4 *Winnemucca Silver State,* March 16, 27, 29, 1875; *Reese River Reveille,* Austin, Nevada, April 1, 1875, p. 2.

5 Portland, Oregon *City Directory*, 1875.

6 *Silver State*, Winnemucca, Nevada, April 28, 1875.

was honestly feared that Has No Horse would relent and accept reservation life. The settlers wanted him killed and Parrish was becoming a threat to Manifest Destiny. He had extended the limits of the reservation—without authorization—to insure that the richest farm land, two hot springs where the Shoshoni had traditionally bathed, and the land cultivated by Pony Blanket would be a part of the reserve. Parrish also built a schoolhouse and constructed more irrigation canals. This was unthinkable!

Gen. Howard, sensing that trouble was brewing, interceded on Parrish's behalf and assured the Indian Department that he was doing a commendable job. It didn't help. The locals were stirring up plenty of turmoil. Settler's petitions to senators and representatives complained of the loss of land to the Indian Department and anonymous letters of criticism appearing in local papers didn't benefit the good standing of Agent Parrish. These complainants found a champion in U.S. Senator James Kelly—ex-Lt. Col. in the Oregon Mounted Volunteers—who had no love for the Snakes.[7]

Parrish attempted to defend his expenditures but the odds were against him.[8] The animosity came to a boil when Sam hired his sister-in-law, Annie Parrish, to teach school and hired Sarah Winnemucca as her assistant. He opened the school in May and when the orphan Snake girl, Mattie Shenkah, became the most apt pupil, white parents considered it a sacrilege that a heathen should be taught to read and write. After all, look what it did for Sally Winnemucca. . . undeniably a trouble-maker, thinking she was as good as any white person.

Parrish, anticipating the final outcome, had called a meeting of the tribal headmen in January 1876 and informed them they had "292 enemies in Canyon City" alone. Sam had it down pat and knew exactly what he was talking about. Led by Col. George Currey (retired)—who suffered his share of defeats at the hands of Snake dog soldiers—these enemies were out to take the richest part of the reservation. "These white

7 Petition to the Hon. James K. Kelly from numerous citizens of Baker County, Oregon, November 11, 1875. Letters Received, Office of Interior Affairs, Oregon Superintendency.

8 Samuel B. Parrish to the Hon. E.P. Smith, Commissioner of Indian Affairs, April 26, 1875, Letters Received, Office of Indian Affairs, Oregon Superintendency.

men," Parrish told the assembled chiefs, "have talked to your Father in Washington saying you are lazy and will not work."[9]

The western writer Owen Wister would sum up the situation in one verse:

Their father in a White House lives,
and in a white house they;
But the father with tomorrow rides,
and the son with yesterday.

And so it was. President Grant, in his last year of office, attacked by liberal Republican reformers and soon to die of throat cancer, would do little to help these wards of the nation. Surprisingly, one report from eastern Oregon directed to the Congress of the United States—which should have been heeded—put the situation quite bluntly. "It would be cheaper to feed the whole flock [on the Malheur Reservation] for a year than to fight them for one week." This message would come back to haunt those involved in less than three years.

More anonymous letters would appear accusing the Snakes of stealing horses. Parrish, taking the charge personally, complained to Howard: "It makes me mad to have some irresponsible person under an alias assail me in the daily prints and virtually call me a thief."[10] But Parrish was bucking tough political odds. Not only George Currey, a lawyer with strong partisan ties to the state legislature but Bill Rinehart, Currey's brother-in-law and local politician; Elisha Barnes, brother-in-law to Dr. Hugh Glenn, the powerful "Wheat King" of California and partner of Pete French who coveted the Malheur Reservation as much as Henry Miller; and of course, Tom Overfelt, silent partner of Henry Miller.

Remember also, the ex-Army officers were not regulars, but veterans of the Oregon Volunteers who had personal axes to grind with the Snake warriors. Another interesting thought: Currey was practicing law in Canyon City and his opposition was attorney Charles Parrish, brother to Sam.

---

9 Hopkins, *Life Among the Piutes*, p. 116.

10 Parrish to Gen. O.O. Howard, April 27, 1876, Letters Received, Office of Indian Affairs, Oregon Superintendency.

Seven days after Parrish leveled his blast at the "irresponsible person" who questioned his integrity, President Grant relieved him of duty and appointed. . . William V. Rinehart agent for the Malheur Reservation!

It would soon surface that Rinehart was cut from the same pattern as most of the Indian agents of the time. The story is told of a prominent politician who went to Washington D.C. and told President Lincoln that he deserved a government-appointed position. There were none available other than Indian agent at the Yankton Agency on the Missouri River. When told that it only paid $1,500 a year, the gentleman complained that at that paltry wage he would be obliged to either steal or starve. President Lincoln looked at him quizzically and replied, "Well sir, you don't look like a man who would starve." He was right. The man accepted the position and in three years resigned. General Sherman visited the agency just after his departure and held a council with the chiefs. They asked Sherman, "You know our agent? The agent great man. When he came he bring everything in little bag. When he go it takes two steamboats to carry away his things." Sherman investigated the matter and discovered that in the three years the agent had saved $50,000 out of an annual salary of $1,500.[11]

At the announcement of Rinehart's appointment, Left Hand talked of war. Quick-witted, ugly in appearance, strange in his conduct, Left Hand wielded the power of a wizard over these people. In council he boasted, "I can defeat our enemies! No bullet can hurt me!" His impassioned oratory swayed his audience into a frenzy for white blood.

Pony Blanket knew that the reservation Shoshoni were in no condition to start another major campaign. Has No Horse, the only sobering influence on these people, had to be contacted. Riders slipped off the reservation to alert the war chief and Bad Face of this new threat. Meanwhile, Pony Blanket did the only thing possible. He challenged Left Hand before the council and for the moment, the medicine man backed down.

As things so often happen, Pony Blanket's messenger found Bad Face but failed to make contact with Has No Horse. In early April, a request from Gen. Crook for Shoshoni scouts to help in the Sioux

11 Slattery, *Felix Reville Brunot*, pp. 144-145.

campaign had reached Fort Bidwell. Has No Horse, seeing a legal outlet for his pent-up emotions, had left the Ochoco for a rendezvous with the man he called Gray Wolf. Bad Face, now on his own and facing new persecution, headed for the Malheur Reserve.

In a desperate move, Sarah, Pony Blanket and Bad Face appealed to the officers at Fort Harney to intercede in Parrish's behalf. The warriors knew anyone was preferable to Rinehart, their sworn enemy. Major John Green—commanding officer at Fort Harney—was genuinely sympathetic but he knew he could do little, for the officers at the military outposts were under as much fire as the Snakes.

The new conquerors of the Ochoco had laid their ground-work very well. These same "anonymous citizens" (one later proved to be Rinehart) also accused the officers at Fort Harney, Fort McDermit and Fort Bidwell of encouraging Has No Horse to stay away from the Malheur Reservation by supplying him with food. The rabble-rousers were working through Gov. Grover, the Hon. Lafayette Lane, Senator Kelly and Senator Mitchell—all good Democrats with the exception of Mitchell who was later indicted in the Willamette Valley and Cascade Mountain Military Road Company land frauds. These gentlemen applied political pressure where it hurt. Major General Irvin McDowell, commander of the Military Division of the Pacific, was forced to admit that the conduct of his officers "if correctly represented, renders them liable to the charge of disobedience or neglect of general orders which could mean Court Martial." In view of this implied threat, Major Green would not push very hard for Shoshoni justice.

On the other hand, Capt. John Norvell, commanding officer at Fort McDermit in 1874 and presently in command at Fort Bidwell, answered the charge in fighting terms. "While I was in command of McDermit, the small issue of stores to visiting chiefs made under authority of the army regulations, have not exceeded in money value five dollars a year. Furthermore, I am sure that not one pound of subsistence has either been issued or furnished by the Government at this post to Ochoco's band of vagabond Indians during the last two years and a half, as I would certainly have known of the fact had it occurred."[12] It appears that Capt. Norvell was ready to take Salem and Washington, D.C. by force.

12 Letter with enclosure of Secretary of War G.W. McCrary to Carl Schurz, secretary of Interior,

On May 26, 1876, Major Green reported to Department Headquarters that Bad Face had told him that if the Snakes had such a man as Agent Parrish to deal with, "the war with General Crook would not have occurred." Green further stated that it seemed strange to him to remove an Indian agent who was doing so much for the Indians and "one whom they are so unwilling to lose."[13] Faced with arguments like this, Gen. McDowell refused to pursue charges against his officers, causing further unrest between the settlers and the army.

On June 28—three days after Custer's ignoble defeat on the Little Bighorn—Major Rinehart with his entourage arrived at Agency headquarters and the Indians never saw Parrish again. Rinehart—a Canyon City whiskey peddler—by controlling the Malheur Indian Agency, could ensure the Shoshoni's downfall. That the government was ignorant of his activity can never be said. Pony Blanket and Left Hand testified to a board of commissioners that Rinehart—when still in Canyon City—had been selling the reservation Indians liquor. Also, Rinehart, who had been in command at Fort Klamath when Paulina accepted the terms of the 1865 treaty, was an avid proponent of Oregon's extermination style of warfare. In dealing with Gen. Howard, Rinehart would speak derisively of the "religious idiocy" of Howard's lenient policy toward Indians.[14] Absolute authority was the principle tool with which he knew how to deal with others and when that authority was breached, even by a child, Rinehart became irrationally brutal and he would conveniently look the other way when his white friends began to trespass on Shoshoni allotments.

At the first meeting with his dependents, Rinehart informed them that the land upon which they lived belonged to the government not, the Snakes or Paiutes but he would be generous and pay them a dollar a day for whatever work they did. Pony Blanket protested, "The man who just left told us the land was ours and what we do on it was ours and you say it is government land." Rinehart, getting hot, retorted, "Egan! I don't give a damn whether any of you stay or not! As for pay, you'll take looking-

---

April 17, 1878, United States Department of the Interior, Office of Indian Affairs, General Files, Oregon, p. 650.

13 Green to A.A.G., Department of the Columbia, May 26, 1876, endorsed by Gen. O.O. Howard, Letters Received, Office of Indian Affairs, Oregon Superintendency.

14 W.V. Rinehart to Mrs. F.F. Victor (author of *Early Indian Wars of Oregon*), April 10, 1881, Bancroft Library.

glasses, shawls, calico and handkerchiefs if I say so and be damn glad to get it!"

The Indians soon learned what he meant by that. At the end of the first week when they returned from the fields to the agent's office to get their money, there was none forthcoming. Posted around the Indian commissary were signs: blankets $6; shoes $3; pants $5 and so on. Out of the $6 earned, Rinehart deducted $4 for rations and the remaining $2 would be applied against anything they wished to obtain from the storehouse. The Shoshoni walked out in disgust. In the meantime, white employees were walking around in new clothes and fed at government expense.

Again Pony Blanket confronted the agent. "Why do you play with us, Rinehart? We are men, not children. . . don't say you are going to pay us money and then not do it. If you had told us you wanted us to work for nothing we would have done it. I don't care for myself but my men want pay, they can buy whatever they like. . . we can go to the soldiers and get better blankets than yours for half the price. You are all wearing the clothes that we fools thought belonged to us."

Rinehart exploded. "Get out," he screamed, "I don't let a white man talk to me like that!" Pony Blanket to prevent more trouble left. Has No Horse would later comment that his brother-in-law, one of the tribe's bravest dog soldiers was now behaving like a child. Bowing to a man who just a few years before, he would have chopped to the earth with one blow of his war axe.[15]

The next morning after this confrontation, Rinehart grabbed a young boy by the ear, knocked him down and then kicked him because the boy laughed in response to an order. The child did not understand English. Rinehart told the watching men that if they didn't instantly obey his orders they could expect the same treatment. That same day a band of starving Paiutes were refused food at the agency commissary. A few days later, another Shoshoni boy was imprisoned and threatened with hanging because "he showed disrespect."[16]

As things simmered on the Great Malheur Reserve, Has No Horse with fifteen warriors crossed Idaho for a union with Gourd Rattler.

---

15 Agnes Banning Philips, granddaughter to Has No Horse.

16 Hopkins, *Life Among the Piutes*, pp. 124-134.

Together, they would join Gray Wolf Crook at Rosebud Creek on the Wyoming-Montana border for the anticipated big Indian war of the year. Had he been aware of Rinehart's arrogance, the showdown may have occurred in Harney Valley. As it was, that brawl would be postponed for a couple of years.

Even to the casual observer it was becoming obvious that long-pent emotions would eventually come to a boil on the Malheur Reservation. A thoughtful eastern Oregon youth, more discerning than most of his elders at that time, had this to say about the reservation policy in 1876:[17]

> This war was provoked by a long series of aggravation, delays and non-fulfillment of government promises, red tape in the affairs of the Indian Department and non-payment of money due them, it being stolen by dishonest agents and the streaming in of great herds and droves of cattle, horses and sheep during the first of the 70s. Their fine meadows were fenced up by the white settlers and their choice hunting sections were over-run by stockmen. The white hunters were killing off the elk and deer for the hides in wintertime. One man told me that he killed over one hundred deer in one winter just for the hides alone.
>
> To offset this, the government tried to supply meat for the Indians by setting up butchering places on the reservations, and hiring white men to kill the cattle purchased for that

17 The memories of Tom Morgan (son of Seth and Margaret Jane Hamilton Morgan) who was no stranger to the Bannock War. The Morgan ranch was located six miles northeast of Fossil, Oregon in what is now Wheeler County. Seth Morgan was running 1,200 head of sheep on Thirtymile Creek at the time. Years later Tom would note that an Indian took a shot as his father and came close to getting him instead; the bullet striking a tree just inches over his head. Tom, only seven years old, and his brother Dan then made a wild ride into The Dalles seeking shelter from the Shoshoni. When they arrived The Dalles was swarming with soldiers from Fort Vancouver. According to Tom, about twenty cavalrymen raced around town most of the day, riding up to the saloons and ordering drinks to be brought out, and bragging what would happen to the poor Indians when they caught up with them. Tom didn't think they ever got close enough to see an Indian.
Young Morgan was also a nephew to Rube Kiger, whose ranch was located at the base of Steens Mountain near Bad Face's hideout in what is now Harney County. Kiger and his wife Minerva (Dolly) Morgan Kiger moved back to western Oregon in 1878 because of the Bannock War. Kiger Gorge in the Steens was named for Reuben by his wife Dolly.

purpose. Thusly the Indian was forced into idleness and inactivity, so about all he had to do was to lay around in the shade. This was entirely out of his nature when he got too hungry. He had not yet accepted the thought that he was not human. When he saw all this closing in on him, and that his liberties were being taken from him the only way out (as he saw it) was to go after white scalps and try to run the whites out of his country. That was the only way he knew how to free himself of this impending slavery. He could not realize that his doom was already sealed, that his love of freedom would be of no avail, his star had set; disgrace and humiliation would follow any move he would make against the Whites. These Indians were once a fierce and powerful people.

CHAPTER 162

A CALL TO ARMS

A long line of glittering lances and brightly polished weapons of fire announced the anxiously expected advent of our allies, the Shoshoni. . . .

Lt. John Bourke
Goose Creek, Wyoming, June 1876

In May 1876 ex-peace commissioner Felix Brunot would quote General Sheridan as saying: "I will send four columns [into Indian country] and we'll make it lively for the squaw, papooses, ponies and villages." Brunot would bitterly comment, "What visions of glory must have floated through the mind of the general as he penned these words! What visions of glory when the brave soldiers in the field should flash over the [telegraph] wires their triumphant dispatches 'We have met the squaws, papooses, ponies and wigwams—and they are ours.' We cannot close our eyes to the fact that the men who enlist in the army in time of peace are among the most vicious of our population."[1] These are the fiery thoughts of a man charged with keeping the peace who detested the government policy of pitting one Indian tribe against another. In fact, blistering outbursts like this may have been instrumental in the firing of the Board of Indian Commissioners shortly before the Bannock War detonated over eastern Oregon.

It would seem that the American mind operated in a vacuum. One might concede it was premeditated but history will bear out it was not intellectual thought but sheer contempt for unsophistication that pitted

1 Brunot would write in this same vein mentioning the Western Shoshoni, Nez Perce and Umatillas in an eight page report to the Hon. William E. Dodge (another member of the old Board of Peace Commissioners), New York City, dated Pittsburgh, May 22, 1876. (Slattery, *Felix Reville Brunot*, pp. 229-236.)

man against man. Therefore, it was quite natural that the French may enlist the aid of Germans to attack Russians; or that Spain would ally itself with Italy to overthrow England for that was progress. But, if the Nez Perce should join with the Americans to subdue the Yakimas, or the Wascos take up the battle against the Modocs, that was just another example of how stupid the Indians were. It never entered the European mind—just because all red skins were the same hue—that to a Blackfoot, a Navaho was as alien as a Norwegian was to an Arabian. As for the American Indian, it was no credit to his intelligence that he allowed Europeans—his true enemy—to pit him against his own kind in the fight for survival. But when the word went out that the army needed help in subduing the Plains tribes, Has No Horse volunteered. From time beyond memory, they had been the enemy. Centuries upon centuries before the arrival of the pale strangers, his people had fought for survival against these people. If the Americans were dumb enough to aid him in their suppression, he would give what little he could—so be it. Gray Wolf was a friend.

While some newcomers to the West were importing all the trappings of European culture, others were busy trying to purge the area of its existing organization. In 1876, the Plains tribes were making their last ditch stand against the forces of civilization. The first complaints had come from eastern Oregon cattlemen who accused the Sioux and Cheyenne of disrupting their cattle drives to the Laramie and Cheyenne railheads, but, as in the case of the Snakes, it was the curse of yellow fever that brought about their final downfall. In 1875, gold was discovered in the Black Hills—the sacred *Paha 'sapa* of the Sioux. All troops in the Military Division of the Missouri were converging on the Plains country. Custer and Gibbon were closing from the east; Terry from the north; Crook with fifteen cavalry companies and five of infantry was moving in from the south.

Crook attempted to enlist local Indians as scouts but was stopped by the Interior Department so he sent requests to the Malheur, Fort Hall and Wind River reservations for help.[2] Fortunately, Capt. Norvell intercepted the Malheur message and got it into the right hands before that summons could add more fuel to the white flames engulfing the Agency.

2 Hebard, *Washakie*, pp. 200-201.

Specifically, Crook wanted one hundred scouts and the enemies of the Sioux, Cheyenne and Arapaho were quick to respond. From the Absaroka Range came the Crows led by the war chiefs Alligator Stands Up and Plenty Coups; from the Blues came sixty-two Snake dog soldiers led by the war chiefs Has No Horse and Buffalo Horn; and from the Wind River Range came two hundred Eastern Shoshoni led by the war chief Gourd Rattler and his son, Dick Washakie, whose brother, Snow Bird (Gourd Rattler's favorite son), had been killed and mutilated by the Sioux in 1865.

On the Owyhee River, the White Knife warrior, Has No Horse, had been joined by the Robber dog soldier, Buffalo Horn, now officially attached to the Fort Hall Reservation. Since Pony Blanket had taken over the reins of command from Man Lost in the early 1870's, it was obvious Buffalo Horn was aware of the problem on the Malheur Reservation. On Green River, the dog soldiers picked up Three Coyotes—fresh from the Apache campaign—with twenty-two Ute warriors disenchanted with The Arrow's capitulation to the citizens of Colorado. Also riding with Has No Horse were three Texas gunmen—known only as Cosgrove, Yarnell and Eckles—who had drifted into eastern Oregon with the great trail herds that were now ranging across the Crooked River basin. Not finding enough excitement to their liking, they had teamed up with the Snake dog soldiers for this fling at adventure. Cosgrove, who held the position of Has No Horse's right hand man in this venture was, during the Civil War, a captain in the Confederate 32nd Texas Cavalry. Riding with Buffalo Horn was Luisant, a French-Canadian half-breed fresh from the Auburn gold fields.[3]

On the morning of June 14, 1876, this dangerous crew joined Crook's column on Goose Creek at the foot of the Big Horn Mountains.[4] Two other Oregonians were already in camp. Joe Wasson and Robert Strahorn, veteran reporters of the Ochoco campaign, were covering this battle as war correspondents for the *Philadelphia Tribune*, *New York Times*, *San Francisco Bulletin* and the Denver *Rocky Mountain News*. Replacing Archie McIntosh as head scout was William F. Cody, better known to the world as Buffalo Bill; and it was whispered that one of the

3 Bourke, *On the Border with Crook*, p. 306.

4 Crook, *Autobiography*, p. 193.

teamsters was a woman—none other than Martha Jane Cannary, better known as Calamity Jane. Aide-de-camp was Capt. Azor Nickerson, who had taken Wolf Dog's surrender statement at Fort Harney in 1868.[5] It was like old home week.

Gourd Rattler, now 72 years old, was riding the war trail to uphold his honor. Earlier some of the younger men had plotted to take over tribal rule blaming his refusal to join Has No Horse's fight for survival on advanced years. With his courage being questioned, the old dog soldier disappeared from camp. Two months later on the night the council was to meet to decide his fate, Gourd Rattler suddenly appeared with six Arapaho scalps taken in a hand-to-hand combat—stopping all opposition to his leadership due to old age. But he was also riding into combat driven by remorse.

His eldest son, Young Gourd Rattler, had been recently killed. . . not in battle but in an Idaho saloon. In a drunken argument, he was beat to the draw by a white man. Gourd Rattler was badly shaken, commenting, "Now my son is dead. For him to die in battle would have made me sad, but for him to die like an Arapaho Indian breaks my heart."

From that day on, Gourd Rattler kept his head covered to remind himself and his friends of his deep sorrow and the fact that his son entered the Spirit Land in disgrace as no Shoshoni should do. Lt Bourke would observe that Gourd Rattler's resemblance in face and bearing to "the eminent divine, Henry Ward Beecher"—one of the first proponents of women's rights—was very noticeable[6] Evidence that the old Shoshoni chief fought bravely in the battle of Rosebud Creek is contained in an interview with Dick Washakie. "Gen. Crook expressed to my father his indebtedness for the service that the warriors rendered the U.S. troops. Gen. Crook highly approved what Chief Washakie and his Indians had done for him on this occasion, and it was through the recommendations of Gen. Crook that my father received a pension from the government for the service rendered at this particular instant."[7]

---

5 Bourke, *On the Border with Crook*, pp. 289, 290, 299.

6 Beecher's sister, Harriet Beecher Stowe, was the author of *Uncle Tom's Cabin*. James Finerty, a Chicago reporter with Crook's forces, saw in the features of Gourd Rattler the image of the Rev. Robert Collyer, another important religious figure of that period. Apparently Gourd Rattler had a reverent face.

7 Hebard, *Washakie*, pp. 200-201.

Upon arriving at Crook's camp on Goose Creek, Wyoming Territory, squads of Snake warriors busied themselves looking after their rifles, which were the latest model .45 calibre and kept with scrupulous care in regular gun racks. Some were sharpening lances, adorning them with feathers and paint thus identifying them as belonging to either the Big Lodge, White Knife, Robber or Bear Killer warrior societies. Others were making coup sticks from twelve-foot willow branches while another group prepared provisions for the fight to come. On their march from Wind River to Goose Creek, the Snakes had killed 175 buffalo on the eastern slope of the Owl Creek Mountains. That night, they offered worship to the moon in a wild frenzied dance.[8]

Crook stalled twenty-four hours waiting for the arrival of Gourd Rattler and to pass time, Has No Horse's troops engaged in horse races with the cavalry and taught the soldiers how to fish Shoshoni style. Fishing with them was not a sport, it was serious business and they brought them in by the hundreds. Placing a dam of woven willows across the stream, a party of warriors would proceed upstream, enter the water and head downstream toward the trap at a gallop driving the trout before them. An average catch usually netted upwards to one hundred fish.

An added attraction was Three Coyotes. When he first started making his tour of the soldiers camp in full war paint and scowling dangerously, the new recruits were a bit nervous. "Ute John" as Bourke called him, "was credited by most people with having murdered his own grandmother and drunk her blood, but in my opinion, the reports to his detriment were somewhat exaggerated and he was harmless except when sober which wasn't often, provided whiskey was handy." Three Coyotes had one peculiarity. The only man he would speak to in regard to the campaign was General Crook (who he knew didn't like him) and his conversations at these meetings would keep the enlisted men in stitches. Cornering the general, he would usually begin, "Hello Crook, how you gettin' on? Where you think Crazy Horse and Sittin' Bull is now, Crook? Don't you worry Crook, me an Ochiho'll find 'em and hang their scalp on your lodge!" Crook, if he had had a choice, would have preferred to miss these encounters.

---

8 Details on camp life and other aspects of the Rosebud battle can be found in Bourke, *On the Border with Crook*, pp. 303, 305, 311, 316, 322, 335, 338, 349, 350.

With the Sioux and their allies amassing their forces on the Rosebud, Crook could no longer wait for the arrival of the Eastern Shoshoni. His long column—1,100 men in all—moved out, flanked by the Crow and Snake scouts. Along the march, they passed many Sioux graves, buried in the same manner as the Shoshoni, the bodies wrapped in blankets and placed on high wind-swept platforms. The Snakes were having great sport tumbling these graves to the ground and looting them for anything of value—getting bows, knives and even nickel-plated revolvers. One day, they came upon one which to the soldiers appeared the same as the others but Has No Horse and Plenty Coups informed them that it was the resting place of a very powerful medicine man and was a bad omen. The Indian scouts were giving it a wide berth when Three Coyotes rode up. Fortified by the grace of his numerous Mormon baptisms (he claimed six) and more than likely by a straight shot of whiskey, Three Coyotes, unrestrained by "vain fears," tumbled it to the ground and unleashed nothing more evil than sixteen field mice.

Nonetheless, the other Indians became morose and Has No Horse confided to Crook that Three Coyotes' indiscretion was not good and it was his belief that the Great Spirit would not ride with them into battle. Crook and his staff officers thought nothing more about the incident until two days later on the Rosebud when Has No Horse's warning was fulfilled.

The head of the strung-out army column hit the headwaters of the Rosebud on June 16, 1876 and here made contact with Gourd Rattler who had over 200 braves—a welcome addition which did much to boast the morale of Has No Horse's troops. Gourd Rattler had been delayed waiting for Wolf Dog and Storm Cloud, who had sent word from the Klamath Reservation that they wished to take part in the war against the Sioux. Riding with Gourd Rattler were two messengers: Black Eagle (Wolf Dog's half-brother), who had been hiding out in the Seven Devil Mountains of Idaho, and Fox (son-in-law to Left Hand), from the Malheur Reservation.

The story was told that Black Eagle and Fox, during the winter of 1875-76, had crossed the Rockies to steal some horses. They had slipped into a Sioux encampment and were in the process of cutting the horses loose when a dog barked, alarming the whole village. During the confusion, the Snakes slipped into a tipi, hid under some buffalo robes and quietly waited for the Sioux to calm down. Unable to locate their quarry, the Sioux returned to camp, ignorant that their lodges were harboring two of the more desperate villains in the western territory. The occupants settled down and when the proper moment arrived the Snakes quietly reached out with their knives, cut the throats of the people closest to them, slipped out of the lodge, ran rapidly to where they had tied the two best ponies and voicing the Shoshoni victory yell, rode away unscathed. More important, they overheard talk of Crazy Horse's plan to rid the Black Hills of white men after the spring break-up.

On June 17, Crook's large force hit Crazy Horse's allied camp on the Rosebud. Bourke, who was riding as military advisor to the Snakes, described what was to follow. "In one word, the Battle of the Rosebud was a trap." Crazy Horse would later acknowledge that he had no less than 6,500 men in the fight and that the first attack was made with 1,500 warriors. . . outnumbering Crook's total force by 400 men. Few whites went in with the Shoshoni that bloody day. One, Pvt. Elmer Snow, trumpeter for Co. M, 3rd Cavalry, rode between the two war chiefs, sounding the charge for special effect. He was seriously wounded in both arms, leaving him crippled for life and escaped death only because of the bravery shown by the Shoshoni in effecting his escape. Another who rode with them, Lt. John Bourke, gave this description of Has No Horse and Medicine Crow as they rode into battle.

> The chief of the Shoshones appeared to great advantage, mounted on a fiery pony, he himself naked to the waist and wearing one of the gorgeous head-dresses of eagle feathers sweeping far along the ground behind his pony's tail. The Crow chief looked like a devil in his war-bonnet of feathers, fur and buffalo horns.

As the Shoshoni and Crows charged into the fray Bourke would remember:

> We moved out in columns of twos at a fast walk, then a trot and finally a full gallop. The ground thundered and rocked beneath our feet as we took sagebrush, rocks, gullies, anything that fell within our path. Only one thought occupied my mind during this charge and that thought was what fools we were not to incorporate these nomads—the finest

> light cavalry in the world—into our permanent military force. With 5,000 such men, we could harass and annoy any troops that might have the audacity to land on our coasts, and worry them to death!

The Battle of the Rosebud was every bit as bitter as Has No Horse had prophesied. Many Sioux and Cheyenne escaped because they were dressed so nearly like the Crows, even the Shoshoni were afraid to shoot for fear of making a mistake and, according to the record, this was the only major defeat Crook suffered at the hands of the Indians. For lack of publicity, Little Rattlesnake's victory at the Infernal Caverns never counted.[9] On the Rosebud, Crook lost 100 killed and wounded not counting the Shoshoni and Crow casualties.

Late in the afternoon when victory seemed sure for Crook, the Shoshoni scouts told him of an ambush and plot to entrap the whole command. Taking them at their word, Crook withdrew and pushed north to join forces with Gen. Terry. On this forced march, the soldiers killed and ate their disabled horses. During the Rosebud setback, Gen. Custer was rushing toward the Little Bighorn Valley in Montana Territory, fearful that all the Sioux would be killed before he could engage them in battle. He would meet this same group.

When Crook's fiery commanding officer, Gen. Phil Sheridan, received Crook's report of the Rosebud encounter, he went ballistic. Burning up the wires, he telegraphed orders to "hit 'em again and hit 'em hard!" Crook read the sharp dispatch and remarked wearily to his officers, "I wonder if Sheridan could surround three Sioux with one soldier."

Crook's disgust with Sheridan stemmed from the Civil War. He had gotten plenty mad at Sheridan during the Battle of Fisher Hill in which Sheridan, who wasn't even in the fight, claimed all the credit and thus gained much of his Civil War fame.[10] Gen. DuPont would remark, "It was fully understood by everyone at Corps Headquarters that Crook suggested the movement and asked permission to move his infantry along the almost precipitous slope of Little North Mountain," which turned the

9 See *Thunder Over the Ochoco*, Vol. III, Chapter 142, for a full account of this battle.

10 Crook was commissioned a Major General in the Army of West Virginia for his service at Fisher Hill, Virginia, October 1864.

Confederates back at Fisher Hill.[11] Gen. Rutherford B. Hayes would agree with DuPont. "At Fisher's Hill, the turning of the Rebel left was planned and executed by Crook against the opinion of other Corps generals. . . . Intellectually he [Gen. Sheridan] is not Crook's equal, so as I said, General Crook is the brains of this army."[12]

Years later when visiting the old battleground, Crook dryly commented,

> After examining the grounds and position of the troops after twenty-five years which have elapsed and in the light of subsequent events, it renders Gen. Sheridan's claims and his subsequent actions in allowing the general public to remain under the impression regarding his past in these battles when he knew they were fictitious, all the more contemptible. The adulation heaped on him by a grateful nation for his supposed genius turned his head, which, added to his natural disposition, caused him to bloat his little carcass with debauchery and dissipation which carried him off permanently.[13]

En route to join Gen. Terry, Buffalo Horn volunteered to take a message from Powder River through enemy country to Gen. Nelson Miles on the Yellowstone, notifying him of Crook's near disaster. In company with Tom Lefarge, a Crow scout and Buffalo Bill Cody, Buffalo Horn successfully completed the dangerous journey. He then decided to stay with Miles.[14]

Back on the Rosebud, Crazy Horse—after defeating Crook—moved north toward Montana. Sitting Bull, who had been camped on Beaver Creek at the foot of the Blues when Crazy Horse's messenger intercepted him, now joined him on the Little Bighorn River.[15] Sitting Bull's first action, to ensure the blessings of the Great

11 General Henry A. DuPont, *The Campaign of 1864*, p. 134.

12 Hayes, Rutherford B., *Diary and Letters*, Vol. V, p. 514.

13 Crook's diary entry December 26, 1889, Crook, *Autobiography*, p. 134.

14 Lefarge, Thomas H., *Memoirs of a White Crow Indian*, pp. 261, 267, 273-74.

15 It appears that the stream called "Beaver Creek" as it appears in most accounts may have been the early fur trade name for Birch Creek. Birch Creek dumps into the Snake River in the

Spirit in coming battles, was to place offerings of tobacco on willow wands stuck in the ground along the trails leading to the Sioux encampment. The following morning after he placed these religious gifts—Sunday, June 25, 1876—the hooves of Custer's horses knocked them down. It was his last mistake for the Sioux say those offerings were not in vain. By noon, Gen. Custer and 276 soldiers of the 7th U.S. Cavalry were dead! Among those killed was Archie McIntosh's brother.[16] The Cheyenne warrior, Two Moons—one of the combatants—said later that the defeat of Custer's cavalry took "as long as it takes a hungry man to eat his dinner."

The lone survivor of Custer's command on the Little Bighorn was Captain Myles Keogh's horse, Comanche—so named because the big war horse (in a previous battle) had taken a Comanche arrow in the hindquarters and kept going. After the battle on the Little Bighorn, Little Soldier (a Sioux warrior) questioned by the Army, told why Comanche was spared. He said the other soldiers had killed their mounts and used the carcasses as barricades. Apparently the bond between Capt. Keogh and Comanche was very strong because he refused to kill his horse and instead knelt under his horse's front legs and fired from there. Keogh died holding onto the reins. It was Little Soldier's belief that no Indian would take a horse when a dead man was holding the reins.[17]

Crook was the first white man to learn of the Custer massacre. It was mid-afternoon, June 25 when his Shoshoni scouts told him, "Yellow Hair and his men have all been killed." They refused to explain how they received information of a tragedy that took place three hundred miles

---

extreme northeast corner of what is now Malheur County, Oregon, which wasn't established until February 17, 1887, eleven years after Sitting Bull camped there.

16 Juana Fraser Lyon, "Archie McIntosh, the Scottish Scout," *Journal of Arizona History*, Vol. VII (Autumn 1966), pp. 103-22; Vestal, Stanley, *Sitting Bull*, p. 161.

17 Still alive two days after the battle, Comanche, wounded in several places, was shipped to Fort Abraham Lincoln in Dakota Territory where he was looked after by Army blacksmith Gustav Korn. He was never ridden again. Gustav cared for the old war horse until 1890. Unfortunately, Gustav Korn was among the casualties at the Battle of Wounded Knee. Comanche died soon after in 1891 at the age of 28. The horse was then stuffed and put on display at the Chicago World's Fair. Today Comanche resides in a glass case at the Dyche Museum of Natural History in Lawrence, Kansas. (A photo of Comanche appears in Nevin, *The Soldiers*, Time-Life Books, p. 219.)

away that very morning. How such communications was possible in 1876 is still an unsolved mystery to historians and scientists alike.[18]

The glorification of Custer began immediately. Within 24 hours of receiving the news of the general's defeat, Walt Whitman had his tribute, "A Death Sonnet for Custer," in the mail to the *New York Tribune*, accompanied by a bill for ten dollars. The fallen soldiers of the 7th Cavalry had not yet received a proper burial when Crook's chief of scouts, William "Buffalo Bill" Cody's play, "The Red Right Hand: or Buffalo Bill's First Scalp for Custer," premiered in the fall of 1876. During this adoration, Has No Horse was shedding no tears.

With the rumor that Sitting Bull might be returning to the Blues, the Shoshoni taking no chances, left the Sioux campaign to protect their families. In late August, Has No Horse and his victorious warriors rode into eastern Oregon loaded with plunder, full of whiskey and infected with venereal disease.

On the Malheur Reservation, Pony Blanket had come to a wise conclusion during the Sioux campaign. In his opinion, Agent Rinehart was the only man he knew who could perform the unbelievable feat of picking an Indian's pocket while his own hands were folded in prayer.

---

18 Heline, Theodore, *American Indians*, p. 29.

CHAPTER 163

SNAKE OR PAIUTE, THAT IS THE QUESTION

No truth in reports of Piute hostility. Winnemucca my father at Idaho wants me and chiefs talk with you. Danger that whites may make trouble for their own benefit. Pay expenses for me and chiefs to come talk at San Francisco. Answer immediately.

Natchez
Telegram to Gen. McDowell

About the same time the Shoshoni scouts entered Wyoming Territory, the ice broke in the Crooked River, flooding the town of Prineville. Across the Cascades, the Willamette went on the rampage flooding Portland. Front Street became a canal, but boats found navigation difficult because of the many wooden walkways thrown across the flooded street. By the time the flood waters receded it was time for the big July 4th celebration commemorating the 100th birthday of the Declaration of Independence.

In Prineville, pistols were used in preference to fire crackers because they were handier and made more noise. Local orators gave flowing speeches and the main topic of discussion was the recent slaughter on the Little Bighorn. This gave rise to much uneasiness about the wandering Shoshoni on the home front and more than ever, the Ochoco citizens voiced approval of total extermination.

Another gentleman destined to become part of the legend of the West died violently on August 2nd. James Butler Hickok was shot in the back by Jack McCall in a Deadwood saloon. Like Custer, it just wasn't Wild Bill's day. It was common knowledge that the early Colt was not a reliable weapon because of misfires. The one McCall killed Hickok with misfired on every cartridge except the first one, which blew Wild Bill through the pearly gates. Even then there was some dispute about how great a loss this was to society.

The big political issue was would that Republican from Ohio, Rutherford B. Hayes, win over the popular Democrat Samuel J. Tilden, governor of New York. To Oregon's dismay—after long contested votes—he did. However, Portland ladies of the Women's Temperance Prayer League and Gen. Howard were ecstatic. Lucy Hayes, with her husband's consent, banished wine and hard liquor from the White House.[1] Another pleased bystander was Gen. Crook, but for a very different reason. Gen. Hayes, who had commanded a brigade under Crook, was (according to the old Indian fighter) "as brave a man as ever wore a shoulder strap." President Hayes would repay this compliment by recommending that Crook be promoted from brevet to full major general, stating that "his appointment will be especially gratifying to all who take an interest in just and humane treatment of Indians."[2]

At Scissorsville things were booming. The Portland Board of Trade would report for the year 1876-77 that gold and silver shipped from Oregon amounted to 1.2 million dollars and a big chunk of this was coming from the Ochoco River strike.[3] Also, more gold on the hoof was moving into the Crooked River basin in 1876. Among the big time cattlemen to arrive was Henry Grimes, who entered Oregon by mule team in 1863. And again, Sally Winnemucca was making headlines.

About the time Has No Horse was heading home from the Rosebud fracas, Rinehart closed the agency school and fired Sarah for insubordination, confiscating her $50 wood stove in the process. Broke and lonely, she fell madly in love with Joe Satwaller, a Canyon City miner, and decided to file for divorce from Lt. Bartlett who had deserted her four years before. The mere thought of an Indian squaw attempting to bring civil action against a white man was laughable until Charlie Parrish volunteered to act as her attorney. This was hardly proper and concerned citizens from Prineville to Prairie City made known their

1 Freidel, Frank, *The Presidents of the United States*, p. 44.

2 Hayes, Diary and Letters, Vol. IV, p. 377; Bourke, On the Border with Crook, p. 321. However, this promotion would not be confirmed until 1885 when Grover Cleveland became the 22nd President of the United States.

3 Reid, *Progress of Portland for the Year Ending 1877*, a pamphlet published in 1879 by the Secretary of the Portland Board of Trade.

disapproval of such irresponsible action. Lawyer George Currey would represent Bartlett for free if he could locate him.

Amidst this furor, Sarah started proceedings against Bartlett on July 10, 1876. A summons for her absent husband was printed in *The Dalles Mountaineer*, the only regularly published newspaper east of the Cascade Mountains at that time. When Bartlett didn't answer the summons, Sarah's divorce was granted on September 21. On November 3, Joe and Sally got a license and were married the same day at Charlie Parrish's house in Canyon City.[4] They then took off for their honeymoon on the Malheur Reservation.

As might be expected, Rinehart made life so miserable for Sarah and Joe that within a few weeks, they moved to the Warm Springs Agency.[5] Apparently things were no better there, for Joe abandoned Sarah and once more she was without a husband.

By spring 1877, Agent Rinehart was getting worried about the Snakes who refused to come to the Malheur Reserve. The few under Wolf Dog and Black Buffalo who did come in were working off the reservation as ranch hands. It was an embarrassment to Rinehart's administration that only a few Paiutes were present when he was supposed to be in charge of at least seven hundred Indians. He went himself to the Steens Mountains to talk to Bad Face but Bad Face refused to return to the Malheur. This rankled Rinehart who then claimed that Has No Horse and Bad Face were pulled away from the Malheur by free food at Fort Bidwell and Fort McDermit and the nightly celebrations at these army outposts which he called "a species of brothel-dances."[6]

Such allegations quickly solicited responses from the officers at Bidwell and McDermit. They testified that the Indians had not been given subsistence at the military posts for years and they "seldom saw Ocheo or Winnemucca who subsist by fishing and hunting."[7] Rinehart didn't

4 Marriage certificate of Sarah Winnemucca and Joseph Satwaller, November 3, 1876, Grant County, Oregon.

5 W.V. Rinehart to Commissioner of Indian Affairs, December 23, 1976, Letters Received, Office of Indian Affairs, Oregon Superintendency.

6 W.V. Rinehart to Commissioner of Indian Affairs, March 23, 1878, Letters Received, Office of Indian Affairs, Oregon Superintendency.

7 Capt. Henry Wagner, 1st Cavalry to A.A.G., February 8, 1878, Letters Received, Office of Indian Affairs, Oregon Superintendency.

believe them. At his insistence, Capt. Wagner called in Has No Horse, who again told anyone who would listen that he was not going on any reservation. "General Crook told me so long as I behave myself, I don't have to go" and that was final.[8]

Crook confirmed Has No Horse's statement. He also warned Gen. McDowell that Has No Horse was well-armed and the country he occupied was easy to defend. If he chose to resist, Has No Horse would be as dangerous and as difficult to overcome as Modoc Jack. Armed with this information, McDowell suggested to the War Department that it would be wise not to yield to any efforts made toward the military to "coerce Ocheo's band onto the Malheur Reservation."[9]

It was prior to these negotiations that Natchez sent his request to Gen. McDowell to bring in the chiefs for conference. McDowell would decline—explaining that he had no money to pay their fare.[10] The general wasn't lying. Oregonians, still clamoring for the complete extermination of the Indians with one hand, were petitioning Congress with the other to reduce the army. At the height of the Sioux campaign, Crook was told by Gen. Sheridan "to push on the Indians as much as possible before the first day of July [1877] as at that date we will be obliged to reduce the army by 2,500 men."[11] So there you have it. Eliminate the Indians, but do it without manpower.

Gen. McDowell did thank Natchez for confirming his own judgment that the Paiutes would remain peaceful. Pony Blanket was not so certain about McDowell's belief—especially if the Paiutes got backing from the Snakes—which he knew they would. He expressed this animosity to a cavalryman at Fort Harney who passed on the information to Senator Newton Booth thinking he might intervene on behalf of the Paiutes.

---

8 Capt. Henry Wagner, 1st Cavalry to A.A.G., March 11, 1878, Letters Received, Office of Indian Affairs, Oregon Superintendency.

9 Irvin McDowell to Adj. Gen. U.S. Army, Washington, D.C., April 16, 1878, Letters Received, Office of Indian Affairs, Oregon Superintendency.

10 Winnemucca, *Nevada Daily Silver State*, June 23, 1877; Telegram from Natchez (Winnemucca) Overton to Gen. McDowell, June 23, 1877, Letters Received, Office of Indian Affairs, Oregon Superintendency.

11 National Archives, Commanding General Division of the Missouri to Commanding General, Department of the Platte, March 16, 1877.

Trooper Burke would write, "From what I have been able to learn, not alone from the Indians themselves, but from white men as well, the cause of the discontent in this locality, is due to the rascally treatment the Indians receive at the hands of the Agent Rinehart. . . . Egan, the 'war chief' of the Payutes. . . cannot speak English very well, but from the interviews I had with him, I am strongly inclined to the belief that he does not propose to bear this sort of treatment much longer. I could read his determination in his countenance."[12]

By mid-April 1877, Rinehart finally observed what had missed the attention of almost every white man since the settlement of Oregon Territory in 1811. The Paiutes were not the same people as the Snakes! In a letter to the commissioner of Indian Affairs, Rinehart wisely observed: "It appears that those bands who have lived along the Blue Mountains and followed the deer, antelope, and bear chase for a livelihood are disposed to look upon the rabbit hunters of the sage plains of Nevada as an inferior people, and treat them accordingly—telling them this is not their country. Prompted by a feeling of independence of their less civilized Snake Brethren, the Paiutes under Winnemucca are looking out for a new home of their own."[13] He would also discover that the Bannocks were Robber Snakes and that Bad Face was a Paiute only by virtue of his daughter's insistence.

As if it wasn't bad enough that the Snakes were being harassed to the point of open hostilities, settlers in northeast Oregon were loudly protesting the presence of Nez Perce in the Wallowa Valley. President Grant had signed a pact agreeing to let them stay there but a few settlers, eager to acquire the high mountain meadows, brought political pressure to bear and Congress revoked the agreement. At that point, the government ordered Gen. Howard to move some five hundred Nez Perce to a reservation in Idaho.

They refused to go and on the night of June 13, 1877—led by the war chief Thunder Over the Mountain (better known as Joseph), the Nez Perce took to the war trail, killing four white men. Frightened by the

---

12 John J. Burke, Saddler, Co. A, 1st Cavalry, Fort Harney to Congressman Newton Booth, March 22, 1878, Letters Received, Office of Indian Affairs, Oregon Superintendency.

13 W.V. Rinehart to Commissioner of Indian Affairs, April 14, 1877, Special File No. 268, Bureau of Indian Affairs, Washington, D.C.

possibility that the Snakes would join the fray, Rinehart confiscated all the guns and ammunition on the Malheur Reservation and sent his employees to Fort Harney for safety. The Paiutes were also alarmed and returned to the agency in droves. They were well aware that it was unsafe away from the agency during wartime because the frontiersmen needed little excuse to take a shot at stray Indians.

With the exception of Fort Harney, all the cavalry companies in eastern Oregon were ordered to the front. Rumors circulated that Has No Horse and Bad Face were on their way north to join the Nez Perce and panic held sway in the Ochoco Valley as settlers fled to Prineville and the Scissorsville mines for protection. This exodus was a wasted effort. Has No Horse and Bad Face were too smart to be set up for the kill by a bunch of disgruntled Nez Perce. Bad Face—always the showman—slipped into Boise City and visited with Gov. Mason Brayman, assuring him that he and Has No Horse had peaceful intentions. During this interlude, Bad Face and some of his warriors were wined and dined by the governor as guests of honor.[14] Has No Horse was feasting on Crooked River beef.

While Bad Face took care of the social formalities, Has No Horse prepared for bigger game. Word was out that Crook had authorized the use of Shoshoni detachments to aid Howard and the Snakes were quick to volunteer.[15] Black Coal with fifty warriors joined Col. Wesley Merritt who led eleven companies of 3rd and 5th U.S. Cavalry into the fray. Buffalo Horn—who had joined Miles' command after the Rosebud affair—was met by twenty braves and attached to Capt. Randolph Norwood's 2nd Cavalry. Has No Horse, now under close military surveillance, dispatched Bloody Antler (his son-in-law) and Yellow Jacket with forty dog soldiers to lead Howard's main command through the Rockies.

In the battle of Canyon Creek, officers of the 7th Cavalry would report that "the Shoshoni of Howard's command kept up a running fight with the enemy most of the day and several scalps and a considerable number of ponies attested to the fact that they had not had the worst of

14 *Daily Silver State*, Winnemucca, Nevada, June 21, 23 and 29, 1877.

15 Crook to A.A.G. Missouri Division, September 23, 1877, House Executive Document No. 1, Pt. 2, p. 90, Series 1843, 45th Congress 3rd Session.

it."[16] Howard would comment about Yellow Jacket and his warriors, "We were as safe in that wild country with the Shoshoni around us as we would have been anywhere else in America."

The *Idaho Weekly Statesman* would report on the battle of Camas Meadows: "Buffalo Horn was with Capt. Norwood in the gallant stand which that officer made against the Nez Perce at the time the hostiles stampeded Howard's camp and drove off his horses. On this occasion as well as others, this Indian stood in with the troops and rendered efficient service. Whatever were the shortcomings of the other Indian scouts, Buffalo Horn always stood bravely and faithfully to his duty and never failed to deliver perfect satisfaction."[17] What the editor failed to point out was that the long experience Buffalo Horn had fighting under different army commanders could make him a dangerous opponent.

Howard several times mentioned the good conduct of "this trusted Indian," but he also noted evidence of independence on the part of Buffalo Horn. One time Buffalo Horn appeared at the General's tent and asked permission to stage a war dance with about 150 Snake scouts. Permission was given. Around midnight, Buffalo Horn and a half-breed came to the General and asked if they could kill three Nez Perce herders who Buffalo Horn claimed were passing military secrets to Joseph. Permission denied. According to Howard, Buffalo Horn became very angry and as a consequence "he never quite forgave me for this refusal."[18] Before another year passed by, Howard would find out just how unforgiving Buffalo Horn could be.

While the Nez Perce blow-up illuminated the eastern Oregon frontier, Crazy Horse surrendered under guarantee of military protection and was assassinated by federal agents on September 7, 1877. Meantime, Sitting Bull had escaped into Canada and this was Joseph's goal. In a 1,300 mile running battle, Joseph made it to the Canadian border but Sitting Bull refused to come to his aid. On September 22, within spitting distance of the international boundary and safety, Joseph was trapped between Miles' and Howard's commands. Fifteen days after Crazy Horse

---

16 Brady, *Northeastern Fighters and Fights*, pp. 191, 221.

17 *Idaho Weekly Statesman*, Vol. 13, No. 39, May 18, 1877.

18 Howard, *Nez Perce Joseph*, pp. 175, 232; Fee, Chester Anders, *Chief Joseph, The Biography of a Great Indian*, p. 211.

was murdered, Thunder Over the Mountain, Nez Perce war chief, surrendered.

Because of this retreat which is often compared to the celebrated march of the ten thousand of old, Joseph is ranked alongside Caesar and Napoleon as one of the great military generals of any age. He was such a clever strategist that his battle tactics were later studied by West Point cadets. . . tactics he learned in battle against the Snake war chiefs Red Wolf, Paulina, and Has No Horse.

With the Sioux and the Nez Perce out of the way, the army settled down for a long needed rest. Then, the floodgates of hell released an overflow of red fury.

CHAPTER 164

GONE TO THE HIGHEST BIDDER

Mr. Rinehart is a good man. . . probably. I think he is a good man. The biggest thief, whether a man or a woman, is good if wealthy.

Sarah Winnemucca
November 26, 1879

While eastern Oregon focused attention on the Nez Perce outbreak, a more critical situation—agitated by Rinehart, George Currey and the influential stockmen of Crooked River and Harney valleys—was brewing under its very nose. Also, strange things were happening. Edmond Veazie, a prominent central Oregon stockman "died mysteriously on the John Day River." Al Lyle, his brother-in-law, who may have known what happened—was afraid to talk. One thing was certain, he didn't blame it on the Indians. Within five years, such mystifying events were becoming a fact of life in the new county named for General Crook. Again, no blame could be placed on the Shoshoni for by late summer 1877, Has No Horse, Pony Blanket and Buffalo Horn were plotting their own self-destruction.

Three Indian holy men—Wovoka, the Paiute dreamer; Left Hand, the feared Snake mystic; and Smoholla, the Nez Perce prophet—were responsible for this state of mind. Smoholla was urging the Indians to give up the white man's mode of living and return to their primitive lifestyle. Left Hand, believed to be bullet-proof, was advocating a war of extermination. Wovoka, known to the Snakes as The Cutter, foresaw divine intervention. Of the three, Wovoka would carry the most influence among the Indian tribes of the West.

Wovoka—ridiculed by the whites as Jack Wilson, the demented son of a Snake shaman named White Man—was troubled by recurring dreams and he urgently wanted to see Has No Horse. Wovoka had been called into the Steens Mountains by a great power and there, five thousand feet above the valley floor, he received a divine revelation. In Has No Horse's lodge, he would reveal that the earth would swallow all white people and the Indians would enjoy their worldly possessions. Has No Horse, although incredulous that an earthquake could distinguish between white and Indian, didn't question The Cutter. In a second vision, Wovoka foresaw that all would be engulfed but the Indians would rise again and enjoy forever an abundance of game, fish and pine nuts. The Snakes welcomed these pleasant tidings but their faith began to waver when fighting continued and Joseph was defeated. At this point, Wovoka received a third revelation according to which only believers in his prophesy would be resurrected while the skeptics would remain buried in the earth with the whites.[1] Any sensible Snake would be wise to believe, but the war chiefs were leaning toward Left Hand's solution to the problem.

Left Hand was advocating not only the killing of all whites, but the destruction of railroads as well. This was sound reasoning. Before parallel rails spanned the continent, hundreds of cavalrymen and Shoshoni dog soldiers had killed each other in various ambushes and skirmishes somewhat on a balance. With the arrival of the iron horse, the scales had tipped heavily in favor of the white combatants. Now Left Hand promised that after the death of the white man and when the Snakes had destroyed the railroads, they would divide both sides of the world among their friends and kill all Indians who had not united with them.[2] A pleasant thought, even if impossible.

Insofar as the whites were concerned, everything seemed to be getting better, especially for those grubbing up the earth. In 1877-78 another 1.28 million dollars in gold and silver was shipped through the Port of Portland with the lion's share coming from eastern Oregon. In the same period, the big cattle drives to the East brought in another

1 Capt. J. M. Lee, quoted by Mooney, 14th Annual Report, Bureau of American Ethnology, p. 700.

2 *Report of the Commissioner of Indian Affairs 1878*, p. 103.

$270,000.[3] The six year period 1873-78—not counting the floating mining population—had also witnessed a significant increase in the Ochoco-Crooked River population.[4] And, some of the more enterprising gentlemen were making money off the Indians at the gaming tables. Pony Blanket was well known as a good poker player but in one high-stake game, he dropped ninety hard-earned dollars to a couple of cattlemen at Harney City. Yellow Jacket was a different story. It is claimed that he sauntered into a Prineville saloon one evening and relieved the local card-sharks of $500 in one hand.

Even with all the hustle and bustle, prices for the finer things in life were not all that high. At Scissorsville the menu at The Antler Hotel was advertising full meals from a dime up; a large tin cup of bourbon, rye or rotgut (take your pick) five cents; a full quart of good whiskey, one dollar; cheaper varieties went for a dollar and a half a gallon; and corked soda water sold for five cents a bottle.[5]

In Prineville, hide-hunting was big business. One old timer would remark, "I will say without fear of contradiction, the first who settled the Ochoco Valley could not have stayed here to become pioneers had it not been for the wild game."[6] Within thirty years of settlement, those who arrived at the turn of the century would swear there had never been any game in the Ochoco. For them, it was sterile hunting grounds and for very good reason.

With the advent of the fur trade, wild game was slaughtered by the hundreds just for sport with little thought of financial gain. Then came the soldiers who continued the butchery in an effort to force the Indians into starvation. And finally the stockmen who would harbor no competition from deer, antelope and elk in the harvest of native shrubs and grass. Through the stockmen's dedicated efforts, a market for wild game—including meat, hides, teeth and horns—was created in the 1870's and continued unabated well into the 1890's.

---

3 Reid, *Progress of Portland for the Year Ending 1878*, a pamphlet published in 1879 by the Secretary of the Portland Board of Trade.

4 For a list of the emigrants of 1873-1878, see page 157-158.

5 Menu found in the walls of Tom Stephenson's log ranch house, which sat on the Ochoco River some six miles west of Scissorsville.

6 Quote of Jasper Wright, whose original log cabin was moved from the upper Ochoco to the Prineville Pioneer Park to serve as a museum where it still stands.

The record gives mute testimony of some of the slaughter that took place. In 1886, smoked deer and elk meat was used as trade to obtain parts for a sawmill at Elkhorn. Bear hides were used for trade in lieu of hard cash. At Camas Valley in the 1870's, William Murray stated, "I have killed hundreds of elk, 1,500 deer. . . . I would dress the elk and deer and take them to Roseburg and sell them to hotels. . . . "[7] Sam Ritter would tell of guiding affluent trophy hunters from the Willamette Valley into the Ochoco Mountains in the early 1900s to kill mule deer, elk, big horn sheep, bear and cougar just for their hides and horns.

Freight wagons loaded with pelts rolled to The Dalles where large scows, containing hundreds of hides on each trip, were towed down the Columbia to Portland where the hides were shipped to various markets and dealers. On one occasion, three hunters killed eighty-five elk in three days, taking only the hides and teeth. This rampant activity was reported from all regions of Oregon that contained deer and elk. The Oregon legislature attempted to at least slow down the practice by passing a law in 1872 that prohibited the killing and selling of deer and elk from February 1 to June 1 each year. Also, the law made it illegal to take deer and elk for the sole purpose of obtaining hides and horns. As usual, the legislature adjourned without appropriating any funds or delegating any person to enforce the law. Needless to say, the law did little to curb the activity.

Star Mealey, reporter for the *Ochoco Review* would note that "on Tuesday, Fried and Sichel shipped 4,000 pounds of deer hides. This makes about 100,000 pounds of deer pelts shipped from Prineville to date since early last fall. It has been a wholesale slaughter merely for the hides." A month later, he would further complain, "Deer hides only bring 20¢ a pound and still the cowardly work of slaughter is kept up. Be it remembered that each hunter would have to kill not less than 10 deer a day to make wages."[8]

In 1877, a movement to create forest reserves was spearheaded by the secretary of Interior. This was the first official recognition of an urgent need to conserve natural resources. At the same time, the Desert Land Act authorized the disposal of 640 acre tracts and arid public lands

---

7 *Oregon Wildlife*, Vol.. 37, No. 4, April 1982, p. 4.

8 *Ochoco Review*, Prineville, Oregon, January 1, 1882; February 4, 1882.

at a $1.25 an acre. There was only one catch—a homesteader had to prove reclamation of the land by irrigation. This difficulty resulted in more than ten relief acts by Congress to aid aspiring settlers.

By now, the Snakes forced—or trying to be forced—onto the Klamath, Yakima and Malheur reservations caused one to bitterly remark, "A dog with three homes has no home at all."[9] It's small wonder that the Snakes held little hope for intervention from Above. Not only were valleys devastated for gold, and wildlife wantonly destroyed, but by the start of winter 1877, stockmen were pushing their vast herds onto the Malheur Reservation and made no secret of their intentions to take up residence on the Indian's land. To stall off any interference from the Snakes, soldiers marched onto the Malheur Reservation and confiscated all guns and ammunition. Word leaked out to Gen. Crook and he applied political pressure in the right places. In February 1878, at the request of the Indian Department, Rinehart reluctantly produced figures that would show that not only had white trespassers cut eighty tons of hay on the reservation, but they were running 545 horses and 10,270 head of beef cattle on Indian allotted lands.[10]

Six months before Rinehart's disclosure, another incident which happened at the height of the Nez Perce war would add more fuel to the flames of unrest. Robert Boyd and John James—Idaho freighters—were crossing Camas Prairie some 200 miles southeast of Fort Harney when they spotted two Indian girls digging camas roots. In the ensuing chase, they caught one of the girls and raped her.[11] It just so happened that she was the sister of Runs Behind, a militant Snake warrior, who was not favorably impressed with this latest transgression. Fortified with whiskey, he rode out with a Winchester rifle and a Colt revolver and gunned them down. Unfortunately, one of the men shot—having a similar name—may have been a victim of circumstances. Whatever, the cry went out that Runs Behind had murdered innocent men in cold blood and the chase was on.

9 *Idaho Statesman*, June 26, 1977.

10 W.V. Rinehart to Commissioner of Indian Affairs, letter dated December 18, 1877 and February 27, 1878.

11 Hopkins, *Life Among the Piutes*, p. 138.

Apparently, only Boyd was killed for on August 8, 1877, Orson James (not John James) wrote to his sister from the Ross Fork Indian Agency: "Dear Sister—I have a sad story to tell you. Today, I lost some of my cattle and was going out to hunt them when an Indian rode up and shot me. The ball struck near the backbone and came out my right side. The wound is not mortal but is bad enough. The Indian before shooting me, shot a boy [Robert Boyd] that lives with and drives for John James of Malad. The ball struck the left side of his neck and came out his shoulder; the wound is very bad but not dangerous. . . . "[12] The bullet wound was more deadly than Orson James thought, for Boyd died from infection.

After a three month hunt, Runs Behind was caught on November 23 by Morgan Morgan, Deputy U.S. Marshall. At the time of arrest Laughing Hawk (Tambiago), a friend of the prisoner, shot and killed Alexander Rhoden, a government beef contractor and another man who was acting as guard for a cattle delivery to the Fort Hall Reservation. In the confusion, Laughing Hawk with his father and two brothers crossed the Snake River and hid out in eastern Oregon, most likely at Has No Horse's camp. By December, federal troops were swarming over eastern Oregon.[13] They would, however be deprived—at least momentarily—of one of the finer attractions on the eastern Oregon frontier. On October 27, 1877, The Dalles City's famed Umatilla House, which boasted the largest bar room on the Pacific Coast, went up in flames. It would be rebuilt in 1878 at the cost of a half million dollars.

During this disruption in social life, Laughing Hawk slipped back to Fort Hall in January and was arrested by Capt. A.H. Bainbridge, post commander. The prisoner was sent to Malad City to await trial. The Snakes became thoroughly aroused over the arrest of Laughing Hawk, spurring the military into more action. In a raid on a Banattee camp, the army captured 53 warriors, 32 guns and about 300 horses. Caught in this round-up was Laughing Hawk's father and brothers who were imprisoned in the Fort Hall guardhouse. They were later taken to Malad City

---

12 Excerpt from the Corrine Record, Vol. 13, No. 1, *Idaho Weekly Statesman*, August 25, 1877.

13 *Report of the Commissioner of Indian Affairs 1877*, p. 78.

and bound over to the U.S. grand jury on $2,000 bail each and sentenced to 20 years in the Idaho Territorial Penitentiary.[14]

While the Robber Snakes languished in the Fort Hall guardhouse, Marian Powell taught the first Sunday school in Prineville on February 3, 1878. Before the summer was over many prayers would be said. During this pious occasion, the yearly trail drives started pouring into Crooked River basin led by Tom Hamilton (who introduced the first shorthorn cattle to central Oregon).

Over at Harney City, Left Hand and Pony Blanket found out that the citizens of Harney Valley had circulated a petition to acquire the most fertile land on the western boundary of the Malheur Reserve. This petition—signed by Capt. George Downey, 1st U.S. Infantry and approximately seventy settlers near or on the reservation—was endorsed by both Gen. Howard and Gen. McDowell and sent to President Hayes in April.[15] According to the tribal chiefs, the area claimed was their only source of camas root, a staple in the Indian diet, and they took their complaint to Fort Harney.

Again, Crook intervened and under pressure of the War Department, the commissioner of Indian Affairs ordered the removal of the rancher's livestock. When news of this decision reached the trespassers, Rinehart found that they were suddenly interested in leasing the land from the government. James Scott, who managed large holdings on the John Day River, was the first to come forward and offered a $100 deposit on a lease for Harney Valley. On the same day, John Devine—part owner of the huge White Horse Ranch—upped Scott's offer by a proposal to rent five hundred square miles of the reservation for $200, paid annually. Two days later, Scott was back with a better proposition than Devine's: $1500 per annum, paid in advance for use of the same acreage that Devine had requested, for a five year period.[16] Oddly, Tom Overfelt—most likely on orders of Henry Miller not to show interest—stayed clear of the bidding.

---

14 *Report of the Commissioner of Indian Affairs 1878*, p. 50; *Idaho Weekly Statesman*, Dec. 1, 1877 and March 16, 1878, Vol. 13, Nos. 30 and 45.

15 Petition to the President of the United States, April 20, 1878, Letters Received, Office of Indian Affairs, Oregon Superintendency.

16 W.V. Rinehart to Commissioner of Indian Affairs, May 18, 20 and 21, 1878.

Rinehart quickly recommended that the Indian Department accept the terms of Scott's offer because, "the Indians have no immediate need for the land except for hunting, root digging and fishing" and he was certain the cattle would not intrude upon those activities. A day later, Rinehart authorized Pete French to start cutting timber on the reservation. Most Indian agents would have at least consulted the chiefs before such major decisions regarding the reservation were made. Such a thought never entered Rinehart's mind. He considered that his charges were incapable of making a determination concerning the land that was now their home and he still insisted that the Shoshoni were on the reservation only through the courtesy of the United States Government.

As it turned out, the eviction of squatters or the leasing of reservation land to cattlemen would be of minor consequence compared to what was facing Agent Rinehart in the weeks ahead.

The emigrations for 1873-1878 included:

1873

Bell, M.H. (family)
Brayman, A.H. (family)
Carey, F. (family)
Carey, Louisa (family)
Christiani, Mike (family)
Circle, William C. (family)
Hedgepath, Manford (single)
Heisler, Jeff (single)
Hendrickson, Rufus (single)
Hill, Taylor (family)
Howard, Howard (family)
Howard, Light (family)
Hunseker, Joe (family)
Johnson, C.J. (single)
Johnson, William (single)
Jory, S.J. (single)
Lytle, Al (single)
Mailing, Charles (single)
Nelson, Press (single)
Van Houten, ___ (family)
Vanderpool, James (family)
Vandervert, J.L. (family)
Wheeler, Henry (family)

1874

Childes, Ben (single)
Thompson, R. (single)
Thorp, John (single)
Wall, Archie (single)
Wilson, Joe (family)
Winters, Jerry (single)
Winters, Dave (single)
Wood, John (single)

1875

Belknap, Harly (family)
Friend, Columbus (single)
Thompson, Amos (family)
Wood, James (single)
Wood, Lee (single)

The new arrivals shown above are from Wasco County files prior to 1882;
Lockley, "Impressions and Observations of the Journal Man,"
Portland Oregon Journal, March 31, 1927; Pioneer Edition, Crook County News, August 4, 1939;
Illustrated History of Central Oregon, 1905.

1876

Calbreath, Clarence (family)
Cleek, Henry (family)
Cline, Dr. (family)
Crandall, Jesse (single)
Davis, Peter (single)
Douthit, J.H. (family)
Elliott, John (single)
Elliott, Kinman (family)
Fogle, Anton (family)
Foley, Lige (family)
Foren, Thomas (family)
Forest, Frank (single)
Fryrear, John (family)
Gray, Henry (family)
Hahn, Henry (family)
Hale, W.S. (family)
Hamilton, William (family)
Haresty, Charles (family)
Harmon, John (family)
Heisler, Monroe (single)
Henry, Allen (single)
Hereford, John E. (family)
Hinkle, M.A. (family)
Hinton, Alex (family)
Hogan, William (single)
Hon, John (family)
Jackson, Oliver (family)
Jaggi, John (family)
Johnson, Jasper (family)
Jones, Ben (family)
Jones, Watt (family)
Kizer, George (family)
Senecal, Dedron (family)

1877

Gerow, Arnie (family)
Glaze, Tilford (family)
Graham, Dick (family)
Grimes, Henry (family)
Maling, C.C. (family)
Thomas, Dan (single)
Todd, Johnny (family)
Turner, George (single)
Turner, Henry (family)
Wilson, Robert (family)

1878

Campbell, John (family)
Chamberlain, Jasper (family)
Curl, Gove (family)
Faulkner, John (family)
Gilchrist, John (single)
Gulliford, Jasper (family)
Gulliford, William (family)
Hackleman, Abe (family)
Hamilton, Sam (family)
Hash, _____ (family)
Hinkle, Joe (family)
Hudson, Harry (single)
Huston, Knox (family)
Ketchum, I.L. (single)
Knighton, Alden (family)
Osborn, George (family)
Pitcher, Billy (single)
Thompson, William (family)
Thompson, S.G. (single)

CHAPTER 165

WAR PAINT

Here lies red Tambiago;
He needs neither camas or sago,
For he is now safe at the head of the stair
With his father, a Bannock dresser of hair,
And his mother, a wild Winnebago.

Inmate, Territorial Penitentiary
June 28, 1878, Boise City, Idaho

As Shoshoni tension mounted, diphtheria raged through the white settlements of eastern Oregon. The plague had barely gotten up a good head of steam when Left Hand predicted that the sky would be filled with fire. "When that happens," he intoned, "it will be the sign to rise up against white oppression." In March, while the heavens blazed with northern lights, earth passed through a meteor belt and the prophesy was fulfilled. Gen. Crook, sensing that big trouble lay ahead, made a hurried trip West. It's interesting to note that Crook, commander of the Platte Department and McDowell, commander of the Pacific Division reacted while Howard, commander of the Columbia Department, appeared to be unconcerned.

Sharing Crook's anxiety, Gen. McDowell again sent out an order to find Has No Horse and put him on the Malheur Reservation where he could be kept under surveillance. On March 11, 1878, Capt. Henry Wagner made contact with Has No Horse and sent the following message to Gen. McDowell:

> Chief Ocheo in obedience to my summons came into the post today and I had a long interview with him. I explained to him the intentions of the government in placing him and his people on the Malheur Reservation. He politely declined and told me many years ago, 'the soldier chief' told

> him to go to the Klamath Reservation where he and his people would be fed and would get red blankets and white blankets and other things. He went but found it was all a lie. His people nearly starved there, and maybe some got a half blanket while some got none at all. . . .

Capt. Wagner then advised his commanding officer that Has No Horse "seems to be fully determined not to go on the reservation upon any terms and in my opinion, it would be well to let him and his people remain where they are."[1] In short, let them continue to roam across central Oregon as they were harming no one.

Other Snake chiefs were being harassed. Throughout this attempt to round up leaders, the *Idaho Statesman* would report that the Snakes were in no way backward in using threats and insults toward the soldiers performing this duty. Lt. Col. Royall, acting inspector general of the Army, visited the Malheur and Fort Hall reservations in March and attributed much of the unrest at Fort Hall to the opposition of the Robber Snakes toward Agent Davidson who he claimed "has lost all influence, and therefore control of these Indians." A more direct threat of war was reported by Agent Rinehart of the Malheur Agency. He revealed that two Snake dog soldiers visited the Malheur in March and stated they would take up the battle lance as soon "as the grass came."[2]

Following Royall's inspection, the secretary of war wrote to Idaho Congressman Hermann, "The alarming reports concerning the hostile demonstration by the Bannock Indians have proven to be without foundation. It may be added that the reservation is now with all appurtenances thereon under the control of the Secretary of Interior."[3] The military was saying in a polite way that if the Indian agencies would clean up their act, there would be no conflict.

Governor Mason Brayman of Idaho would tend to agree with Secretary McCrory. Both knew that the spark which ignited the powder

---

1 Capt. Henry Wagner, Camp Bidwell, March 11, 1878 to Gen. Irvin McDowell, San Francisco, Letters Received, Office of Indian Affairs, Oregon Superintendency.

2 The Idaho Statesman, June 11, 1878; W.B. Royall to Adjutant General Department of the Platte, March 19, 1878, United States Department of Interior, Office of Indian Affairs General Files, Idaho, W10281; Report of the Commissioner of Indian Affairs, 1878, p. 11.

3 *Illustrated History of Central Oregon*, 1905, p. 934.

keg was struck in 1868 when the Banattee Snakes were forced onto the Fort Hall Reservation, which was to include Camas Prairie in southwestern Idaho. . . less than two days horseback ride from the Malheur Reservation's eastern boundary. Through a clerical error, the treaty referred to Camas Prairie as "Kansas Prairie," a nonexistent region as far as the government was concerned. When the reservation boundaries were surveyed, Camas Prairie—containing 600,000 acres of choice grazing and farm lands—was omitted from the Indian's allotment. The Snakes fought inch by inch to retain it for their ponies and the camas root which was their bread, but white settlers paid little attention to the intent of the treaty and fattened their hogs on camas roots.

Gov. Brayman would write to U.S. Senator W.J. McConnell, "No protection was given to the treaty rights of the Bannocks, and when they discovered their harvest being destroyed by the white man's hogs, forbearing ceased to be a virtue and they appealed to the only arbiter they knew, the God of Battle. The writer, being one of the first trespassers on Camas Prairie, must admit that the Indians under their code of morals and government, had ample justification for the methods they pursued."[4]

With the building clouds of war, Gen. Crook arrived at Fort Hall to the accompaniment of Indian drum-beats. Two days later, on April 2, he visited the Bannock Agency on Ross Fork of the Malad River. Here, he issued a stern warning to the settlers of southern Idaho and eastern Oregon criticizing the management of the Fort Hall and Malheur reservations, which he found to be in deplorable condition. In reference to the Indian's food allotment he would comment, "I telegraphed and the agent telegraphed for supplies, but word came that no appropriation had been made. They [the Snakes] have never been half supplied." He would emphasize that there was nothing for the Indians to live on.

> The buffalo is all gone and an Indian can't catch enough jack rabbits to subsist himself and his family, and then, there aren't enough jack rabbits to catch. What are they to do? Starvation is staring them in the face, and if they fully appreciate what is before them. . . I do not wonder, and you will not either that when the Indians see their wives and

4 Haily, John, *Early History of Idaho*, p. 364.

> children starving, and their last source of supplies cut off, they go to war. And then we [the military] are sent out to kill them. It is an outrage!
>
> All the tribes tell the same story. They are surrounded on all sides, the game is destroyed or driven away; they are left to starve, and there remains one thing for them to do—fight while they can! Some people think Indians do not understand these things, but they do, and fully appreciate the circumstances in which they are placed.[5]

To the settlers absolute horror, Crook urged—for their own safety—that the horses, arms and ammunition taken from the starving Indians be returned so they could hunt wild game and thus avert war. No way was that going to happen.

While Crook argued for relief, Sarah Winnemucca—who had left Warm Springs to work for a family near Prairie City, Oregon—was visited by three starving Paiutes from the Malheur Reservation begging her to come back and reason with Rinehart. Having had her fill of his arrogance, she refused to go. Again in May, six more delegates came and told her many Robber Snakes were moving onto the Malheur. This time Sarah went with them and met with Pony Blanket, Left Hand and Three Coyotes. It was becoming obvious that the Snakes were preparing for war.

Before Sarah arrived at the reservation, the inevitable happened. The citizens of eastern Oregon were screaming for more blood. Howard, who had just returned to Fort Vancouver from the Nez Perce campaign, knew what was happening and he also knew the Indians, even though the Oregonians were accusing him of dilatory tactics for delaying immediate action.

Howard was certain that the only thing holding Has No Horse in check was that he was stalling for the Army to send troops into eastern Oregon, thus giving him an excuse for war—and as usual would strike to kill in the white settlements. Howard also knew from past experience that once hostilities began, the ranchers who were now howling for Indian blood would be the first to suffer the consequences.

---

5 *Army and Navy Journal*, Vol. XV, No. 47, June 29, 1878, p. 758.

By the first of May, 200 Snake dog soldiers were gathered near Payne's Ferry on the Snake River and Buffalo Horn was having difficulty controlling them.[6] As they had done in the past, white men—oblivious to the winds of war—were herding hogs, cattle and horses onto Camas Prairie. On May 22, Buffalo Horn told some of the white herders he wanted the livestock removed immediately. Before they could leave, the son of Three Coyotes—on a drinking and gambling spree—shot three of the herders.

That night a courier from Harney Valley reached Boise City with a message to Gov. Brayman from a mountain man named James Dempsey. Dempsey and his Shoshoni wife had been living with the Banattees for many years. He warned that war was eminent and that the Banattees were acting in concert with the Umatillas and White Knife Snakes. No doubt Dempsey knew what he was talking about. Laughing Hawk, in his last confession to Father Archamboalt, would state that a white man, James Dempsey, had been counseling the Robber Snakes to go to war for more than a year. In October 1877, Dempsey bought guns and ammunition from the Mormons at Salt Lake City which he traded to the Indians, giving ten rifles to Buffalo Horn in exchange for a woman, and he also sent fifteen rifles to The Climber who, true to form, went to the side of the whites.[7]

Dempsey's message also indicated that war might still be avoided if the governor would come with a few men to talk to Buffalo Horn. The Idaho executive refused to go. Brayman then came under media attack because he had granted Buffalo Horn permission to buy some ammunition about two weeks before the outbreak on Camas Prairie. In his own defense, the governor claimed that the war chief had promised he would return to Fort Hall after digging camas and he had been given only 100 cartridges and a small amount of powder for hunting purposes.[8]

As the Governor and the press exchanged broadsides, Laughing Hawk's father and two brothers—on Gen. Crook's order to protect them from a lynch mob—were placed under heavy military guard and taken in leg irons to Salt Lake City. At Salt Lake City, they were locked in a

6 *Idaho Statesman*, May 11, 1878.

7 *Idaho Statesman*, June 29, 1878.

8 *Idaho Statesman*, June 1, 1878.

railroad car and shipped to Omaha Barracks for imprisonment. Back at the territorial prison, Laughing Hawk told officials that Buffalo Horn intended to rendezvous in the "Juniper Mountains" (the Steens) with Bad Face where he planned to make contact with Has No Horse.[9] This information was ignored.

Meanwhile, remnants of the Snake war tribes were engaged in a council of war that led to the killing of James Dempsey, the gun trader-informer. Ten years almost to the day had passed since the first Shoshoni war ground to a halt on the sun-baked Fort Harney parade grounds. Now, on May 27, 1878, with bullets whizzing like angry hornets over eastern Oregon, the second Shoshoni war was unofficially declared. A month later with firm tread, Laughing Hawk stoically mounted a scaffold at the Boise Territorial prison and dropped to his death at 1:00 p.m. for the shooting and killing of Alexander Rhoden, a government beef contractor. His only resistance was at the placing of the black hood over his head.

As Laughing Hawk was being led to the place of execution, one of the penitentiary inmates seized an old newspaper and scribbled his epitaph:[10]

Here lies red Tambiago...
For dealing a grave to young Rhoden.
He dreamed not his own should be trodden,
Nor thought 'ere the snow drift had covered the dead,
He should bleed as his own innocent victim had bled;
Till his own heart grew silent and sodden.

And so, another Snake warrior paid for his sins. More blood would flow before 1878 staggered to a close. The historian Bancroft would comment that the coming struggle was one of the last human hunts of civilization and the basest and most brutal of them all. In his opinion, the final phase of the Shoshonean wars was "in the worst tradition of the native race and the response was in the worst tradition of the American race."

9 *Salt Lake Tribune*, June 16, 1878.

10 *Idaho Weekly Statesman*, June 29, 1878, Vol. 13, No. 45.

The Shoshoni uprising would go down in history as the Bannock War. On June 10, 1878, the United States Congress officially declared war on the Western Shoshoni Nation. The Snake war council had beaten them to the punch by fifteen days. Even so, never before in the annals of U.S. military history had federal troops moved against an Indian revolt so quickly.

CHAPTER 166

SIX DAYS

The silly twaddle about this land belonging to the noble red man and that we have no right to rob him of what was given him by the Creator, and a great deal more of like nonsense, should cease!

Editor
Idaho Herald, Pocatello

On May 27, 1878, the call again went out, "Where's Ocheo?" Has No Horse, who had been camped in Warner Valley northeast of Fort Bidwell, had disappeared!

On this quiet Monday evening—some ten miles east of Plush in Warner Valley—Nehemiah and Rose Fine were settling down to supper when a war whoop rent the air. Rufus Funk—cousin of Gen. Crook—was hunting on the head of the Blitzen River when a rifle cracked and he headed for Fort McDermit. On Beaver Creek, some one hundred and twenty miles to the north in Paulina Valley, William Noble was coming in from the barn when an arrow struck a corral pole as it grazed his shoulder.[1] Forty miles to the west, Joe Hunsaker, rounding up cattle on Combs Flat within rifle shot of Prine's Saloon, barely made it into Prineville ahead of a Snake war party.[2]

---

1 Sarah Noble Allyn, William Noble's wife, would recall that 20 wagons were loaded with families and gathered at George Noble's ranch (William's brother) planning to build a fort. "The men started digging breastworks, but some of the women began to cry, saying it looked like they were digging their graves. Then all but George and Tom Maupin started down the road to Prineville." Most of these refugees went on to the Willamette Valley. It was Sarah Noble's opinion that "General O.O. Howard and the band of soldiers were after the Indians, but he [Gen. Howard] did not seem in any great hurry to catch them."

2 Names of people involved in the Indian raids and their location are taken from personal biographies in *Illustrated History of Central Oregon 1905*, pp. 619-894.

Over on Thirty-mile Creek, near Fossil, Seth Morgan shot an Indian dog. Ten minutes later, a bullet tore bark from a tree three inches above his head—a grim reminder that the Indians were no longer turning the other cheek. Rube Kiger, taking a herd of cattle to Canyon City, was attacked and brought word of an Indian uprising to Harney Valley. Joe Smith and his son hurriedly left Harney City to protect their ranch against Indian attack. A few days later, Rube and Doc Kiger found their bones in the ashes of their cabin.

Pete French was directing branding operations when a rider galloped up with news of raiding Indians. French had the only rifle so he sent his men back to the ranch while he stood off the advance, fighting a fourteen-mile running battle. Joined by fifteen armed buckaroos, French made the ninety miles to Fort Harney in fifteen hours, fighting all the way; several of the men were killed in the retreat including French's Chinese cook, Ah Wong. Even so, during this skirmish French and his allies delivered a telling blow. One of the warriors lying in ambush who was shot out of a juniper tree by Pete French's cowboys was. . . Little Rattlesnake, the first warrior to defeat Gen. Crook in his purge of the Ochoco.

Michael Christiani, soldier of fortune who fought with the Crow scouts on the Big Horn, and who made money in mining and lumber from Pike's Peak to the Kootenai in British Columbia, would lose a fortune. In 1873, he came into Prineville trailing thousand's of head of sheep. In this week of terror, he would see them ground into mincemeat under the slashing hooves of a hundred Snake war horses. And he was not alone in this destruction of livestock.

Up on the Columbia Plateau, Ben Snipes' cattle took a beating as trained buffalo killers slaughtered hundreds of head. Ben is reported to have said, "I've very likely got more dead cattle than any man in the world but I'm still a very live cattleman."

Joe Delore was riding the range in Nevada when word arrived from Fort Harney that his brother Pete needed scouts and he headed north dodging hostile patrols. George Coggons and four teamsters were killed in Deadman Pass between Pendleton and La Grande. Jim Street, a Paulina rancher known as an expert rider and roper, made one of the most famous rides on record. Jumped by a Snake war party south of Hampton Butte at three o'clock in the afternoon, he galloped into Prineville at nine the next morning, covering a 120 miles in eighteen hours.

Another endurance rider—changing mounts as he went—thundered into The Dalles City packing a rather pathetic message signed by the citizens of Prineville, Mitchell and Canyon City. The telegram sent to the governor of Oregon simply said: "An Indian war is upon us. Come, we entreat you. Come to our help!"

It appears that extermination of the Snakes was not as much fun as anticipated by the white population in eastern Oregon.

Charles Williams—who at age fifteen took charge of a freight outfit—was trapped in Canyon City where he laid out the entire summer of 1878 unable to move his wagons. His brother Richard was scouting for Gen. Howard at the battle of Murderer's Creek where Joe Aldridge, another scout, was scalped and his mutilated body found near what is now named Aldrich Mountain.[3]

All cattle were driven off from Joe Crook's ranch near Grizzly Mountain. He and his wife, America Jane—the daughter of Eliza Spaulding Warren (the first white child born in Oregon Territory)—hid in the willows on Lytle Creek until they could make their escape into Prineville.

Jim Faught, first sheepman on Trout Creek, rushed over the mountains with his family to the safety of the mining tunnels at Scissorsville. They were soon joined by refugees from Paulina Valley. John Faulkner, who had opened a general store and taken over as postmaster at Paulina in 1877, had all of his property confiscated by the Indians. He, his wife Charity, and the two Noble families (George and William) arrived at Scissorsville on Friday, May 31. With them was Knox Huston, who had been driving sheep into Little Summit Prairie when he was attacked. This cured Huston of sheep grazing and he later became county surveyor.

William Adams—son-in-law to Howard Maupin—who had struck it rich at Silver City, Idaho, was running cattle on Beaver Creek. He and Nancy, with their two-year-old daughter, escaped over the mountains to the Ochoco stockade on Mill Creek. During the excitement, Howard Maupin, the old Indian fighter, died of natural causes. Thomas Belfour was attacked forty miles west of Paulina. Belfour and one other

---

3 Aldrich Mountain was named for Oliver Aldrich, another casualty of the Bannock War. He may have been Joe's brother.

family were the only people between Prineville and Burns who didn't seek safety at one of the forts.

North of Prineville, William Libby Baker and four men were the only people left between Cherry Creek and the Columbia River. The rest had fled to The Dalles. For the next three weeks, Barker and Company slept with their horses' picket ropes in their hands.

Apparently one person was enjoying the excitement. In later years, a weathered board marker was found at one of the abandoned homesteads inscribed:

Sacred to the Memory
of
Ephram McDowell
Who during his life time killed 98 Indians
that had been delivered into his hands by the Lord.
He had hoped to make it 100 before the year ended
When he fell asleep in the Arms of Jesus in his home
In Ochoco Country, 1878

The inscription didn't say if old Ephram had help or not when he made the last call but in view of the times one could speculate that he may have had some assistance from his red brethren.

From all over eastern Oregon reports of Indian depredations were pouring in and everyone, including the military, was guessing as to where Has No Horse would surface next. They didn't have long to wait. One jump ahead of the army, Has No Horse leisurely rode in of his own accord. Pitching his lodge in full view of Fort Harney, he apparently settled down to await the outcome of the war. His deception worked.

Earlier, the Snake head men had met in council and without exception, Has No Horse was looked upon as the man to save his people in this last conflict for survival. Again, he came up with the element of surprise so customary of the Shoshoni style of warfare. It was common knowledge that Has No Horse would be the accepted leader, hence all eyes would be on him. Also with Has No Horse riding at the head of these warriors, the army would be sure to bring in the best shock troops they possessed including Crook. Has No Horse, knowing Crook's method of fighting, didn't particularly want to subject his people to that type of warfare again. So a plan was made. The military tactic was deceptively simple. Has No Horse would voluntarily ride to Fort Harney and set up camp within sight of the Army parade grounds. Once there, he would nonchalantly await the outcome of the war.

Meanwhile, his brother-in-law, Pony Blanket, would lead the pack. The Snakes knew that next to Has No Horse, Pony Blanket was the most capable leader they had, another surprise for the whites. They had gotten to know Pony Blanket on the reservation where he appeared to be a very mild mannered man, loved and respected by the Indians but hardly the kind of person to lead a major uprising. Perhaps not, but with a military strategist in the background, he would make a good showing for himself.

Five days had passed since the opening guns of the Bannock War were fired. On the morning of the sixth day as Has No Horse leisurely rode into Fort Harney, a rider burst out of the army compound and disappeared in a cloud of dust. It was now Saturday, June 1, 1878.

With no more worry about Has No Horse's whereabouts, Gen. Howard—within the next two weeks—would puzzle as to how Pony Blanket knew all troop movements. Had he taken the time to put Has No Horse's lodge under close observation it wouldn't have been hard to determine. Almost nightly lithe riders slipped into the lodge unnoticed, picked up their orders and rode out under the protective cover of darkness. Lone army scouts returning to the fort with urgent messages never arrived. Why? A lone chief out for an afternoon outing was in a key position to pick off any communications with the fort. . . an easy job for as crafty a warrior as Has No Horse. Neither was it uncommon for the Indian seen strolling about the distant camp, tending horses or just lounging by a camp fire to be someone other than the war chief.[4] That's how confident the military was that Has No Horse was under wraps.

Not only were vindictive dog soldiers riding roughshod over eastern Oregon but diphtheria—in epidemic proportions—was raging across the land. This highly contagious disease was striking extremely hard among the children and in some cases entire families were wiped out.[5] It is certain that the infected settlers would generously share the seeds of pestilence with the advancing red wave.

4 Testimony of Tom Ochiho at McDermit, Nevada.

5 Morgan, *My Story of the Last Indian War in the Northwest,* p. 1.

CHAPTER 167

THE SELL OUT

To all good citizens in the country——Sarah Winnemucca with two of her people, goes with a dispatch to her father. If her horses should give out, help her all you can and oblige.

Captain Reuben Bernard
1st U.S. Cavalry

Two years had passed since Alexander Graham Bell patented his new invention called the telephone and Portland acquired its first crude instruments in the spring of '78. Even as these symbols of progress jangled in Portland, puffs of smoke and mirror flashes directed activities in eastern Oregon.

On Saturday, June 1, the greatest one-horse ride in the history of the West was beginning at Fort Harney. Sgt. Maurice Fitzgerald clutched an important dispatch and saddled his horse, Fandango. Horse and man covered the 148 miles to Baker City—the nearest telegraph office—in 23 1/2 hours! The message carried that fateful Sunday morning was the outbreak of the Bannock War. . . ahead of The Dalles communiqué by some six hours.

Gen. Howard was just sitting down to breakfast at his Portland home when he received word of the outbreak. No sooner had this dispatch arrived when he received a telegram from Idaho Gov. Brayman. "One hundred fifty Indians hit the King Hill Station in Jordan Valley [Oregon]. The Overland Stage road raided; all horses carried off. The right to Big Camas Prairie evidently the cause." He was correct, and the Indians found one ally in Oregon Senator H.W. Corbett.

Corbett stirred up a hornet's next when he stressed the need of individual holding of land by the Indian. "If," he advocated, "there be not sufficient lands upon the reservation suitable for homes and cultivation let them choose other lands off the reservation for homes under the homestead act like white people."[1] Only a few weeks before the Snake uprising, Corbett's recommendation had been laughed off as a joke.

With horse raids in progress, the word went out that the army was in need of cavalry mounts, artillery horses, mules and wagons and they were paying top dollar. Advertisements soon appeared throughout the west: Wanted, cavalry or artillery horses, $121.54; mules, $145; oxen, $80; six-mule Pennsylvania wagons, $99.25; high-wheeled ambulance wagons, $169.90; two-horse Leavenworth wagons, $92.50; six-mule harness sets, $67.49; four-horse ambulance harness sets, $57.84. Many contractors were becoming wealthy overnight.

Howard wasted no time sending orders to all army outposts for quick mobilization of troops. His promptness undoubtedly prevented a larger concentration of hostiles than otherwise would have been the case, though great numbers of Indian allies did join in the war. Before it was over, the Bannock War affected the Military Departments of the Columbia, the Platte and the Dakota.

Eight days after the official declaration of war, Gen. Crook—commander of the Department of the Platte—was asked by a reporter from the *Omaha Herald* if there was any "serious apprehension in regard to trouble with the Indians." He quietly replied, "There are good grounds for it. As long as the muzzle-loading arms were in use we had the advantage of them, and 20 men could whip a hundred, but since the breech loaders came into use it is entirely different; these Indians can load on horse-back and now they are a match for any man."[2] This was not pleasant news for the eastern Oregonians.

Down in Arizona, Archie McIntosh volunteered to head the Arapaho and Crow scouts that were rushed to the battle front but was told by Crook that the situation was not yet serious enough for his services.[3] Local scouts from Prineville, Paulina, Mitchell and Scissorsville were being mustered in at a rapid rate—Pete, Joe and Baptiste Delore (sons

1 Brimlow, George Francis, *Bannock War of 1878*, p. 215.

2 *The New York Times*, June 23, 1878, p. 5, reprinted from *The Omaha Herald*, Nebraska, June 18, 1878.

3 National Archives, No. 2598, Department of the Platte, July 3, 1878.

of old Pete); John Blevins; Jim Street; Jake Stroud; Joe Aldridge; John Luckey; Jerry Luckey and John Jaggi to name but a few.

During this confusion, two gunmen—Van Allen and Jeff Dripps—rode into Prineville and attempted to take over the town. Following a street fight in which three citizens were wounded, a warrant was issued for their arrest and Deputy Jim Chamberlain was ordered to serve it. In the exchange of gunfire, Allen was killed but Dripps escaped. Later that evening Dripps was captured by Jerry Luckey and taken in chains to The Dalles for trial where he was acquitted of any wrongdoing.[4]

While Prineville was being shot-up, Sarah Winnemucca left for the Malheur Agency and arrived on the evening of June 5 to find many Banattee Snakes on the reservation. Her cousin, Jerry Long—agency interpreter—sent for Pony Blanket, Left Hand, Dancer and Three Coyotes to come speak with her. The word was not good. Neither Rinehart nor Danilson at Fort Hall were providing the Snakes with any food. Pony Blanket would bitterly ask, "What does the praying agent mean by not giving us our rations?" Long would report that he tried to buy some flour but Rinehart "won't sell me any." He would also reveal that Rinehart had not issued any clothing since he had been at the agency and had taken all stray horses for his own and shot Paiute horses if they chanced to stray into the fields.[5]

Three Coyotes told Sarah what had happened at Fort Hall; the rape of the Indian girl, the jailing of Laughing Hawk, and the military confiscation of all weapons and horses in retaliation against the Snakes. He then asked Sarah to write it down and notify Washington, D.C.

At this meeting, Pony Blanket, in his white cotton farmer suit, straw hat and short-trimmed hair, was in stark contrast with the Banattee warriors whose long, braided hair was arranged in a pompadour at the forehead, while feathers and beads hung from their fringed leather garments. Pony Blanket collected $29.25 from the assembled dog soldiers and gave it to Sarah for expenses to go to Washington and talk to President Hayes.

Like Has No Horse, Dancer—a Bear Killer medicine man—was being very closely watched. On June 7, two days after Sarah's meeting

---

4 *Illustrated History of Central Oregon 1905*, p. 724.

5 Hopkins, *Life Among the Piutes*, pp. 140-46.

with the Snakes, Rinehart would report that Dancer was at the fish traps on the Malheur River and that Pony Blanket had passed on downstream to the Snake. He would further state that Pony Blanket got his permission to buy some ammunition and asked "me to say on paper that he wanted to trade a horse for a gun, which I did." Rinehart then noted that Black Eagle (Paulina's brother) with fifty-five braves picked up supplies and left immediately going east. "Everyone nervous."[6] The next day, Sarah left for Elko, Nevada to board a train. She would never arrive at her destination.

By now Buffalo Horn, with 300 mounted warriors at his back, was moving west to link with Has No Horse (through Pony Blanket). Captain Reuben Bernard, a Civil War veteran and experienced Indian fighter, wired a message to Howard: "This is the strongest outbreak I have ever known!" and he had seen many. Now in command at Boise Barracks, Bernard was the first to take the trail with a detachment of 50 1st U.S. Cavalry. Crossing Camas Prairie, he found two sheepherders wounded. They had been shot in their tent without apparent cause. It never dawned on them that their sheep were trampling into the ground the starving Indians' last food supply. . . for the once proud hunters of the mountains were now forced to the position of root-diggers for survival.

Although classed as one of the best planned uprisings in the Pacific Northwest, the Bannock War was doomed from the start. On June 8, scarcely more than a week after the rebellion had gotten off to such a hell-raising start, 26 volunteers led by Capt. John B. Harper rode out of Silver City and found Buffalo Horn 80 miles out from the southern Blues near the Idaho-Oregon border. This force encountered 60 hand-picked dog soldiers under the personal command of Buffalo Horn. This was a raiding party, well-armed and in a strong defensive position. Knowing they were outnumbered, Capt. Harper nevertheless ordered a charge, losing two men killed and three wounded. Facing an Indian cavalry advance, the volunteers broke and ran.

Buffalo Horn leaped toward the retreating militia, his warriors rallying to the assault which would have spelled annihilation to Harper's company. A volunteer whirled and fired blindly. . . Buffalo Horn plunged

6 Rinehart to Commissioner of Indian Affairs, June 7, 1878, Office of Indian Affairs, General Files, Oregon, R406, 1878.

from the back of his pony. The dog soldiers circled their fallen chief to protect him, giving the enemy a chance to escape.[7] Bleeding freely from a gaping chest wound, Buffalo Horn managed to remount his horse and head his men toward Pony Blanket's waiting forces on Silver Creek south of Snow Mountain, in what is now the Ochoco National Forest. For two days the dying chief, by sheer will power, stayed on his horse. Then, as he led his men into the foothills near the southern base of Snow Mountain his spirit gave up. Buffalo Horn had bled to death. His warriors, fearful of being overtaken by the cavalry, hurriedly hid his body in a ravine. Making certain no evidence could be found of their loss, they continued on.[8]

At the Malheur Agency, Rinehart was aware that all was not right on his reservation. Pony Blanket had returned from his rendezvous with Buffalo Horn and was asking for food when a courier arrived reporting that the Snakes had captured government wagons loaded with ammunition for the front. On this unhappy note, Rinehart abandoned the Agency and with all government employees made a dash for Canyon City.[9]

En route to Fort Lyon, Sarah was unaware of what was happening. The day she left the Malheur Agency, Capt. Bernard—in pursuit of the hostiles—caught up with them on the Idaho-Oregon border. In the fight, Black Buffalo and Old Bull were wounded. These warriors were in the process of isolating the war zone from the outside world. Before all the telegraph lines were pulled down, Gen. McDowell got a message through to Fort McDermit asking for confirmation that Bad Face and Natchez would help to keep the peace. Both professed their friendship to the whites and announced their intention to leave for the Malheur Reservation to talk to the hostile Snakes.[10] In truth, they intended to join them.

Sarah's first warning that she was in danger came when a messenger told her the stage from Elko to Fort Lyon had been ambushed, the

---

7 Glassley, *Pacific Northwest Indian Wars*, pp. 229-30.

8 As related to Scout John W. Redington by Yellow Jacket, one of the Snake hostiles, after the conclusion of the war. Yellow Jacket was riding with Buffalo Horn at the time. *Idaho Daily Times*, June 18, 1931.

9 Rinehart to Commissioner of Indian Affairs, June 7, 1878, Letters Received, Office of Indian Affairs, Oregon Superintendency.

10 Gen. Irvin McDowell, telegram to Gen. Sherman, June 4, 1878, Letters Received, Office of Indian Affairs, Oregon Superintendency.

driver killed, a passenger wounded and "the Bannocks were killing everyone in their way." When she arrived at Stone House—a stage stop west of Fort Lyon—the Oregon militia accused her of hauling ammunition to the hostiles. Fortunately, Capt. Bernard arrived and believed Sarah when she said that she was opposed to war.[11] During her dash from the Malheur Agency to Fort Lyon, a lathered rider galloped into Prineville with a request for Jim Blakely from his father, for Jim to come to Brownsville and supply the army with beef. Jim, with Clanic (a Warm Springs Indian) and five cowboys set out for Fort McDermit with 450 head of yearlings. Skirting south of the war zone, they made it without mishap.

It was now June 12 and Howard had arrived in the field to take command. One of his first official acts was to assign Major Joseph Stewart to take command of the Malheur Reservation. This didn't sit well with Agent Rinehart and he would stridently complain to the commissioner of Indian affairs ". . . the general commanding arrived [at the Malheur Reserve] and proceeded at once to give Major Stewart such instructions and administer to me such a rebuke, by threatening to place me in [military] arrest, so as to give free license to the whole command and to take such public property as could be found. . ."[12] Rinehart—who had his own desires for the public's assets—was quite miffed at this disruption of his plans. It would soon become obvious that he was at the bottom of all the settler's criticism being heaped upon Howard's military strategy. And no doubt, Rinehart coined the degrading term (which was blamed on the Shoshoni) of calling the general "Day After Tomorrow Howard."

Four days before Howard's arrival on the battlefront, the mortally wounded Buffalo Horn began his ride toward a union with Pony Blanket on Silver Creek in what is now the northwest corner of Harney County. Things were looking gloomy for the military when Sally Winnemucca—for a promise of $500 if successful—offered her services as an army courier and a spy. This was the woman whose baby brother—still

11 Hopkins, *Life Among the Piutes*, p. 78.

12 Annual Report of the Commissioner of Indian Affairs to the Secretary of Interior 1878 (from the content of this report, one could suspect that Rinehart was attempting to cover his own tracks in the misuse of government supplies intended for the Shoshoni); Annual Report of the General of the Army to the Secretary of War 1878.

in his basket cradle—was thrown into a blazing fire by Capt. Almond Well's cavalrymen in the same 1865 battle where her mother and sister received bullet wounds that eventually led to their deaths.[13]

Sarah volunteered for this mission with a personal objective in mind, and that was to find her father and keep him from joining the hostiles at any cost.[14] Howard eagerly accepted her offer and granted Bernard permission to send the Princess into hostile camps as a peace messenger. Sarah knew this was a foolhardy move for if the Snakes ever suspected that she had turned traitor, her life was about as uncertain as a candle flame in a windstorm. Nevertheless, she accepted the risk on the hope she could reach Bad Face, now moving to join Has No Horse, before she got caught.

Sarah, packing a written warning to all white men not to interfere with her mission, left Bernard's camp at 10 a.m., June 13. Fifty-five hours later at the end of a 223 mile ride, the mission was completed. Her father had defected. What Bad Face's real reaction was will never be known. Only Sally's version reached the ears of the whites.[15]

In a small valley north of Juniper Lake at the eastern base of the Steens, Sarah located a hostile camp composed of over 300 lodges and numbering 450 warriors. Attempting to slip through the cordon of guards, she was caught by her brother, Lee Winnemucca. Quickly she told him of her latest madcap scheme. Lee, shaking his head in disbelief, disappeared into the gloom soon to return with an Indian dress. He then painted her face and together they went to their father's lodge. All night long Sarah argued with Bad Face and before dawn broke, she had her way and was long gone. Throughout the next day, Bad Face's family deserted the hostile camp one by one. Even Mattie Shenkah, Pony Blanket's and Has No Horse's niece, defected. Dutiful wife that she was, Mattie followed her husband Lee Winnemucca to the side of the whites and with her sister-in-law, Mattie became a guide, messenger and interpreter for the army.

---

13 *Virginia Union* (Virginia City, Nevada), March 17, 1865; Bancroft, *Scrapbooks*, Vol. 93, p. 12. Sarah would claim that her mother and sister died of famine and cold. Hopkins, *Life Among the Piutes*, p. 78.

14 Hodges, *American Indians*, p. 962.

15 Hopkins, *Life Among the Piutes*, pp. 154,164; Howard, *My Life and Personal Experiences Among Our Hostile Indians*, p. 391.

On the evening of June 15—perhaps in an attempt to save Pony Blanket from punishment—Sarah reported that he was being held prisoner by the hostiles. Seven days later, Howard's force was brought to a standstill on Silver Creek. . . stopped by the White Knife dog soldier, Pony Blanket! Sarah's report was not very accurate.

Howard was beginning to have doubts as to the integrity of his Indian informers. At Sheep Rock Station, he would report that Black Spirit—who he called War Jack—was a double agent. "During the campaign of '78, this Indian rode into my headquarters and so won my regard and the confidence of those about me that I decided to send a message by him from this point [Sheep Rock Station] some 200 miles west to Fort Harney. As he was more loyal to the other side, he carried my dispatch straight to Chief Eagan [Pony Blanket], the enemy in the Steens Mountains, instead of Fort Harney."

Actually, Black Spirit delivered the message to the master of intrigue, Has No Horse. Howard would grieve that the spy, Black Spirit, was "the only Indian in the Northwest that I had to do with directly who played me false!" He would later concede, "The Snakes were outrageous as they possibly could be during the activities of what they called 'war' but after the war was over none of them entered into a deliberate plan to deceive and injure me and mine as many educated white man has done!"

On June 18, two days after Howard's disappointment with Black Spirit, Pete Delore, Jr., captain of the Warm Springs scouts and Prineville scout John Blevins, under the direct command of Col. J.W. Forsyth, surprised three warriors in the Steens building a signal fire. When ordered to surrender, the Indians shot Pete's horse out from under him. During the fight, the Warm Springs scouts were joined by Jim Clark and seven more Prineville scouts.[16] In the exchange of gunfire, two of the Snakes were killed and one escaped. One of those killed was Wolf Dog. . . recognized head chief of the Western Shoshoni Nation.[17] The Bannock War was increasing in tempo.

Sylvester Smyth—whose father and brother had been shot and burned to death in their Happy Valley ranch house—kept a handwritten

16 The Prineville scouts with Clark were: Jerry Winters, John Thorp, Harry Hodson, John Jaggi, Henry Allen, Manford Hedgepath and Dan Thomas.

17 As remembered by Captain Delore's brother, Baptiste Delore, also an army scout.

journal detailing hostile activity in what is now southern Harney County. He, if no one else, was aware of who the ranking Shoshoni war chief really was. Smyth would carefully note, "All the Indians knew that most of the bloodshed to the south was caused by Ochoho [Has No Horse]."[18]

18 Handwritten manuscript now on file with the Harney County Historical Society, Burns, Oregon. Harney County was carved out of Grant County in 1889, eleven years after the end of the Bannock War. Smyth's statement would also apply to the southern part of Wasco County which became Crook County in 1882.

CHAPTER 168

TOWNS UNDER SIEGE

Sent fifty well-armed men with needle guns over the mountain road to Ochoco under command of Major Herren with 5,000 rounds of ammunition. Will be at Portland tomorrow morning to try to take remainder of organized companies up the Columbia.

Gen. M.V. Brown,
Oregon Volunteers
Telegram dated July 8, 1878

Howard, the praying general, entered the Ochoco with heavy artillery and a brace of Gatling guns. On Saturday, June 22, his forces caught up with Pony Blanket on Silver Creek, some two miles east of the present Crook County line. Orlando Robbins, a colonel in the Idaho militia and former U.S. marshall of Idaho Territory, estimated the hostiles at 2,000. It appears that the Snakes had called in all detached war parties and concentrated their forces in the southern Ochoco Mountains. If Robbins' estimate proved correct, this was the largest concentration of warring Indians since the defeat of Custer on another June day in 1876.[1] With this memory still fresh in their minds, Robbins' troops—who had been the first to arrive—decided to wait for the arrival of Capt. Bernard with his 250 cavalrymen who were believed to be in the near vicinity and for Howard's infantry, which was one day's march to the south.

Bernard arrived late that evening with four companies of 1st U.S. Cavalry and decided that Robbins and his scouts should investigate the Indians' position more thoroughly. Under a full moon, Robbins rode out at midnight and succeeded in getting into a location from which he could carefully appraise the Shoshoni camp and decide the best avenue of

1 Glassley, *Pacific Northwest Indian Wars*, pp. 229, 232.

attack. Reporting back to Bernard, he again placed the hostiles at 2,000. . . 1,500 of whom were dog soldiers. They also had a mighty herd of upwards to ten thousand horses picked up on their push from the Idaho border to Silver Creek.

At 2:00 a.m. Sunday morning, Bernard broke camp and reached the hostile encampment just at daybreak. He didn't arrive unannounced. Already, Bearskin, the Banattee medicine chief (known to the soldiers as "Little Bearskin Dick") was riding toward the advancing cavalry column under a white flag of truce. Apparently Pony Blanket wished to confer with the soldier chief, perhaps to evacuate the Shoshoni camp of women and children before the battle started. Whatever he had in mind will never be known. As Bearskin rode up, Bernard spoke to Sgt. Jim Street and asked if he was going to "let the black rascal ride over him." Instantly several carbines rang out and Bearskin—for the first time in his life—was a "good Indian" as Col. Bud Thompson sarcastically put it.[2]

At the same instant Bearskin fell, a bugle sounded the charge and troops bore down upon the encampment, firing their rifles first and then drawing their revolvers, kept firing as they swept through the great camp. Oddly, Bernard had decided to attack without Howard's help. Though taken by surprise, half-naked warriors threw out a line of skirmishers. Mostly chiefs and sub-chiefs, they bore the brunt of the fighting. Armed with 12-shot .44-40 calibre Winchester carbines—the first truly practical repeating center-fire rifle—they could produce more fire-power than the soldiers, who where armed with Model 1873 Springfields.

Bernard was in for another jolting surprise. Robbins' scouts were not fully informed regarding the lay of the camp. After sweeping through, Bernard discovered to his dismay that the Shoshoni were encamped on the edge of an impenetrable swamp and he could go no further. Wheeling around, the cavalry charged back through the Shoshoni lines, this time using their sabres as the dog soldiers stood their ground, fighting like demons with many engaging in hand-to-hand combat. Sgt. George Richmond had his rifle knocked from his hands as he raised it to fire at close range. The sergeant whipped out his pistol and shot his opponent in the neck who, severely wounded, was rescued by his comrades. About

2 Thompson, *Reminiscences of a Pioneer*, pp. 137-38. James Street, a sergeant in the Prineville militia, was serving as scout for Capt. Bernard.

the same time, an army scout took an arrow in the throat, knocking him off his horse. Pulling it out, he remounted only to choke to death on his own blood minutes later.

Then Pony Blanket and Robbins—sighting each other at the same time—charged head-on. Both were veterans of many battles. Both were courage at its best. Pony Blanket slid to the far side of his horse and fired under the horse's head. Robbins sat his horse erect. Both animals were plunging and rearing, interfering with the aim of the contestants, but Robbins position on his horse made his aim more certain. Several bullets passed through the colonel's clothing and some grazed his body but none hit home. Then with a lucky shot Robbins hit Pony Blanket in the wrist, causing him to fall from his mount. As he arose, Robbins shot him in the chest. Still the wiry chief refused to go down. In a leaning position he started for his mounted enemy. Again Robbins fired and with a .45 calibre bullet ripping into his right groin, Pony Blanket plowed to the ground. Robbins in disbelief watched him try to struggle to his feet. He was then carried away by the intensified fighting of the dog soldiers when they saw their chief go down. However, Robbins did capture Pony Blanket's well-known buckskin war horse and it was believed that Pony Blanket's wounds—if he didn't die—would make his capture comparatively easy.

By now, the fighting was so intense that the soldiers had to retreat. During this retreat, Bernard was reinforced by Pete French with 65 ranchers and cowboys. French's volunteers rode into a "hot box," suffering the loss of two men killed and several others seriously wounded. Already, Bernard had lost four men not counting the wounded. In desperation, the cavalry dismounted and fought the Indians for several hours with carbines.

Black Eagle, the first to reach Pony Blanket, quickly packed him to safety where his limp form was covered with his favorite red blanket. His wife and children, seeing what had happened, attempted to reach him. Only his daughter made it. Evening Star, his wife—sister to Has No Horse's first wife—and two sons lay dying on the banks of Silver Creek riddled with bullets.

A rider was dispatched for Has No Horse as skilled, dark, leathery hands cleaned Pony Blanket's wounds. Dancer worked feverishly to stop the flow of blood while other hands whittled splints. Pony Blanket would live but his leadership was lost. Left Hand, the prophet, was elevated to the position of war chief backed by his son-in-law Fox; the Lohim head chief, Yellow Jacket; and Black Eagle, brother to Paulina and Wolf Dog.

That evening, Gen. Howard (with 400 infantrymen) was still seven miles from the battle front when Left Hand rallied his troops and the game of hide and seek began. That night, a big fire was built to make the soldiers believe the Indians were still standing their ground. The next morning, army scouts found they had departed from Silver Creek. The scouts found only ten bodies, including women and children, but estimated that fifty Indians may have been killed. Col. Thompson would claim that the soldiers pulled forty-two bodies out of a crevice in the rimrocks and among those was Buffalo Horn.[3] As a fitting memorial to Buffalo Horn's final resting place, perhaps within rifle shot of where he died, the largest known Rocky Mountain Douglas fir in the world paid silent tribute to its fallen brother.[4]

It was now June 24. Taking out on the Indian's trail, Bernard jumped them again at Sage Hen Springs and once more the Shoshoni outwitted their pursuers. All the army succeeded in doing was capturing some women who told Sarah that Pony Blanket was still alive and that Left Hand was now in command and headed for the Umatilla Reservation in hopes of recruiting more men. Sarah quickly passed this information on to Gen. Howard.

Meantime Has No Horse began a desperate attempt—reminiscent of his path of destruction from the Ochoco settlements to the Idaho border in 1868—at a flanking attack to draw fire away from Pony Blanket who was trying to reach the Columbia River and ultimate escape into Canada. Swinging wide of the main line of march, Has No Horse (with a hand-picked group of 150 warriors) began striking the whole countryside, causing further confusion to Howard's troops who had no way of

3 Monaghan, *The Book of the American West*, p. 244; Thompson, *Reminiscences of a Pioneer*, 138-39.

4 This 155 foot tall giant had been growing on the headwaters of Silver Creek near Delitment Lake in the Ochoco National Forest since the time of Columbus. The mammoth fir had attained a diameter of nearly eight feet at the time of Buffalo Horn's death. Another 117 years would pass as the towering fir stood guard over the Silver Creek battle site. Growing old and highly vulnerable to the forces of nature, this monarch of the forest would topple in a violent windstorm on July 3, 1995. Fortunately the historic tree will be left where it fell to serve as useful plant and animal habitat through most of the coming century. In final tribute, it will now mingle with the dust of the first inhabitants of the Shoshoni Ochoco.

knowing that a new commander had joined the fray. He first rode toward Canyon City then turned west, leaving havoc and waste in his path.

Prior to this, the hostiles—in deference to the holy man, Wovoka—had done little in the way of property damage. It was Wovoka's belief that when the white men were removed by Divine intervention, all they possessed, including houses and land were to revert to the original owners of the country. Consequently, few buildings were destroyed throughout the initial raid of several hundred miles. The Smith home in Happy Valley, on the north side of Steens Mountain; the French ranch in Harney Valley; and the Cummins house on the John Day River were exceptions. Even fences around fields were left intact to serve their intended purpose when the hated white man was no more. When Has No Horse took to the field, this preservation of property came to a halt. If the Sky Father wished the Indians to have wooden houses and fences, *He* could jolly well provide them! As for cattle, his dog soldiers were butchering them by the hundreds, taking only the tongues for food. Now, let the white man see what it was like to starve.

Many settlers, some men and women still in their nightclothes and mounted bareback, made miraculous escapes. By July 1, every eastern Oregon town from Prineville to Baker City was crowded with refugees. Homes were abandoned so hastily that no provisions or clothing were taken. Several cattlemen and sheepmen were caught in the mountains and killed before they could reach safety. Reports were circulating that 200 to 300 Indians were riding behind the advance and that the cavalry was a hundred miles away.[5] Isolated ranchers and their families were murdered, their houses burned and their livestock slaughtered. Has No Horse was providing every diversion he could for Left Hand and Pony Blanket to escape with the women and children. For reasons unknown, Howard was leaving him strictly alone to concentrate his efforts on Pony Blanket's flight.

On July 4, Sam Baker—a special courier from Prineville—galloped into Salem with a message addressed to Gov. Stephen Chadwick. Prineville citizens were urging the Governor "to use all possible haste in dispatching a military company" for the relief of this threatened commu-

5 W.V. Rinehart to the Commissioner of Indian Affairs, July 1, 1878, Letters Received, Office of Indian Affairs, Oregon Superintendency.

nity. According to the express rider, Ochoco residents were deserting livestock, abandoning harvest fields and fleeing homes in search of more secure localities.

On July 5, Gov. Chadwick in response to this petition, sent Gen. M.V. Brown—commander, 2nd Brigade Oregon Militia—to Portland where he arranged for arms and ammunition to be transported across the Cascades from Albany to Prineville, A 50-man rifle company was organized by Capt. N.B. Humphrey and ordered to be ready to march to the Crooked River Valley by July 8. Brown himself returned to Albany and accompanied the Linn County Volunteers to the battlefront. Other rifle companies recruited in Portland never made it to the front for lack of arms. In fact, most of the rifles and ammunition destined for eastern Oregon were shipped to Prineville in the center of the great livestock industry; and to Canyon City in the heart of the rich mining district. The citizens of Prineville would acknowledge this contribution with a message to Gov. Chadwick expressing their heartfelt gratitude.[6]

At the outbreak of the great Snake uprising—as those in eastern Oregon called the Bannock War—Prineville lawyer George Barnes and Bud Thompson (serving on jury duty) were in The Dalles. They loaded a two-seated buggy with several hundred rounds of Winchester ammunition and headed for Prineville 150 miles to the south. By the time they arrived in central Oregon, many settlers had buried their personal effects and forted-up at the Baldwin Ranch on Hay Creek, while Prineville was barricading the city streets. This was the condition when the Oregon Militia marched into town.

Accompanied by Gen. Brown, a Civil War veteran, this elite group was under the direct command of Major James Herren, who at the age of three, was a member of the lost 1845 emigrant train. Other members of the rifle company were Capt. Humphrey, a prominent Linn County businessman; First Sgt. George Chamberlain, who would become a United States Senator; and chief scout, Warm Spring Johnny, a white man who had been raised by the Snakes since infancy, captured by the army in 1864 and imprisoned as a Snake dog soldier. In Prineville, at the request of Gen. Brown, Thompson joined this company at his old rank of colonel in the Oregon Militia.

6 *The Morning Oregonian*, July 6, 9 and 19, 1878, Vol. 18, Nos. 131, 133 and 142.

By the time the militia arrived the displaced settlers had completed construction of a log fort on the west end of town which was intended to repel anything the Snakes could throw at them. This stockade, the size of a city block, consisted of 14-foot logs stood on end and buried 4 feet into the ground after the fashion of other forts throughout eastern Oregon.[7] When the fortification was considered to be battle ready, one of the defenders fired into the fort with one of the needle guns furnished by the U.S. Army. Upon investigation it was found that the .51 calibre bullet passed through both walls of the log stronghold. Fortunately for the refugees, Has No Horse with his firepower didn't attack Prineville.[8]

As Gen. Brown and Major Herren set up a perimeter of defense around Prineville, a report came in that Left Hand, accompanied by the White Knife war chief Dead Deer, had doubled-back and was attempting a retreat into Nevada. Col. Thompson and Capt. Humphrey were immediately dispatched to cut off the Snakes at the Elkins Ranch on Grindstone Creek, a tributary of Crooked River. The report proved to be false. Left Hand and Pony Blanket were still forging to the north. Moving into the South Fork of the John Day, the volunteers saw signal flashes from two high points. They were now under hostile surveillance.

Interestingly, Warm Spring Johnny told the soldiers how the Snakes could make those highly visible fire flashes. A pile of dry grass was collected and then surrounded by blankets. The grass was then ignited and when the blaze was brightest the blanket on the side they wished to signal from was quickly raised and again lowered, giving out a bright orange flash of light. Once detected, the Linn County volunteers had the good sense not to engage the Snakes in battle, although Thompson claims he and a young boy attacked the Indians' horse herd against all odds and captured nineteen ponies. [9]

---

7 This fortress was bounded on the north by West Third Street; on the south by West Second Street; on the east by North Claypool Street; and on the West by North Deer Street.

8 William Tweedie, "Some Aspects of the Early Development of Crook County," Thesis Paper, August 1939, p. 60. An early settler would recall that "one bullet [when fired at the stockade wall] knocked off the hat of Rick Powell, who was a small boy at the time. We concluded that the fort wasn't any good, but we kept watch for the Indians every night until the alarm died down. At the time the Shoshoni were camped on Crooked River just a few miles east of Prineville." Lewis Hodges' description of the Prineville stockade as written by his daughter, Dolly Hodges Fessler, for the *Central Oregonian's* 1975 Heritage Edition.

9 Information on the Linn County Volunteers found in Thompson, *Reminiscences of a Pioneer*,

With Left Hand's estimated 1,000 warriors still knifing toward the Columbia, reports of Indian depredations began pouring in from all over eastern Oregon. Has No Horse's ruse was highly successful. Although he never actually struck the towns, the mere rumor of raiding Snakes was enough to put the townsfolk into hiding and no amount of begging on the military's part could secure enough volunteer riflemen to do them much good. Local people were staying at home to protect their own. Thus, Has No Horse kept that many more men off Left Hand's advance.

Aided by Bad Face, Has No Horse was hiding his activities quite well. Whenever the army suspected that Has No Horse was missing from his Fort Harney lodge, Bad Face would explain that the chief had ridden into the Steens Mountains to visit with him. He would also report that Has No Horse told him he wanted to go back to Fort Bidwell but "was afraid of the settlers and soldiers." Warming up to the subject, Bad Face would swear that both he and Has No Horse had never entered the hostilities, although "the Bannocks had come urging them to do so."[10] No sensible military man could doubt the sincerity of Sarah Winnemucca's father at a time like this.

In Prineville, breast works were being thrown up around the city and a company of mounted riflemen were ordered to report to Col. Bud Thompson on the South Fork of the John Day and from there, to join the Grant County Guards under the command of Capt. F.C. Selk. As the Prineville recruits marched east, more refugees from the upper Ochoco Valley and Mitchell area headed for one of two places, whichever was the nearest: the schoolhouse stockade at the mouth of Mill Creek or the mining tunnels at Scissorsville. Among the late arrivals at the Mill Creek stockade were John and Mary Frier. Although they lived on West Branch Creek near Mitchell, Mary (the daughter of Bluford Marks who had taken a claim on Marks Creek in 1869) wanted to be with her parents so the Friers bypassed Scissorsville.[11]

A fortress built at Long Creek under the command of Capt. Charles Ballance was approached by the war chief Red Willow—son of

pp. 149, 152, 154-55.

10 Capt. H.C. Hasbrouck to Asst. Adj. Gen., Military Division of the Pacific, July 9, 1878, Letters Received, Office of Indian Affairs, Oregon Superintendency.

11 *The History of Crook County*, Oregon, p. 109.

Has No Horse—under a flag of truce but Ballance refused to let him in.[12] Red Willow then drove off all the livestock in Long Creek Valley and burned the ranch houses. It was claimed that Tom Keeney's ranch house (the first to be put to the torch) was burned in retaliation for him having cheated Red Willow in a horse trade some time before. At that time, if Red Willow could have foreseen that his grandmother would soon be scalped alive, it's doubtful if anything in Long Creek Valley would have escaped his wrath and it is certain that Has No Horse would have committed mass destruction. During this eternity of panic, Charley Williams, mistaking Henry Blackwell for an Indian, shot his horse out from under him.

At La Grande, a force of men and boys (directed by U.S. Senator James Slater) prepared rifle pits around the three-story brick building of Blue Mountain University and barricaded the building. A volunteer company formed by Gen. J.H. Stevens and Col. Micajah Baker stood guard around the town night and day. Everywhere in the threatened region, fear and uncertainty reigned.

It was during this period that the hue and cry went out that Gen. Howard was afraid to fight the Indians. . . an unsupported rumor that was quickly circulated by the press. It is questionable that an officer praised for "gallant and meritorious service" in the Civil War and who was awarded the Congressional Medal of Honor for distinguished bravery at the Battle of Fair Oaks—where he lost his right arm—was intimidated by a force lacking in military power who, by the very nature of current conditions, were unable to wage their normal type of guerrilla warfare.[13] O.P. Cresap, one of the earliest settlers in Grant County who served as an army guide and scout for Gen. Howard throughout the Bannock campaign, would place the general's actions in proper perspective.

Howard was well aware of who would suffer the most if the fighting escalated with the very real possibility of dozens of battle-hardened Snake dog soldiers, now hid out over five western states, joining

---

12 This fort was constructed at the Charley Dutten ranch, about one-half mile northeast of the present town of Long Creek. (Information given by Mabel Wilson Binns and Norma Macy Smith, descendants of James Macy who was a volunteer Indian scout in General Howard's command.)

13 For more on Shoshoni military operations, see *Thunder Over the Ochoco,* Vol. III, Chapter 41, pp. 21-24.

the fray. As it was, the Army had already brought in Apache scouts from Arizona, which was like waving a red flag in the Shoshoni's face. Cresap would observe, ". . . as to General Howard's ability as an Indian fighter, opinions differ, but that he was sincere in his belief that it would be a disastrous policy [with respect to the white settlers] to push the Indians too hard, there is no doubt in my mind. The Indians did not go very far out of their way to commit depredations but confined themselves strictly to their line of march [to Canada]."[14]

Seven-year-old Tom Morgan, who rode 100 miles bareback to The Dalles in two days seeking safety, had this to say: "The Indians killed a lot of unsuspecting travelers, sheepherders and cattlemen, but I never heard of these Indians scalping or mutilating anyone. If they had, we would have heard of it for the whites never missed a chance to spread bad news about them."[15]

Now, you have the other side of the story. Perhaps Howard was doing the settlers a favor by not pushing the enemy too hard.

In Pendleton, settlers were pouring into town with wagon loads of women and children where they set up camp in the courthouse yard. Men and boys were issued arms and put to work digging and erecting fortifications, with the main stockade being built near the intersection of Willow and Webb Streets. Later, soldiers from Fort Vancouver bolstered the defenses. Scouts who rode out from Pendleton were ambushed at Willow Springs near Pilot Rock and all were killed or wounded.

In June, several families of mining Finns from Michigan's Copper Range had settled east of Pendleton, lured there by Elias Peltopia, a California gold rush prospector from Finland. These unfortunate homesteaders found out that Peltopia had neglected to mention one very important item. . . Indian raids! They paid for their ignorance with blood.[16]

On July 1, Lt. William C. Brown rode into Canyon City with the purpose of recruiting volunteers—leaving his pack train guarded by eight cavalrymen on the outskirts of town—but when he reached the main

---

14 Morgan, "O.P. Cresap's Memories," *The Last Indian War in the Northwest,* p. 17.

15 Morgan, *My Story of the Last Indian War in the Northwest,* p. 7.

16 Albert Horalo who, at the age of two, arrived in this settlement in 1878 told of the Finlanders misfortunes to Dorothy Lois Smith, staff writer, Portland *Oregon Journal,* May 1959.

section he heard screams of, "Here they come!" Brown reported that "men were yelling, dogs barking, women and children screaming; one woman was running wildly down the street with her luxuriant tresses streaming in the wind. . . " the cause of all this confusion was because Brown's men decided to bring the pack train into town either for safety or to get a glass of beer, and had been mistaken for the first onslaught of the hostiles who were hovering on the edge of town.

Having achieved his objective of mass hysteria, Has No Horse veered west to cause more panic. The following day, he struck Major Narcisse Cornoyer's troops on the John Day River, forcing them to turn back to the Columbia. Twenty-two days had elapsed since the official declaration of war on June 10, and the Snakes had driven the citizens of eastern Oregon to the brink of nervous collapse. What might have happened if the war chief of the old Paviotso Confederacy had been pushed to the limit is anyone's guess.

CHAPTER 169

THE TRAIL OF NO RETURN

When we challenge the white man, we like to challenge the white man. Gambling is our oldest profession.

Russell Means
Sioux Indian Activist

To the beleaguered occupants of eastern Oregon it would seem as though an eternity had passed in those three terror-ridden weeks. The countryside had been raked with guerrilla warfare which, to the distraught recipients, appeared to have no connection to the actual frontal assault of the Shoshoni main column forging steadily toward the Columbia River. In an effort to understand what had transpired, it is necessary to backtrack to the first big military strike on Silver Creek some 70 miles southeast of Prineville.

During this engagement, Gen. Howard arrived at the battle site on June 24, adding his 21st U.S. Infantry and 4th U.S. Artillery to Capt. Bernard's 1st U.S. Cavalry and Col. Robbins' Idaho Volunteers. On Silver Creek, Howard split the command, mainly to appease the disgruntled civilians caught up in a full-scale Indian offensive. For some vague reason, these anti-Indian protesters had difficulty understanding why they had been chosen as prime targets.

Bernard, with the fast moving cavalry and volunteers, would continue pursuit of the main Shoshoni forces while Howard with the infantry and artillery would take flanking action to prevent any hostiles from escaping the cavalry; and also to alleviate the reported Indian depredations raging from the Crooked River Valley to the lower John Day.[1] Both commands moved out at dawn on June 25 with Bernard riding

1 Brevet Colonel Reuben Frank Bernard, captain of Company G 1st U.S. Cavalry, had a

toward the South Fork of the John Day River as Howard took a zigzag course across the Ochoco Mountains. The cavalry would be stalled by heavy fighting while Howard's column became bogged down in a land that offered little encouragement to full-scale military travel. Artillery wagons were not making good progress.

The first day out, the infantry marched 30 miles in an all-day rain. The supply wagons and artillery (some pulled by oxen) covered only 13 miles in fourteen hours. Col. Thompson would report that the use of heavy artillery was "Gen. Howard's first fatal blunder. His men were mostly employed in grading roads through the rough, broken country to enable his ox teams to follow. Some have questioned this statement. But I saw with my own eyes the road down Swamp Creek and the mountain road leading to the South Fork of the John Day River, seven miles south of the mouth of Murderer's Creek."[2] It was not a pleasant journey for either man or beast.

On the morning of June 26, snow began to fall and fell steadily until the evening of the 29th. Before daybreak on the 26th, a courier from Bernard reported hundreds of Indian pony tracks were just a short distance north of Howard's light column, the artillery wagons now being a day's march to the rear. At 6:00 a.m., the mounted infantry moved out to intercept the reported hostiles. Along the edge of Little Summit Prairie, they found hundreds of pine trees stripped from the base up as high as a person could reach. Sarah's explanation to the General was that the Shoshoni used the inner bark for food. The outer bark helped cover the frozen ground for beds and also added to their fuel. From appearances, there had been between 1,500 and 2,000 Indians encamped on Little Summit Prairie.[3] On a stump near the remains of a lodge, the soldiers picked up a white man's scalp. Howard had stumbled on to Left Hand's

---

remarkable military record. By the time of the Bannock War, having risen from the ranks in the 1st Cavalry, Bernard already had taken part in 98 of the "103 fights and scrimmages" he was to boast of in the Civil and Indian wars—a record not challenged by any of his contemporaries. (Monaghan, *The Book of the American West*, p. 244).

2 Thompson, *Reminiscences of a Pioneer*, p. 139.

3 Howard to McDowell, October 1878, House Executive Document 1, Serial 1843, 45th Congress, 3rd Session, Part 2, p. 219. Later, Charlie Prindle of Mitchell would report that he was herding sheep on Wolf Mountain when he stumbled upon Left Hand's camp and gave the information to Howard's artillery unit, *Illustrated History of Central Oregon 1905*, pp. 697-98.

main force and his scouts would report that the Indian's trail had veered sharply to the west.

The next day, two prospectors who claimed they were familiar with the country joined the column seeking employment. Howard lost no time in engaging them as army guides. In the highland lodgepole jungles of North Pisgah one of the professed scouts became panicked by the pressing thickets and deserted; the other confessed he had lost the way so the soldiers followed along the high ridges to Lookout Mountain. Howard would note that it was very cold and snowing all day. He would also describe the area through which they had passed. "What a diversified country! Jagged rocks, precipitous slopes, knife-edged divides, deep canyons with sides steep and difficult, the distance from a crest to the mountain streams that tumbled over the rocks far below being sometimes four or five miles."[4] He didn't exaggerate. From the crest of Lookout Mountain to the Ochoco River at its base, the distance is six miles. . . almost straight down. From this vantage point, Howard saw where the Indians reversed course and watched them as they crossed Big Summit Prairie, once again moving toward Bernard on the South John Day River. On this epic chase, the infantry was adding names to local landmarks such as Howard Point, Howard Valley and Howard Butte. By June 30, Left Hand had drawn Howard's infantry into Black Canyon as Has No Horse continued his commando raids along a 250-mile strike zone.

Traveling a direct course, Lt. J.B. Hazelton's 4th U.S. Artillery reached the South Fork on June 27, three days ahead of Howard's 21st Infantry. From the west rim of the John Day Canyon—dragging logs fastened to the heavy artillery wagons—it took eight hours to make the descent, arriving at Bernard's camp at ten o'clock that night. Ironically, Prineville scouts Joe Combs and Jake Stroud accidentally found the Yreka Trail entrance to the South Fork Canyon too late to stop the hazardous downhill plunge.

At the South Fork camp, Howard overtook the cavalry and artillery units on July 1 and assumed full command of field operations. While the army got its second wind, the dog soldiers were doing the same at the abandoned Stewart Ranch south of Dayville. Meantime, Jim Clark in command of 26 Ochoco riflemen marched up the South Fork to

4 Howard, *Life Among Our Hostile Indians*, p. 400.

discover which way the Shoshoni were headed. He found out the hard way. En route, Clark (of Burnt Ranch fame) led his volunteers to believe that the Snakes were nothing more than "skulking thieves armed with bows and arrows." To the home guard's consternation, what they encountered were fierce horsemen armed with modern firearms. Closing in on the Stewart Ranch at the mouth of Murderer's Creek, the volunteers found the bodies of two sheepherders. They also blundered into 50 Snake warriors. It wasn't a friendly meeting. Oliver Aldrich received a fatal shot in the head; W.C. Burnham, Bill Milliron, Jerry Winters and Billy Pitcher were wounded. Clark and two others escaped on foot after having their horses shot from under them. At least Capt. Clark had a good idea as to where the hostiles were located.

The next morning—it was now July 2—the U.S. Regulars found where Jim Clark's Prineville volunteers had been routed by the Indians, leaving their dead behind to be buried by Howard's advance. By midnight, Howard's weary troops (who had covered 112 miles since June 28), set up camp at the Cummins Ranch near Dayville to await delivery of supplies from Canyon City.

Already over a hundred volunteers from the Crooked River and John Day valleys had gathered at the Cummins Ranch to quell the great Snake uprising. Some were horseback, some in wagons, and some on foot—but all were determined to wipe out eastern Oregon's native population for all time. It seems that the irregulars fully intended to carry out this sinister threat. Moving down the South Fork of the John Day River, the volunteers trapped about thirty Indian women and children in a cave. One of the home guards (who for obvious reasons shall remain unnamed) said he could not bear to kill the children with his .56 calibre Spencer rifle because "it tore them up so bad." . . . So he did it with his .38 Smith and Wesson revolver. Maybe that wasn't as messy.

Meantime when Jim Clark and his home guards came up missing, a search party was quickly organized. During this activity, a man thought to be a sheepherder was seen riding along the side of a mountain east of the ranch. Screened from the ranch by tall Cottonwood trees it was difficult to tell what was up there so Warren Cassner—a John Day rancher—volunteered to investigate. Once he cleared the trees, Cassner couldn't believe what he saw. The whole mountain slope was blackened by Indians and horses. He estimated their numbers at 1,200 Indians and

8,000 horses. At the same instant that Cassner spotted the Snake advance, he saw a party of dog soldiers attempting to cut him off from the ranch and yelled to the volunteers, "For gawd's sake get out! We're surrounded by Indians!"

Then, as Col. Thompson of the Oregon Militia put it, "There began a race seldom witnessed in Indian or any other kind of warfare." Men on horseback scattered in all directions; wagons careened into each other; men on foot were running for dear life attempting to jump aboard bouncing wagons—some of which overturned in the flight for safety. Emil Scheutz, one of the few men that made a stand, took a .50 calibre slug across his chest, ripping a trench one could lay his arm into. By a stroke of luck, Bernard's cavalry—eight hours ahead of Howard's ox teams and army of road builders—arrived in time to prevent a complete massacre. As it was, the volunteers didn't stop running until they reached Canyon City, each imagining the fellow behind was an Indian.[5]

Seeing the demoralized volunteers pouring into town, the citizens of Canyon City rushed to the mine entrance and more than one hundred families hid in the tunnels as word spread that the Shoshoni were riding toward the settlement. To make matters worse, the rumor was now out that 600 Umatilla braves were gathered in Fox Valley, some twenty miles north of Canyon City, to add their support to the Snakes. What started out as a pleasant interlude to inoculate eastern Oregon from the red plague was turning into an epidemic of nightmare proportions.

Shortly before the Dayville rout, word spread that Howard had stopped the hostiles on the South Fork of the John Day River and that they were now in retreat. This encouraging news prompted the settlers of northeast Oregon to abandon their fortifications and return home. When the volunteers stampeded into Canyon City it became obvious that this was a false report. Joe Blackwell—an army scout—headed north to alert the settlers of the South Fork defeat. He had barely gotten out of sight of Canyon City when his horse was shot out from under him. Continuing on foot he met a Chinese prospector who loaned him his horse so Blackwell could warn the Long Creek inhabitants that the Shoshoni were not only undefeated but advancing in that direction.

---

5 Thompson, *Reminiscences of a Pioneer*, p. 140-41.

Meantime on a scouting mission, Jim Macy and the Curl brothers (Tom and Doug) rode up Flower Gulch to the top of Ritter Butte and saw nothing suspicious in the way of Indians. Moving some nine miles to the south, the scouts rode to the crest of a ridge and discovered that the earlier report of hostiles gathering in Fox Valley was not a rumor. New arrivals kept coming in until dark and the scouts saw that the main group was now engaged in a spiritual war dance. Abe Lamb, returning to Charley Dutten's fortified ranch house about one half mile northeast of Long Creek, also saw the Indians gathering in Fox Valley. Lamb had a band of sheep grazing on the hills near the Indian big encampment. The sheep were being tended by a Dutch herder who apparently became curious as to what the Indians were doing and rode down among them where he was killed. The dog soldiers—showing their contempt for animals that stripped the land of all forage—then rode among the sheep and cut off their legs, leaving them to suffer and die.[6] General Howard would later comment that of all the Shoshoni war tribes, the Robber (Banattee) were the most cruel.

Mable Macy Binns would recall a pleasant memory from this hectic period:

> In the midst of all this fright and turmoil, one romantic incident took place. James Macy and Elizabeth Miller, having fallen in love and having planned their marriage before the Indian uprising took place, decided to let neither earthquake, floods and much less Indians interfere with "loves sweet young dream." James accompanied by Tom Curl and Charley Dutten, rode to Canyon City for the marriage license. They returned safely and the marriage was performed inside the [Dutten] fort by Preacher Harrow.[7]

Rushing to Gen. Howard's aid, Col. John Grover (commander of Fort Boise) with 400 troopers had reached Prairie City, some 45 miles

6 Information give in a letter from Tom Black, a descendent of James Macy, dated November 21, 1997, Baker City, Oregon.

7 As remembered by Mabel Macy Binns and Norma Macy Smith, daughter and granddaughter of James and Elizabeth Macy.

east of the Cummins Ranch, at the time of the volunteer's rout. Here, he received an express from Howard ordering him to proceed to Fort Harney in anticipation of a further outbreak from the Paiutes who remained on the Malheur Reservation. It was now becoming increasingly obvious that Has No Horse was making a lot of unexplained visits to Bad Face's camp. In view of this, Gen. Brown and Col. Thompson with the Oregon State Militia were ordered to reinforce Col. Grover at Fort Harney.

At the same time. Col. Grover marched into Fort Harney, Brig. Gen. James W. Forsyth arrived from Chicago to take command of the 1st U.S. Cavalry Regiment now led by Col. Bernard. And, for the first time in history, Oregon and Washington had a navy in action on the Columbia River. Steamships armed with howitzers, Hotchkiss guns and Gatling guns, under the command of Captain W.A. Wilkinson, were patrolling the Columbia to prevent warring Shoshoni from crossing the river and eventual escape into Canada. The summer of '78 would be long remembered by Oregonians who thought the rebirth of the Paviotso Confederacy was a joke.

After Howard's advance across Big Summit Prairie, Left Hand's heart began to weaken when his scouts reported more than a thousand U.S. Regulars moving in on their back trail. Gaining strength daily, Pony Blanket once more took over command, continuing the advance which was sweeping a belt 30 miles in width through the state of Oregon—spreading death and destruction in its path. Although his warriors were heavily encumbered with women, children, baggage and the infirm, Pony Blanket steadily advanced deeper and deeper into the rugged Blues. No white caravan of like size could withstand such tremendous strain and fatigue and still survive. In a desperate forced march to Camas Creek—a tributary of the North Fork of the John Day River—he covered 90 miles without engaging in battle. Then, on July 4 near Ukiah, Pony Blanket again struck a lethal blow.

Pendleton was now in the line of march and most foresaw its complete destruction. The town had 150 inhabitants living in 30 to 40 houses scattered along Court and Main Streets, but refugees had swelled the population to over 300. Gen. Forsyth hurriedly set up army headquarters at the Golden Rule Hotel as a wagon barricade was stretched across Main Street to the Pendleton Savings Bank. Women and children were barricaded in Byer's Grist Mill in an effort to protect them from flying bullets. Frank Vincent, captain of a hastily organized militia, rushed south to intercept the Indians. J.H. Kunzie, appointed assistant adjutant general by Gov. Chadwick, rushed to Umatilla City—now guarded by two steamers outfitted as gunboats—and set up state military headquarters there.

William Lockwood, veteran stage driver on the Salt Lake City-Umatilla City run was holed up at Meacham. He decided to run the 25-mile Shoshoni gauntlet to Pendleton and deliver the mail. Loading the mail into a light carriage, he hitched four horses to the vehicle, put an expert rifleman in the back seat and took off. Soon after a war party took pursuit but the rifleman pumped enough lead to discourage an attack and Lockwood made it through. The big news was that the Sheep Killer Snakes had staged a new outbreak in Idaho.[8] They would soon be joined by Black Eagle and his Bear Killer dog soldiers.

At La Grande, four heavily-loaded freight wagons drawn by 16-horse teams were standing by to make the run to Pendleton with badly needed supplies. Four tough drivers, Wallace McLaughlin, John Doe, A. Smith and "Whispering" Thompson volunteered to make the hazardous run. Before reaching Meacham, they were attacked by Black Eagle's warriors. McLaughlin was instantly killed and then scalped. Thompson ran into the forest where he was also killed and scalped. Doe hid in a thicket where he was found, tortured, killed and mutilated. Smith, badly wounded, hid in some willows near a spring. Desperate for water he tried to reach the spring and was caught. The Indians tied him with a horsehair rope and dragged him back and forth just out of reach of the spring until he died. The teams were killed, the freight scattered and the wagons burned.

The pent-up hatred nursed by years of white domination was being expressed in raw brutality and the military was reacting in kind. From time to time, soldiers captured small bands of Shoshoni, hanged some of them and returned others to the Malheur or Fort Hall reservations to die a slow death from starvation. Prison wagons were rolling daily toward Fort Harney. If women refused to enter, they were dragged to the wagons and pitched in. Families were separated with the children loaded in the rear wagons and the men herded like cattle behind the prison wagons.

8 Glassley, *Pacific Northwest Indian Wars*, p. 237.

From Fort Harney, the wagons packing the dangerous war criminals passed through Prineville en route to Vancouver Barracks for shipment east.[9] And the fighting was relentless.

Marching south from Pilot Rock, Capt. Frank Vincent in command of the Pendleton volunteers and Captain Joe Wilson (a Yakima War veteran who settled in Prineville in 1874) in charge of the Prineville volunteers, reached the battleground on July 4. Shortly before noon, Vincent's group was attacked at what they named Wilson Spring. At the first volley, thirteen volunteers (including Capt. Wilson) sprang on their horses and deserted for Pendleton. This left army scout Jacob Stroud in command of the Prineville volunteers. Others tied their horses in a sheep corral and hid in the shed which was soon riddled by bullets. William Lamar—a schoolteacher engaged to Dr. William McKay's daughter—was killed. Henry Howell took seven bullets but lived and seven more volunteers were seriously wounded.[10] The Indians cut out Lamar's heart and roasted it over a slow fire in view of the volunteers. That night Walter Harrison and Harrison Hale were killed while trying to escape.

After Joe Wilson reported back to Pendleton, Sheriff J.L. Sperry organized a company under Lt. William Blakely (Jim's brother) and started for the Camas Prairie front on July 5.[11] Major Joseph W. Magone (veteran of the Yakima War) volunteered to accompany Lt. Blakely and to serve as guide and express messenger for Gen. Howard. Although considered past his prime, Magone was in good shape. In 1891—at the age of 70—Magone walked all the way from Canyon City to Chicago to win a bet. It seems that he wanted to see the World's Columbian Exposition.[12]

At the outbreak of hostilities, the *New York Times* predicted that the Shoshoni outbreak might extend into a larger war encompassing the entire Pacific Northwest and offered the opinion that, "The War Department and the Interior Department, between whom the responsibility is

9 They were shipped to places such as Fort Keogh (Montana), Fort Omaha (Nebraska), Fort Washakie (Wyoming), and Indian Territory, Oklahoma.

10 The wounded included S.I. Lansdon, A. Crisfield, G.W. Titsworth, C.R. Henderson, Frank Hannah, Jacob Frazer, J.W. Salisbury and H.H. Howell.

11 Camas Prairie in northeastern Oregon should not be confused with Camas Prairie in southwestern Idaho where the Robber Snakes fired the opening guns of the Bannock War.

12 *Oregon Historical Quarterly*, Vol. III, p. 276, and Vol. IX, p. 309.

divided, are seldom capable of effectively assisting each other."[13] As the fighting escalated it appears the *Times* was right on target.

Pony Blanket, trying to make contact with the Cayuse war chief Four Crows, had taken possession of the Oregon Camas Prairie on July 4. Had he continued his march on Pendleton, there was no organized resistance. Instead, he frittered away time killing sheepherders and skirmishing with Capt. Vincent's volunteers, who again engaged the Indians on July 6 near Albee, north of Ukiah, and were now in full retreat to Pendleton. During this withdrawal, Prineville scouts John Jaggi, Jerry Winters, and John Luckey out on patrol heard cougar screams and thought it to be a woman. They narrowly escaped death when they blundered into a hostile camp.[14]

At this time, the big sheep outfit of Jewell and Morrissey had a large band in Camas Prairie. When Charlie Jewell—Oregon state senator—heard of the attacks, he took off for Camas Prairie and succeeded in reaching the herder's cabin. He then went to Pendleton for arms and on July 5 returned to Camas Prairie with several needle guns. When Jewell hadn't returned to Pendleton by July 8, Morrissey went looking for him. En route, he met Capt. Frank Maddock with a volunteer company from Heppner who informed him that two ranchers—Nelson and Scully—had been killed. Still no sign of Jewell. Continuing to search, Morrissey found a piece of wood in the middle of the road with the message that Jewell was wounded and hiding in the brush. He called and got a faint answer. Jewell was found with a bullet lodged in his left side and a broken left arm. He had arrived at the sheep camp the night of the 5th, was shot and had crawled into the brush where he had lain for three days without food or water. Jewell was taken back to Pendleton where he died on July 12.

On July 3—one day before Pony Blanket's attack on Camas Prairie—with Col. Miles closing from the east and Gen. Forsyth from the west, Has No Horse hit Cayuse Station on the Umatilla Reservation.

---

13 *New York Times*, July 6, 1878, p. 5, Col. 3 and 4.

14 As remembered by John Luckey's wife, Sally Hodges Luckey. Other civilian scouts attached to Howard's command were the Blackwell brothers—Dick, Joe, Clem and Henry; the Curl brothers—Tom and Doug; Sherman Keeney, John Blevans, Al Morgan, Couch Dicky, John Austin, Murat Blevans and Johnnie McBain. All were from the Fossil, Echo and Long Creek areas.

Shortly before his mid-morning attack, four freight wagons rolled into the agency compound loaded with supplies for the front. By the time the battle smoke had drifted away, Has No Horse had captured all the supplies (including five barrels of whiskey), killed seven men and burned the government buildings to the ground. Five days later on July 8, Has No Horse with five sub-chiefs appeared at Fort Bidwell—300 miles southwest of the Oregon front—and assured the commanding officer he had taken no part in the fighting.

By July 5, Gen. Howard's 21st U.S. Infantry, Gen. Forsyth's 1st U.S. Cavalry and Major Throckmorton's 4th U.S. Artillery had united south of Pilot Rock. The army was now using Arapaho and Crow scouts against the Snakes while Col. F.J. Parker was dispatched to Fort Boise to bring in more federal troops. Riding in advance of Parker's detachment, army scout George Frohman was ambushed on the North John Day River. In a dash for safety, Frohman was killed and Jack Campbell with three other scouts were all wounded. On word of this loss and the defeat of the volunteers on Camas Prairie, Howard drew more rations and began an advance on Pony Blanket's main column. At the same time, he sent an express rider to intercept Miles' advance from the east with orders to proceed to the Umatilla Reservation in an attempt to cut off Has No Horse's raiders. Miles was marching with 500 troopers at his back.[15] They arrived at the burned out Umatilla Agency on July 9 and instead of encountering Has No Horse's small guerrilla force, Miles was hit by a war party 1,000 strong.

During this engagement, the Snakes' Umatilla allies sat their horses atop a hill overlooking the fighting waiting to see which side would win. With howitzer shells and Gatling guns ripping their ranks to shreds, the Snakes abandoned the fight and treachery was born. On the advice of the medicine chief Dr. Whirlwind, the Umatillas (in a move to secure forgiveness) began negotiations with Miles and his staff officers to either kill or capture Pony Blanket. The army officers were more than happy to agree to the terms of betrayal.[16] Meantime, moving in two columns, Howard with two batteries of artillery, one company of infantry,

15 Miles' force was made up of four companies of 21st U.S. Infantry, two batteries of 4th U.S. Artillery, one troop of 1st U.S. Cavalry, and 100 Oregon Volunteers.

16 Glassley, *Pacific Northwest Indian Wars*, pp. 234-36.

one troop of cavalry and twenty of Col. Robbins' scouts, headed up Birch Creek while Forsyth with seven companies of cavalry, one battery of artillery and 100 volunteers marched up Butter Creek on July 6.

The next day, Gov. Ferry of Washington rushed into Walla Walla and raised a company of 40 volunteers under Capt. W.C. Painter where they embarked on the steamer *Spokane* under the command of Major John Kress to patrol the Columbia. A few miles down river, the *Spokane* fired a volley into a Snake encampment—destroying it—while a landing party confiscated all Indian property including blankets and buffalo robes. Hearing the bombardment, Capt. Wilkinson with 32 men boarded the steamer *Northwest* with a Gatling gun and two howitzers, adding their firepower to the naval battle.[17]

On Sunday, July 7, as the Columbia River Navy shelled Shoshoni refugees, Howard, Forsyth and Col. Throckmorton made a three-pronged attack on Pony Blanket's main column entrenched on Battle Mountain at the headwaters of Butter and Birch creeks. Moving up Birch Creek, Howard's troops were greeted with a loud shout. Sarah identified the voice as that of Left Hand and interpreted his message as: "Come on you white dogs! What are you waiting for?"

As usual, when the Indians taunted them, the American boys had to poke up their heads, revealing their positions. With the Shoshoni, just the opposite occurred. When the soldiers called out, they hugged a little closer to the ground. Bullets whistled all around, falling like hail on the infantry and cavalry holed up in the rocks. The 1st Cavalry's regimental history claims that part of this fight was the first example of cavalry fighting on foot without separating the men from the horses—each trooper advanced firing his carbine while he led his horse by reins thrown over his forearm.[18]

Howard cautioned Sarah to stay down but Sarah didn't wait to be told to hide. When the shooting commenced she slid off her pony and dug into the ground in a hurry. As bullet-riddled cavalry horses lay screaming in pain on Battle Mountain, Sarah told Mattie Shenkah, "We will see a great many of our people die today, and soldiers too." She spoke

17 *New York Times*, July 9, 1878, p. 1, col. 3; July 10, 1878, p. 1, col. 3.

18 Monaghan, *The Book of the American West*, p. 245.

the truth.[19] The Snakes kept the army pinned down all day and again escaped. In fact, the women and children, along with the best war horses, were beyond danger before the battle began.

Gen. Howard, the self-proclaimed "Messiah of the Indian," was performing a task he didn't particularly relish. With Col. Throckmorton it was a different story. As his Gatling guns spewed destruction on Battle Mountain, Throckmorton told a news reporter, "Indian agents may cry peace but there can be no peace until the last one of the red demons whose fingers are dripping with the blood of Mary Ward, the Perkins and others, are numbered with the good Indians who have fallen. They must die and every time one of them bites the dust every good citizen will say amen! So be it! Bless the Lord! Hallelujah!"[20]

And die they did as Dr. Gatling's unholy weapon—condemned by Crook and other military commanders—finally ripped the backbone out of the Snake war tribes on Battle Mountain. In a 24-hour battle, three Gatling guns blasted Pony Blanket from a seemingly impregnable position on top of a bluff and went down in history as the crux of the Bannock War. As one author would comment, "Its the type of tribute Richard Gatling would have liked."[21] Not counting loss in human life, this one-day conflict alone cost the Military Department of the Columbia $127,000.

Capt. Bernard, with a Gatling gun and a detachment of Cayuse scouts led by Cut-Mouth John, had accompanied Howard up Birch Creek. The scouts spotted a Shoshoni war party going up a steep hill and alerted Bernard who started after them on a trot. Seeing that Pony Blanket was still alive and could sit a horse, the cavalry pursued him for three miles. Each time they thought he was trapped, Pony Blanket would appear triumphant on the next ridge. All of the cavalry got out of this chase was a few old horses and played-out mules. Like a flock of sparrows, the Shoshoni flew ahead from one pinnacle to another. . . and in the bluffs above Willow Springs they made a stand.

---

19 Howard, *Life Among Our Hostile Indians,* pp. 404-05.

20 *The Eastern Oregonian*, Pendleton, July 27, 1878.

21 Lt. Col. George M. Chinn, *The Machine Gun*, Vols. I and IV, Navy Bureau of Ordinance; J. David Truby, "Hailstorm of Death," *VFW Magazine*, February 1972, pp. 17-18.

Meanwhile, Left Hand—looking for other openings in the game of war—was surprised by Capt. Rodney's 4th U.S. Artillery who, besides his two companies of artillery and infantry, also had a troop of 1st U.S. Cavalry under Capt. Bendire. Umapine (the Umatilla head chief who had joined forces with the Snakes) was riding with Left Hand. Not as well schooled in the art of guerrilla attack, Umapine charged Capt. Rodney's column and was badly defeated while Left Hand flew on to fight another day. After this failure, the Umatillas were ready to dissolve their Snake partnership.

During this battle many residents had abandoned their ranches and herds to seek safety in Pendleton. With the owners temporarily away and their livestock unprotected, white rustlers were cashing in on the Indian scare. Two local entrepreneurs, Hank Vaughan (a recent graduate of the Oregon State Penitentiary) and Billy Moody, hoping to get rich selling stolen horses in Nevada, got caught. Taking advantage of the Indian situation, they had reined in at the deserted Battle Mountain stage station and were in the process of corralling some local mustangs when they were surprised by a rancher posse scouting for horse thieves.

This unexpected visit separated Vaughan and Moody from their mounts so they made a dash for the barn. Although the ranchers fired a barrage of lead into the barn, the horse rustlers successfully held off the posse until dark. During the night a couple of stray horses wandered into the barn corral. These horses had never been ridden before, but the trapped outlaws caught and saddled them. What followed was a furious bucking contest which the posse members only heard because in the darkness they couldn't see what was happening and the suspected thieves escaped in the night. The next morning when the barn was searched it was found riddled with so many bullet holes it seemed impossible that Hank and Billy had escaped without injury.[22] Perhaps they didn't. After all, both were mighty tough characters who survived several bullet wounds in their comparatively short lives. Vaughan was only 44 years old when the horse he was riding stumbled and fell on him. It would take 17 days for him to die.

On July 8, the united commands of Howard, Wheaton and Forsyth hurled back the advancing Shoshoni, forcing them out of the mountains

22 Interview, John Waseese, September 26, 1959, Ukiah, Oregon. Waseese is a Umatilla Indian.

and driving them toward the Columbia River. Once more Pony Blanket united with the women and children who had been shunted from the battlefield. Armed steamers cut off their flight and the main body of hostiles swung back to wreck injury and death upon more settlers. In spite of heavy shelling, one wing of this force mounted on their best war horses and led by the desperate Old Bull, attempted to swim the Columbia. A few succeeded in reaching the Washington shore, including Old Bull, and from there continued their flight into Canada and safety.

Then, on the morning of July 14, Umapine—now convinced that the Snakes were fighting a lost cause—sent a messenger to Col. Evan Miles with a unique request. If the United States government would pardon the Umatillas from all war crimes committed, he would waylay Pony Blanket and his leading war chiefs and deliver them to the army. After a quick consultation with generals Howard, Forsyth and Wheaton, the terms of sedition were accepted.[23] That afternoon, a Cayuse warrior rode into Pony Blanket's war camp asking that he and his lieutenants meet with Umapine on a matter of grave importance.

Already seriously wounded from the battle on Silver Creek and in a desperate state of mind, Pony Blanket and sixteen dog soldiers left the war camp to meet with Umapine, Dr. Whirlwind and Four Crows. In war, Umapine—known to the Snakes as Deceitful Dog—had displayed profound treachery and positive enjoyment in his acts of brutality. After committing atrocities, he would strut with pride and boast of his brutal powers. The Paiutes had leaned upon him as a friend. The Snakes hated him but they were now in dire need of assistance.

On July 15, eighty Umatilla braves joined Pony Blanket some two miles southwest of the Meacham Stage Station. In a high mountain glade on the crest of the Blues—just an arrow shot from heaven—Pony Blanket was delivered into the hands of an enemy. He had just entered his 40th year on earth. Riding at Pony Blanket's side on this fateful day was his brother-in-law Pipe, scourge of the Applegate Trail. As the dog soldiers dismounted and walked toward the council ring, several Umatilla warriors attempted to seize Pony Blanket. In the struggle, he was killed—supposedly by Umapine. With a dozen rifles exploding in chorus, twelve

23 Captain N.A. Connoyer to Commissioner of Indian Affairs, July 19, 1878, Letters Received, Office of Indian Affairs, Oregon Superintendency.

Snake dog soldiers died and five wounded were held as prisoners of war to be delivered to Miles' command. The next morning, Umapine rode into the Umatilla Agency with ghastly proof of his undercover work. Displayed on poles were the heads of Pony Blanket, Pipe, Fox (son-in-law to Left Hand), Storm Cloud (the Tuziyammo war chief), and Spotted Elk (the Banattee medicine man).[24] It's worth noting that Henry Robie—a Harney Valley stockman—before he died from exhaustion after being chased by the dog soldiers had placed a $1,000 reward on the delivery of Pony Blanket's head to any military outpost.

Rumor quickly spread that Umapine, for all of his bragging, didn't have the nerve to kill Pony Blanket. The claim was that Pony Blanket had been betrayed by the Tebechya (Sun Hunter Snake) dog soldier, Little Foot, who did the actual killing.[25] True or not, at the end of the war when Has No Horse turned himself in at Fort Bidwell, his rifle was adorned with Little Foot's fresh scalp.[26]

Accompanied by a party of Cayuse scouts attached to Miles' command, who were herding five wounded Snake dog soldiers and 300 horses ahead of them, Umapine rode up to Lt. W.C. Brown's tent. From the lances of the Cayuse dangled eight fresh Shoshoni scalps. In Umapine's hand was a burlap bag. When Lt. Brown walked forward, Umapine tossed the sack at his feet and out of it rolled the head of Pony Blanket and his left arm.[27]

To make certain it was indeed Pony Blanket, Capt. John McGregor—attached to Gen. Frank Wheaton's command—and army surgeon, Major J.A. Fitzgerald rode out to the scene of slaughter to identify the body from wounds inflicted by Col. Robbins in the fight on Silver Creek. They were led by Prineville scout John Blevins, who was with the party that brought in Pony Blanket's head and arm.

Major Fitzgerald, the army doctor who examined the body, decided Pony Blanket would have died in any case from the Silver Creek

24 Howard, *Famous Indian Chiefs I Have Known*, p. 277; Brimlow, *Bannock Indian War*, pp. 150-54.

25 Hanley, *Owyhee Trails*, p. 147.

26 Dave Chocktote's testimony as told to him by his father, Black Buffalo. It was also believed that Little Foot killed Big Man by his own request.

27 Howard to McDowell, October 1878, *House Executive Document 1*, Serial 1843, 45th Congress, 3rd Session, Part 2, p. 229.

wounds. He had Pony Blanket's head preserved in alcohol and sent to the Army Medical Museum in Washington, D.C. as "a fine specimen of an Indian head of large brain." Accompanying this grisly token of war was the head of Pipe—known to the whites as "Charlie"—whose wife, Honey Bear (Pony Blanket's sister), had been shot to death on Silver Creek.[28]

On the night Pony Blanket died, Sarah Winnemucca dreamed of his murder. When she learned a few days later that he was indeed dead she packed the word to the Snakes. This last and greatest humiliation to a leader they loved and respected was keenly felt. Upon hearing of Pony Blanket's death from Sarah, Leggins threatened to kill Umapine. He and Natchez with some twenty warriors rode into the Umatilla camp where Natchez, in a voice dripping with contempt, told the assembled tribesmen, "We have never taken our own brother's scalp [Pony Blanket was born a Cayuse] and fastened it on a pole and danced around it to show the whites how brave we are. . . . "[29] From this point onward, even though the Snake war tribes were vanquished, no Umatilla dared to venture from camp alone.

At the close of the war, Sarah too, would get in her digs to an American audience who believed the Western Shoshoni were not yet far enough along the white man's road to take advantage of their good fortune in defeat and go meekly onto a reservation. Speaking in San Francisco during the Christmas season of 1879 Sarah would tell them, "Some say I am a half-breed. . . . I would be ashamed to acknowledge there was white blood in me. . . . I call upon white people in their private homes. They will not touch my fingers for fear of getting soiled. That's the Christianity of white people."[30] Sarah was taking a hard look at her utopian days of racial harmony and a harder look at her Shoshoni ancestry.

In the aftermath of Pony Blanket's death, the army was apprehensive that the Snakes—still in a militant mood—would try to "carry out their insane project of going to the buffalo country and thence to Sitting

---

28 J.F. Santee, "Egan of the Paiutes," *Washington Historical Society Quarterly*, January 1935, pp. 22-24.

29 Canfield, *Sarah Winnemucca of the Northern Paiutes*, pp. 148-49.

30 *Daily Alta California*, December 24, 1879, p. 1, col. 5.

Bull."[31] There was ample justification for this fear. Under the leadership of Black Eagle, the attempt was made and more blood would flow in 1879.

Meantime Gen. Brown's Oregon militia was issued 200 rounds of ammunition each on orders to escort prison wagons from Fort Harney to Fort Vancouver. During this interlude Col. Thompson, certain in his own mind that the war was "a rank failure" decided to remain in Prineville. However, he did concede that he and Gen. Brown "probably saved some lives" and that was worth all the hardships they had endured. According to Thompson, among those misfortunes suffered during the first two weeks of the campaign, his eyes became so badly affected from the dust and glare of the sun reflected from the white alkali plains on the head of Crooked River that he nearly went blind. His savior, who bathed and bandaged his eyes with wet cloths and led his horse was the boy, Eugene Jones, who was the only soldier to accompany him on the Snake horse raid on Murderer's Creek. All who knew young Jones claimed he was a soft-spoken, decent and honorable man. Then came the awakening.

On arrival back in Prineville with the volunteers, a letter from Sheriff Hogan of Douglas County was awaiting Col. Thompson notifying him that the Jones boy was none other than Eugene English, a notorious highwayman and stage robber—a brother to the infamous English boys, well known as desperate characters. The sheriff's letter further asked the colonel to place English under military arrest. In view of past events, Thompson thought this would be "the depths of ingratitude" so he laid the matter before Prineville's resident politician, the Honorable Frank Nichols. "By George, Colonel, I would not give him up." A second opinion was solicited from Art Brayman, a Prineville merchant, who agreed with the judge. On these gentlemen's advice, Thompson quietly procured a voucher for the young soldier's service from the militia quartermaster; had English sign it over to Brayman for hard cash; and told him to get lost.[32]

---

31 Howard to McDowell, October 1878, *House Executive Document 1*, Serial 1843, 45th Congress, 3rd Session, Part 2, p. 229.

32 Thompson, *Reminiscences of a Pioneer*, pp. 165-66.

That night the young outlaw disappeared and was never seen again. Thus ended the colonel's and the private's contribution to the great Snake uprising.

CHAPTER 170

OUTLAW STATUS

We are not now speaking of the horrors of war and the courage of battle. We are referring to the calculated annihilation of Indian communities, the heartless slaying of men, women and children in order to appropriate their lands.

H.H. Bancroft
Oregon Historian

Their leaders killer or captured, the Snakes had little else ahead but to hide in the isolated canyons of eastern Oregon in an attempt to postpone final surrender. With the prison wagons rolling into Fort Harney, a few such as Black Eagle, Dead Deer and Half Horse fled to the Seven Devil Mountains, stronghold of the Sheep Killer Snakes. And the campaign was becoming more and more treacherous.

Sarah would report that she saw a Shoshoni woman still alive blinded by gun power at close range and scalped. She was clutching a baby in her arms (possibly her grandchild). This would be confirmed by Andy Blackwell, a John Day rancher who took the woman under his personal care. She had been shot through the loins in addition to sustaining nasty head wounds. A wide flap of skin cut loose in scalping fell forward over her eyes. Blackwell, having no surgical instruments, took a pair of sheep shears and clipped off the flap of skin and dressed her wounds as best he could. This was Agent Rinehart's official report to the commissioner of Indian affairs.[1]

Perhaps a more factual account of this tragic incident would emerge from those who were there. On a scouting mission accompanied

1 Rinehart to commissioner of Indian affairs, September 18, 1878, United States Department of Interior, Office of Indian Affairs, General Files, Oregon, R710/1878.

by John Said, described as "an unprincipled and cruel renegade," Joe and Dick Blackwell found the bodies of several Shoshoni woman and children in Flower Gulch, who they thought had been scalped and left for dead. She was still alive and trying to crawl to the nearby stream for water. It was at this moment that the Blackwell brothers suspicioned that John Said was responsible for the brutal killings. The scouts took the wounded woman back to the Long Creek fort where Eva Harrow (wife of the minister) and Mary Blackwell (Joe's wife) cared for her. For the Shoshoni woman's safety she had to be hidden from the other white settlers so the Rev. Harrow and Joe Blackwell built a small pen in which she was kept out of harm's way.

Not being familiar with the Shoshoni language, the only word her benefactor could understand was "Egan"—the American's name for Pony Blanket—which she kept repeating over and over again. Because of this, Eva and Mary decided that she must be either the mother or the wife of Pony Blanket.[2] They were wrong on both counts. Pony Blanket's wife, Evening Star, had been killed on Silver Creek several weeks before this incident and he had never known his birth mother. This woman was Butterfly (Buli) his mother-in-law, the wife of Lost His Arrow (Paiakoni) and the mother of Evening Star and Dawn Mist, Has No Horse's first wife who was murdered in the upper Ochoco Valley in 1866. She was also the maternal grandmother of Red Willow. The perpetrators of this atrocity couldn't have chosen a more respected Shoshoni woman to mutilate.

As soon as Butterfly was past emergency care, soldiers from Fort Harney took her back to the Malheur Reservation. From then on Butterfly always wore an oil cloth cap to hide her scarred head.

At the height of the fighting, three self-styled Indian fighters from Linkville (Klamath Falls) drifted into Prineville. Well-armed, dressed as army scouts and displaying fresh scalps, they were given a hero's welcome. They identified themselves as John Said, Sam Rush and William Richards—better known on the frontier as Rattlesnake Jack, Arizona Sam and Texas Dick. It was later found out they followed the

---

2 As remembered by Mabel Macy Binns, Norma Macy Smith and Wallace Blackwell. The government later paid Mary Blackwell and Eva Harrow for nursing the Shoshoni woman back to health. A literal translation of the Shoshoni word Eheganti means the Blanket Owner.

trail of the retreating hostiles and murdered Indian woman and children too old or too young to keep up the line of march. These were the scalps that they displayed in Prineville, Canyon City and Harney City. Heralded as protectors of humanity, they headed for the Steens Mountains presumably to lay siege to Has No Horse's secret camp. In reality, they were out to stir up more trouble with the Harney Valley ranchers.

Within a short time, the Grant County sheriff received a telegram from the sheriff of Winnemucca, Nevada wanting him to arrest John Said for the theft of 150 head of horses owned by Pete French. Captured, Said was returned to Canyon City to stand trial—not for murder but for horse theft. He arrived wearing the infamous Oregon Boot, as handcuffs were of little use on his small hands. The Reno *Evening Gazette* would report that he got off with a light sentence because his "poor old dad came across the Cascades to plead leniency in his behalf."[3] On release from prison, Said tried to kill a bartender in Weiser, Idaho and was gunned down by the town deputy.

Meanwhile, the "white-eyes" and the "red-skins" were wreaking havoc upon each other. In an effort to stop civilian interference in military affairs, Gen. Howard divided his command and began a systematic search of eastern Oregon, sweeping across the Crooked River and John Day valleys to the Idaho border. His stated objective was to capture all remaining Shoshoni in the Ochoco and surrounding country and place them on the Yakima Reserve in Washington Territory. But there was more than met the eye on this purge of the timbered slopes of the Ochoco.

Obviously, the ranchers wanted the range cleared of intruders but if the Homestead Act of 1862 was tailored for the stockmen, the Third Amendment of the Homestead Act—the Timber and Stone Act of 1878—was made for the West's lumbermen. This act applied only to those lands in California, Nevada, Oregon and Washington that were "unfit for cultivation" and "valuable chiefly for timber and stone." It allowed any citizen or "first paper alien" to claim and buy 160 acres of timberland for $2.50 an acre. This was less than the price of a single saw log in 1878. . . a very good incentive to open up timberland. Company agents rounded up gangs of men to file their claims for a quarter section then go to a notary public to sign over their deeds to the corporation and

3 *Evening Gazette*, Reno, Nevada, November 3, 1878, item on Rattlesnake Jack.

then were paid off. Fifty dollars was the usual fee but it soon dropped to $10 then $5 and finally to the price of a glass of beer. And thus, another 3.6 million acres of Indian lands were confiscated.

Under the leadership of Lt. Col. Forsyth, Major Sanford, Capt. Bernard and Capt. Winters (with Sarah and Mattie acting as army couriers), as many as ten separate military columns plowed into the wilderness. In the next few weeks, small bands of Snake refugees were gathered and brought into the government detention camps.[4] On the flanks of Lookout Mountain, Forsyth's column captured 99 prisoners—72 of whom were women and children—confiscated 30 rifles and 200 horses. At about the same time on September 5, the Oregon Militia seized twenty Snake lodges (nearly 100 people) and all were killed. This wanton slaughter by volunteers was having its affect on both the regulars and the hostiles.

Prior to this murderous attack the general's son, Lt. Guy Howard, with a detachment of 12th Infantry and a troop of Major George Sanford's Nez Perce scouts were cutting across country from Boise Barracks to join the fray. On July 18, three days after the betrayal of Pony Blanket, the scouts were ambushed by the Oregon Volunteers and one scout was critically wounded. The Oregonians would later claim that they thought they were Snakes. The Nez Perce disagreed. Dressed in army scout uniforms and moving in an orderly fashion, they concluded that the white men, knowing that they were Indians, deliberately fired upon them. At this point, army officials refused to believe the Volunteers. In the week it took him to die, the Nez Perce scout identified the white man who shot him but the damage was irreparable.

Now the tide of battle took on a new dimension. As the regulars scoured the Blues to dislodge the few remaining dog soldiers, Sarah would describe this final fight. "Sometimes I laugh when I think of this battle. It was very exciting in one way and the soldiers made a splendid chase and deserved credit for it; but where was the killing? I sometimes think it was more play than anything else. If a white settler showed himself he was sure to get a hit from an Indian; but I don't believe they ever tried to hit a soldier—they liked them too well—and it certainly was remarkable that with all these splendid firearms, and the Gatling gun,

4 Hopkins, *Life Among the Piutes*, p. 196.

and General Howard working at it, and the air full of bullets, and the ground strewn with cartridges, not an Indian fell that day."[5]

There was a message in that statement. The soldiers couldn't help being in sympathy with the beleaguered Shoshoni.

Of the estimated 510 Paiutes still living on the Malheur Reserve, all were forcibly removed and added to the prisoners at Fort Harney. By now, the Shoshoni had earned "outlaw status," throwing the reservation open to white occupation—if not legally, by force—for the Malheur was not officially opened to white entry until 1883. Nonetheless, white speculators occupied the Malheur Agency, stealing Indian supplies, destroying Indian property and selling farm equipment and improvement claims to the highest bidder.

Tom Overfelt (who had coveted Agency Valley for years) at least had the decency to wait until the government officially opened the reservation to settlement. But, in so doing, he nearly lost his dream after making one of the most famous endurance rides in western history.

Squatters were in full possession of the Malheur Reserve when an exhausted rider galloped into Overfelt's LF Company headquarters in Silvies Valley and told him that Agency Valley was to be sold to the highest bidder "at noon tomorrow." There was only one obstacle, it was now noon and the auction was to take place in Lakeview, Oregon. Overfelt had but twenty-four hours to make the 200 mile ride or lose Agency Valley and his silent partnership with Henry Miller. He accepted the challenge grabbing fresh mounts—with or without permission—along the way and at high noon the following day smashed through the door of the Lakeview land office. Bidding was already in progress but Overfelt topped all offers and paid the full amount with a draft bearing the famous Bull's Head brand of Miller and Lux Land and Livestock Company.

In an unprecedented move, the government land office clerk refused to accept the draft, demanding cash—which was quickly produced by another buyer. In a state of shock, Overfelt dashed to the nearest telegraph office and wired Miller of the unexpected outcome. It worked. Miller appealed to the commissioner of the General Land Office in Washington, D.C. and Overfelt got his prize.

5 Hopkins, *Life Among the Piutes*, p. 177.

After all, this was no big deal for Henry Miller, who had bought off California state legislators and with a little manipulation of the Swamp Lands Act of 1850 had acquired a hundred mile strip of land on both sides of the San Joaquin River in the Central Valley for $1.25 an acre which was then refunded to him upon his sincere claim that he had spent a like amount on reclamation.

Unfortunately, Tom Overfelt didn't live long enough to enjoy his victory. One day in 1886, mounted on a rough-broke horse, his saddle turned and he was dragged to death. His coveted Indian holdings were merged into Henry Miller's vast domain.[6]

Overfelt's property loss was trifling compared to what the Snakes had to forfeit now that they had achieved official outlaw status. In return for lands lost—1,775,000 acres (equal to 2,285 square miles)—they were given 18,240 acres (28.5 square miles) of arid sagebrush land in Harney County. By 1973, this had been reduced to 800 acres or 1.25 square miles on the outskirts of Burns, Oregon.[7]

Eighty-five years after the fact in August 1964, the U.S. Senate passed a bill to set up the machinery for distribution of about $550,000 to descendants "of the Snake Indians who once lived on the Malheur Reservation in Oregon." The bill, which would have permitted the Interior Department to draw up a list of Indians eligible to receive the money, got stalled in the House on a disagreement over technical amendments.[8] At the time of this writing in 1998, it is still stalled.

Back on the eastern Oregon front things were happening rapidly. On August 13, 1878, Left Hand, Red Willow and Leggins (Natchez's son) with 60 warriors gave up at the Malheur Agency and were immediately clamped in irons.[9] Under heavy questioning, Leggins identified the ranking war chiefs as Oytes (Left Hand), Bannock Joe (Race Horse), Captain Bearskin (Little Bearskin Dick), Paddy Cap (Yellow Jacket), Boss (Spotted Elk), Big John (Three Coyotes), Eagle Eye (Black Eagle), Charley (Pipe), D.E. Johnson (most likely a squaw man[10]), Beads and

6 Hanley, *Owyhee Trails*, pp. 110-12.

7 *Oregon Guide*, pp. 467-69; *Oregonian Sunday Magazine*, July 13, 1947; Brimlow, *Harney County, Oregon*, pp. 147-48.

8 "Malheur Indian cash bill wins nod in U.S. Senate," *The Oregon Journal*, August 11, 1964.

9 *New York Times*, August 14, 1878, p. 1, col. 6.

10 Squaw man was the term used to describe a white man who married an Indian woman.

Elisha Barnes,
first mayor of Prineville,
circa 1880.

Courtesy Crook County Historical Society

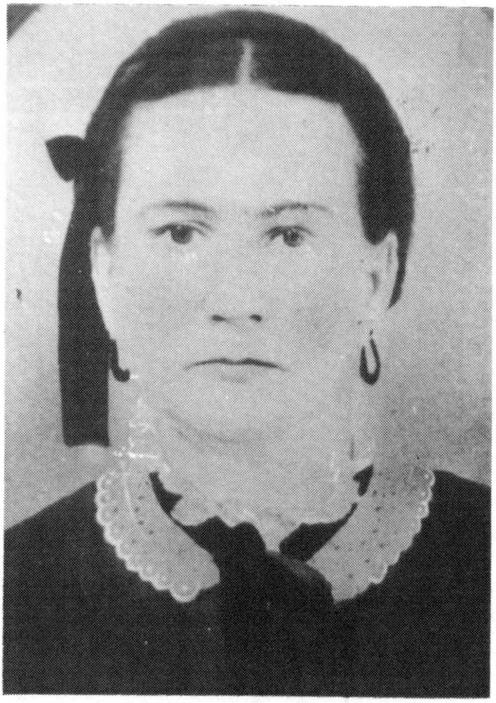

Suzanna Barnes,
wife of Elisha.
One of the first white
women in central Oregon,
circa 1880.

Courtesy Crook County Historical Society

Dr. Lark Vanderpool, one of the first doctors in Prineville, circa 1880.

Courtesy Crook County Historical Society

Dr. Lark Vanderpool and his famous remedies. Prineville 1880.

Courtesy Crook County Historical Society

Billy Smith, member of the first homestead party into the Ochoco in 1866, standing in front of his second cabin. The first cabin built is standing to the left. Both were located on Mill Creek, about a mile upstream from its confluence with the Ochoco River.

Courtesy Crook County Historical Society

First school in central Oregon, on Mill Creek in 1870.

Courtesy Crook County Historical Society

Ng Ah Tye,
an early Chinese doctor in
central Oregon, circa 1900.

Courtesy Crook County Historical Society

Leander "Lee" Liggett,
a settler on the South Fork
of the Crooked River
and known for his attempts
to cultivate alfalfa,
known derisively as
"Liggett's Weed."

Courtesy Crook County Historical Society

Henry Miller
of the Miller and Lux Cattle Co.
at age 40 in 1880.
Courtesy Steve Lent

William and Mary Marks,
early settlers in the
Upper Ochoco country,
circa 1880.
Courtesy Crook County Historical Society

Left to right: Abraham Zell, Libby Zell, George Millican, and Ewen Johnson.

Courtesy Crook County Historical Society

At left:
Barney Prine,
saloon keeper,
blacksmith
and founder of
the city of
Prineville.

Courtesy Steve Lent

At right:
Frank Prine,
brother to
Barney Prine.

Courtesy Crook County Historical Society

The grave of Howard Maupin, who killed Chief Paulina in 1867.
Maupin died at Ashwood in 1887.

Courtesy Gale Ontko

James Miller,
founder of the
Keystone Ranch east
of Prineville and
the brother of Joaquin Miller,
world famous poet.

Courtesy Steve Lent

Ashwood, Oregon, nerve center of the Trout Creek mining district, located about three miles northeast of where Maupin killed Chief Paulina.

Courtesy Steve Lent

Stagecoach in Prineville standing in front of the stage office and the Poindexter Hotel, circa 1900.

Courtesy Gale Ontko

Prineville, looking south down Main Street from Ochoco Heights, 1895.

Courtesy Steve Lent

Manford Nye, wife Adell
and daughter Wilda
It was claimed that Nye,
a horsebreaker, was never
thrown from a bucking horse.
An early Bear Creek rancher,
he made 800 mile cattle drives
to San Francisco from the
Bear Creek area.

Courtesy Steve Lent

August Schernickau's store at Cross Hollows in 1885. Cross Hollows was later named Shaniko, the world's largest shipping point for wool.

Courtesy Steve Lent

Jones sawmill on the upper Ochoco River in 1910.

Courtesy Steve Lent

An ox-drawn logging wagon on Willow Creek.

Courtesy Crook County Historical Society

Frances "Frank" Forest.
Forest Crossing on
the Crooked River
was named for him.
Courtesy Steve Lent

James Hawkins,
early sawmill operator
on the upper Ochoco River.
The Hawkins mill sat about a
half mile west of the
Smith Brothers mill,
both on the Ontko Ranch.
Courtesy Steve Lent

Mitchell, Oregon in 1900; photograph taken between floods.

Courtesy Steve Lent

Smith Brothers sawmill on the upper Ochoco River in 1928.

Courtesy Steve Lent

Henry Koch,
a casualty of the range war.
Courtesy Gale Ontko

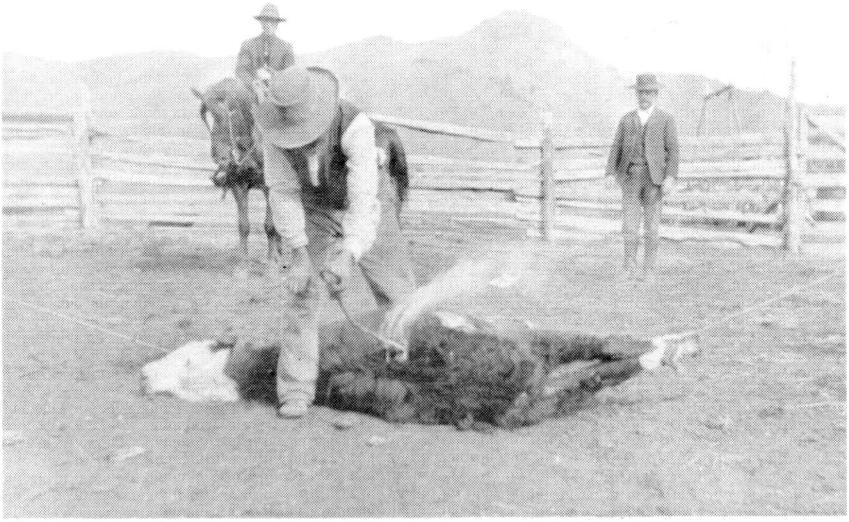

Branding a calf to turn out on the range.
From left to right: Gilbert Lawson (on horse), Charlie Lister (branding) and Jake Johnson (standing). Berkhart Butte is in the background.
Courtesy Crook County Historical Society

Walt Demaris operation on McKay Creek
loading a big log with the rolling hitch method.

Courtesy Gale Ontko

Sherar's Bridge.

Courtesy Gale Ontko

Oldest homestead and largest barn
on the upper Ochoco (the Ontko Ranch).

Courtesy Gale Ontko

Oldest homestead and largest barn
on the upper Ochoco (the Ontko Ranch).

Courtesy Gale Ontko

Iron Mouth,
Shoshoni war chief during the Bannock War, and sometimes called Pete Burns. He rode for the Suplee ranchers as a cow hand.

A typical ranch house in the Ochoco Mountains.

Stagecoach in front of the Canyon City Commerce Co.

Hauling bags of wool to Shaniko.

Scissorsville (lower town), Oregon. Discovery Cabin is on the right, Ryle Thompson's Pay Dirt Saloon on the left. Circa 1885.

Courtesy Crook County Historical Society

The Quicksilver Mine in the Ochocos, circa 1920.

Courtesy Crook County Historical Society

Andy Ontko and O.M. (Bud) Koch,
hard-rock miners.

Courtesy Gale Ontko

Andy and Bud enjoying themselves after
a hard week's work in the mines.

Courtesy Gale Ontko

Louie Beirl,
Hard-rock miner.
Courtesy Maxine Stocks

Art Champion, discoverer of most of the cinnabar mines in eastern Oregon, including Horse Heaven, Mother Lode and Blue Ridge.

Courtesy Gale Ontko

Louie Beirl cutting wood for his cabin with a Vaughan drag saw in 1918.
Invented and patented by Elbert Vaughan, his daughter,
Mildred Draper, still lives in Prineville.

Courtesy Maxine Stocks

Louie Beirl at the entrance to the Sunshine Mine.

Courtesy Maxine Stocks

Remains of the Mayflower gold stamp mill
at Howard, Oregon, taken in 1954.

Courtesy Gale Ontko

Oregon Mayflower Co. mine.

Courtesy Gale Ontko

Art Champion on the cover of *Mining World,*
examining a piece of cinnabar ore.

Courtesy Gale Ontko

General view of the Horse Heaven Mine looking east. The glory hole that now marks the outcrop can be seen between the peak and the mine dump. Below the plant is the burned-rock dump.

From Quicksilver in Oregon by C.N. Schuette
(State of Oregon Department of Geology and Mineral Industries publication, 1938)

View from just below the glory hole towards the northwest along the Horse Heaven Fault. The fault crosses the saddle of the ridge. White flags in the foreground mark diamond drill holes.

From Quicksilver in Oregon by C.N. Schuette
(State of Oregon Department of Geology and Mineral Industries publication, 1938)

Close-up of the Horse Heaven Plant from the burned-ore dump. The tunnel in the foreground leads to the furnace pit. Power House is on the right.

From Quicksilver in Oregon by C.N. Schuette
(State of Oregon Department of Geology and Mineral Industries publication, 1938)

Close-up of the mouth of No. 1 level of the Horse Heaven Mine.

From Quicksilver in Oregon by C.N. Schuette
(State of Oregon Department of Geology and Mineral Industries publication, 1938)

The furnace plant at the Mother Lode Quicksilver Mine, Crook County.

From Quicksilver in Oregon by C.N. Schuette
(State of Oregon Department of Geology and Mineral Industries publication, 1938)

Reduction plant at the Champion Mine. A.J. Champion, the owner of the mine, is the discoverer or co-discoverer of many of the quicksilver mines in the Ochoco District.

From Quicksilver in Oregon by C.N. Schuette
(State of Oregon Department of Geology and Mineral Industries publication, 1938)

Rotary furnace at the Blue Ridge Mine.

From Quicksilver in Oregon by C.N. Schuette
(State of Oregon Department of Geology and Mineral Industries publication, 1938)

This shows the Condenser System of the Rotary Furnace shown above. It was way too small for the size of the furnace.

From Quicksilver in Oregon by C.N. Schuette
(State of Oregon Department of Geology and Mineral Industries publication, 1938)

General view of the Maury Mountain Mine.

From Quicksilver in Oregon by C.N. Schuette
(State of Oregon Department of Geology and Mineral Industries publication, 1938)

Mine entrance of the Maury Mountain Mine.

From Quicksilver in Oregon by C.N. Schuette
(State of Oregon Department of Geology and Mineral Industries publication, 1938)

Surger (Fox).[11] Leggins did not identify Has No Horse as a chief; whether out of fear or loyalty, we will never know.

Six days later, Has No Horse rode into Fort Bidwell. A fresh scalp rumored to be that of Little Foot dangled from his rifle barrel. He was immediately placed under arrest and taken under armed guard to Fort Harney.

The most dangerous prisoners were shipped out of Oregon country. Fort Keogh, Montana would receive 64; Fort Hall, Idaho, 47; Fort Vancouver, Washington, 38; Fort Washakie, Wyoming, 17; and Fort Omaha, Nebraska, 3. Before the winter was over, Fort Simcoe, Washington would receive 543 survivors of the death march—most of whom were women and children charged with lessor crimes against the government.[12]

The war was over. In the past two decades more than 100,000 army personnel saw action against the Snakes in eastern Oregon and victory was bought at a staggering price. Between 1865 and 1868—not counting Oregon's contribution to the war effort—it cost the federal government 1.6 million dollars to establish and hold military posts encircling the Ochoco. Add to this the Bannock outbreak of 1878 and the total costs to defeat the Snakes is in excess of 2.2 million dollars. By contrast, the combined total of the Modoc and Nez Perce wars comes to 1.3 million dollars.[13]

The number of Shoshoni killed will never be known nor that of American civilians, but the army would estimate that nearly 2,000 whites died from Shoshoni-inflicted wounds. For all its fanfare, the Modoc War would claim 63 white casualties and the Nez Perce War would claim only 123.[14]

Those who escaped the final round-up lived in the most remote reaches of the Ochoco—to be shot by ranchers like predatory animals.

---

11 Canfield, *Sarah Winnemucca*, p. 153.

12 Brimlow, *The Bannock War of 1878*, pp. 189-91.

13 Report of Quartermaster General, December 20, 1879, Senate Executive Document 15, Series 1941, 46th Congress, 3rd Session, p. 3. The actual cost of the Bannock War was $556,636.19.

14 Adjutant General Report, October 18, 1880, Senate Executive Document 15, Series 1941, 46th Congress, 3rd Session, p. 20. The known number of Shoshoni killed during the period of 1865-68 was 545. Another 78 were killed in 1878. This is all that the army will admit to. In 1872-73, 21 Modocs were killed and in 1877, the Nez Perce lost 151 tribesmen.

Their lands were now the unchallenged possession of the invaders. Whether the new occupants would prove to be better managers of the land's great bounty, and thus justify the agonies of the change, remained to be seen.

Bear in mind that the ranking chiefs of the Western Shoshoni Nation—with the exception of Paulina in a distressed state of mind—have never signed any treaty with the United States relinquishing their right to remain upon tribal lands. The Treaty of 1863 (known as the Treaty of Peace and Friendship) is, in reality, a consolidation of several treaties obtained by Lt. Col. Reuben Maury, First Oregon Cavalry. Accompanied by Gen. Patrick Conner, Third California Infantry and James Doty, Utah superintendent of Indian affairs, Maury swept across eastern Oregon, southern Idaho, northern Utah and northern Nevada, negotiating three separate treaties with the Western and Eastern Shoshoni signed by Man Lost (Pocatello), Gourd Rattler (Washakie), Stiff Finger (Taghee) and the Great Rogue (Le Grand Couquin)[15]. Then, on October 1, 1863 at a meeting in Ruby Valley, Nevada, these treaties were lumped into one document as the Treaty of Peace and Friendship signed by Fish Man (Numaga), a minor Paiute headman.

Nearly three years later on June 26, 1866, this treaty was amended and signed by the headsmen of three clans of Northwestern, Western and Goship Shoshoni as witnessed by Lt. Col. J.B. Moore, Third Infantry California Volunteers; Jacob T. Lockhart, Indian agent Nevada Territory; and Henry Butterfield, interpreter. The Ruby Valley Treaty of 1863 was again revised on June 17, 1869. This amended agreement was ratified by Congress on October 21, 1869. The men who signed these various documents were considered traitors by the leaders of the Paviotso Confederacy. Even so, the Western Shoshoni have never broken the 1863 treaty while on the other side of it, it seems as though the United States is constantly searching for some excuse to breech the contract.

The questionable treaty entered into at Fort Klamath, Oregon on October 14, 1864 was—at best—an agreement between the United States and the Klamath/Modoc tribes; and at the worst, was a fraudulent signing by two men incorrectly identified as Yahuskin Snakes (who most likely

15 See *Thunder Over the Ochoco,* Vol. III, pp. 143-144.

were visiting Washoes)[16]. There is no Shoshoni tribe or clan named Yahuskin, which in the Shoshoni language means "a person with a large stomach."

The 1865 Treaty also concluded at Fort Klamath with the Wall-pah-pe (Walpapi) tribe of Snake Indians signed by Paulina—who had no intention of honoring this piece of paper which he did not understand—and marked with an X by a motley crew of Snake warriors (Paulina's bodyguards) was a meaningless document to the Western Shoshoni. For the treaty to have been valid in their minds, the 1865 Treaty would have had to been signed by Wolf Dog, Has No Horse, and Big Man. It wasn't.[17] It would not have made any difference if they had signed as the 1865 treaty was still a shady transaction.

As the Civil War was grinding to a bloody end, J.W. Perit Huntington—a minor federal bureaucrat—was exiled to Oregon and placed in charge of Indian Affairs. In Washington D.C. he was known as a drunkard who conducted business in an unprofessional manner. It seems that Huntington was dedicated to obtaining fraudulent treaties. Shortly after Paulina signed the 1865 Klamath treaty on August 12, Huntington rode into the Warm Springs Agency. Here, he rounded up 21 Indians and had them sign the Warm Springs document on November 15, 1865. . . a treaty which is still stirring up trouble between the Confederated Tribes of Warm Springs, the United States Congress and the state of Oregon some 130 years later.

At the end of the 20th century the Western Shoshoni still have no reservation set apart for their exclusive use either by treaty or by executive order and they receive no government annuities.[18] The only concession made by the United States—and it amounts to nothing—is contained in Article VII of the amended Ruby Valley Treaty of 1866 and ratified by Congress on October 21, 1869. On that date and for the next 20 years the government would provide the Western Shoshoni with such articles as the president of the United States deemed suitable for their wants and conditions to sustain life "as full compensation and equivalent for the

16 For more on the 1864 Treaty see *Thunder Over the Ochoco,* Vol. III, pp. 241-243.

17 Signers of the 1865 Treaty were the ten warriors who accompanied Paulina to Fort Klamath to free his wife from imprisonment. For a list, and more on the treaty of 1865, see *Thunder Over the Ochoco*, Vol. III, pp. 283, 341, 450.

18 Jackson, *A Century of Dishonor*, pp. 437-438, 444, 447-448.

loss of game and the rights and privileges hereby conceded." If it wasn't so pathetic this endowment granted by the richest nation in the world would be laughable.

The Nevada lands where the Western Shoshoni now attempt to eke out a living are considered to be the most contaminated on earth from atomic experiments. From 1957 to 1992, the United States has detonated 934 nuclear explosions on property claimed by the Western Shoshoni Nation.

Based on the interpretation of the 1860s treaties and the devastating outcome of the Bannock War, the reign of the Saydocarah war lords had come to an end. . . but the rain of tears had just begun.

CHAPTER 171

DEATH MARCH

> *What! In this cold winter and in all this snow? Why they will die! My people will never believe me again.*
>
> **Sarah Winnemucca**
> Fort Harney, December 1878

In October orders arrived from army headquarters that all Paiutes were to be gathered at Fort Harney, presumably so they could be returned to the Malheur Agency for the winter. Sarah, accompanied by a company of cavalry, was directed to bring them in. It is doubtful that she would have worked so hard rounding up the stragglers if she had known what her "kind soldier fathers" were planning.[1]

Once assembled, Capt. Cochran (fort commander) told Sarah the Paiutes, along with the Snake hostiles, would be taken to the Yakima Agency in Washington Territory. He also ordered her to keep quiet about the transfer until a few days before departure.[2] Jim Blakely—who had just delivered 450 yearlings to Fort McDermit—rode into Fort Harney in the wake of a blizzard. He would note that "the soldiers had all the Indians rounded up there. It was a great sight—a quarter-mile of Indian camps."[3] In mid-December the mandate arrived for immediate delivery of the prisoners to Rev. James Wilbur, Indian agent at Fort Simcoe, Washington Territory. Ironically, the transfer was to be carried out by an officer of the 1st U.S. Cavalry named Capt. William Winters.

Sarah was stunned. She had been led to believe the action would take place the following spring. By now it was frigid cold with four-foot

1 Hopkins, *Life Among the Piutes*, p. 200.

2 Ibid., p. 203-05.

3 *The Sunday Oregonian*, March 12, 1939.

snow drifts blanketing the Fort Harney stockade. Agent Rinehart, aware of the army's orders, refused to issue blankets or even clothing to the half-naked prisoners.[4] In a fit of anger, Sarah shouted, "No human being would do such a thing as send people across the fearful ice clad mountains in mid-winter!" She was mistaken.

The eastern Oregonians were jubilant at the prospect and a festive Prineville filled with the Christmas spirit laughed when the report came in that Sally Winnemucca—in a voice brimming with passion as her belief in human equality was shattered by reality—accused the whites of taking "all the natives of the earth into your bosom but the poor Indian who is born of the soil of your land and you say he must be exterminated!" A year later this impassioned comment would appear in print when Sarah addressed a crowd of San Francisco's elite in her final lecture on the genocide of the eastern Oregon Shoshoni.[5]

A later philosopher would observe (and rightly so) that "human beings are not equal, least of all in the eyes of God. If Judas Iscariot is equal to John the Baptizer, Christianity can close shop." He would also note that Jefferson's remark that we are "created equal" is, unfortunately, "the words of a slave-owner who merely wanted to point out that our British brethren are not superior to Americans and have no right to rule over them."[6] The same could apply to the American brethren having no right to rule over the Shoshoni, but that was a mute issue in the winter of 1878-79.

Then, in a fitting tribute to the holiday season, thirty prisoners of war led by the desperate Has No Horse escaped from Fort Harney in a blinding snow storm. . . on the night of December 25, 1878. In a frenzy of confusion, two cavalry companies took pursuit and managed to capture all but the illusive war chief and his son Red Willow.[7] Sarah and

4 Letters of Capt. M.A. Cochran, dated November 18 and December 6, 1878, Annual Report of Commissioner of Indian Affairs 1879, p. 129.

5 *Daily Alta California*, December 4, 1879, p. 1, col. 3.

6 Erik von Kuehnelt-Leddihn, "Utopia and Ideologies," *Chronicles* Vol. 12, No. 12, December 1988, p. 21.

7 *Daily Silver State*, Winnemucca, Nevada, January 2, 1879. Has No Horse and Red Willow were to be imprisoned at Fort Omaha, Nebraska.

Mattie (who accompanied the cavalry) were after five women who also escaped, one of whom was Has No Horse's second wife Bessie.[8]

Apparently, Butterfly also escaped. A few years after the Fort Simcoe death march—a trauma she could not have survived in her weakened condition—Butterfly returned to Long Creek Valley with some Shoshoni hunters. She stayed at the Blackwell ranch while the men and younger women continued on looking for big game. Upon hearing gunfire and thinking it was the Indians on the rampage again, Mary Blackwell with her children and Butterfly hid in the thick willows along the middle fork of the John Day River. Wallace Blackwell, then a small boy, would remember the gamestalkers sudden misfortune. "After the war, the Indians would come back to hunt elk in the mountains above Long Creek. A group of white men, whose identities were not known then nor later, decided to wreak vengeance on the Indians for past wrongs. So [they] went up into the mountains and killed the entire hunting party.[9]

During the pursuit of the woman escapees at Fort Harney, Mattie's horse slipped on the ice and fell on her, causing massive internal injuries. Unconscious and bleeding from the mouth, Sarah tried to keep her warm as help was summoned from the fort. When the post surgeon arrived, he did little to help Mattie.[10] On January 6, 1879, Mattie Shenkah—in agony—was carried out to a four-horse wagon and the journey to Fort Simcoe (350 miles to the north) began.[11]

Tom Morgan would give a graphic account of the Shoshoni women and children's pathetic attempt to avoid imprisonment. It is best told in his own words:

> A friend of mine was there [Fort Harney] at the time and told me what he saw there in getting all the Indians started

---

8 The name Bessie is a corruption of two Shoshoni words, doezeeaup and ibidsii. Bessie's given name was Flower Blossom (Doezeeaup) but many tribesmen would call her "mother" (Ibidsii) because she was now the step-mother of Has No Horse's two living children. . . Red Willow and Mourning Dove.

9 Information given by Wallace Blackwell to Mabel Wilson Binns contained in a letter from Bob Black to the author dated November 21, 1997, Baker City, Oregon. Mabel Binns is Black's great aunt. Norma May Smith is his mother-in-law. Bob Black and Tom Black are brothers.

10 Hopkins, *Life Among the Piutes*, pp. 206-07.

11 W.V. Rinehart, unpublished manuscript, Bancroft Library.

> on the long, heartbreaking trip. The bucks were all herded off to one side by the soldiers and held there [at gun point]. The large government wagons were lined up. They had high top covers with doors in the rear ends. The squaws were ordered to get in, this they refused to do. The soldiers grabbed them, dragged them to the wagons and threw them in while others held the doors open. The poor creatures fought like wildcats, kicked, scratched and screamed. The children were loaded after the others were quieted. I have never heard how they got through that trip. It was getting late in the season, some had about 1500 miles to their destination [the dangerous war criminals who were being taken to Indian territory in Oklahoma] and it must have been terrible. Strange as it may seem, the next year several bucks [Has No Horse, Bloody Antler, Red Willow, Wolf Jaws and Tobacco Root] showed up in hiding in the Blue Mountains. The stockmen secretly killed them wherever found.
>
> After some years when so many had died down there [Fort Simcoe] the Indian Department brought back about five hundred and placed them out on Cottonwood Creek a few miles from Burns, Oregon. There they can be seen today—a pitiful wreck of a once proud and independent people.[12]

Guarded by 160 cavalrymen, fifty more wagons loaded with refugees would complete the column while the warriors—shackled two-by-two in leg irons with a steel ball in the middle—would trudge the entire distance across the snow whipped desolation of two mountain ranges.[13] At The Dalles, the captives were ferried across the frigid

12 Morgan, *The Last Indian War in the Northwest,* p. 11.

13 These leg irons were hand-forged by W.W. Johnson, the Malheur Agency blacksmith. W.W. (Broady) Johnson, later a U.S. deputy marshall, should not be confused with W.J. (Jake) Johnson, first deputy sheriff of Harney County. Both men had brothers named Frank. Broady's brother Frank Johnson was a schoolteacher at the Malheur Agency. Jake's brother Frank Johnson married Jennie McPheeters in 1898. Jennie was the daughter of Burns pioneer physician, Dr. Samuel B. McPheeters. Jake and Frank Johnson were the sons of Ewen Johnson, one of the first settlers in what is now Crook County, Oregon. Jake Johnson is buried in the Mill Creek Cemetery some eight miles east of Prineville and Frank and Jennie McPheeters

Columbia to be imprisoned on the land of their centuries-old enemies, the Yakima Indian Reservation. This trip alone would cost the government $50,000.[14]

The prison wagons were held up for two days at Canyon City where a telegram awaited Capt. Winters, ordering him to bring in Leggins and his followers who had been promised amnesty due to Leggins identification of the ranking war chiefs.[15] During this halt, a blizzard raging across the Columbia plateau caught up with the outcasts. As they struggled northward, women died in childbirth, infants died from starvation, oldsters died of pneumonia, men died of gangrene from wounds suffered in battle—they died in anguish racked with pain.[16]

Twenty-five days out of Fort Harney, the exiles arrived at the Yakima Agency on January 31, 1879. Eighty-seven would die along the way. Out of the 630 who had started the death march only 543—in starving condition—would arrive at the Yakima Agency in snow waist-deep where they were housed in a 150-foot-long shed without heat.[17] Without food, all hope died. As they slowly starved to death, Agent Rinehart complained that 65,000 pounds of beef and flour lay unused at the Malheur Agency.[18]

At The Dalles, Left Hand under heavy guard was taken straight to Fort Vancouver where he stood trial as a dangerous war criminal. On the witness stand, he shouted in rage, "Do what you will with my body

---

Johnson are buried in Juniper Haven Cemetery, Prineville, Oregon. (Brimlow, *Harney County and Its Range Land,* pp. 99, 160, 192; *The 1981 History of Crook County,* Oregon, p. 154; *The 1994 History of Crook County, Oregon,* p. 141.)

14 James Wilbur to Commissioner of Indian Affairs, July 21, 1879. Letters Received, Office of Indian Affairs, Oregon Superintendency, Special file No. 268, Bureau of Indian Affairs.

15 Hopkins, *Life Among the Piutes*, p. 207.

16 Among the casualties was Left Hand's first wife, Spotted Kitten (Phtoksie) leaving her infant son motherless. He too ended up on the Warm Springs Reservation and was named Calvin Johnson. Apparently Left Hand never talked to him as Calvin was only vaguely aware that he had an older sister who was killed by the Warm Springs Scouts in 1867, and knew nothing about his brother-in-law who died as a Snake dog soldier in the 1878 Bannock War. (Deposition given by Calvin Johnson to Stuart H. Elliott, examiner of inheritance at Warm Springs Agency, April 16, 1915.) At the time of the interview, Calvin Johnson was 37 years old.

17 James H. Wilbur to Commissioner of Indian Affairs, February 6, 1879, Letters Received, Office of Indian Affairs, Oregon Superintendency.

18 W.V. Rinehart to Commissioner of Indian Affairs, March 3, 1879, Special File No. 268, Bureau of Indian Affairs.

because I will return and show you a much greater battle. More white blood will be spilled!" After three years in solitary confinement, Left Hand had a change of heart. When he was released from prison in 1882, he vowed never to return to the Ochoco where Shoshoni blood had gushed like water down a dry wash after a summer's storm. And he never did. Left Hand was sentenced to life on the Warm Springs Reservation, which to him was worse than death.[19]

During Left Hand's one-sided trial, the Shoshoni sentenced to the Yakima Reservation were facing equally grim odds. Although doggedly clinging to life, Mattie's condition was deteriorating daily. Dr. Kuykendall, the agency medical officer, operating on the theory of "give 'em something good to eat before they die" prescribed a little sugar, rice and tea to soothe her wounds. After five months of suffering, Mattie Shenkah—the angel of mercy to Broken Knife and Big Man—died May 29, 1879.[20] She was only 19 years old.

Eight days before Mattie gave up her spirit, The Dalles City, gateway into eastern Oregon and the original breech of the Ochoco, felt the wrath of God. On May 21, at 2:00 p.m. a raging inferno exploded between the Pioneer and Kiss hotels. Pushed by vagrant winds in all directions, entire blocks melted away before the onrushing flames. Property damage would exceed one-half million dollars. Victory over Shoshoni land was not coming cheap.

In April it was reported that Has No Horse, in final defeat and starving, would abandon his Ochoco retreat and return to the Malheur Reservation. This was a government ruse intended to lure Bad Face out of his Nevada hideout.[21] It didn't work as neither man showed up.

By now, the desperate bureaucrats were open to suggestion and willing to try any means to corral uncooperative Indians onto some

---

19 Oits, or Johnson as Left Hand was officially named, died at the Warm Springs Reservation on March 16, 1915 at the age of 84. He was survived by a half-brother born in 1849 called William Johnson and five children by three different wives, two of whom were sisters. The sisters—his second and third wives—were named Sallie (Yellow Flower) and Pukugie (Water Woman). (Approval of heirship, estate of Oits or Johnson, Warm Springs Agency, Oregon, dated May 26, 1915, signed E.B. Meritt, assistant commissioner of Indian affairs, Department of the Interior, Office of Indian Affairs.)

20 Hopkins, *Life Among the Piutes*, pp. 212-14.

21 W.V. Rinehart to Commissioner of Indian Affairs, May 12, 1879, Special File No. 268, Bureau of Indian Affairs.

holding reserve. Believing that the army was too lenient in its enforcement of reservation policy, another shake-up in the Indian service took place. In July 1879, Congress passed legislation that excluded the practice of appointing military personnel to manage the agencies. Indian welfare was turned over to churchmen of various religious faiths and, as Captain John Smith (agent at Warm Springs in 1879) caustically put it, "the agencies were shuffled among the church denominations like so many cards in a deck."[22] This realignment of supervision didn't correct the problem, it only served to create more difficulties with the reluctant Snakes.

Once the different orthodox denominations got involved in agency administration, bewilderment set in. Hell-bent on converting the Indians to Christianity, Methodists would preach one route to the road of redemption; Baptists another; and Roman Catholics yet another. Trapped in the limited environment of a reservation, boredom soon cooled the Indian's intellectual intensity, starved his remarkable physical qualities and fatally affected the code of morality which he undoubtedly possessed. In curbing his wilder passions, the civilizing process usually developed the meaner ones.

During the attempt to track down Has No Horse and Bad Face, Sarah had been shipped to Fort Vancouver to speak for the Snake war criminals. The *Idaho Enterprise* would complain that "Sally Winnemucca, the corpulent queen of the Paiutes has just been paid $75 per month as interpreter for the prisoners."[23] She would also conduct school for the children, teaching them English. Daily the prisoners were let out of the guard house to whitewash fences, make pathways, build and improve roads to put the entire fort in prime condition. Three escaped, swimming the broad Columbia and disappeared forever into the dark forests of Oregon. One of the escapees was Bloody Antler, son-in-law to Has No Horse.

Once again, The Cutter (Wovoka) lay in a trance in a hut in Mason Valley, Nevada where he was transported to the Spirit World and received

22 As told by the descendants of Captain Smith who settled in Crook County in the early 1900s. Captain Smith was a church-going man and he continued as agent at Warm Springs until he died in 1884. Some of his descendants settled in Sisters, Oregon and one, Percy Smith, was a jeweler in Prineville in the 1930s.

23 The *Idaho Enterprise*, September 11, 1879, Vol. 1, No. 15.

a divine revelation. The Indians would once more rule North America.[24] Now the Paiutes possessed two leaders who would draw national attention to the plight of the Indians. Sarah would travel the continent to affect a political change while The Cutter stayed in Mason Valley prophesying the rebirth of Indian supremacy and Indian leaders from as far east as the Dakotas would come to hear him speak. And in 1884, the Yakima-held Shoshoni would be promised 160 acres of land in return for the reservation they had lost. Many walked back to central Oregon—but none received any land.

24 James Mooney, *The Ghost Dance Religion and the Sioux Outbreak of 1890*, p. 3.

CHAPTER 172

PEACE MISSION

Once nature gave him everything he wanted, now the agent gives him bib overalls, hooks his hands around plow handles and tells him its a good thing—push it along. Maybe it is but they're having a hell of a time proving it.

Charles Marion Russell
Western Artist

While the survivors of the Oregon death march starved in a communal shed on the Yakima Reservation, Oregon (whose population had nearly doubled since 1870) observed its 20th birthday at the banquet tables. With the Snakes defeated more important matters would occupy the minds of the victors. As the rest of the world speculated on the success of the Panama Canal Company organized under Ferdinand de Lesseps and the birth of Albert Einstein went unnoticed in Germany (people were more interested in the first electric street car exhibited at the Berlin Trace Exhibition), the main topic of conversation in the cow towns and mining camps of eastern Oregon was the arrival of the double-action Colt. Before the summer had passed, they would fervently wish that they had one.

Advertised as the "Peacemaker," it could be acquired for $15 to $20 and for the fancy price of $45 you could get an engraved pearl-handled model. Gunmen were further intrigued when Ned Buntline (his real name was Edward Zane Carroll Judson) ordered five special Peacemakers with 12-inch barrels and detachable stocks to give to five well-known frontier lawmen—Charlie Basset, Bat Masterson, Bill Tilghman, Neal Brown and Wyatt Earp. Buntline had sacrificed speed for accuracy, but Earp claimed he could draw the long-barreled Buntline Special as fast as he could the gun of standard length and in his duties as town marshall often pistol-whipped a desperado into submission with this weapon.

Despite this new innovation, tranquillity on the eastern Oregon front was to be temporarily side-tracked. In the spring of 1879, a handful of Snake dog soldiers under the command of Black Eagle and the medicine chief Black Spirit, swooped in on a mining camp on the Oregon-Idaho border, killing a number of Chinese laborers. While Gen. Howard issued the necessary orders from Fort Vancouver to set the military forces into motion, the Sheep Killer Snakes continued their reign of terror on other mining camps and isolated ranches—killing and burning as they went. Although hard-hitting veterans such as Captain Bernard and Col. Aaron Parker had been dispatched, Howard in desperation was organizing a commando unit to round up the escaped refugees.

For this unique assignment he chose 2nd Lt. Edward S. Farrow of the 21st Infantry, a young officer just out of West Point. His orders were to enlist a company of Indian scouts and add to that a detachment of expert army riflemen to be selected for their endurance. Further, the commandos were to operate independent of the regular army command.[1]

Howard was not disappointed in his choice of a leader. Lt. Farrow, enlisting 20 Umatilla scouts and seven army sharp-shooters, started his campaign with only 28 men counting himself. Attacking in six to eight feet of snow at elevations averaging a mile above sea level, Lt. Farrow fought the dog soldiers on their own terms and it was brutal. During this action, Farrow claimed to have found Big Man's fresh tracks in the snow. If he did, the old Snake warrior was wearing ghostly moccasins. While the main command floundered back and forth across the Snake River chasing shadows, the commandos knifed ever deeper into the Seven Devil Mountains. Black Eagle and Black Spirit—known to the Americans as Eagle Eye and War Jack—were engaged in a death struggle with a white pony soldier. It appears that Lt. Col. Forsyth's report that his troops had killed Black Eagle on July 31, 1878 was so much wishful thinking. Neither had they killed the Sheep Killer warrior known as Eagle Eye.[2] In late August on the South Fork of the Salmon River, Black

1 Glassley, *Pacific Northwest Indian Wars*, p 241.

2 The name Eagle Eye—shared by two different men—is another English translation of Black Eagle's name. This rendition of a Shoshoni word has caused its share of confusion when attempting to trace the two warriors through the murky corridors of historic documents. Both men were Mountain Shoshoni. The difference being that Black Eagle (Wahweveh or Kwahu) was an Oregon Walpapi (Mountain) Snake and Eagle Eye (Igrai or Kwahu) was an Idaho

Eagle—last of the "Paulina Boys"—joined his brothers, Wolf Dog and Paulina in the spirit world. Black Spirit was now in full command of the Sheep Killer insurrection. This final phase of the Snake rebellion, in the last Indian war in the Pacific Northwest, would creep into history as the Sheepeater War—another insult to the Shoshoni war tribes.

In an effort to help the beleaguered Snakes, the White River Utes under command of the war chiefs Douglas and Antelope, staged a violent outbreak in September 1879. Among those killed was Indian Agent Nathan Cook Meeker, considered by some to be "one of the best and most honest men ever assigned to the Indian Service." During this fracas, Ouray (The Arrow), serving as a peace commissioner, lived in constant fear that he would be assassinated by one of his own tribesmen. Gen. Crook immediately dispatched Major Thomas Thornburgh with three troops of cavalry and one of infantry from Fort Fred Steele, Wyoming Territory to quell this disturbance at its birth. On September 29, this column was ambushed and Major Thornburgh was killed. Col. Wesley Merritt—covering 170 miles in 48 hours—scattered the Utes into the mountains.[3]

Back on the Oregon-Idaho front, the supporting cast in a 20-year war drama was facing its final curtain call. Hounded into the ground by Lt. Farrow's guerrilla tactics, the Sheep Killer dog soldiers were losing heart. Short on arms, ammunition, food and horses, they could fight no more. But in taking their last bow, Black Spirit and his battle weary troops brought down the house.

In stark contrast to Lt. Farrow's strategy of hit and run, Lt. Henry Catley of the 2nd Infantry and a battle-wise veteran of the eastern Oregon

---

Weiser (not a Shoshoni name) Mountain Snake. More correctly they were Seewookie Snakes, a Shoshoni term for people who lived in a mountainous and forested area. The Oregon Walpapi were a minor offshoot of the powerful Hunipui (Bear Killer) Snake war tribe. The Idaho Weiser were an offshoot of the equally powerful Tukapui (Sheep Killer) Snake war tribe consistently called Tukaricka or Sheep Eaters by the white men. Eagle Eye and his followers could not avoid Central Oregon's Shoshoni war that affected Idaho from 1864 to 1868 and was forced to seek refuge on the Malheur Reservation. Like Has No Horse, Eagle Eye refused to accept reservation life and after the "Sheep Eater" war, he successfully hid out in the area of the Seven Devil mountains where he died in 1896. His followers escaped detection until shortly after 1900. (Brimlow, "The Life of Sarah Winnemucca," *Oregon Historical Quarterly,* June 1952, p. 130; Corles, *The Wiser Indians,* pp. xii-xv, 6, 40.)

3 Monaghan, *The Book of the American West*, p. 246; Sprague, *Massacre, the Tragedy at White River*, pp. 289-97; Crook, *Autobiography*, p. 227.

campaign, chose to ignore the advice of his Indian scouts. In the Salmon River country Lt. Catley was ambushed, caught in a Shoshoni-set forest fire and under enemy guns attempted a disastrous retreat. For this escapade, he was court-martialed and found guilty of misbehavior in the presence of the enemy and sentenced to be dismissed from the service under less than favorable conditions. On recommendation of the Judge Advocate General, President Hayes intervened and set aside the sentence. Catley then resigned from the army in disgrace.[4]

At the close of the campaign, Farrow had a total of 80 men in his command counting army sharp-shooters, volunteer riflemen, Indian scouts, civilian guides and packers. Black Spirit—the last surviving war chief—surrendered on October 6, 1879 and was relieved of command by an army firing squad. Farrow would later claim that his elite corp captured 388 hostiles, the largest number of Indians captured at any time by United States troops.[5]

Perhaps Lt. Farrow overestimated his contribution to the punitive action. In 1879 three separate tactical units totaling 186 combat veterans under the overall command of Col. Reuben Bernard were sent into the mountains to apprehend an estimated 200 Shoshoni men, women and children. The official Army record states that they captured 51 prisoners—15 of whom the commanding officer classified as "warriors." Pursued for three months by the U.S. Cavalry, U.S. Mounted Infantry, enlisted Umatilla scouts and civilian volunteers, the armament of this formidable foe totaled four carbines, one breech-loading rifle, one double-barrel shotgun and two muzzle-loading rifles. This pathetic affair is committed to history under the arrogant title of the "Sheepeater War."

During this disruption in eastern Oregon's peace of mind, Sarah Winnemucca in a last ditch effort to stall off more bloodshed tried to solicit enough funds to gain passage to Washington, D.C. with her entourage consisting of brother Natchez, papa Bad Face and cousin Jerry

---

4 Glassley, *Pacific Northwest Indian Wars*, p 248. During the Shoshoni war, Henry Catley (a regular Army hospital steward holding the rank of 1st Sgt.) was with Lt. James Waymire on the first military push into the Ochoco. He also served as a hospital steward in Drake's command during the Crooked River offensive. (*Thunder Over the Ochoco*, Vol. III, pp. 151, 165, 173, 225.)

5 *The Evening Press*, Asbury, New Jersey, May 13, 1909, speech delivered by Major Edward S. Farrow, U.S. Army.

Long. Wiser heads thought that a more appropriate spokesperson (the highly respected, albeit belligerent, Snake warrior Has No Horse) should accompany them. In Sarah's opinion, this was unthinkable. Still trying to divorce her father from his Snake heritage and more important (in her eyes) from the bad influence of Has No Horse, she balked. Actually Sarah had little to worry about. A brace of Gatling guns couldn't have dislodged Has No Horse from his hideout in the Warner Mountains. When Long dropped out of the planed tour, a Snake non-entity called Captain Jim filled the vacant spot.[6]

A solution to the proposed journey turned up in an unexpected manner. The Department of Interior, smarting under this latest act of disobedience by its Snake foster children, sent special agent J.M. Haworth into the territory in an effort to persuade Has No Horse and Bad Face to gather the outcasts and take them back to the Malheur Reserve. Seeing the futility of this assignment, Haworth volunteered to pay railroad fare for Sarah and her hand-picked group to Washington, D.C. and also arranged for an audience with President Hayes. In return, Natchez assured Haworth that if they were treated fairly in the nation's capitol, on his return he would "go to Ochiho's at Bidwell and try to get him to be the first to go to the reservation."[7]

Throughout the course of these negotiations, Indian leaders from all over the West were riding boxcars into Nevada to confer with The Cutter and learn his secret for returning the land to Indian occupation. As Haworth wisely observed, it was a period of extreme tension for the white settlers.

Having set up an appointment with Secretary of the Interior Carl Schurz, Sarah and company boarded a Central Pacific train for

---

6 In the cease-fire agreement with the Snakes concluded and signed at the Fort Hall Indian Agency November 7, 1873, Captain Jim was the first to sign. (House Executive Document 129, Serial 1608, pp. 4-5, 43rd Congress, 1st Session.) Special peace commissioners were John P.C. Shanks; Henry W. Reed; and T.W. Bennett. To dignify his signature Captain Jim (now being called Jim Collins) was bally-hooed as the headman of "a large contingent of Shoshoni." It was also duly noted that when Buffalo Horn took to the war trail, Captain Jim chose the path of peace. Ironically, many Shoshoni thought that Has No Horse did accompany this peace mission. In a 1997 interview at Fort Bidwell, Jimmie Washoe (then 93 years old) said, "I remember Old Chief Ochiho and I think they [Sarah and company] also took him to Washington. I don't know when." They didn't.

7 *Daily Silver State*, Winnemucca, Nevada, December 30, 1979.

Washington on January 13, 1880, three months after Black Spirit's surrender to the army.[8] Unknown to Sarah, her peace mission would be scuttled before she ever arrived in the national capitol. Acting on the advice of concerned citizens in central and eastern Oregon, Agent Rinehart obtained and sent numerous affidavits to the commissioner of Indian affairs attesting to the fact that Sally Winnemucca was "a trouble-maker, a notorious liar and malicious schemer."[9] Three stockmen from the Burns area were equally unflattering. Two wrote that Sarah was untruthful and "generally regarded by those who know her as a common prostitute and thoroughly addicted to the habits of drunkenness and gambling." The other pillar of the community—perhaps from first-hand knowledge—stated that "Sarah could be bought for a bottle of whiskey."[10]

On arrival in Washington, Sarah was thoroughly disappointed in her efforts to gain a responsive ear. President Hayes spoke to her briefly—not in the Oval Office—but in a hallway. Secretary Schurz was less than sympathetic. However, on the promise that Sarah would make no attempt to lecture to a Washington audience, he promised the Snake and Paiute refugees would be returned to the Malheur Reserve without further punishment. Sarah honored her end of the bargain.

The only one impressed with the Washington reception was Bad Face. After seeing Washington D.C., Bad Face came to the conclusion that the white man was like the sun, whereas the Indian was no more than a campfire. Upon his return from the nation's capital, he immediately visited Has No Horse and piled sand into two mounds—one big, one small. "This white man. This Indian. No use to fight!" Has No Horse, suspecting that his old friend and battle companion had reached the age of senility, was of a different opinion. He was not going onto a reservation. With Has No Horse's refusal to take up residence on the Malheur, the reservation was abandoned forever.

---

8 *Daily Silver State*, Winnemucca, Nevada, January 4, 1880.

9 These affidavits signed by nine gentlemen of Canyon City, Oregon were sent to the Honorable T.H. Brents, January 14, 1880. Special File No. 268, Bureau of Indian Affairs.

10 W.V. Rinehart to the Honorable E.A. Hoyt, January 15, 1880 enclosing three affidavits by William Currey, Thomas O'Keefe and W.W. Johnson (all dated and sworn and subscribed to Rinehart, January 13, 1880.) Special File No. 268, Bureau of Indian Affairs.

Some of the Snake war prisoners were shipped to the tiny town of Mountain City, Nevada and placed on the Duck Valley Shoshoni Reservation. One hundred years later news headlines would announce to the world: "Reservation has nation's highest suicide rate." And so it did—twelve times the national average![11] This situation would not improve. Nine years after the self-destruction revelation, the national press would blare: "Corruption on reservation exposed by Senate probe." A Senate committee would find that Indian programs run by the federal government were "riddled with shocking corruption including contract fraud, illegal gambling, organized crime and sexual abuse of children."[12] Not a very high mark for the stewardship of the Interior Department.

Even Rinehart—haunted by guilt in the twilight of his life—would question his role in the mistreatment of the Shoshoni. Completely out of character for him, Rinehart would meditate, ". . . after all, savages as they were, who can have the heart to blame them for fighting for their homes and the lives of their people? . . . I cannot say I know them . . . although they joined the Bannocks in 1878 and were nearly all exterminated, they left our handful of whites unmolested at the Agency. They went against General Howard's troops when they might have slain us and taken all the government stores. Despite their savagery in war, there is a deep tinge of pathos pervading the history and decline of the Indian race."[13]

And so by 1880, the Ochoco was finally free of Indian depredation but her favorite son, the notorious Has No Horse, was still roaming the mountains—fair game for any white hunter crafty enough to frame him in his gun-sights.

In September 1882 President Arthur restored to the public domain all of the Malheur Indian Reservation, making it open to entry except for 320 acres of the Fort Harney military reserve. This paved the way for the politically powerful Pacific Livestock Company (controlled by Miller and Lux) to acquire thousands of acres of former Shoshoni lands while squatters claimed the remainder. Less than seven years later, on

---

11 *The Bulletin*, Bend, Oregon, December 19, 1979.

12 Senator Dennis De Comcini, Chairman of the Senate Select Committee on Indian Affairs, *The Bulletin*, Bend, Oregon, January 30, 1989.

13 W.V. Rinehart, "War in the Great Northwest," *Washington Historical Quarterly*, April 1931, p. 97.

March 2, 1889, President Cleveland—in his last official act before Benjamin Harrison seized the reins of command—restored the remaining 320 acres of military reserve to the public domain. The seeds of greed planted during the Shoshoni storm would now take root.

INTERMISSION

The following seven chapters contain vital information on the final destruction of the Shoshoni Ochoco and must, by necessity, drift out of sequence as to when these events actually took place. This will serve to warn you that there are rough times ahead. It may be dry reading for some perhaps, but it is a necessary evil to set the stage for what is about to transpire in the evolution of the Ochoco from a primitive society to a citadel of greed which in some respects continues to the present day. To set the mood for the coming production, we must go backstage and open the trunk of economic growth in central Oregon which may not appeal to some readers. However, if you wish to follow the program, the actual performance will be meaningless without this background material. So relax and enjoy. If for no other reason it will give the actors an opportunity to rehearse their lines and they will certainly need it. As Alan Keyes (assistant secretary of state in the Reagan administration) once commented: "If we are a people who can no longer tell right from wrong, who can no longer stand for justice, then we will be a people no longer capable of governing ourselves." And that statement could apply to the new landlords of the Ochoco. With that in mind, don't wander too far away as the scenery is being moved into place for the opening curtain of a drama steeped in intrigue, covert dealings . . . and death. But that is yet to come in Volume V of *Thunder Over the Ochoco.*

The Shoshoni, now drenched in a rain of tears, continue their struggle to avoid oblivion. In so doing, they will witness absolute domination by the new landlords.

CHAPTER 173

LET'S BUILD TOWNS

Everywhere busy workmen were plying ax, hammer and saw; and the voice of the artisan was heard in the land.

Albert Richardson
Reporter for the *Boston Journal*

Title to the Ochoco had been bought with Shoshoni lives, not to mention a few gallons of Anglo-Saxon blood. Now the new occupants would cleanse the land with economic growth. Industry would transform this heathen outpost into a new garden of Eden. The current landlords never doubted for a moment that they would be more competent in the development of resources than their backward predecessors. Henry Villard—*New York Tribune* reporter and economic leader of Oregon in the 1870's and 80's— would note that everybody was making money. One busy merchant hung on the door of his establishment a sign saying, "Gone to bury my wife—back in half an hour." And thus it went. Speaking for Has No Horse and all Indians in 1904, the Sioux chief Red Cloud would note: "The white men made us many promises but they never kept but one. . . they promised to take our land, and they took it."

Now that the war games were over, the settlers took a brief time-out to assess their ill-gotten gains. If vitality had slowed to a stand-still in eastern Oregon, the rest of the world was clipping along at a lively pace.

In 1880, Sarah Winnemucca and her court were still en route to Washington, D.C. when the Gilbert and Sullivan's comic opera, "The Pirates of Penzance," opened to standing applause in London's Savoy Theater. New York City was boasting its new Edison electric street lights and Gen. Lew Wallace—his epic biblical novel, *Ben Hur*, winning international acclaim—was basking in glory. Just a few months earlier life had not been so rewarding. With little warning, President Hayes had appointed Wallace governor of New Mexico and shipped him west to settle lawlessness in the Lincoln County range war. As if that wasn't enough to take his mind off fiction writing, Gov. Wallace was further jarred back to reality when his first official visitor, gun in hand, was the notorious Billy the Kid.[1] But the biggest highlight of 1880, insofar as Oregon was concerned, was the arrival of the first president of the United States to set foot on Oregon soil. Grant, being a lowly captain in the army at the time of his Oregon tenure, didn't seem to count.

Perhaps President Hayes' curiosity was piqued and he wanted to witness firsthand Sarah's accusation that Oregonians were inhospitable. Whatever, in September the presidential coach thundered out of California and plowed to a halt at the Jacksonville Hotel in southwest Oregon. Traveling with the president was his wife, a cheerful woman in her late forties known throughout the land as "Lemonade Lucy," because she refused to serve alcoholic beverages in the White House.[2] This title held little appeal to Oregon's upper-crust who privately claimed that her son, young Webb Hayes, slept on a pool table in the west wing sitting room of the White House and they actually believed that.

All was pomp and circumstances as the president and first lady stepped graciously down and entered the hotel lobby. The night was serene but come next morning, it was a furious President who faced a high-spirited frontier lady in one of the lesser known showdowns of the Old West.

Madame Holt, French proprietress of the Jacksonville Hotel, had just presented President Hayes with a bill in the amount of $300. Gold miners lining the dusty street looked on with obvious relish as a flushed Hayes spluttered, "Madame, I did not wish to buy the place!"

---

1 This meeting took place in Santa Fe on March 17, 1879. It was guessed (but never proven) that Wallace promised amnesty if the Kid would surrender and stand trial for the various killings he was accused of committing. Whatever promises were made, if any, Billy the Kid did surrender to the law four days after his encounter with Gov. Wallace. Of all the aliases Billy the Kid assumed, including Kid Antrim, William H. Bonney was the one which stuck with him. His real name was Patrick Henry McCarty. (Book of Marriages, William H. Antrim to Catherine McCarty (Billy's mother). Santa Fe, New Mexico, March 1, 1873; McLoughlin, *An Encyclopedia of the Old West,* pp. 17-18, 55, 338; Wayne Gard, "The Law and the American West," *The Book of the American West*, p. 282.)

2 Margaret Brown Klapthor, *The First Ladies*, p. 46.

Pay he did, however, and as one wit observed, "It was probably a good thing that no army under Hayes ever faced a French woman of the calibre of this daring creature for the army would surely have lost the battle."[3]

The best the President could do was to climb sullenly into his coach and leave the southern Oregon mining town which had greeted him royally without saying good-bye. Maybe Sally Winnemucca was more truthful than originally thought.

Other things besides presidential ire were growing in Oregon. By the 1880's, Prineville boasted a stable population of 300 which supported three general stores, a drug store, a planing mill, a grist mill, three livery stables, a millinery and dress shop, two newspaper offices, a general land office, a restaurant, three hotels, a brewery, five saloons soon to expand to nine, a stage station, an opera house, a bakery, a harness and saddle shop, a shoe shop, a bank, and a Japanese novelty shop. Actually, the shop was owned and operated by a Chinese gentleman. Obviously it was more civilized to call it a Japanese shop.

In 1880, with new construction going on daily, Prineville was "the treasure house of a vast pastoral empire" as one enthusiastic promoter would put it. And, if the Ochoco cattlemen had anything to do about it, they were going to push meat-packing from the ninth place it presently held in Oregon's industries to the number one slot. At this time over 10,000 square miles of livestock country paid tribute to Prineville, the acknowledged hub of eastern Oregon. "As a trading center it stands alone and holds undisputed control of the largest region of country in the United States not traversed by a railroad," boasted another proud Prinevillite.

Within two years it was debatable as to whether Prineville was the garden spot of earth, or at least as a mecca for newcomers. As the deadly coils of vigilante gun smoke encircled the land, they told this story of a family who was preparing to leave the safety of the Willamette Valley and plunge into the high country beyond the Cascades. When their little girl was told that she was moving to the Ochoco country, she closed her night's prayers with, "Good-bye, God. We are going to Prineville." But prideful Prineville maintained she had actually said, "Good! By gawd we are going to Prineville!"

3 "Centennial Countdown 1880," *The Oregon Journal*, April 18, 1959.

In the 1880's killings in Prineville were something that went along with the times. . . an annoyance that one had to face, something like smallpox or the Shoshoni. Murder in this land of cattle, gold and pretty dance hall girls didn't create nearly as much displeasure as the theft of a first class saddle horse. The motto of the vigilantes was simple and to the point. "Give 'em a good honest trial, then hang 'em!"

Sixty-five miles to the southeast Prineville's sister city of Paulina was also boasting and trying its best to take away some of the glory from the "Queen of Oregon cow towns," as the townsmen called their fair city. Paulina's residents glumly referred to it as "The Bucket of Blood," a wicked city for women and youngsters to stay clear of.

Paulina was located in the center of some of the finest natural meadow land in the Pacific Northwest. Nestled under the protective shoulder of the southern Blues in Chief Paulina's old hunting grounds, it sat on the southwest edge of Beaver Creek Valley. . . a valley 20 miles long consisting of one great natural meadow. Said one satisfied Paulina resident, "The day is not far distant when Beaver Valley is known for what it really is—the best dairying and stock farming country in the Indian empire. And not only is it a great dairy section but lately discovered in the foothills near the Grant County line ore-rich outcroppings of gold both base and free milling and also cinnabar."

Actually, gold had been discovered in the vicinity of what is now named Powell Mountain some 15 years earlier. At that time Powell Mountain was known as Gold Hill and often called Treasure Butte, indicating that rich deposits of gold were believed to be found in that area. During this period John Calbreath—a pony express rider for the Canyon City mining companies—was carrying gold shipments to The Dalles City and Sacramento, California. One day Calbreath, his saddlebags stuffed with gold dust and nuggets bound for Sacramento, galloped out of Canyon City by way of the Yreka Trail. When the pony express rider didn't show up at his scheduled relay station, a search was begun. Calbreath's body—minus the gold shipment—was found in Bear Creek Gulch, a tributary of Beaver Creek and there he was buried.[4] It was never known whether he was killed by Indians or road agents.

---

4 Testimony of Jess R. Calbreath descendant of John Calbreath, November 4, 1971. Calbreath's grave is located in T165, R. 25E., Sec. 3 (within sight of the present Forest Service road 1577)

Whatever, gold and quicksilver were not exactly the blessing needed for the then sedate Paulina. For gold and silver bring along some mighty rough customers as the local citizens were soon to find out.

On May 23, 1881, the Red Bluff Stage pulled out of Hardin Corral on the edge of Twelvemile Table and headed for Canyon City. It had a scheduled detour to swing north to Treasure Butte (now called Powell Mountain) and pick up a shipment of gold. The miners guarding the gold had gotten into a poker game, paying little attention as to what was going on around them. When the stage arrived, the miners were loading the strong box when three masked men appeared out of nowhere and politely relieved them of their burden. The miners took after them but soon gave that up when on the head of Jackass Creek, Dave Pollard took a rifle slug through the chest which lifted his spirit into heaven.

Blamed for this mishap was one Charles Fallon, better known as "Rattlesnake Jake."[5] The description of the leader as being over six feet tall, straight as a ramrod, unkempt brown hair, fit Fallon to a tee—as it did about fifty other gentlemen in the Paulina vicinity. The only thing the miners couldn't identify was Fallon's buck tooth because of the mask but undoubtedly this guy had one. Anyway, Sheriff Luckey was notified and Luckey dutifully stayed out of the Paulina area for a few weeks.[6]

A couple of years later Fallon ran afoul of the law again in Lewiston, Montana and on July 4, 1884, he and Edward Owens tried a shoot-out with the Montana Vigilantes. Fallon headed up the trail with twelve bullet holes in his carcass while Owens gave up on the ninth bullet. It was claimed that at least two of the slugs that tore through Fallon were made by a .50 calibre Sharps buffalo rifle. He was believed to have been around forty years of age at the time of death.

---

almost on the survey line between sections 3 and 10. The burial site is approximately 1 1/2 miles north of the old Yreka Trail and some three miles north of Gold Hill (Powell Mtn.). The grave site now consists of a headstone engraved "John Calbreath" and a narrow mound of stones with a small wooden pole corral around it constructed by John Arriaga in the summer of 1970.

5 Charles Fallon is sometimes confused with John Said who was known as "Rattlesnake Jack." Fallon's buck teeth were said to have been rather pointed, which may have led to the nickname of "Rattlesnake Jake." (McLoughlin, *An Encyclopedia of the Old West,* p. 160.) John Said, after serving a prison term for horse rustling in eastern Oregon, was gunned down in Weiser, Idaho in the early 1880s.

6 Sarah Hodges Luckey, wife of Deputy Sheriff John Luckey, September 7, 1956.

Seeing what kind of characters these were, maybe it was just as well Paulina hadn't enjoyed a gold strike. Over the divide at the twin cities of Canyon and "Tiger Town," as John Day was called, they could vouch for it. And Scissorsville could tell how a town based on gold could rise and fall in ten fleeting years.

Straddling the Ochoco River some 35 miles east of Prineville, the boomtown of Scissorsville was dying. . . at least insofar as its reputation was concerned. The placer claims were on the decline and with the high-graders and pocket hunters taking over, it was rumored that the "Golden Goddess" of the Ochoco was about to become a company town with its inherent social graces—not a pleasant outlook for saloon keepers, road agents, hurdy-gurdy girls or card sharks. In 1885, the Oregon Mayflower Company was formed consisting of six placer claims and eleven lode claims, causing Scissorsville to give way to the company town of Howard. All too soon, the clicking of poker chips, the tinkling of bordello pianos, and the clinking of whiskey glasses would be gone forever.

Thirty miles due east of the Golden Goddess, the sprawling shanty town of Spanish Gulch clung to the north slope of Spanish Peak. It was facing a more immediate death. The 1870 census would reveal that Spanish Gulch sported a hotel, saloon, Thornburg's general store, post office and 13 houses. The population of 30 was counted as twelve miners, six farmers, two horsepackers, one hotel keeper, one merchant, two Chinese, one Portuguese, one Norwegian sailor, one Swede (also a sailor) and three ladies. Quite impressive. However, by 1880 Spanish Gulch was deserted but strung around the hillsides, the census taker found, "Thirty-three adult males and thirteen wives in 18 households." So much for the budding metropolis of Spanish Gulch.

To give an idea of just how fleeting a gold rush could last, just one year earlier in 1879 the census lists 960 whites and 2,468 Chinese miners in the eastern Oregon gold fields. Besides miners, the census would also reveal that the Chinese population consisted of cooks, laundrymen, merchants, doctors, a shoemaker, one tailor and four prostitutes.

Then in 1895 a new gold rush was in progress. Chinese miners moved into Spanish Gulch operating under the Loy Yick Company and began hydraulic operations with a lease to develop a reservoir "situated in said Spanish Gulch up the canyon just south of the site of the old town of Spanish Gulch," thus providing further evidence of the town's existence.[7] This latest gold rush lasted about as long as a Chinese dinner.

Sandwiched between Scissorsville and Spanish Gulch, Mitchell took root on the south bank of Bridge Creek. It was no boomtown—like Harriet Beecher Stowe's Topsy, Mitchell had just grown since 1867 when Fred Sargent threw up a log cabin alongside The Dalles-Canyon City Military Road and proceeded to peddle his wares to the tourists. In some respects, it was not a pleasant location. Polk Butler on first seeing the country surrounding Mitchell exclaimed, "My gawd! This is Hell with the fire put out!" Others claimed it possessed an "artistic beauty" and one went so far as to state that the Mitchell countryside "presents a repulsive appearance." No doubt, the stage had been pursued by Indians that day.

Bill Cranston, who turned Sargent's stage station into a saloon, had to wait until 1875 before a store would add dignity to the saloon. This store was built by R.E. Edmandson who had found competition in Prineville just a little too tough.

By 1881, two general mercantile stores graced the banks of Bridge Creek, plus a blacksmith shop, one hotel, and steps were being taken to construct a grist mill on the eastern city limits. This was almost a necessity as it cost $10 a barrel to get flour from Prineville. In fact, things had been looking up when at 4:00 p.m., Friday, September 12, 1881, Ike Richards was awakened by the smell of smoke. He barely had time to alert his wife and another young lady who was sharing their sleeping quarters before the house was enveloped in flames. Richards lost an estimated $7,500 in property besides cash, notes and accounts amounting to $3,800.

Three years passed quietly then in 1884, the heavens opened and water poured down Bridge Creek, filling Main Street in front of Howard and Thompson's Mercantile Store. The flash-flood also carried away Fred Sargent's house, cut a deep gulch through the livery barn, carried away three wagons and proceeded to wipe out every homestead from Gable Creek to the John Day River.

The townsfolk were beginning to wonder if their fair city was cursed. Deep-thinkers were quick to note that the town's namesake, John Hipple Mitchell—one time Portland city attorney—was somewhat of a

7 Grant County Mining Records, Canyon City, Oregon.

scoundrel. When Mitchell became deeply involved in illegal land transactions his good friend Ethan A. Hitchcock (secretary of the Interior) would blandly state, "The land frauds only involved several hundred thousand acres."[8] No big deal.

Four times elected Oregon's U.S. senator, Mitchell was charged with financial dishonesty, bigamy, living under an assumed name (his original surname was Hipple) and wife desertion among other things. It was also noted that his conduct in the Senate was grossly mercenary and corrupt. He died December 8, 1905 while appealing a conviction for bribery.[9]

At the very least, the town of Mitchell's supposed curse was food for thought as calamities kept plaguing them. By 1893, Mitchell was again going full tilt. Now it sported Stella's Millinery and Dress Shop, a carpenter and cabinet shop, a flour mill, two general stores, a saloon, one drugstore, a shoe shop and a spanking-new city jail.[10] It also would concede that the town had three vacant buildings.

But this new growth wouldn't last long either. On March 25, 1896, a Wednesday afternoon, fire broke out in lower town. The inferno created so much heat that burning shingles raised in the convection column which could be seen in Prineville nearly 50 miles to the west, floated four miles up Bridge Creek, igniting additional fires. Two hours and twenty minutes later, Mitchell was in ashes. Among the buildings destroyed were two saloons and the new town hall.

On August 4, 1899 children touched off a blaze that caused $20,000 in property damage and seared half of the rebuilt town. Then, the weather spirits decided to take a different approach on the harassment of Mitchell.

On July 11, 1904, a cloudburst hit the head of Bridge Creek and passed over into Keyes Creek. This alone lessened the terrible destruction for the Bridge Creek wave struck first and was partly abated when the Keyes Creek torrent arrived. At 6:30 p.m. a distant roar was heard and townspeople ran for the hills. In an incredibly short time a wave of yellow

---

8 *The Pacific Monthly*, February 1904, p. 121.

9 Senator Mitchell's terms of office were 1873-79, 1885-91, 1891-1897, and 1901-05. Corning, *Dictionary of Oregon History*, pp. 167-68.

10 *Antelope Herald*, April 14, 1893.

water thirty feet high swept around the rocky point at the flour mill gouging out a channel, tearing buildings to pieces, grinding some to shreds, and throwing others into the air. Everything in the path of the raging waters was destroyed. Twenty-eight buildings with all contents were swept away. Agnes Bethune was carried away in her hotel along with Martin Smith who had just retired for the night. Like a chip, the hotel danced along on the crest of the wave for almost half a mile before being dashed into kindling, as a rider galloped ahead of the flood to warn people downstream.

Scantily clad, drenched to the skin in the driving rain, men, women and children gathered on the sullen hills to console each other. It was an overpowering scene as the very heavens blazed with blinding lightning and the thunder crashed. Some were terrorized at the destruction before them, others were given to joy that they had escaped death; all were silent. Had they looked more closely, they may have seen Shoshoni ghost-riders in the stormy Ochoco skies.

Strange things happened. Fragile items sometimes escaped undamaged; iron cogs were stripped from gears; metal polished as if by an emery wheel; and the sickness and disease was yet to come. When the sun rose next morning, Mitchell presented an awful sight. Men were ruined financially. Happy homes were gone never to return. Still, there was a strain of thankfulness that so few had perished.

Only a year before, their neighbors at Heppner had not been so fortunate. On June 14, 1903, a cloudburst originating in Willow Creek Valley descended as a wall of water on the small farming community, nearly destroying it. In a period of twenty minutes, following the collapse of a local dam, the flood waters poured through town and swept all life before it. Classed as one of Oregon's worst natural disasters, 225 people lost their lives.

But the siege wasn't over for Mitchell. On September 25, 1904 (76 days after the first onslaught) another flash-flood struck at 8:00 p.m. flowing down Nelson Street from a gulch south of town. Excitement ran high but no lives were lost and since there was little left to damage after the July flood, property loss was only $1,000.[11]

---

11 *The Illustrated History of Central Oregon*, 1905, pp. 652-53.

A half-century of tranquillity slipped by as Mitchellites convinced themselves that their hard luck days were buried in the past. Then came Friday, July 13, 1956. On a muggy afternoon a summer shower increased in tempo as Bridge Creek began to rumble. Within minutes all hell broke loose as a 50-foot wall of water wrenched the town from its moorings. The *Bend Bulletin* would say it all in screaming headlines: "Mitchell heavily damaged when cloudburst-swollen creek plunges through southern Wheeler County town on Friday."[12] A reporter for the *Oregonian* would describe the event in these words: "Big water came out of the skies, rolled off the hills and in one brutal blow smashed half the town to smithereens. . . . So crushing was the blow that it spewed pieces of what had been the business section [of town] more than five miles over the countryside."[13]

The business district was totally destroyed and 200 residents—out of a population of 400—were left homeless. Twisted wreckage of cars, logging trucks and farm equipment were strung out downstream for eighteen miles. Power poles were uprooted; telephone lines were down; and U.S. Highway 26 along with ten steel and concrete bridges were obliterated, leaving the town cut off from the outside world. Mitchell town marshall A.W. Helms, who had survived the earlier onslaught, shook his head in disbelief. "This was quicker, this was more cruel than the 1904 flood."[14]

Facing over one-half million dollars in property loss, the townspeople received little help from government agencies, causing extreme bitterness. Help would arrive from an unexpected source. Prineville rallied to their stricken rivals' cause sending in hundreds of boxes of groceries, first-aid supplies, blankets and clothing to feed and comfort the homeless. Harvey Lollor, a Mitchell timber faller, was overwhelmed. "I never expected it from those folks in Prineville but I got to take my hat off to 'em this day." And so went the fortunes of Mitchell.

North of Prineville where the Ochoco Mountains rubbed shoulders with the Columbia plateau, the town of Shaniko was growing like a weed. Located at the great freight terminal where the Prineville stage

---

12 *The Bulletin*, Bend, Oregon, July 14, 1956.

13 *The Oregonian*, Portland, Oregon, July 15, 1956.

14 *The Oregonian*, Portland, Oregon, July 15 and 16, 1956.

road wedded with The Dalles-Canyon City Military Road, it was soon hailed as one of the most wide-open towns in the West. . . a reputation that kept town marshall, Dell Howell, on his toes. It was named for the first stage-station operator, August Schernickau, except his first visitors (raiding Snake dog soldiers) couldn't pronounce such a name so they called him "Shan'i-ko," a name that stuck.

As one early supporter recalled, "The town expanded until there were two, four, six full blocks filled with hotels, saloons, stores, gambling houses, livery stables, freight warehouses, bawdy houses and land offices."[15] Shaniko became the largest wool shipping station in the world. Here, the huge freight wagons drawn by eight to ten horses rolled down the dusty streets twenty-four hours a day. A boomtown filled with thirsty freighters, miners and sheepherders, it too would become a ghost town only to be revived some 70 years into the future as a tourist attraction.

Between Shaniko and Prineville in a rock-walled canyon where the war chief Paulina was murdered, another frontier town was taking shape. Dating back to the early 1870's, Ashwood, nerve-center of the Trout Creek mining district, exploded with activity following the discovery of rich deposits of cinnabar, the parent ore of quicksilver. The Silver King mine would soon be praised as "the richest in mineral of any mine in the Pacific Northwest."[16] Leading the prospectors in search of new diggings was James Wood.

On the slopes dotted by ancient volcanoes—the most prominent being Ash Butte, which combined with Wood gave Ashwood its name—new strikes were being made daily. Among the more productive were Disappointment, Juniper Ledge, Morning Glory, Red Jacket, Ohio and Horse Heaven—which became the richest strike of all.

Virtually overnight, saloons appeared followed by livery stables and a fine hotel. Promoters would brag that "the location of the town is all that could be desired in the very heart of a mining district and in a beautiful level valley through which flows a mountain stream. . . . Ashwood is just the place that is destined to become one of the leading

15 Giles French, publisher of the *Sherman County Journal.*

16 *Ashwood Prospector*, Vol. 1, No. 1, March 30, 1901. Published by Max Luddermann who launched the *Antelope Herald*, *The Shaniko Star* and *The Bend Bulletin*, all of which were central Oregon newspapers.

towns of eastern Oregon." A population of "thousands of people" was forecast.[17] The prediction was overly optimistic, for Ashwood, like Scissorsville, would soon fade from memory.

And so it came to pass that the centers of population in central Oregon from 1870 to 1900 were: Prineville, perched in the heart of Oregon's cattle country, fast living up to its title as *The Bucket of Blood, U.S.A.*; staid and respectable Paulina, hanging on the edge of the southern Blues just a hop, skip and a jump from the Great Basin, soon to be known as *Outlaw's Roost*; Spanish Gulch, doggedly clinging to the windswept north slope of Spanish Peak and *The Mecca* for a Chinese mining company; Shaniko, *The Wildest Town in the West*, teetering on the brink of the Columbia plateau; Ashwood, *The Metropolis* that never came to pass, squatting on the grave of a Snake warrior; Mitchell, *Hell With the Fire Out*, hidden in the twisted, sun-baked corridors of the northern Ochoco Blues; Scissorsville, *The Golden Goddess*, bawdy tramp of a mining town gone tame, snuggled in the upper Ochoco Valley. . . and *Tiger Town* (soon to be known as John Day), that other eastern Oregon city polluting the John Day River.

There were other frontier settlements in central Oregon such as Meadow in Big Summit Prairie which boasted a school, a saloon, a general store and a tourist resort. Fife, a minute dot on the edge of Misery Flat near the present GI Ranch flaunted a general store which peddled hard liquor in a back room. And then there was Hay Creek—headquarters for the massive Hay Creek Land and Livestock Company. Clustered around the three-story headquarters building (lavishly furnished with beautiful mahogany and marble-topped tables) were a commissary, blacksmith shop, livery stable, bunkhouse and a fashionable hotel. This company town was threatening to take away all of Prineville's trade.

It could be said of these frontier towns that some grew, some vanished and some just stagnated. A quarter of a century would fade into the dust of time before Bend, Redmond and Madras made their belated debut on the central Oregon scene. These latecomers have shaped the destiny of central Oregon for better or for worse and they continue to do so. As one sagebrush philosopher would put it, "The fate of the world is entwined with the fate of its cities." Perhaps he was right.

---

17 *Ashwood Prospector*, March 30, 1901.

CHAPTER 174

SOME CALL 'EM RANGE MAGGOTS

After months of herdin' woollies you imagine lava rocks are lumps of gold; bitter alkali water is wine; arid sagebrush plains are covered with grass; and falling snow is butterflies of summer.

Roy Leonard
Ochoco Sheepherder

By 1870, just three years after settlement, the Ochoco country had 21,000 cattle, 18,000 sheep, 8,500 branded horses, 900 mules and God alone knew how many board feet of merchantable pine. This was the nucleus that one day would attain full stature as the Central Oregon Sheep and Cattle War.

In the beginning most of the stockmen doubled in at least two and sometimes all of these commodities but as the battle lines became drawn they soon made their choice and no one, no matter how hard he tried could remain neutral. All had something at stake and ultimately the war was to drag four factions into the fracas—the stockman with his droves of cattle, horses, and sheep trampling unrestricted over the public domain; the homesteader with his vow to break all rangeland to the plow; the timber baron with his unchallenged access to billions of board feet of virgin pine timber; and the United States government, a disinterested bystander who belatedly took up the thankless role of mediator and hopelessly bound the whole mess with the strangling ropes of bureaucracy.

Ewen Johnson, Elisha Barnes and William Marks are credited with bringing the first sheep into the Ochoco Valley in 1868—five hundred head in all. From this insignificant start, sheep had blossomed into big business by the 1880's. Big enough that men were amassing large fortunes and willing to die for the opportunity. But back in '68, sheep-raising wasn't so inviting. The original herd had grazed across the middle Ochoco Valley less than a year when they gained the doubtful honor of having acquired the first case of scabies in the settlement although at the time no one knew exactly what the poor critters had. Many guesses and related cures were tried as the sheep herd continued to deteriorate. Finally somebody came up with the inspired suggestion that the sheep were suffering with mange, although it was believed mange was a hog disease unique to the Willamette Valley. Nonetheless, Johnson and company religiously greased the stinking woollies with bacon rind (which was a rank waste of bacon as it didn't do a bit of good). The dejected sheepmen also deducted that whatever the condition was, it was a native of the Ochoco. The rims had it, the sagebrush had it, it was in the grass, on the rocks, in the air, even coyotes were totally naked because of it.

By the fall of '69, the JBM sheep were a sight to behold as were all other sheep in the community. The wool was hanging in patches exposing red-blotched skin. In desperation, they called on Dr. Vanderpool for advice. While sheep were somewhat out of his line, Doc promised he would give them a try. Meantime Left Hand, the Snake medicine man, drifted into Mill Creek on his annual trek to Spirit Caves. He came up with an immediate cure. . . "kill 'em!" By this time, the pioneer sheepmen were ready to go along with his suggestion. They might just as well have taken Left Hand's advice for by the time Dr. Vanderpool diagnosed the case all the wool was lost and most of the sheep. After this episode most of the sheepmen retired from the business in disgust but from this feeble beginning, the multi-million dollar sheep industry was born.

On November 5, 1874, Dr. David M. Baldwin of Oakland, California, after negotiations through LaFayette Tyrrill, purchased land on upper Hay Creek from William Allen as a start for a sheep ranch in the very backyard of Teal and Coleman's cattle empire. This transaction caused little excitement. Then twelve days later on a Thursday afternoon, Tyrrill filed on an adjoining tract with Dr. Baldwin acting as witness. Dave Baldwin immediately bought this tract and before he was through laid claim to Foley Creek and amassed 50,000 acres of land operating under the name of Hay Creek Company. Unknown to the cattlemen, while Baldwin was purchasing land, his great herds of pureblooded

Spanish merinos were already moving up the Sacramento Valley headed for the Ochoco. As a blind, 1,000 head of longhorns were preceding them and before it all ended, Baldwin was running 3,000 head of blooded shorthorns and 50,000 head of sheep.

Having brought in the first merinos, Baldwin spared no expense in laying the foundation for the biggest purebred sheep ranch on the north American continent. During this period, Hay Creek Company was importing pedigreed sheep from France by the thousands. Baldwin was also exporting blooded sheep to the rest of the world. On one occasion he shipped 10,000 sheep to Russia and a year later another 15,000 head. As late as 1931, Hay Creek sheep were being transported by boat through the Panama Canal to Italy. John Minto—commissioned by the secretary of agriculture to report on the western sheep industry—called Hay Creek Ranch the greatest merino breeding station in the world.

Of more importance to Prineville's businessmen, Baldwin's headquarters ranch just over the Grizzly divide was threatening a trade war with local merchants. This was not idle bluster. Baldwin put in a general store, blacksmith shop, livery stable, post office and hotel. With the addition of a saloon, Hay Creek Ranch soon became a bustling frontier town. And that wasn't all it became. It was soon known locally as a sanitarium for a bunch of nuts!

One of Baldwin's first business ventures was to set to work growing "Liggett's Weed" as the local citizens called the then little understood alfalfa. Lee Liggett had grown some on the South Fork of Crooked River a year earlier and killed half the cows in central Oregon. Why any sane man would deliberately try to cultivate a plant that was a proven killer of livestock was beyond them and it did little to make Dr. Baldwin a popular man with the other stockmen.

In 1882, Baldwin sold his interest in the Hay Creek Company to Cartwright and Van Houten who expanded the business and made a further success financially. During this exchange, Baldwin's sons went into the banking business in Prineville and with papa's backing, they had the where-with-all to do it.

Meanwhile Allen and LaFollette, with headquarters on Allen Creek, followed Baldwin's lead and in a short span of time were running pureblood merinos on a very large scale. To help block off the northern Ochoco, Henry Hahn and Leo Fried formed the Prineville Land and

Livestock Company in 1887 with headquarters on Muddy Creek and holdings stretching into Big Summit Prairie where they clashed with Merritt and O'Kelly's cattle spread. Famous as the "Muddy Company," Hahn & Fried ran sheep and as a side-line dabbled in cattle. These enterprising gentlemen were also connected with one of the largest businesses in Portland—the firm of Wadham & Company—which conducted one of the biggest wholesale grocery establishments in the Pacific Northwest. Coupled with this, Hahn & Fried opened a large mercantile firm in Prineville.

Sandwiched between these outfits was Thomas Hamilton, who came to the Ochoco in 1878. To keep up appearances (as did all the sheepmen in the area), he trail herded in 500 registered shorthorns and was a pioneer in the introduction of blooded cattle. But his big item was blooded rambouillets. From his Trout Creek ranch, Hamilton ranged deep into the Ochoco Mountains and pushed dangerously close to the cattle operations in the upper Ochoco and Paulina valleys.

On the south, the same conditions prevailed. The big sheep outfits such as William's California Company and Cosgriff Brothers were moving herds up from Nevada, California and southern Oregon to compete with local sheep outfits such as Roscoe Knox on Newsom Creek, who was bound in by the big cattle ranches.

Unfortunately, the men who would get hurt in the power struggle were not the owners but the ones who lived with the sheep; the men who loved the bleating critters enough to die for them. These were the herders and camp tenders. . . such men as John Knox, Henry McCoy, Jake Koch, Tom Prine and dozens more who felt the bite of the cowman's long rope before the game was called off for lack of players. And they certainly didn't sacrifice their life for love of money. A foreman of a sheep band might receive $50 a month and herders, if lucky, would get $40 and all the mutton they could eat. This, at a time when sheep bought for a dollar and a half in the Ochoco sold for three dollars at Laramie and the lambs were pure profit.

Many young men fresh out of Scotland, Ireland and the western Pyrenees of Spain and France came west to herd sheep. They battled cattlemen for range, fought for water and endured the harsh weather and rugged terrain of the Ochoco. It wasn't an easy or pleasant existence and many gave up. An old aspen tree at Hahn Spring (located in the upper

Ochoco Valley) bore this inscription carved by a herder in 1901: "It is better to be dead than to live thus."[1] When not dodging bullets, life on the range was monotonous. Some passed the time piling huge monuments of rock which can still be seen today;[2] others became master craftsmen with a pocket knife whittling intricate items out of wood; and a few like Roy Leonard expressed their lonely thoughts with pencil or pen.

By 1882, thousands of sheep were being trailed out of the Ochoco for the eastern market. On these drives, young John Knox would remark that he was "in the saddle every day for half a year." Trailing was the economical way to deliver livestock for they could feed on the way and the cost of a drive was but a few cents per head. The sheep were fed out in Nebraska where corn sold for 14¢ a hundred pounds and a pound of corn per day was all it took to fatten a sheep before shipping it on by rail to the Chicago market. In those days you could ride out of Prineville in any direction across eastern Oregon, Idaho and Nevada without striking a fence. This impediment didn't arrive until the homestead rush of the 1890's. One drawback to trail-herding was the scarcity of wood on the Great Plains. On his last trip east, John Knox paid 75¢—over half a day's

---

1 Many Basques from the Pyrenees of Spain and France came to America (they called it Amerikanuak) because only one son could inherit the family farm. The rest had to find their own way in the world. Sheepherders were needed in the American West and a network of family connections helped bring Basques to the High Desert of central Oregon. For most Basques herding sheep wasn't an occupation they enjoyed. Many worked the sheep just long enough to save up money and return home.

2 These works of boredom have served to confuse present government archaeologists to no end. Piles of crumbling rock having no more significance than the whim of the idle herder who made them, have been identified as the obscure efforts of native American craftsmen and dutifully protected for posterity—which, after all, is a commendable tribute to the unoccupied sheepherder. Unfortunately these meaningless mounds of rocks have successfully detracted, perhaps even obscured, important archaeological discoveries. Years ago I discovered a mound of stone that didn't fit the pattern of sheepherder monuments. Most noticeable, there were no other rocks in the immediate area. Neither did this marker bear much resemblance to a loafing herder's idle efforts. Unless he possessed the strength of an ox, no herder in his right mind would have attempted to move the rocks which formed the base of this cairn. Should he have been dumb enough to try, about all that would have been accomplished is a double hernia. In 1997, a Western Shoshoni told me that monuments of this dimension—requiring group effort—are authentic Shoshoni markings of the boundaries of clan hunting grounds and are placed in strategic locations such as mountain passes, well-traveled game trails and other vantage points spaced many miles apart.

wages—for three old railroad ties to use for kindling in starting buffalo chip camp fires.

Most of the herds were bound for the railhead at Omaha, Nebraska. One band alone in 1894 totaled 25,000 head and, had the drive been completed, it would have taken six months. As was, when the herd reached Idaho, news arrived of a devastating drought in Nebraska and the decision was made to hold the sheep in Idaho. All available grass hay, oats and wheat was bought up to feed the sheep. Shortly thereafter, Cosgriff Brothers (with only eleven herders) arrived in Idaho with three big bands totaling over 15,000 head and got caught in a blizzard. Unable to buy feed, they were forced to sell, nearly bankrupting the company.

In early 1902, 500,000 sheep were bought by an eastern outfit and trailed out of the Ochoco. They were the lucky ones. Before the year was over, the central Oregon range would reek with the rotting carcasses of slaughtered sheep.

CHAPTER 175

LONGHORNS, SHORTHORNS AND MUSTANGS

This was a pretty country you took away from us—now it is only good for red-ants, coyotes and cattlemen.

Quanah Parker
Comanche War Chief

In 1854 when young Sam Grant headed up into Oregon country, he picked his best cavalry mount out of a herd of 40,000 mustangs. Ten years later there were more than two million wild horses north of the Rio Grande and the wild long-horned cattle were so thick, they were crowding out the buffalo. All one had to do was catch, brand, drive and sell them to get rich. Sam Maverick had even a simpler plan. He let others do the catching and branding. What was left over he claimed, thus adding "maverick" to the vocabulary as the word for unbranded cattle.

A ranch was as large as the man who could hold it and a herd as big as the man who could drive it. The only limit he faced was himself, drought, Indians, rustlers and a few hundred miles to market. As Jim Miller, founder of the big Keystone spread east of Prineville put it, "Stampedes, bad food, rotten whiskey, floods and the hydrophobia from being bit by a mad polecat" were all in a day's work. His brother-in-law, John Luckey, would strongly agree.

The millions of free roaming buffalo were more of a problem but thanks to Bill Cody and others of his humanitarian desires, not for long. Although buffalo didn't directly affect herds in central Oregon, they were certainly a bother when the big trail herds headed east for market. The herds had to go through them and as any cowhand could attest, buffalo didn't drive worth a damn. For example, in later years, Leonard Lundgren saw fit to import buffalo from the Black Hills of South Dakota and turn them loose on the GI Ranch on the South Fork of Crooked River. A couple of his prize buffalo charged through the Barb-Wire Ranch on Hampton Butte, crashed through some feed lots on Lizard Creek and drifted off toward Pringle Flat, taking out every fence as they came to it. With irate cowman Bob Monical hot on their trail—.30-.30 Winchester rifle in hand—they led him on a chase that would cover five eastern Oregon counties and this occurred in the wild old days of 1961. The chase finally ended when one of the buffalo was beefed down by Silver Lake and the other was last seen surveying his domain at Benjamin Lake just south of the Deschutes-Lake county line.

George Millican and John Latta had brought the first cattle into the lower Ochoco Valley in 1868 for a rapid beginning in the beef industry. Not even the Oregon legislature could hold it back. As early as 1864, Oregon had enacted a law which made owners who drove cattle in from other states liable for the trespassing of their cows and damage caused whether lands trespassed upon were fenced or not. Too bad the Shoshoni weren't aware of this legal action. . . they could have sued instead of rustling 50 head of prime beef belonging to Millican.

Millican and Latta were immediately followed by the big outfit of Teal & Coleman who, on the strength of a government contract to furnish beef to the eastern Oregon military posts, pushed into the Ochoco and set up headquarters near the mouth of Hay Creek in the fall of 1868. The firm included Col. Joseph Teal, his brothers-in-law Henry and Frank Coleman and Barney Goldsmith, a silent partner who financed the operation from Portland. Teal & Coleman claimed most of north central Oregon from Trout Creek to the Columbia; and from the Deschutes to the John Day River while maintaining supply points in the Tygh, Klickitat and Yakima valleys.

They moved into the Ochoco with William Gates—who organized and led the first pack train into the Idaho gold strike in 1861—as company foreman. Accompanying Gates were Harmon Simpson and Richard Williams who would serve as administrative bookkeepers. Ahead of them, 750 head of bawling shorthorns would form the nucleus of the herd. In February 1869, Hank and Bill Coleman (another brother) pushed 1,200 head of shorthorns into Hay Creek, Trout Creek and the Grizzly Mountain area. Hank and Bill Coleman immediately filed additional claims to the original Teal & Coleman land grab of 1868. Joe Teal, Jr., the colonel's son and later a noted Portland attorney, took over as ramrod of the Trout Creek Ranch and a cattle empire was born. Within ten years, Teal & Coleman grew to such size that local markets in Oregon, Washington and Idaho couldn't absorb the beef shoved at them and the big cattle drives began.

Teal & Coleman's first competition would come from a couple of young cowboys out of the Willamette Valley. Jim and Joe Blakely had hit the saddle at an early age. In 1865, Jim was only thirteen years old when he joined his father, Captain James Blakely and Billy Smith (member of the first Ochoco homestead party) to deliver 500 head of longhorns to the military posts in northern California. They crossed the Santiam Pass—soon to be known as the Chisholm Trail to the Ochoco—and first laid eyes on the lower Crooked River Valley. Skirting Snake war parties, they slipped through Little Rattlesnake's hunting grounds on the Pitt River and sold the cattle at Fort Bidwell for $20,000 in gold which they hid in sacks of flour.

In 1868, Jim and his brother Billy Blakely drove 600 head of shorthorns over the Santiam to the army posts in eastern Oregon and spotted the lush grassland west of Prineville. Later that same year, Jim and Joe pushed 1,500 head into Willow Creek and wintered them on the edge of the big Teal & Coleman spread. The following summer they drove 500 of these steers to Chico, California where they sold to Miller and Lux and made a big enough profit to return to Prineville and set up headquarters on Willow Creek. They soon were grazing cattle from Grizzly Mountain west to the Deschutes River; and from Crooked River north to Hay Creek, taking in all of Agency Plain. Blakely's big spread would include Opal Springs on the lower Crooked River, which discharges over 80 million gallons of water each day. At the time, Blakely would observe that "there was plenty of range then for everybody and even when the sheep came there was no trouble. Sheep always crowd you a little but there was so much open range that nothing serious happened."[1]

Soon to follow the Blakely boys were the Thompson brothers, Bud and George, who by fair means or foul took over six ranches in the

---

1 Interview, Jim Blakely, August 1950 in Prineville, Oregon.

Crooked River basin. During this period of expansion most of the cowhands were Mexicans and Indians. . . a carefree roving lot who lived and died on the range, men who had drifted out of the southwest with French, Teal, Miller and Devine. By the mid-1870's, they were being replaced with young adventurers from back east. For all the romance attached to his memory, the American cowboy was in fact only a little above the cow itself in the social scale of his time. Like the sheepherder, he worked for $30 or 40 a month and all the beef he could eat.

One interesting buckaroo at the turn of the century was Annie Gregg, a Modoc maid who at seventeen dressed like a man, tucked her braids under a Mexican sombrero and hired out to any cow outfit that would take her. She was reputed to be a wildcat in a fight and there were men with the scars to verify this. Her Scot-Cherokee father, Fred Gregg came west from Indian territory in 1884 and married Betty Schonchin, daughter of the Modoc war chief and second cousin to Captain Jack. This is the same Modoc Annie who, on April Fool's Day 1959, led the well-publicized Owyhee gold rush out of Vale, Oregon—which discovered nothing.

And then there was Iron Mouth, a full-blood Shoshoni, who rode for the big cattle outfits in the Paulina-Suplee area. As a war chief during the Bannock War, he was sentenced to the Fort Bidwell reservation in northern California. After spending several years at Fort Bidwell, Iron Mouth returned to the Paiute Indian Colony on the outskirts of Burns, Oregon, where he was known as Pete Burns. Longing for the old way of life, Iron Mouth was one of the fortunate few who found a safe haven in the upper country where many of the French-Canadian settlers also had Indian blood flowing in their veins. Being a top cowhand and bronc buster, the old Shoshoni warrior was readily accepted as one of the crew. He was the kind of buckaroo that the large cattle outfits treated with respect and this at a time when an Indian was placed in the same unwanted category as sheep and poison larkspur.[2]

---

2 The Paiute Indian Colony, located northwest of Burns, Oregon was allotted ten acres in 1897. In 1935 a 760 acre parcel was purchased for them under authority of section 208 of the National Industrial Recovery Act of June 16, 1933. These parcels were not designated as a reservation until October 13, 1972. Iron Mouth's daughter, Suzie Burns, married Picking Up (Tibuood), a Paiute living at the colony. Suzie died there in 1928. Her son, Cato Teeman (Iron Mouth's grandson) about 84 years old in 1997, was still living at the old Paiute Indian Colony.

By 1873, Tom Logan and son Sanders Logan had carved out a spread between the Middle Fork of Camp Creek and the South Fork of Crooked River branding with the 96 iron. Logan would recall that on one trip up Crooked River and back to Prineville down Antelope Creek, he killed 24 rattlesnakes.[3] Logan's next door neighbors on Camp Creek were Grant Mays and Charlie Brown operating under the Pot Hook brand. To the east, on the South Fork of Crooked River was Abraham Franklin Hackleman's big Q ranch and John Gilchrist running the GI iron.

During the final Shoshoni outbreak in 1878, Gilchrist—trailing 600 shorthorns to Winnemucca, Nevada—found half the settlers in southeast Oregon forted up at the Shirt ranch with 500 saddle horses held in a corral. Two freight wagons loaded with supplies for Fort Harney had just been attacked by the Snakes but, by cutting loose the teams, the drivers escaped and made it to the ranch. Young Pete Delore, army scout who was also holed up at the Shirt ranch, along with a dozen heavily-armed cattle drovers attempted to rescue the wagons. When a rifle bullet grazed Delore's head, cutting off some hair, the cowboys decided this wasn't such a hot idea and high-tailed it back to more peaceful surroundings.

In 1869, following in the Blakelys' tracks, Bill and Jasper Foster with a team and wagon, two saddle horses, one longhorn bull and 30 head of scrawny cows, crossed the Santiam divide and erected a juniper log cabin on a rye grass flat east of Crooked River near the south end of present Fairview Avenue. For two years, they ran their herd on the high desert and wintered them on the Crooked River bottoms a few miles south of Prine's Saloon and each year increased the herd's size. In 1872 with the Shoshoni relatively quiet, they transferred their cattle operations into the Bear Creek country—the first cattle to range there. The Foster spread expanded rapidly running into Paulina Valley and the Suplee country on the east—grazing off 96 and Pot Hook grass—and by 1877 was crowding against John Todd's Farewell Bend Ranch on the west. In fact, Foster ran longhorns on the present site of Bend and pushed Todd to the limit. By now, Billy Foster was a cattle baron.

3 *The Crook County News*, Prineville, Oregon, August 4, 1939, p. 2.

On December 28, 1876, Billy Foster married Mary Allen, daughter of Ben Allen thus tying him in with the big Allen & LaFollette sheep outfit on the Ochoco River. Allen was also the first stockman to introduce Jersey cattle to central Oregon. The Fosters lived for a short time at Allen's headquarters on Allen Creek before moving into Prineville in 1884, building a house on West 4th Street where the Hometown Laundry now stands. Ben Allen, who was associated with the Baldwin brothers in establishing the First National Bank of Prineville, would remark that "10% interest beats the sheep business."[4]

In 1873, Edward Conant, a native of Cuba, moved into an unclaimed high basin on Foster's cattle range and started a herd of draft horses which also crowded Roscoe (brother of John) Knox's sheep range. By 1890 this herd had grown into hundreds of head. Conant was his own overseer and nature was his farmer. His horses ran wild in the natural meadows up to the dead of winter. Punctually on the first day of January without variation, Conant threw open his fenced pastures in the basin and the hungry horses wallowed in knee-deep uncropped grass. Fencing one end of a high-walled plateau, Conant provided spring pasture for his brood mares. Before his death in the '90s, a homesteader or two had fenced off a bit of this great monopoly.

By 1874, proceeded by two years of severe draught, beef prices fell to 3¢ a pound delivered at The Dalles City. If herded over the Cascades to Eugene City, prime beef would sell for 5¢ a pound. It would be seven years before cattle prices rose. Rustling became prevalent, which brought on the cattle associations, but the most destructive enemy to the stockmen were the bleak eastern Oregon winters. Many cattlemen like Billy Foster, in an effort to cover their hole card, headed for Scissorsville and the awaiting gold.

Meantime down in California, John Devine crawled up into his silver-mounted saddle, rode up from the Sacramento Valley and established the Alvord Ranch—16,000 acres of meadow between Alvord Desert and the Steens Mountains in Bad Face's hunting grounds. He then built White Horse Ranch and gradually collected another 150,000 acres

---

4 *The History of Central Oregon*, published by the Crook County Historical Society, 1981, p. 48.

of prime rangeland while controlling an additional 30,000 acres simply by owning or holding the creeks, springs and desert water holes.

In 1872, passing himself off as a land buyer, John William French (better known as Pete) rode into southeastern Oregon to scout out the country. It wasn't long until French and his Mexican vaqueros drove a large herd of longhorns and horses from northern California into the Blitzen Valley, claiming everything west of the Steens Mountains and north to Harney Lake. This chunk of real estate he christened the P Ranch. He was also crowding Has No Horse's latest hideout on Warner (Hart) Mountain.

Nephew by marriage to Elisha Barnes—another prominent Ochoco stockman—Pete French held a special dislike for sod-busters and it was a well known fact that he was anything but gracious in his dealings with the dirt-poor homesteaders. Then on February 17, 1883, Dr. Hugh Glenn (French's business partner and actual owner of the P Ranch) was gunned down by a gentleman named Miller only 17 days after his daughter Ella married Pete French—placing French in control of Dr. Glenn's vast operation. Fourteen years later, French was shot and killed by Ed Oliver—a homesteader—the day after Christmas, 1897. Charged with murder in the first degree, a sympathetic jury could find no evidence to convict Oliver of any wrong-doing. Their verdict. . . not guilty![5]

In the fall of 1874, eight years before Crook County was created from Wasco and thirty years before Bend was to take shape as a frontier village, a dusty rider known only as Homesteader No. 2896 galloped into The Dalles and filed claim on a strip of natural meadow on the upper Deschutes River.[6] A desirable piece of real estate, others soon filed on adjoining claims and a group of Prineville businessmen purchased the tracts from the legal owners. Within two years, these tracts were consolidated into one chunk by Tom Geer and called the Farewell Bend Ranch.

About this same time Henry Gray and his brother-in-law Dick Breese moved into the rimrocks between the Ochoco and Crooked rivers in 1876 claiming all of Combs Flat as their range and establishing the

5 *The Portland Oregonian*, December 29-30, 1897.

6 U.S. Land Office, The Dalles City, Oregon Series No. 2896, October 21, 1984.

Bonnieview Ranch with holdings stretching into Gray's Prairie on the south side of Lookout Mountain, in Wolf Dog's old hide-out.

Then, John Young Todd, a lone rider and a hard one, entered the scene and in 1877 acquired the Farewell Bend Ranch for two saddle horses and $60 in gold. Immediately after buying the place, Todd rode into the Wapinita country with his foreman, Felix Dorris, rounded up 1,200 unbranded cows and moved them into the upper Deschutes, setting up headquarters on Squaw Creek north of Camp Polk.

In 1878 at the height of the Bannock War and with cattle prices sky-rocketing, Todd rounded up another 800 head of wild ones and put them on the Farewell Bend range, moving his headquarters there and wintering the herd in Tepee Draw, his desert range east of Powell Buttes. Here, he clashed with Billy Foster. While this quarrel was in progress, John Stors, Wasco County sheriff, filed a preemption claim on Todd's ranch. In a swift move, Todd bought a herd of cattle from Barney Springer, hired Springer as ranch foreman and put the Farewell Bend Ranch in his name in an effort to hold it. Springer then married Todd's daughter in a civil ceremony in Prineville.

With the Indian war placing a premium on beef, Teal & Coleman sold 5,000 head to a big Texas outfit and trailed them through the heart of the Shoshoni battleground to Abilene, Texas. More company cattle were being trailed to Cheyenne and Council Bluffs to reach a railhead.

However, there was more than domestic military contracts pushing the price of beef out of sight. In 1878 the newly invented refrigerator car and the adaptation of refrigeration to shipping gave the cattle industry a big boost. By 1879, with a rash of small wars raging across Europe, the foreign market had exploded. Seven million dollars worth of beef from the western range was shipped to England from New York City alone, and nearly twice that amount was sent overseas the following year.

At the same time, Captain Blakely and young Jim with six Indian cowboys moved 450 head of prime yearlings from Brownsville to Jim's Willow Creek ranch for shipment to Fort McDermit to feed soldiers. Everything was peaceful when they left Prineville but out on the desert, they ran head-on into a Snake war party. At the time, the army was engaged in a big fight at The Narrows near Fort Harney.

In the running battle, young Blakely took an arrow through his arm. He would later recall that, "we had to turn our steers loose on the range. Later in the fall we went back and rounded them up. We didn't lose many. We then drove them to the Oregon-Nevada line between White Horse Ranch and Fort McDermit and delivered them to soldiers on a government contract."[7] On this trip, Blakely saw much evidence of Shoshoni raids. The Indians had choked horses to death instead of wasting ammunition and had hamstrung 500 sheep in one corral. It was Blakely's belief that white men riding with the Snakes had put them up to it.

During the heat of battle, William Walter Brown, a teacher at Willamette University, rode into central Oregon looking for land. Temporarily discouraged by the Indian outbreak, Brown bided his time until 1882 when he again returned to central Oregon with his brothers—Ellis, George and Bob—all of whom were college graduates. The Brown boys arrived with $2,700 apiece—good money for those days—and spent the winter of '82-83 camped on the north slope of Wagontire Mountain beneath an over-hanging cliff. According to Bill, "we near froze!" They didn't even have a tent.[8] That spring, they established Gap Ranch and later would headquarter on Buck Creek in the GI spread's backyard.

The Brown brothers soon pushed the $10,000 they had between them into a fortune, acquiring nearly 38,000 acres in what became Crook, Lake, Deschutes and Harney counties, and on which they ranged 10,000 head of horses and 22,000 sheep. In the winter of '88-89 when 3,000 sheep froze to death, Ellis, Bob and George gave up and sold out to Bill. Ellis became a medical doctor in Portland; George a banker in Oregon City; and Bob a "potato king" in Klamath Falls.

A colorful character, Bill Brown rode horseback without boots, wearing only socks on his feet and he wrote checks on anything that came handy. Checks were honored at the First National Bank of Prineville written on shingles, wrapping paper, strips of cloth, used envelopes. . . even one for a thousand dollars written on a tomato can label.[9] Brown branded with the horseshoe bar iron which put the clover leaf outfit in business. By making a few simple strokes with a running iron, the  horses soon became  horses. "Peculiar Bill" was the undisputed horse

7 *The Sunday Oregonian*, March 12, 1939.

8 "William Walter Brown," *Central Oregonian*, Centennial Edition, 1968.

9 Interview with Harold Baldwin of the First National Bank of Prineville.

king of the West, running his horses from Foster's Suplee range all the way to Todd's Farewell Bend Ranch at the eastern base of the Cascades.

One who signed on with Bill Brown was Jim Johnson—the ninth of Ewen and Nancy Johnson's eleven children—who was the first white child born in the Mill Creek Valley on Thanksgiving Day, 1870. While with Brown, young Jim learned to shear sheep and it got him into big trouble. Quitting the horseshoe bar spread, Johnson organized a crew and moved around southeastern Oregon shearing sheep. A union man tried to "organize" Jim's crew. After politely asking him to leave several times, Jim shot and killed him. Jim's sheep-shearing crew (along with the influence of old Ewen Johnson) kept him from being convicted of murder but he immediately joined the army and got out of the country for awhile.[10]

Bill Brown may have been the horse king of the Old West but beyond any doubt, Henry Miller—kingpin of Miller & Lux whose Midas-touch turned the silver sage to gold—was the monarch of the cattle barons. Reported to own a million acres of land and a cow for every acre, Miller boasted that he could drive his herds from the Kern River in southern California to the Malheur River in eastern Oregon and not spend a night off his own land. Miller bought out Devine's White Horse Ranch when the drought of '88-89 killed thousands of his cattle. He then hired Devine as ranch foreman. A big mistake. As ramrod of a big cattle outfit, Devine was about as helpful as a sheep tick. It was money that had made Devine a cattle baron, not his knowledge of ranching operations. Because of this, he was smart enough to hire the best ranch managers available. Devine himself, couldn't handle the job—the day-to-day administration of running a big cattle operation was beyond his capabilities.

In 1879, sixteen-year-old William Hanley pushed out of the Rogue River Valley, drove a herd of cattle across the high desert and lit on the edge of Harney Valley. Grabbing what French, Devine and Brown hadn't already claimed, he established the Double O and the Bell A ranches. He too, would make his mark on eastern Oregon history.

By 1880, the Ochoco was overrun with livestock but the winter of '80-81 would take care of that. With the exception of the sheltered

---

10 As told by Jim Johnson when the author was just a lad. Also see *History of Crook County*, 1981, p. 155; *History of Crook County*, 1994, p. 141.

Ochoco Valley, the arctic front slammed into central Oregon with the destructive power of a runaway freight train. Pushed by swirling snow, large herds were rushed to the Ochoco Valley where they wintered along the Ochoco River from mouth to head. What animals didn't starve in the over-grazed valley died an agonizing death on the bleak wind-swept ridges of the Crooked River plateau. With western markets in decline and the range deteriorating, Col. Teal organized the largest cattle drive to ever leave the Pacific Northwest for the eastern market. It would also be one of the largest cattle drives in history. Following the general route of the Oregon Trail, this cattle exodus would span 1,200 miles—one-third the width of the United States.

Col. Teal contacted all the big cow outfits in central Oregon and offered to take their herds to market. Young Joe Teal would be over-all manager of the undertaking and somehow, the colonel persuaded John Todd to act as trail boss. As such, Todd would take the lead with 3,000 head (1,500 company steers and 1,500 head of Todd's longhorns). Hank Coleman would assemble the company herd on Trout Creek while Todd rounded up his herd on the upper Deschutes. They then would take separate routes, picking up other ranchers' livestock along the way and merge the herds east of Burns for the trek east. Altogether, 58,000 cattle took to the trail. . . nearly 2.5 million dollars worth of beef on the hoof.

Out on the Great Plains disease struck the trail herd and they suffered heavy loses. Between them, Todd and Coleman lost a thousand head of their own stock. Finally when the depleted drive reached Cheyenne, Todd turned his cattle over to Joe Teal for marketing. To legalize this transfer, John Teal formed a new cattle firm named the John T & Company. When this action was completed, Todd returned to his Farewell Bend ranch.

When Todd failed to receive any word from Teal or money for his cattle, he returned to Cheyenne. There he learned that the cattle had been trailed to Nebraska to fatten. Many of them had broken through the ice crossing the Platte River and drowned. Then the man who wintered the dwindling herd sued Coleman—now trail boss—and the court awarded the plaintiff a judgment of $75,000. When Todd, Coleman and Teal returned to central Oregon, their neighbors also brought suit for payment of the cattle entrusted to them. This litigation went all the way to the Supreme Court. The decision in favor of their neighbors bankrupted the company, which went out of the cattle business and broke Todd, forcing him to sell the Farewell Bend Ranch to pay off, leaving him with only squatter's rights to the Squaw Flat Ranch near Sisters, Oregon.

In the late summer of 1881, Todd sold the ranch to John Sisemore without title. Sisemore, an ex-Scissorsville miner, scout for Gen. Crook and Prineville stockman was leading a packstring into California when he made camp at the Farewell Bend Ranch. A desperate Todd spent half the night by a blazing fireplace discussing the merits of his ranch as a cattle operation. All this talk paid off. Sisemore bought Todd's homestead relinquishment for a mere $1,400. In one respect, it was a fair profit over two saddle horses and $60 cash but extremely small considering that Todd—just six months before—had been one of the major cattle-operators in eastern Oregon.

While Todd was pushing 58,000 bawling steers across the plains, Bernard Markam, a dispatch rider in the 16th Kansas Regiment, brought a herd of purebred Durham cattle into the Ochoco in the summer of 1880. He would also run competition to Brown's mustangs. Not only did Markam raise thoroughbred horses but he also ran the wild ones. Markam so loved horses that his wife Harriet, an invalid who opened the first millinery and dress shop in Prineville, traded her business property to Frank Zell for a band of wild horses. Incidentally, there were three influential gentlemen living one mile west of Prineville who gave rise to the town's slick-ear battle cry of "catch 'em, mark 'em and brand 'em!" Their names. . . Isaac Ketchum, Bernard Markam and Jim Brandam (a slick-ear was an unclaimed or unbranded calf).

Then there were the Yancey brothers who rode up from Nevada in 1880 and made their stake as freighters before going into the cattle business. As they rightfully figured, a cowhand had little chance of making it on a dollar and a half a day. During the sheep and cattle war, they went into the wool business. Perhaps brother Steve's reputation as a dead-shot kept them from losing many sheep. It was also a known fact that as sheriff, Yancey shot and killed a half-breed Shoshoni who tried to break jail. The Shoshoni didn't stand a chance even in peace time.

During the livestock invasion, sheepmen would complain bitterly that "cows" was just a shortened name for "Central Oregon Watershed Strippers." Maybe so, but sheep weren't doing much to improve the range either. Along with the sheepmen and cattlemen, there were other tough operators entering the Ochoco. They too would leave their scars on the countryside.

CHAPTER 176

TIMBER!

With the bull pine practically gone, the old pine logger leaned on his axe and took a squint around him. To his horror, the plow was creeping into the choppings behind him. He took a fresh chew of snoose—lifted his nose to the wind and headed for the Pacific slope.

Earnest Swift
The Glory Trail

With all its other troubles, a new plague would strike central Oregon. In 1873, fanned by the constant burning of Portland and The Dalles, the demand for lumber skyrocketed. By mid-spring the lumber baron would challenge the cattle king and the mining czar for exploitation of the Ochoco. The frontier logger—a species first recognized in the New England states—became the lumber baron's first line of defense and a hell-roaring time would be had by all. With the possible exception of the mountain man, the West never produced a rougher, tougher customer. The man with the double-bit axe had a violent dislike for any type of restraint and he held no doubt that "with my bare hands and caulked boots I can whip any breed of animal that walks on its hind legs." And he would add to the western vocabulary such terms as spar-tree, steam donkey, cat-skinner and bull of the woods.

Whatever the original motive that sent men into the Blue Mountains of eastern Oregon, it was not to cut trees for a living. At that time lumber had little or no value. About all trees were good for was to hide Indians from civilized folks and therefore were another element of nature to be reckoned with. The Hudson's Bay Company followed by the Methodist missionaries and the U.S. Army did cut a few trees but it was merely done as a way to sustain life. These pioneer loggers—mostly

French-Canadian trappers, Scandinavian soldiers and Indian converts—did so because they were forced into it. Through their trial and error, the first techniques of West Coast logging were worked out. From their mistakes, the lumber industry began to emerge as a business of specialties such as cruising, felling, skidding and hauling logs to the place of manufacture. In the words of the logger, "this is where he got the feel of her."

The first determined start of logging as a business in Oregon Territory came in 1852 when Wilmer Hutchins and William Littlejohn shipped sawmill equipment from San Francisco to Astoria and took on the cedar of the coast range. They lasted for a year in a high-risk operation where amateurs were fortunate to survive a week. Whether they were killed in the woods, ambushed by Indians or died of sickness no one knows but the lumber industry was born and the specialists were on the way.

At the start of the westward migration it was never doubted—least of all by the die-hard loggers—that the state of Maine had enough timber to last the nation "until the hinges of hell rusted off." It came as a shock that corrosion was complete by the 1830's and the lumberjack had one choice if he desired to chop down more trees. Hacking his way westward across Ohio, he found the mother-lode in the Great Lake states and settled in for some serious cutting. Twenty years later, he again faced the setting sun. He had cut his own throat with a cross-cut saw.

In 1855, the professional logger swaggered onto the Oregon scene—the land of the giants. When he saw the "big stuff" he was somewhat taken aback but that didn't slow him down. Lengthening his saw and notching a couple of planks—he called them "spring boards"—he got up to "where she would fit" and from there on, it was the devil take the hindmost. Burying his axe in the Port Orford cedar, he roared that he could hold his own against all comers and clear the country in the process. He didn't lie.

By the end of the 1860's the West Coast forests were gutted from California to British Columbia. The billions of board feet of lumber harvested for an expanding nation are almost beyond comprehension; and the 800 mile swath of slash, sawdust, saloons, dance halls, ghost towns, tax delinquency and forest fires the logger left behind him was a hard price to pay. It was so bad that the surveyor-general of Washington

Territory earnestly recommended to the General Land Office that all the forest lands in the territory be "sold immediately while there is still anything left to sell."

The lands were not sold for no one was eager to pay taxes on land when its by-product was free for the taking and more billions of board feet of lumber in Washington and Oregon disappeared from the public domain. It became a different matter when, in 1871, a million board feet of West Coast lumber disappeared from a Boston Navy Yard never to be seen again. Congress lurched to its feet and introduced the first bill to reserve and protect timber stands on the public domain.[1]

Two years later with the army tacking up clap-board shacks on the Modoc treaty grounds and the gold-strike town of Scissorsville mushrooming on the banks of the Ochoco River, the stampede for more logs was on. The Ochoco contained the largest stands of Ponderosa pine in the world and it was now up for grabs.

Immediately Jim Marshall and Ike Swartz, who had built a modest sash mill on Mill Creek in 1868, faced competition from the most modern equipment located a few miles to the west. Within days after his newfangled head rig arrived on the scene, Charlie Maling started operations on Johnson Creek followed by Press Nelson, who put in a saw mill on Combs Flat. It didn't take long to cut out the available timber and Nelson sold out to Bill McMeekin. McMeekin moved the operation to the head of McKay Creek. Here, for some unknown reason, McMeekin came up with the idea that it was easier to haul logs than it was to haul rough lumber so, in 1874, he moved the milling operation into town, setting up on the Ochoco River where the *Central Oregonian* office now stands and gained the distinction of having constructed the first sawmill in Prineville.

Of more importance, something else would evolve from this venture. It didn't take Mac very long to determine that hauling logs thirty miles by horse and wagon was a costly operation so, knowing his loggers... he quietly converted the sawmill into a more lucrative business in 1875. The town folks (inwardly greedy for capital but outwardly

1 *Historical Highlights of Public Land Management*, pp. 33-34.

projecting pure Christian desires) were dutifully dismayed. McMeekin's sawmill became a brewery. . . likewise, the first in Prineville.

This enterprise was soon reinforced with Loeker's Brewery and then came the saloons. Seven to be exact. In no particular order, these dispensers of distilled spirits were: Dick Graham's *Longhorn*; Joe Kelly's *Last Change*; Smith and Cleek's *Silver Dollar*; Dave Rowan's *Dew Drop*; Fred Goulet's *Electric*; Henry Burmeister's *Stockman's Exchange*; and Til Glaze's *Singer,* better known as *The Bucket of Blood.*

Accustomed to endless backbreaking toil and daily staring death in the face, the logger broke this monotony when he hit town with an explosive energy beyond the comprehension of the ordinary mortal. He wanted whiskey, he wanted women and he wanted to howl. And if some sod-buster, cow-puncher, sheepherder or hard-rock miner was dumb enough to call him a brush-ape the fight was on. When he had "rimrocked the town" as he phrased it, he returned to his forest solitude at peace with the world.

But not always. Jack Miller, bull of the woods for a logging operation in the Snow Mountain area, had hired Matt Egan from one of the big cow outfits as camp cook. One day Miller fired Egan and Egan took off for Burns in a mean frame of mind. According to Egan, Miller "canned" him so he could hire a woman cook whose company he liked better. Egan began drinking and the more whiskey he downed the more he brooded. One day, he jumped Miller on a Burns street and in typical cowhand style pulled a gun on him. Miller was quicker and pumped four bullets into Egan's stomach. He then took Egan's gun and brandishing both weapons charged in to the nearest saloon and in true logger style bellowed, "if any of you sonsuvbitches don't like what I've done get out here and try your hand!" Nobody stepped forward and the shooting was ruled justifiable homicide.

A short time later a warrant was issued on Miller for horse-stealing. He got out of Burns ahead of the sheriff, cutting the telegraph lines on the way. He then dropped out of sight not to be heard from again until the Klondike Strike of 1897. Suddenly he was back on his old stomping grounds with a new name. As Jack Dalton, he formed a partnership with Ed Hanley to drive cattle from eastern Oregon to the Yukon—making them a fortune. The route they took with the cattle drive became known as the Dalton Trail.[2]

Soon after Bill McMeekin converted his sawmill into a brewery, John Hamilton built a planing mill on the corner of Third and Beaver Streets. This manufacturing plant produced the finished lumber for the first courthouse and first schoolhouse in Prineville. Meantime in 1877, the innovative Charles C. Maling—a native of England—put in the first steam driven sawmill on Blakely's cattle ranch on Willow Creek. This done, he bought Hamilton's planing mill and then sold the operation to Edward Harban. Harban took in John Shipp as a partner who bought him out. To keep up with the demand, Harban started another sawmill which burned in 1879, putting a finish to Harban's lumber enterprise. Bluffed out by fire, he went into the metal business by building the first machine shop in town.

That same year, with Snake warriors cleaning out the sheep and cattle herds and the homesteaders clamoring to open up the creek bottoms, Ben and Watt Jones established the first sawmill and logging camp on the upper Ochoco River at the mouth of Duncan Creek. This operation was followed by Jim Hawkins' mill at the mouth of Douthit Creek and Vic Blodgett's sawmill on Scissors Creek. Over on Trout Creek, Maling had formed a partnership with Charles Durham and was constructing yet another sawmill. And Samuel Compton, who had set up a plant on Mill Creek in 1876, was now operating out of Ashwood and by 1917 had expanded operations into Coon Creek. Joe Smith was hacking his way across Grizzly Mountain and the Carson brothers—Lew and Kit—were logging the Maury Mountains. By 1880, Oregon was boasting it had 228 sawmills in operation and nine of these were in the

---

2 In 1898, two thousand beef cattle were driven to Dawson City over the Dalton Trail, which ended at Fort Selkirk on the upper Yukon River. Dalton also charged $250 toll to anyone who wanted to use the trail. Others had tried to collect toll for the use of roads, bridges and trails in this rough and lawless country, but only Dalton was tough enough to collect, sometimes at gunpoint. Dalton was described as "a mean man to tangle with possessing a compact, powerful body and a quick temper." He once almost beat a man to death with his bare fists for trying to start a saloon on his property; and fatally shot another for attempting to turn the Indians against him. The wife that he had left behind in Harney County—Mae McClintock, the woman who replaced Matt Egan as cook at the Snow Mountain logging camp—later followed Jack to Alaska where she died a few years after rejoining him. (Information taken from *Harney Historical Highlights,* the Harney County Historical Society newsletter, published monthly at Burns, Oregon.)

Ochoco drainage alone. Several years later, two of Joe Smith's sons—Alonzo and Thomas—purchased the W.F. King sawmill on Mill Creek and milled the lumber used in construction of the Ochoco dam. They too, would move their operation to the upper Ochoco Valley.

A few of the settlers witnessing the mass destruction of valley bottoms and eroding hill sides voiced their concern but the logger was little given to sentiment or to philosophical discussion on the result of his violent attack against the yellow pine. About the only breath he wasted was to roar against some mild protest regarding his methods and to staunchly maintain that he was the forerunner of progress.

But the logger would clash with the biased citizens of the Ochoco. He was not of the genteel class and once he had cleared the creek bottoms—in short, the tillable land—he was not welcome, *persona non grata* so to speak. The locals would take over which was probably just as well. That way, the rape was prolonged for sixty-five years. . . long enough for the federal government to take over and spurred by the Second World War, the earnest harvest began. One old central Oregon logger said it all when he was interviewed by a local newspaper reporter in 1983. Born in 1885, Luther Metke was asked what he would do in today's world if he were 28 years old instead of 98. Metke immediately responded: "I'd try to wreck the U.S. Forest Service."[3]

Others would not be so kind in their comments. "To the unknowing," said one critic who referred to the Forest Service as the bastard child of Gifford Pinchot, "the image is that of a benevolent bureaucracy protecting wilderness and replacing the rape and ruin logging of the past with enlightened conservation." Instead, he would continue, "This agency is the primary force behind the destruction of wilderness ecosystems and healthy habitat."[4] Harsh words yes, but they have the ring of truth.

As late as 1938 one of America's largest and longest log drives began on the Deschutes River when Shevlin-Hixon floated more than 20 million board feet of logs down a 40 mile stretch of wild river to Benham Falls where they were placed on logging trains for removal to Bend.[5]

3 *The Bulletin*, Bend, Oregon, November 30, 1983.

4 Howie Wolke, *Save Our National Forests*, Kalispell, Montana, May 1988.

5 *The Bulletin*, Bend Oregon, December 25, 1938.

Left in the wake of this massive log drive was a naked land stripped of all dignity.

It was ordained that the plow should follow the axe and it did. The sod-buster soon found out that the Ochoco didn't take kindly to farming. Cultivated crops had about as much chance for survival in this harsh environment as a snowball in hell. Native plants were the natural lords of the Ochoco and they intended to maintain that supremacy. By the late 1890's those farms on Marks Creek, Wolf Creek and Canyon Creek (main tributaries of the Ochoco River) had given up completely. The land was created for grass, pine and grazing animals and the latter could survive only so long as the grass held out.

But the logger had done his job "high, wide and handsome." In his terminology, he had "let daylight into the Ochoco thickets" and they would never be the same again.

CHAPTER 177

BELCHER GULCH

—— CLAME NOTISE ——
Jim McClure of Mitchell takes this ground;
jumpers will be shot!

Mining Claim Notice
Belcher Gulch, June 2, 1873

In 1862, the editor of *The Oregonian* would comment, "What a clover field is to a steer, the sky to a lark, a mud-hole to a hog, such are new diggings to a miner." In a sense that was true. To many, the grip of gold fever was more than just a yearning for wealth. While that was a pleasant benefit, discovery became the all-important goal.

A good example of this obsession involved Texan Ike Guker. Working on the side of Canyon Mountain in 1862, Ike sluiced $50,000 from a 10' x 20' hole in a single day. He believed the strike was so rich that he let visitors pick up nuggets and keep them. Guker then spent thirty-five years of backbreaking work looking for another bonanza and by 1897 had found only $17,000 total in dust and nuggets to show for his years of effort.

The tools of the trade were simple—a shovel, a pick, a gold pan, a bottle of quicksilver, a rifle, food for a couple of weeks and a mule to carry it all. Cash to equip himself was of minor concern since the prospector could usually persuade someone to give him a grubstake. In frontier towns, grubstaking was a common business arrangement. A backer would supply the prospector with supplies for a share—often half—of any strike made.

It wasn't an easy life but like the logger, buckaroo and sheep-herder, the miner took hardship as his normal lot and not many who sampled the prospector's life willingly relinquished its freedom to settle down. Even the bleakest winter could find him building a big fire on some frozen gravel bar, thawing it to the point where he could pan for gold, picking out each color with a knife or fingernail and stashing it in a bottle or can. When he quit work at nightfall, he would transfer the day's gleanings to a leather pouch.

In a long day squatting in a mountain stream, a prospector could process about fifty panfuls of gravel and would make ends meet at high boom town prices if he averaged ten cents worth of gold per pan. In rich placers, miners sometimes washed panfuls of sand worth $50 each and at the Canyon City strike on rare occasions an individual pan yielded as much as $500.

When prospectors ventured into new country, they looked first in the stream beds, which they called poor man's mines because any gold that accumulated there could be collected without costly equipment. The sand and gravel often contained other yellowish or glittering minerals such as iron pyrites (fool's gold) which confused greenhorns. But gold was unmistakable to anyone who had hefted it and clenched a bit of it between his teeth. Soft and malleable in its pure 24-carat form, gold was the only yellowish metal that would not break when it was pounded or beaten. Under almost all conditions, pure gold stubbornly maintained its own identity.

Gold would not rust or tarnish even after lying for centuries in mineral laded water. But for all the gold's resistance to change it did have one compliant property that aided prospectors. Gold had a strong affinity for mercury (or as the miners called it, quicksilver) and would readily unite with it on contact. Thus tiny particles of placer gold could easily be picked up with a blob of mercury and mercury was readily accessible in the Ochoco. In some places native quicksilver was even beaded to the grass roots. After amalgamation, the two metals could be separated easily by squeezing them in a wet deerskin bag; the mercury would pass out through the pores of the leather but the gold would not.

Canyon City had accumulated a large, exportable surplus of miners and they were on the prowl. The inner Ochoco was still virgin territory, the Shoshoni had seen to that. Although many prospectors had tried for twenty years to break the trade barrier few lived to reveal what they may have discovered. Now, like the vast stands of yellow pine and the endless sea of grass, its underground riches were waiting for the man bold enough to claim it.

At the height of the Modoc War with gold at a premium, the search began. However, the exploration of the Ochoco would be profoundly different. In all prior western gold strikes, the prospector had paved the way into the wilderness for civilization to follow; the roles were reversed in the Ochoco, the granger having proceeded the argonaut and in typical Oregon fashion the outcome would be cloaked in concealment.

For Sam Fischer (whose luck had run out at the Whiskey Flat strike), temptation was too strong to ignore. For security's sake, Fischer rounded up five partners—including George and Lewis McAllister, a couple of hard-rock miners—to accompany him on this foolhardy mission. Timing their arrival to coincide with the spring run-off, these reckless gold-seekers got a grubstake and headed for the Indian-infested Ochoco in May 1873.

Meantime Bill Cranston (a Mitchell saloon keeper) had been hearing rumors from various prospectors that the big bonanza was still to be found in the Ochoco Valley. On May 30, a day set aside by Congress to decorate the graves of those killed in the Civil War, Cranston closed the saloon and along with everyone else in the Bridge Creek country headed for the Fort Watson cemetery to attend Memorial Day services. Here, the crowd was joined by a circuit rider fresh from Canyon City where his quest for converts had met with only marginal success. At the cemetery, he found a more receptive audience and they adjourned to Tone Cannon's ranch for some soul-searching. Cranston went deer hunting.

Under the north rim of Mount Pisgah, Cranston ran into six men leading a packstring of mules loaded with mining supplies. Curious, he asked where they were going. A close-mouthed bunch, they admitted they were from Canyon City but gave no indication as to their destination. Cranston quickly decided there must be gold nearby and headed for Cannon's ranch on Mountain Creek to spread the word. His earth-shattering news fell on deaf ears.

The Rev. James Mansfield was just warming up to redemption when Cranston burst onto the scene. Most, fired with newborn Christian zeal, figured Bill had been communing too freely with his own spirits and dismissed his glorious revelation as wisdom from the bottle. Finally Cannon, Milt Belcher and Jim McClure decided "what the hell, we ain't got nuthin' better to do" so they rounded up some shovels, a pick and a frying pan and followed Cranston into the mountains. With the prayer meeting in shambles, preacher Mansfield, hoping to gather more strays in the Ochoco Valley settlements and not looking forward to crossing Indian territory alone, asked if he could tag along. Permission granted.[1]

Skirting the north side of Pisgah, Cranston picked up the prospectors' trail next morning and followed it to the head of Ochoco River. Some two miles down stream, the intended claim jumpers came to a halt. Deep in Shoshoni country, the bottle dry and—in their opinion—mighty sterile ground for a gold strike, the earlier excitement was beginning to fade. As Cranston brewed a pot of coffee, Cannon remarked that they might as well look for gold in an anthill. McClure laughed and pointed, "there she is boys, start diggin'!" Playing along with the joke, Belcher scooped up a frying pan full and found it rich with gold. He had located the Belcher Gulch strike.[2]

Wealth beyond their wildest expectation lay at their feet. Thirty years later, the *Prineville Review* would still boast that hidden in the upper Ochoco Valley "there is gold from the grass roots down."[3] The Canyon City boys were completely forgotten as plans were hurriedly made for exploration. Reverend Mansfield swore on the Bible that he wanted no part in this sinful enterprise. Sworn to secrecy, he immediately departed for the Willamette Valley and apparently he told the truth for there is no record of him filing a claim and he didn't return to the Ochoco until 1879.[4]

In their excitement, the new discoverers neglected to see a lonely cabin sitting a quarter of a mile down river. In time, another story would unfold dating two years into the past.

James Howard had followed the golden goddess into eastern Oregon. Having no luck in the gold fields, he took a contract to haul wheat from the Mitchell area to the government grist mill at Warm Springs Agency. Working with him were Bill Uttinger and Henry Evans, also veterans of the gold fields. In the fall of 1871, they crossed the Blues on the Vowel Trail passing over the divide at the head of what became Howard Creek into the head of Ochoco Valley and camped on a small

---

1 Art Champion, June 1941; Earl Hereford, August 1969.

2 Henry Stephenson letter to the editor *Crook County News*, Prineville, Oregon, April 13, 1939.

3 *Prineville Review*, May 21, 1906.

4 Silvia Mansfield Mizener (Mansfield's daughter), Paulina, Oregon, June 1980.

stream which emptied into the Ochoco River some thirty miles east of Barney Prine's trading post. That evening Howard observed that "the ground around here looks like what I worked in California."[5] With nothing better to do, the freighters grabbed frying pans and headed for the side stream. Uttinger struck pay dirt in the first panful so they named the tributary Uttinger Creek in honor of the occasion. By 1874, this creek would become the "Scissors Creek" site of the Ochoco gold rush.[6]

Well-educated in the short-comings of advertisement, the freighters decided to keep quiet about the strike, continue on to Warm Springs and then return home for the winter before trying to develop their discovery. There is evidence that Jim Howard slipped back into the area in January 1872 and did some heavy prospecting.[7] At that time he constructed a rough log shelter on Uttinger Creek which became known as "Discovery Cabin" and also filed a homestead claim some nine miles down river to throw off any suspicion as to his activities in the area.[8] Uttinger returned in the spring of '72 but there is no record that Evans did. If he did, it is possible his share in the discovery was bought by Howard. Whatever happened, the strike was kept a well-guarded secret until Cranston and Company arrived in 1873.

When the Belcher Gulch gang spotted Discovery Cabin things went into turmoil. It got even more chaotic when a mile downriver they discovered the Canyon City prospectors sinking a hole to bedrock. Fischer's group had struck gold where "Fisher Creek" dumped into the Ochoco. It was obvious that a stampede for riches was forthcoming but it would die at birth. . . simply because the farmer, the merchant, and the school teacher—the more refined element of frontier life—had preceded the Ochoco strike. They were already on the scene, organized, primed and waiting for battle. The outcome would be vastly different than other gold strikes of the Old West. As one old-timer put it, if you wanted to survive in the white man's Ochoco "you damn well better be a hard shell

---

5 "History and Resources of Crook County," *Crook County Journal*, 1905; *Wheeler County Chronicles*, "The Mayflower Mining District," December 1938.

6 Ochoco Mining Register, Crook County Clerk's Office, Prineville, Oregon, p. 44.

7 McArthur, *Oregon Geographic Names*, p. 371.

8 Discovery Cabin stood for 92 years before collapsing into Scissors Creek during the 1964 flood which inundated most of Oregon and everything else in the Pacific Northwest.

baptist and a staunch democrat." Few, if any, of the denizens of gold strike areas fit into either of those categories.

A later historian puzzling over the lack of publicity would accurately observe that the fact many of the miners were local people who had some acquaintance with each other "must have been a factor." He further concluded that the first to arrive at the strike "were ranchers with families who would have been in the area whether there was gold or not and this had to lend some stability to a fairly frenzied gold rush situation."[9] It certainly did. Cannon would make sure of that.

Some word did leak out. Maybe Mansfield, but more likely influential citizens in the Ochoco settlement made contact with political friends in the Willamette Valley. It is of some interest that within two months from the Belcher Gulch discovery, the Oregon legislature—anticipating more gold flowing into state coffers—authorized construction of a new capital building at Salem with a dome copied after the national capital in Washington, D.C. It would be four years before it was completed and it would stand for 63 years before being destroyed by fire.

Blue-nosed western Oregon quickly slipped a $100 a month tax on dance halls specifically aimed at eastern Oregon's anticipated boomtown on Scissors Creek. Whether enforced or not is hard to say but an enthusiastic Montana politician suggested that the territorial legislature follow Oregon's lead. The way Sidney Edgerton, Montana's territorial governor, put it, "If Oregon dance houses have to pay $100 per month, why not Virginia City?" The legislature couldn't see why they didn't either so Montana dance halls were licensed for $400 a year which was a bargain compared to Oregon's $1,200 assessment to operate a place of relaxation.[10]

In 1871, Tom Stephenson became the first settler in the upper Ochoco Valley, constructing a two-story log cabin on what is now the Ontko Ranch.[11] Stephenson and Cannon had been boyhood companions in Kentucky and he lived only a few miles down river from the Belcher Gulch strike. Cannon had an idea. Leaving McClure to guard Belcher

---

9 Burr Henly, *Gold From the Grass Roots Down, An Historical Profile of the Ochoco Mining District,* p. 10.

10 Joan Swallow Reiter, *The Women*, Time-Life series of the Old West, p. 141.

11 Ironically, this historic landmark erected in July 1871, celebrated its 100th birthday by burning to the ground in July 1971.

Gulch, the rest would go to Stephenson's ranch, alert him to the strike, borrow a team and wagon, load up on supplies and get a jump on the Canyon City boys.

When Cannon's party arrived at Stephenson's there was no one home so they decided to await his return. By some quirk of fate—it now being Sunday—Stephenson and his family had gone to visit Jim Howard, whose ranch was a quarter of a mile west of the present Howard School. The next morning Stephenson and Cannon headed back to the diggings while Cranston and Belcher left for the nearest source of supplies, Hiram Gibson's trading post in the area now covered by Ochoco Lake. They cleaned him out of picks, shovels and groceries as the word spread throughout the community. Meantime, Cannon and Stephenson started digging in a ravine north of Belcher's strike. They named this gully Stephenson Gulch and the first claims were filed on June 4, 1873.[12]

Well aware of new mining legislation passed by Congress the year before, here was a neat way to acquire more land. The 1872 General Mining Law promoted private prospecting and development of metallic minerals on public lands by protecting private interests in mining claims. Under this act, all mineral lands were declared open to exploration and occupation; and patents to such land could be obtained from the federal government. All that was necessary to gain title was: (1) make a valid mineral discovery; (2) invest $100 in improvements annually for 5 years; (3) pay for a boundary survey; and (4) apply for the surface area of the lands included in the survey boundary at $2.50 an acre for a placer mine or at $5 an acre for a lode mine.[13] Within days 69 local residents filed on 93 placer claims.

Howard knew immediately what happened and he moved fast. With a stroke of the pen, he formed the James Howard Mining Company which included his five sons—James Jr., Lytle, John, Howard and Markus—and within the next few weeks purchased and consolidated claims until he controlled more land than any of the other companies.[14]

---

12 Those filing were G.W. Cranston, A.L. Cannon, Thomas J. Stephenson, Milton Belcher and James McClure. *Ochoco Mining Register*, p. 12.

13 *Historical Highlights of Public Land Management*, p. 34.

14 *Ochoco Mining Register*, pp. 11-21.

In an eight day period beginning May 31, 1873 and ending June 7, 1873, a major gold strike was made and suppressed in the Ochoco Valley.

It is obvious that Howard worked the claims he acquired hard and fast. In less than a year, he sold a half interest in the Howard Mining Company along with tools, sluice boxes and a house for the sum of $160 which indicates he believed the claims were played out and then unloaded them.[15] With more miners moving in, the local ranchers lost little time in uniting and on June 7 appointed a committee to devise laws for governing the claims. The primary purpose of this meeting was to make it difficult, if not impossible, for outsiders to push the strike into a full-blown rush and to this extent, they were somewhat successful. The fact that production lasted until the early 1900's with little fanfare indicates the strike was deliberately played down. What gold was admitted to be taken out and what was really produced are two different matters.

Many of those involved with the committee—men such a Elisha Barnes, John Sisemore and Jim Marshall—were reformed prospectors, veterans of the earlier gold strikes and they knew the ropes. Following the June meeting, the committee met two days later at the house of John Douthit and, in a effort to discourage newcomers, drafted some stringent rules. Other than a new strike, a person would be limited to one creek claim extending 200 feet in length up and down said creek with a sluice head of 30 inches of water; and one hill claim 300 feet square. . . and that was it, period! However, the discovery of a new strike "on any creek, gulch or hill *not known to contain mineral*" would be allowed to hold one extra creek claim and one extra hill claim as "discovery claims."[16]

The strike area was to be know officially as the Ochoco Mining District and James Howard Sr. was appointed as the first recorder of mining claims. For this, he would receive 50¢ for recording each entry or bill of sale as provided for in Article 16 of the Articles of Confederation. Not much but it would give him the inside track on what was going on. One of the more interesting transactions which Howard recorded was

15 Ibid., p. 35.

16 The men present at the June 9, 1873 meeting were: Henderson, Chonor, Douthit, Howard Sr., Addis, Light Howard and Cannon. *Ochoco Mining Register, Articles of Confederation.*

William Uttinger's purchase of Ed Ratcliff's claim in 1874 for the novel consideration of one dozen steel traps.

Article 17 contained a warning to trespassers: "The settlement of all disputes not provided for in the foregoing Articles in regard to mining shall be left to arbitration, each party choosing one man and they choose an umpire in case of disagreement." This was a polite way of saying the quarrel would be resolved on the field of honor at the end of a six-gun.

Almost as exciting as the discovery of gold, 1873 saw the advent of the Winchester .44 and the Springfield .45-55 carbine, both popular items of equipment in the Ochoco mining district. The army also coveted them and Custer carried an 1873 Springfield to his grave. Has No Horse put his 1873 Winchester to better use.

Prineville was also benefiting from the strike. The summer of 1873 saw the first flour mill constructed by James Allen. Monroe Hodges opened the first hotel and livery stable and the more pious element organized the First Baptist Church. To take care of the increased activity, Prineville was granted recognition as an official U.S. Post Office with Dan Thomas in charge of seeing that the mail was distributed in a timely manner. Thomas would readily admit that bad weather, hostile Indians and good whiskey interrupted his appointed rounds.

In the late fall of 1873 a large party of Canyon City miners drifted in to Belcher Gulch packing enough supplies to carry them through the coming winter. Faced with approaching storms in an unfriendly environment, it didn't take the local vigilance committee long to convince the intruders that this was not a wise decision. Leaving most of their supplies behind with the understanding that they would return the following spring, the Canyon City boys headed for home.

When the Canyon City miners arrived at the Ochoco mining district, they were accompanied by Collard Blue and Frank Pett, a couple of John Day merchants loaded with trade goods to start a business venture. Part of their inventory consisted of 30 barrels of first-class whiskey. These entrepreneurs began construction of a combination log store and saloon but with winter coming on, Pett and Blue decided to abandon the project until spring. They dug a long tunnel into the side of a hill on the north side of Ochoco River opposite the mouth of Scissors Creek; stashed the 30 barrels of whiskey inside; blockaded the tunnel entrance with a blast from a keg of gun powder; and returned to John

Day with the Canyon City miners. Both parties left with the agreement that their private property would not be disturbed.

Following a year of drought, the winter of 1873-74 was exceptionally severe. With cattle prices at rock-bottom due to the drought—3¢ a pound delivered to The Dalles City—the big cattle and sheep operators swooped in on the Ochoco strike, investing heavily in mining claims. But as winter engulfed the Blue Mountains, the little mining district became isolated from the world. Cut off from supplies by six-foot snow drifts, the desperate inhabitants resorting to "miner's rights," called a meeting and voted to loot the Canyon City prospector's food cache. A clerk was appointed to take charge and check each item "purchased" so if the need should arise, the purchaser could account for his sins to the Canyon City absentee creditors. It is recorded that the Ochoco debtors were never called upon to explain their use of the Canyon City cache.[17] Likewise, the prospectors trapped in Belcher Gulch vehemently denied any desecration of Blue and Pett's whiskey tomb. Since most of them were local residents who professed (at least publicly) to be staunch supporters of the Baptist Temperance League, there is an outside chance that they were telling the truth. According to Earl Hereford, who as a young boy lived in Discovery Cabin, the distilled spirits are still buried in the caved-in tunnel. If so, the whiskey would be well aged. . . 120 years old at this writing.

Belcher Gulch was paying $20 a day per man with a gold rocker. The rocker method was used almost entirely during the first summer and since it was dependent upon a flow of water, water would become one of the main issues of dispute. Water was all-important and hard to develop in the strike area due to steep terrain. It was impossible to placer without water flowing through the sluice boxes or to hydraulic without water to jet through the hoses and wash raw material down from the hillsides. Stephenson Gulch—for lack of water—was the first to play-out and Cranston, the only one who had any money, bought out the other partners in the fall of 1873. He immediately began construction of a dam across Ochoco River and by spring of 1874 had put a ditch around the head of Belcher Gulch. In a matter of days he took out $20,000 in gold. The

17 "Mayflower Mine dates back to fall of 1871," Old Timers' Edition, *The Central Oregon Shopper*, August, 4, 1949.

saloonkeeper had discovered the answer to gold mining. Within a few days of each other, Cranston and Att Marks both claimed all the water on Scissors Creek and the fight was on.

Adding to the discord, drought again struck in the summer and fall of 1874. The mining register shows that virtually every claim was shut down for "want of water." This sparked the initial phase of ditch digging and the call went out for Chinese laborers.[18] This was not an easy decision to make. Chinese were not considered the cream of western society. . . just cheap hard workers. A Virginia City reporter pretty much voiced the sentiment of all westerners when he reckoned that upon the arrival of a stagecoach full of Chinese looking for jobs, they "should not be killed unless they deserve it but when they do, why kill 'em lots." Over at Spanish Gulch the miners specified that "no Mongolian shall be allowed to hold any claims in this District for mining purposes by location or preemption."[19] Twenty-one years later, the so-called Mongolians ruled Spanish Gulch backed by the Loy Yick Company.

The search for Chinese labor alerted the outside world that something was going on in central Oregon besides ranching, logging and Indian fighting. It also upset the mental calm of some west-side politicians. The wise men in Salem, by legislative act of 1866, had decreed that no Chinaman not born in the United States (which sort of limited Oriental opportunity) could mine in Oregon. Then realizing they had overlooked a possible source of revenue, the lawmakers tacked on an exception to the rule. If said Chinaman could obtain a license from a local sheriff and then pay $4 per quarter he could be issued a work permit. However, should he fail to pay such tax the sheriff "might seize and sell his property." As an added precaution, the law further stipulated that "any person employing Chinamen to work the mines is liable for this tax on all so employed." Eighty percent of the revenue collected would go to the county and the remaining 20 percent to the state. For prompt payment of this tax, any Chinaman complying with the law "should be protected

18 Lem and Betty Houston, December 1949; Earl Hereford, September 1966.

19 Rock Creek Mining District, *Articles of Operation* filed in Grant County Records, Canyon City, Oregon.

the same as citizens of the United States."[20] How much more generous could you get.

Then in 1882, over President Arthur's veto, Congress passed the Chinese Exclusion Act which barred Chinese immigrants from the United States for 10 years.

The moment the paid-up Chinese laborers arrived in the upper Ochoco Valley, they were put to work constructing a large dam on the Ochoco River above the mouth of Ahalt Creek. From here, they gouged a high ditch some three miles long to Scissors Creek. One of the construction gang, Ng Ah Tye, made a modest strike during his off-duty hours and opened a Japanese Bazaar in Prineville's Cary House restaurant located at Main and Third, next to the present day Bank Drug.[21] Apparently the Japanese designation was more acceptable to the townsmen than Chinese.

Within three weeks after the high mainline ditch was completed, the Belcher Gulch community attained a weedy but rugged growth and its population was such that organization would soon follow. Before water started flowing down the Ochoco ditch, Eli and Lea Watkins sold the water in their ditch from Judy Creek to John Douthit for $100. It should be remembered that dollar amounts paid for claims and ditch-rights recorded in Douthit's mining records are not necessarily the true figures. It's like looking at a real estate deed in which 5,000 acres of land sold "for one dollar and other consideration." It doesn't tell you the whole story. Anyway, a provision of the Judy ditch sale stipulated that for two years, the Watkins could continue to use 50 inches of water from the ditch for their hydraulic operation on Scissors Creek. After the two years were up, they still hadn't played out their claim. Douthit then agreed to let them use some water from their old ditch for $50 a year.

As it turned out, the Ochoco River middle ditch (200 feet above the valley floor) came in about ten feet below a major gold vein. No problem. With the ground below the middle ditch line paying as high as $1,200 a day per man, Scissors Creek was literally moved west for half a mile into Judy Creek. Some of the claim names tell a story unto themselves. Just imagine the Midnight Tramp, the Bashful Youth, the

20 *Oregon Laws 1866*, pp. 41-46.

21 Ng Ah Tye's picture appears in *The History of Crook County, Oregon*, p. 293.

Four Horsemen, the Big Bonanza, the Rustler, the Blue Bucket, the Glory Hole and the I Don't Know—to name just a few. One miner named Davis came up with an ingenious method for describing his claim. It ran, he wrote, from a stake marked **TOM** to one marked **D**, to one marked **A**, to one marked **V** to one marked **I**, to one marked **S** and then back to **TOM**.[22]

It wasn't long before some half-dozen houses clustered on either side of the rough trail which up until 1952 was U.S. Highway 28.[23] By this time a sizable camp had grown on the south side of Scissors Creek straddling the Ochoco River. This rowdy camp would soon expand upriver for another half mile. "Such prosperity," according to one prospector, "called for the usual mining camp activities" and whether the local ranchers liked it or not, it came.[24] By the end of summer 1874, Scissors Creek flat—known as Lower Camp—boasted the Antler Hotel; Henry Cleek's Silver Slipper Saloon; Ryle Thompson's Pay Dirt Saloon; Olsen's Mercantile Store (which sold whiskey by the bottle in a back room); Charlie Riqua's Look Out dance hall complete with hurdy-gurdy girls; a red-light district (discreetly hidden across the Ochoco River); a livery barn; blacksmith shop; and a sawmill.[25]

It's worth noting that young business women who lived on the edge of town didn't fare any better than Chinese laborers when it came to taxation. It was hinted that one of the duties of the Wasco deputy sheriff was to pay periodic visits to the sporting houses to make certain everything was going smoothly. Of course it never was because law officers,

---

22 *Ochoco Mining Register*, p. 65.

23 In 1952 the highway was diverted up Marks Creek to avoid crossing the mile-high Ochoco pass (5,289 feet) and the dangerous hair-pin curves, 100 in all, on the northeast side of the pass. The author, who ran snow plow over the Ochoco pass during the winter of 1948-49, can vouch for the number of curves. The new highway became U.S Highway 26. Old U.S. Highway 28 in the upper Ochoco Valley became Forest Road 1222 leading into Walton Lake.

24 Art Champion, "The Mayflower Mining District," *Wheeler County Chronicle*, December 1938.

25 As remembered by Earl Hereford, Art Champion, Roy Davenport and Lem Houston. Ryle (short for Riley) Thompson, owner of the Pay Dirt Saloon was the son of Amos Thompson who settled in the upper Ochoco Valley in 1874 one mile southwest of where the Ochoco Ranger Station is presently located. Ryle and Bud Thompson were cousins. The Thompson wagon train of 1852, organized by Bud Thompson's father, consisted of the William Thompson and John Thompson families of Missouri; the Amos Thompson family of Iowa; Littleton Younger; John Gant; and five Welch men under the leadership of a man named Fathergill. Thompson, *Reminiscences of a Pioneer*, pp. 2-4; *The History of Crook County, Oregon*, 1981, pp. 241-42.

the courts and other powers felt that they had to extract a tribute. Most working girls paid a monthly fine for "operating a disorderly house" which amounted to a license to stay in business.

By 1877, with a floating population that varied between 250 and 1,700 people, this frontier outpost would be identified on the first survey map of the area as "Scissorsville, Oregon. . . a mining town located near the center of section 30."[26] The survey would also mark the ancient Shoshoni trade route from the southwest to the John Day River where it crossed the township two and a half miles northeast of Scissorsville. Prineville's population in 1877 was about 200.

Running competition to Scissorsville was Upper Town—scene of the Mayflower strike—known as Howard, Oregon. Equally as big as Scissorsville (but more sedate), Howard sported the Ochoco Hotel; Lite Howard's Dance Hall (it is unknown whether he or Riqua paid Oregon's sin tax on dancing); George Jennings' Mayflower saloon; Cady and Ben Ahalt's Mercantile store; a stage station; a post office; and Jim Howard's livery barns. Down on Fisher Creek, George and Lew McAllister were peddling mining tools from a tent.

John Douthit, pushing Jim Howard for control of the gold fields, laid out the largest amount of recorded cash when he bought out cattle baron Billy Foster for $200, acquiring his mining claims, equipment, horses and lumber in 1875. This deal made Douthit a kingpin at the mines and by 1876, the strike area was referred to as the Douthit Mining District.[27]

One of the cooks at the Ochoco Hotel went out one afternoon between meals and discovered a pocket of gold about 300 feet from where the Mayflower tunnel entered Gold Hill. He sluiced $10,000 from this hole in one month.

It is very difficult to determine just how much gold was found by the early placer miners as they kept it secret. But the estimate is that over half a million dollars in gold was taken from the Ochoco River alone in the first ten years from discovery. Oddly, mint records do not show any production before 1885. However, there is little reason that they should

---

26 E.A. Thatcher, *Field Notes Survey T.13S, R.20E.WM, Dec. 1-Dec. 10, 1877*, BLM Microfilm, Prineville, Oregon, p. 193.

27 *Crook County Mining Register*, Prineville, Oregon, p. 28.

for there was no incentive for the Ochoco settlers turned miners to send their easily spendable placer gold to the mint.

During that period Scissors Creek was placered from the head to its junction with the Ochoco River, a distance of nearly four miles. It was worked 150 to 200 feet wide to a depth of 20 feet, moving over 1.6 million cubic yards of dirt and it paid out 2.5 million dollars. Other placers on Judy, Fisher, Cady, McAllister and Davis creeks yielded $623,700. One gulch was placered to the top of Gold Hill—a distance of 1,800 feet—and returned nearly a million dollars ($970,200). Ochoco River, worked solely with rockers and gold pans, was never placered as it was considered to be too deep to get to the bedrock.[28]

Scissorsville was based on hydraulic mining. Howard would grow from hard-rock mining and this would draw the professionals—the men who worked for wages for the big companies and were considered to be on the same level with the Chinese laborers.

Placer mining continued up until 1884. By that time the high-line ditch from Spring Bench on the head of the Ochoco River was completed and mining was started at the summit of Gold Hill. During this period Josiah Williams—who had arrived in the Ochoco Valley in 1869—purchased the Belcher claim which crossed the Mayflower vein. He began placering and by so doing discovered the Mayflower lode. He also discovered that it would take more than surface mining to get at it. So, in 1886, he sold out to the McAllister brothers—the hard-rock men from Canyon City—and a new method of mining would emerge.

28 Kimerlin, *History and Geologists Report of the Mayflower Group of Mines*, Berkeley, California, September 4, 1926.

CHAPTER 178

FIRE IN THE HOLE!

We heard yells comin' from the tunnel. . . in a few seconds there come the sounds of breaking timber. . . our carbide lamps went out but we did not need light to know the tunnel had caved. . . .

Frank Crampton
Hard-rock Miner

In 1883, the high graders and pocket hunters—mostly local ranchers and loggers—started to work Scissors Creek. In a few weeks, they took out another $100,000 but it was apparent the mother lode was not near the surface and that presented a problem. Things were heating up at Scissorsville when Josiah Williams bought Cranston's Belcher Gulch claim and they came to a boil when, in 1884, he struck the Mayflower vein. Running a placer operation, Williams soon lost the vein but excitement was running high. Then began a two year struggle of amateurs attempting to wrest the mineral from the ground with picks and shovels. To help dig, Williams took in John Counters as a partner. About all they accomplished was a 100 ton accumulation of rock which without sufficient manpower and proper equipment refused to give up its riches in paying quantity. What was needed were experienced hard-rock miners; but with the vigilantes riding rough-shod across central Oregon no one in his right mind would suggest such foolishness.

While Counters and Williams dug, Fred Gilliam took a claim about 100 feet down river from Louie Beirl's Sunshine Mine. Beirl, an experienced hard-rock miner, was hand-drilling a tunnel into the face of a solid rock bluff. A little strange, or so most prospectors thought, and they pretty much stayed clear of him. This didn't bluff Gilliam. After some exploratory digging, he took a chunk of ore into Prineville, gave it to Dr. Horace Belknap who sent it to the Colorado School of Mines. The ore assayed $96 a ton, not enough for a placer miner to make wages but it gave the doctor an idea and also prompted Gilliam to abandon his claim. A few days later some Canyon City hard-rock miners sunk a shaft between Gilliam's claim and the mouth of the Sunshine tunnel. They dug until they hit a huge boulder, tunneled under it and calmly removed $80,000 in gold.

Meantime, Doc Belknap—undoubtedly with some backing from influential merchants and livestock men—made a trip to Scissorsville, inspected the Mayflower tailing pile and offered to buy the whole works for $10,000. The offer was eagerly accepted and within days, Dr. Belknap made a deal with the Yancey boys' freight line and started hauling the rock to The Dalles for shipment by barge to Tacoma, Washington for processing. . . a distance of 400 miles! It was a paying proposition and a new era in mining had begun. It also alerted the Ladd Company, a Portland investment firm that something was afoot in the Ochoco.

Then, on July 10, 1886, John Counters located the main Mayflower vein and within four months, Lew and George McAllister had control.[1] Immediately, William McAllister joined his brothers and was listed in the mining records as Lew's "attorney and agent."[2] It was then that the McAllisters came to a logical conclusion. The Mayflower vein went deep underground and they couldn't touch it with hydraulic nozzles. There were but two alternatives—give up or go to hard-rock mining which would require heavy financing. Undaunted, they formed the Oregon Mayflower Company consisting of six placer claims and eleven lode claims. Not on the best of terms with the local population, and short on funds, they started a shoe-string operation.

Charlie Lowry—a man with a vocabulary of a mule-skinner and suspected agent for the Ladd Company—on the promise of producing some working capital, acquired an interest in the Mayflower claim. Apparently it was a promise only, for soon a notice informing him he had 90 days to contribute "his share or risk foreclosure" began appearing in the *Crook County Journal*. It ran for thirteen weeks and was ignored. It wasn't long before the Ladd Investment Company took over the claim, beginning a 15 year cycle of mismanagement by company lessees who

1 *Crook County Mining Register*, Vol. I, p. 92; *Ochoco Mining District Records*, p. 126.

2 *Crook County Mining Register*, Vol. II, p. 170.

were heavily subsidized by local backers with orders to make a fast profit and then get lost.

Because most of the hard-rock miners were company men, in short, common wage earners as opposed to the free wheeling placer miners, their numbers could be easily controlled. Lew McAllister was a different story—a man who packed a gun and wasn't afraid to use it. McAllister was soon branded as a trouble maker. Eventually, he too would be eliminated but for now, he was just a thorn in the side to be ignored and hopefully shoved into a quiet corner where he couldn't disrupt plans.

Americans were expert placer miners but they knew little about hard-rock mining. It would take men from Europe who had centuries of experience in deep tunneling and following elusive veins to do the job. By 1875 when dynamite replaced black powder, the principal tools of the trade were hand driven drills held by men with nerves of steel, and sticks of dynamite.

No one, least of all the mining companies, kept track of all the casualties. For decades a miner's life was regarded by his bosses as no one's responsibility but his own. It was thought if a man spent ten years in the mines, he stood one chance in three of suffering a serious injury, and one in eight of getting killed. In one terrible explosion and cave-in at a Utah mine in 1903, thirty-five miners lost their lives. In the 1890's at the Goldfield Nevada mine, twenty men—including Frank Crampton[3]—were trapped in a cave-in for fourteen days. They were lucky, all but one survived. All told, possibly 7,500 men died digging out the silver and gold on the western mining frontiers—with another 20,000 crippled for life. Many of the Ochoco hard-rock miners had fingers and/or an eye missing. Not even logging exacted such a frightful human price for its treasures.[4]

Yet the only way to get at the precious metal deep underground was to descend into the dangerous depths and dig it out. If the miners could not reach the lode by tunnel, they sank a vertical shaft to a point below the proposed mining area, dug laterally until they got under it and

---

3 The author's father Andy and Art Champion were both friends with hard-rock miner Frank Crampton.

4 Wallace, *The Miners*, p. 94.

again worked their way upward. This, in itself, was a dangerous process as the rock overhead dropped down on the men boring upwards. Jack Simpson, drilling to place a dynamite charge in the Whiting mine on the upper Ochoco River, got crushed in this manner. He was lifted 150 feet up a vertical shaft to the surface in an open ore bucket and survived.

Miners developed their own vocabulary to describe these underground passage ways. A *stope* was a step-like excavation formed by the removal of ore from around a vertical shaft. A *winze* was a slanted shaft or inclined passage from one level to another in a mine; and a *drift* was a horizontal passageway driven into or along the path of a mineral vein. Underground, these terms were used to identify strike areas called lode claims in the same manner as placer claims were identified on the surface. For example when the hard-rock miners arrived at Howard, we find recorded strikes bearing such names as The Mayflower Stope; Blue Bucket Tunnel; Fraizer Winze; Ophir Shaft; and The South Drift.[5]

Blasting holes were cut in the rock by "single jacking" in which a miner held a drill in one hand and swung a 4 pound sledge with the other or by "double jacking" in which one man held the drill while a companion or two drove it with 8 pound sledges. The drills had to be constantly turned in the holes so they wouldn't stick. A good team of double jack men could deliver as many as sixty blows a minute and drill two inches into solid rock in that time. Should a hammer man miss his mark, the drill holder usually lost his hand. After a drill cut about six inches of hole it had to be reshaped and tempered by one of the busiest and highest paid men in the mine—the blacksmith.

In ordinary rock they would drill seven holes 30 inches deep into the face, placing a stick of dynamite in each hole. In very hard rock it would take sixteen holes filled with dynamite to do the job. With the traditional warning of "fire in the hole!" the powder monkey would ignite the fuse and run for his life. Progress was very slow. With luck, they could advance the tunnel three feet at a blast. Work on the Frazier winze (which was sunk to a total depth of 112 feet with several drifts and a second winze 35 feet deep) took 20 men three years to complete. Earl Hereford, single jacking in the Frazier winze would remark, "Drilling was the easy

5 Kimerlin, *History and Geological Report of the Mayflower Group of Mines*, September 4, 1926.

part. After that, the real work began. You had to muck out all that rock to the surface."[6]

Dynamite was dangerous not only from a premature blast or even worse, a charge that failed to explode one or two sticks—but its detonation also released clouds of nauseating fumes. Two powder men—Andy Ontko (the author's father) and Bud Koch (the author's uncle)—told that when handling dynamite, they had to be extremely careful not to wipe sweat from their foreheads. Nitroglycerine from the sticks would get on their hands and when rubbed on the head would cause splitting headaches that could last for hours or even for days. Also a misjudgment in length of detonating fuses which were attached to each stick of dynamite could spell death.

To this day, a large tailing pile at the mouth of The Sunshine Mine—two miles upriver from Scissorsville—marks where Louis Beirl single-jacked a tunnel 600 feet through solid rock into the northern base of Gold Hill. It took 15 years to reach that depth and he was still drilling when he was bitten by a tick and died of spotted fever. The baffling thing about this back-breaking labor was that Beirl was not looking for gold. Taking orders from a spiritual medium in Tacoma, Washington, Beirl believed that an angel was directing his diggings and he was told "to search for uranium," a powerful radioactive element found in pitchblende and carnotite. At that time in the Ochoco mining camps no one had ever heard of uranium.

Uranium had been discovered by a German chemist in 1789 but it wasn't until 1896 that the French physicist Antoine Henri Becquerel demonstrated its radioactive properties which led to the discovery of radium and to the concept of atomic fission; and eventually to the development of the nuclear bomb. Louis Beirl was years ahead of his time.[7] The mere fact no one knew what earthly value there was in uranium

---

6 At the time of this interview, Earl Hereford at age 86 was the only miner still living who worked the Mayflower mine. He went to work for Frazier, manager for a Los Angeles company, in October 1920.

7 By the end of World War II, serious uranium exploration was being done in central Oregon, continuing throughout the 1950s and early '60s. Found in this area in carnotite bearing ore—lemon yellow in color—one of the more extensive diggings was located on the southwest slope of Powell Buttes.

or for that matter what the ore even looked like didn't deter Louie one bit.

Because of his knack in dealing with "the other world," most miners were a little nervous in Beirl's presence. Louie had gained somewhat of a following among the local residents and on occasion would hike (he walked wherever he went) for miles to hold a seance at some farm house. He did stop traveling at night however when one evening near midnight a cougar followed him from Jim Johnson's ranch to his shack at the entrance of the Sunshine Mine. . . a distance of fifteen miles.

Henry Koch (the author's grandfather), who bought Stephenson's ranch from J.N. Williamson and was doing some placer mining on the Ochoco River, told of one such visit. A dignified old-country Russian of german descent, Hank was not one to let his imagination play tricks. In fact his father-in-law, a frontier marshall in Washington Territory, was a noted "ghost-buster."

One evening, Louie stopped by the diggings and Hank invited him in for supper. During the course of conversation, Louie remarked that there were spirits present. Not necessarily friendly ones either. Hank chose to ignore this revelation but on Louie's command there were loud raps on the window followed by others on the wall. Hank maintained his composure but as the evening wore on inanimate objects mysteriously moved from one place to another. Hank was more than relieved when Louie finally decided to head home.

Shortly after Louie's departure, Hank went to bed. In telling what then happened, Hank's German accent came to the fore which I won't attempt to put into writing.

> I had just crawled into bed and was about to fall asleep when it felt like someone at the head of the bed and one at the foot lifted it a couple of feet off the floor. I jumped out of bed, lit the lamp, grabbed my rifle but there wasn't nothin' there. I decided I must be goin' crazy and got back in bed. Then came a bangin' at the window. My old dog damn near tore the door off its hinges tryin' to get out so I ran outside and looked around. Nothin! The dog took off yelpin' and I didn't see him again for two days. Anyhow, I went back inside, sat down on the chair tryin' to figure it

> out when the chair with me in it rose to the ceiling and slowly came back down! Gott Tam! I never let Louie back in the house again.[8]

A few days later, Henry Koch was shot in the back by an unknown assailant using a .30-.30 Winchester rifle.

Other interesting sidelights were surfacing in the upper Ochoco Valley. One woman in the gold camps must have worked herself to death to receive the following praise from an admiring male at her funeral: "Magnificent woman that, sir. A wife of the right sort, she was. Why she earnt her old man $900 in nine weeks, clear of all expenses, by washin' clothes. Such women ain't common, I tell you. If they were a man might marry and make money by the operation."

By 1886, other hard-rock miners besides Lew McAllister and Louie Beirl were arriving on the scene but unlike the free-wheeling prospectors, they required a steady employer and that would be arranged. Capricious spirits and the departed soul of a laundry woman were not responsible for the early demise of that rowdy settlement at the mouth of Scissors Creek. It would suffer a more ignoble death at the hands of a fly-by-night highly suspect hard-rock mining operation. Soon this outfit would take up residence at Upper Town but it would arrive with arms shackled.

Hard-rock mining—if done properly—required large capital investment to erect the necessary crushing mills and sink shafts through solid rock. Backing would be forthcoming but in the beginning it was local money put up by central Oregon livestock outfits and Prineville merchants which financed mining operations. . . and this money would dictate the outcome of the Ochoco gold strike. By necessity, mining companies would import hundreds of skilled and unskilled laborers to do the job but there would be no economic boom in central Oregon in the conventional sense of the word nor would there be any concern over the sudden influx in population. This in itself seems strange when considering at the time, influential citizens were discouraging new settlement—by force if necessary. Most likely, the disposition of the new arrivals was the reason for tolerance.

---

8 Henry Koch, September, 1948.

Wrenching gold from veins buried deep within the earth was monotonous and back-breaking labor requiring the miners to put in a ten hour shift below ground mucking and drilling for $2.50 a day. When they got off work, they returned to primitive shacks for uninviting meals of coffee, beans and greasy pork. Under such conditions they suffered from many diseases; among them diarrhea, dysentery, chills, fever and malaria. Men in this position—undernourished, underpaid and often chronically ill—would pose no threat to the cattle, sheep and timber industry of central Oregon.

The first in a succession of suitors who attempted to lure the golden goddess from her underground bed chamber was the secretive Portland-based Ladd Investment Company which knew nothing about hard-rock mining but was operating under the name of the Oregon Mayflower Mining Company. The McAllister brothers who formed the original Oregon Mayflower Company were lost somewhere in the shuffle. Trying to trace the web of well-concealed agreements pertaining to mining operations leads to blind alleys, but the sequence of deals to come are roughly like this.

By the end of 1886, the Ladd Company had control of 27 claims, 5 lines of ditch, 3 large storage reservoirs and all available water rights. How big the Ochoco Mining District really was at this time is anyone's guess. At the very most 27 mining claims—600 feet by 1,500 feet—can fit into a square mile and by 1890 there were hundreds of claims recorded in the district. It was now obvious to the legitimate mining corporations that something was being withheld. The Oregon Mayflower Company—with suspected local and very influential backing—was exclusively run by leasees and no systematic exploration or development was attempted. Only the high grade ore was mined and it had to be extremely valuable as the high cost of transportation by horse-drawn wagons and river barges to Tacoma, Washington precluded any shipment except that of high grade ore. With just a small capital outlay—less than the freighting costs of one year—equipment could have been installed on site to process the ore at Howard but it wasn't. Neither was any advantage taken of the 1872 mining law.

The first thing the Ladd Investment Company did was to construct a huge oven called a smelter to melt down the gold-bearing rock and about 40 tons of ore were smelted before the smelter overheated, caught fire and melted the brick furnace. This forced the company back to freighting ore out of the area for processing. These huge ore shipments attracted the attention of the professional hard-rock miners and the chase was on. With the Ladd Investment Company paying all expenses, the Oregon Mayflower Company became a Washington Corporation formed by the Thronson brothers. Thron Thronson, an assayer, geologist and mining engineer was president and manager of the Mayflower Company; J.A. Thronson, secretary and C.J. Thronson, treasurer.

In a series of puzzling leases, the Thronson brothers held the mining property for a time; then the Chicago-based Ochoco Mining Company entered the scene loaded with eastern money; the Gatewood Mining and Trading Company backed by Kansas capitalists; a Salt Lake City firm financed by the Mormon Church; and somewhere in this paper-maze, Stockman and Owens—Medford, Oregon speculators—gained control of the mining property.

With outside capital flowing in, the Oregon Mayflower Company shifted activity from Scissorsville to Upper Camp, adding to the already established town of Howard another blacksmith shop, storage sheds, mess hall, sleeping quarters, company office and assay office. Lucy Helms, a sixteen-year-old waitress at the Ochoco Hotel dining room, would note that by 1901, there were "only about a half dozen houses left in lower town." Unfortunately, many Scissorsville buildings—perhaps by company order—were demolished by hydraulic operations between 1895 and 1900.[9]

In a flurry of activity, a stamp mill with crushing plates and concentrating tables was under construction. The dull roar of dynamite shook the upper Ochoco Valley as tunnels were expanded and huge ore-wagons rumbled through Prineville bound for the port of The Dalles and Tacoma, Washington. Five 750-pound stamps were used to crush the gold-bearing rock for shipment, requiring a 500 foot head of water to

---

9 Lucy Helms, Fossil Oregon, 1979; Emery Oliver, *Mineral Survey No. 411 of Mayflower Group of Mines 1900*, Bureau of Land Management files, Portland, Oregon. In the late 1950s, to complete the desecration of a time when the golden temptress held sway in the Ochoco, our guardians of the forest—in the name of public safety—destroyed what remained of the Howard dance hall and saloon with its ornate log porch running the full width of the building; the two story log Ochoco Hotel; and the one-of-a-kind historic stamp mill clinging to the steep timbered north slope of Gold Hill.

drive them. More water was needed to power a mighty steam engine capable of lifting ore from a depth of 600 feet. Vic Blodgett was brought in from the Yukon to supervise mining operations. Jim Fuller, a hydro-engineer, was placed in charge of reservoir construction. For back-up, Fuller hired Mike Mulvahill, a native of Ireland out of Chicago, to oversee reconstruction of the upper Ochoco dam (now Walton Lake) while he personally took over construction of a lower dam at the mouth of Ahalt Creek which fed water into the vital middle ditch, the main source of power for the stamp mill and hydraulic operations still in progress on Judy Creek and Scissors Creek. This work entailed importing Chinese laborers from Portland, Seattle and San Francisco.

Mining engineers soon located the main zone of ore some 700 feet above the valley floor. Hard-rock experts drove a tunnel over a quarter of a mile into Gold Hill in search of the elusive golden goddess. On the south side of Gold Hill, the Ochoco Mining Company (incorporated by Prineville merchants Frank Elkins, Fred Wilson, A.H. Lippman and Granvel Clifton with a capital stock of $3,125) was also driving a tunnel into the mountain.[10] The Mayflower drift and the Elkins tunnel came within a few feet of connecting—which would have opened a passage-way completely through Gold Hill.

At a point 330 feet from the Mayflower entrance, a charge of dynamite misfired and blew out a hole 90 feet back from its intended target and the glory hole—named the Mayflower Chute—was found. This pocket alone produced $220,000. It was enough to encourage railroad surveys up the Ochoco Valley with an estimated 4.5 million tons of gold-bearing ore yet to be tapped.[11] During its heyday, from 1886 to 1906, the Oregon Mayflower Company would have a record production of 2.5 million dollars in gold and silver bullion.

By 1897 more scheming was going on. Whether it was Mulvahill (the Chicago transplant) who tipped off Illinois benefactors or Vic Blodgett tampering with a new idea or both is hard to say. Whatever the cause, that year the Ochoco Mining Company was organized in Illinois

---

10 *The Pacific Monthly*, Portland, Oregon, February 1903, p. 134.

11 As late as the 1930's these railroad survey stakes were still in evidence on the north side of the Ochoco River where it passed through the Ontko Ranch some seven miles southwest of the Mayflower mine.

financed by Chicago money and its purchasing agent was Victor Blodgett.[12] This raised the possibility of the Ochoco Mining Company going into hard-rock mining on a massive scale. Instead, Blodgett quietly purchased from the different owners all the placer ground on Judy, Fisher and Scissors creeks. He then hired Frank Hereford to begin logging operations on Scissors Creek and began construction of a sawmill on Judy Creek for the purpose of cutting lumber for flumes. By now, it was obvious he was going back to hydraulic operations on a grand scale using the water system earlier constructed for the operation of the Mayflower claims.

Placer mining was renewed with vigor until 1901, averaging $100,000 a year.[13] During this active period, Blodgett kept as many as ten 5-pound lard pails filled with gold nuggets and dust in his Scissorsville office, which was build like a jail.[14] This historic landmark withstood the rigors of time until the mid-1970s when it was destroyed by the Forest Service.

In 1898, control of the mining property passed from the Ladd Investment Company to the Thompson brothers of Ashwood, Oregon after they had sold their interest in the Oregon Queen Silver Mine to the Oregon King Mining Company. To further entice outside capital, the *Blue Mountain Eagle* reported new discoveries of rich placer ground some thirty miles east of the Mayflower strike in the head of Spanish Gulch.[15] This was confirmed by geologic surveys reporting $100,000 in placer gold and "at least two good prospects of hard rock mines."[16] The *Blue Mountain Eagle's* latest gold scoop would also throw the Chinese controlled Loy Yick Company into turmoil by cluttering Spanish Gulch with Occidental pocket hunters.

Finally, with Prineville banker Tom Baldwin and Prineville M.D. Horace Belknap hovering in the background, the Oregon Mayflower Company reverted to Lew McAllister who made a deal in January 1903 with Thron Thronson, president of the Washington corporation, to serve

---

12 *Crook County Mining Register*, Vol. I, pp. 216-18.

13 Champion, "The Mayflower Mines," *Central Oregon Shopper*, August 4, 1949, p. 3.

14 Earl Hereford, son of Frank Hereford, June 8, 1965.

15 *The Blue Mountain Eagle*, John Day, Oregon, February 11, 1898.

16 Walhemar Lindgren, *The Gold Belt of the Blue Mountains of Oregon*, 1901, U.S. Geologic Survey; A.J. Collier, A Geologist with the Oregon Bureau of Mines and Geology, 1914.

as manager. For his part in the take-over McAllister received $26,000 and one share in the operation.[17] By April, the Oregon Mayflower Company incorporated with a capital stock of one million dollars and shares selling at one dollar each. Oddly enough, one month later, the *Pacific Monthly* was advertising shares for 25¢ with a minimum of 10 shares to purchase plus easy payment on the installment plan.[18] Eight months after this announcement, the *Monthly* would give a glowing account of the Mayflower mine in an article entitled, "On the Ochoco."

According to the Portland magazine: "Capital is going into that region by the hundreds of thousands. . . the attention of mining men recently has been attracted to the Ochoco in Crook County. . . evidence abounds for heavy faulting movements. . . the greatest area of extreme depression being the confluence of Ochoco, Scissors and Judah creeks, the location of the mines." The article continues: "Although Gold Hill rises to an altitude of 4,500 feet above sea, and 500 feet above Ochoco Creek level, you look down upon its crest much as you would look into a great crater." It would conclude: "This region will, in the near future, prove a valuable addition to the many rich mineral districts of the Blue Mountain region, and will add millions to the wealth of the shrewd and wide-awake mining men of the coast."[19]

Within a year, a new stamp mill and concentrating table were added to the operation in 1905 in an attempt to cyanide the gold-bearing ore but owing to lack of fine grinding it was not successful. Even so, 2,000 tons were treated and yielded nearly $300,000. Then in March 1912, George McAllister and W.T. Davenport—agents for the Washington Mining Company—entered into a rather unusual contract with Richard King and T.F. McNamara. For the sum of one dollar McAllister and Davenport agreed to sell the Mayflower Company to King and McNamara at any time within one year of the contract date for one million dollars in gold coin, "or such less sum as the parties heretofore may hereafter agree upon."[20] However, if King and McNamara didn't buy the mine in that time period and it sold to someone else, King and

17 *Prineville Review*, February 5, 1903.

18 *Prineville Review*, April 16, 1903; *The Pacific Monthly*, Portland, Oregon, June 1903.

19 *The Pacific Monthly*, Vol. XI, No. 2, February 1904, p. 138.

20 *Crook County Mining Register*, Vol. III, pp. 506-07.

McNamara were to receive 10% of the purchase price. Rather a neat agreement but apparently no sale was made to any interested party.

In keeping with these shadowy transactions, three gentlemen from Canyonville in Douglas County, Oregon were granted a lease on a portion of the Mayflower vein and made "an excessively rich strike."[21] In a span of four days working the Swank stope, they extracted $6,000 in gold dust using a mortar and pestle. After that the mineral went base but the Canyonville miners sacked and shipped ore until June 1917 and took between $80,000 and $100,000 in dust and nuggets.[22] And so it went.

When Lem and Betty Houston spent their last cent in the 1950s to acquire patent to the Mayflower gold claim it was a futile effort. Prineville attorney Harold Banta summed up the Houston's situation when he wrote that "they have literally sunk every cent they could beg or borrow into this patent application and they still owe some $3,000."[23] The Houston's submitted as evidence samples of ore taken from the turn of the century diggings but the court's decision was not based on whether a "prudent man" would have invested in the mine at that time but whether a "prudent man would now invest in the mine" and the samples held no influence in the judge's decision. Using that line of reasoning it could be argued that sensible people never engaged in mining in the West. They stayed home and became clerks or if they did go to the gold fields it was to be shopkeepers or some other rational occupation. The point is, any of the early miners would have had an easy time acquiring a patent before 1918. Forty years later after the high-graders got through, the Houston's application went down in flames.

Needless to say, the *Pacific Monthly's* glowing report of 1904 didn't pan out. The total amount of known gold and silver produced between 1885 and 1918 was 6.84 million dollars. It was believed by Kimerlin who made a survey of the mine in 1926 that there remained some 4.5 million tons of gold and silver bearing ore which at the 1920 gold standard was worth 13.5 million dollars. . . and this was still in the

---

21 Champion, *The Central Oregon Shopper*, August 4, 1949, p. 3.

22 Champion, who worked in the Mayflower mines, claimed they took $100,000 in gold. Kimerlin in his *Geological Report of the Mayflower Mine*, September 4, 1926 claims $80,000.

23 Letter from Harold Banta to Hearing Officer Felton, May 19, 1955, p. 2.

ground! By the end of the 20th century this same amount of gold-bearing ore would be worth 270 million dollars.

The Ochoco Mining District has gone from being touted as the golden goddess of the Ochoco to a barren landscape without even a sign to inform passersby of its existence. As one observer would lament "surely its proper status lies somewhere in between."

CHAPTER 179

LIQUID SILVER

I worked up to the saddle above White Rock gulch, pulled up some bunchgrass and there it was—native quick beaded to the grass roots!

Arthur Champion
Discoverer of the Horse Heaven Mine

The earliest known discovery of quicksilver in Oregon was the Bonanza mine in Douglas County in 1865 but production was not undertaken until 1879 at the close of the Bannock War. In the collective minds of western prospectors, quicksilver was useful for only one purpose and that was to separate gold from rock. Although a major product long before the birth of Christ, the United States knew little to nothing about its economic value. Therefore, a short history of quicksilver production is in order to give some idea as to what could have been a booming central Oregon industry had international politics not entered the scene.

Because of a lack of knowledge of quicksilver's potential value on the world market, the protectionists who ruled central Oregon would allow the cinnabar miners to operate in obscurity. After all, there was no danger of a population influx as production was mainly done on an individual basis or at most, three or four men might be involved in the operation. Besides, with the sheep and cattle war in full swing, there were more important things to occupy the mind. And so, central Oregon's quicksilver industry blundered into existence. The forerunners—men like Art Champion, Frank Towner, Ed Staley and Bill Westerling, the major discoverers—developed reduction processes working with brick furnaces and iron pipe called retorts which were not noticeably safer than the hooded bonfires used by early Cro-Magnon man. In two words, they were damned hazardous. At least all the retort men had to worry about was being "salivated" by their own hand instead of being gunned-down by an irate stockman. Beirl, still gouging out rock for "mysterious uranium" was also ignored, but Hank Koch, who stubbornly stuck to gold, did suffer that indignity.

The quest for cinnabar was an evolutionary step followed by discovery of gold. After crushing the gold-bearing rock, the gold had to be removed by amalgamation with quicksilver. Then the quicksilver was boiled off in a smelter. This led to the search for cinnabar, or mercury-bearing ore. Aside from the danger involved, quicksilver was easy to process and required little capital, so most exploration and development was done by hard-rock miners. Getting off to a late start, it soon became obvious that the ancient Clarno lava flows covering the Ochoco were underlain with high-grade cinnabar, something the Spanish were aware of at the turn of the 18th century. Not only were these rich deposits known to Charles II of Spain but they were also suspected by his cousins, William II of Great Britain and Louis XIV of France. . . two hundred years before the Ochoco prospectors stumbled onto a discovery. When they did, in a 30-year period beginning in 1906, quicksilver mining eclipsed the gold industry in eastern Oregon.

The Ochoco quicksilver mining district—geologically known as the Round Mountain Quadrangle—was shaped like a half circle with Prineville serving as the mid-way point. In a 35 mile radius from Prineville were twenty producing mines, anchored on the north by Horse Heaven and the Oregon King mines; on the east by Blue Ridge and the Mother Lode; and on the south by the Sundown and Bear Creek mines. Within this 2,000 square mile arc lay all the rest.

There was also a geologic reason for this configuration. The Ochoco strike area sitting on the ancient cinder cones of Lookout, Horse Heaven, Bear, Maury and Round mountains would give proof to this. On the Ontko claim in the upper Ochoco Valley, the weathered remains of the Columbia lava flow can still be traced to this day.

The occurrence of quicksilver is definitely associated with volcanism during the Tertiary and Quarternary periods of the Cenozoic era. It was during this period that Lookout Mountain, the Maurys and Mt. Pisgah were ripped by violent eruption. It is thought that quicksilver is a common property of magma deep within the earth. It is also one of the most volatile metals. Because of this characteristic, if special conditions don't trap the metal upon release from the parent magma, it exists at the surface. Great quantities of quicksilver—along with sulfur and water vapor—escape into the atmosphere in a volcanic explosion.

If trapped near the surface, quicksilver can show up in very high grade bodies of ore but without much reason for doing so. This makes it harder to locate than other metals but this same irregularity can also carry the possibility of finding a high-grade ore pocket. About twenty-five minerals carry quicksilver but the most important are cinnabar followed by native quick. Most of the rest which include meta cinnabrile—black in color and confused with iron ore—and calomel, a white to yellow brown ore, are rare.

Quicksilver itself is a rare metal, a fact not often known to central Oregonians in view of the abundance in which it occurs in the Ochoco. In the small amount produced in any given year quicksilver ranks next to gold and in value per ton of ore it ranks third among the precious metals, exceeded in value only by gold and silver. The Ochoco prospectors soon learned that to the professional miner who extracted the precious metal from cinnabar there was no such thing as mercury except maybe a name applied to the Roman god of trade. The miner may refer to it as "quick" or maybe even "silver" but he never called it "mercury." The liquid metal he produced was quicksilver. When the consumer got it, he called it mercury—a silver white metal which was liquid at ordinary temperatures and the heaviest liquid known to man.

Some quicksilver is found in all parts of the world but the productive areas are confined to three regions: the countries bordering the north coast of the Mediterranean, the West Coast of South America and the West Coast of North America. In those areas, four large mines have produced the bulk of quicksilver used world-wide.

If the Ochoco miners went at it like a bunch of amateurs, it was because they hadn't done their homework. Having taken a backseat to gold on the western frontier, the search for cinnabar exploded across central Oregon like a case of dynamite and it had centuries of technology to guide it. With beginnings that preceded written history, the mining of cinnabar was an ancient and lucrative business. In all likelihood pre-historic man may have accidentally built a fire on a cinnabar vein and discovered quicksilver. This theory may not be as far-fetched as it sounds.

On a chilly spring evening in 1933, Bill Westerling, who had been tramping over Round Mountain for days prospecting for cinnabar, set up camp near the 5,000 foot elevation. The next morning as he stirred up the fire to warm some coffee, he was elated to see beads of quicksilver in the ashes. Westerling had discovered the Round Mountain mine.[1] In the next few years, he drove a tunnel 500 feet into the mountain, established nine surface claims and was producing quicksilver.

By 415 B.C. Callias, a Greek scientist, had discovered a reduction process for quicksilver and in so doing became a wealthy man. China mined cinnabar which was used as vermillion ink and paint in the arts and by 210 B.C., they record the use of metallic quicksilver, giving proof that a Chinese engineer had also perfected a reduction process.[2] Both Greek and Chinese would discover that playing with mercury fumes was a hazardous sport.

By the 1980s, mercury poisoning became a prime environmental issue but the risk of contamination is pretty much limited to the production process. Retorting or cooking cinnabar as the miners called it, is still being done about the same as it was 2,000 years ago. The first processing was accomplished by building a fire under a pile of ore and placing a hood overhead to trap the fumes. Then came clay retorts which are still used in China. The first furnace invented for exclusive quicksilver reduction was built in Peru at the Huancavelica mine in 1633. Owned by the Spanish government, the mine was in operation for over 300 years before it finally played out in the mid 1800s, having produced 1.5 million flasks of quicksilver.

Thirteen years after its invention in Peru, the reduction furnace was introduced at Almaden, Spain. Ten furnaces built at the Almaden mine between 1646 and 1654 are still being used at the present time. The Almaden, owned by the Romans, the Moors and then Spain has not only been in continuous production for over 2,000 years but is still the largest producer in the world. By the start of World War II, it had produced over 6 million flasks and by the end of the war it had taken over world production. The Idria mine developed in the early 1500s by Aus-

---

1 William Westerling interview at Log Cabin Service Station on old Mitchell Highway, 1939.

2 For a detailed account of quicksilver's role in history see C.N. Schuette, *Quicksilver in Oregon*, State Department of Geology and Mineral Industries, Bulletin No. 4, 1938, pp. 10-25.

tria—held for a time by France and taken over by Italy after World War I—has been in production over 400 years and at the time of the Italian take-over had produced 2 million flasks. The first iron retort was installed in Spain in 1641, just 57 years before the Spanish pierced western North America to 43° 12' latitude east of the Sierra del Nortes (Cascades) and began smelting operations at Silver Wells on Camp Creek in central Oregon just a few miles south of the Maury mines. By 1879, some 125 people were living at or near Silver Wells, never once realizing they were sitting on the site of the first quicksilver reduction plant to be erected in what would become the United States of America. No one will ever know how much quicksilver was produced at Silver Wells but it was a high-tech operation until put out of business by the Shoshoni.

Once condensed, the quicksilver had to be contained and that was no easy task. It was also discovered that only black iron, enamelware, stoneware or wooden buckets could be used in handling quicksilver as anything else will contaminate it. So containment was accomplished by sealing the quick in iron flasks for shipment and a unit of measurement was established. Unlike gold and silver which are weighed in ounces, quicksilver is measured by the pound. Each flask holds 76 pounds of quicksilver (which is equal to 1/2 of a liquid gallon) and a flask became the standard unit of weight for marketing. Fifty dollars a flask was considered the break-even point at the start of Ochoco production. By the 1930s when the rest of the country was gripped in depression, Ochoco quicksilver was selling for $100 a flask and fifty years later it would bring $600 on the world market.

Both cinnabar and quicksilver were used in international trade from very early times. At the birth of Christ, Venetian trade ships were transporting some 10,000 pounds of cinnabar annually to Rome from the mines in Spain. The Roman artisans were especially fond of finely ground cinnabar, not only for polishing metal and glass, but for a preparation to beautify the skin. They were using mercury for the recovery of precious metals and shrewd Neapolitan merchants washed silver coins with mercury to give them more luster. Following a few experiments which involved the union of quicksilver with tin, craftsmen created a household article in common use today. By applying this mixture to one side of a pane of glass, the style-conscious Latins produced the mirror, perhaps to view first-hand the cosmetic effect of powdered cinnabar. French ladies called it *rouge*.

Around 700 A.D. when alchemists practiced their black arts, it was believed quicksilver was the answer to their quest for the elixir of life and the transmutation of metals. One theory held that quicksilver was a compound of all metals and by adding the right amount of sulfur and other (secret) substances while muttering the correct words almost any desired metal could be produced—including gold. Needless to say, they wasted an awful lot of tax payer's money during that period of research.

Use of quicksilver increased in the succeeding decades. Even so, up to the 16th century world consumption was small. Then, in 1557, the Spanish developed a process in Mexico for the recovery of gold and silver by using mercury and the first industrial process using large amounts of quicksilver had arrived. More exploration led to Spain's thrust into central Oregon. Since that discovery, the consumption of quicksilver increased century by century and by 1950 had overtaken production with a world demand of well over 100,000 flasks per year. Ironically, only about 100,000 flasks are produced annually and the U.S. consumes 35% of the world production.

Even though it was known to be poisonous, mercury was—and still is—widely used in medicine, especially in the treatment of skin diseases. Combined with chlorine, it is used in antiseptics, as a disinfectant and for the purification of drinking water. Amalgamated with silver, gold and tin, it became dental fillings highly frowned upon by the health gurus of the 1990s. In the early 1700s, the mercury thermometer was invented which measures not only atmospheric temperature but body temperature.

A hundred years earlier, the mercury barometer—used to measure atmospheric pressure—was invented and became a boon to modern science. Industrial use includes leather tanning, dying of cloth, embalming, photography, electrical switches and electroplating to name but a few of its current applications. With a minus 40° F freezing point (72° F lower than that of water) quicksilver had never been seen in the solid state until 1760 when a Russian scientist observed that it solidified at that temperature.

The next big jump in the use of quicksilver came in the final days of the Washington administration when, in 1787, an American chemist produced mercuric fulminate used to detonate explosives! The significance of this discovery can be appreciated when you consider no modern war can be waged without quicksilver. It is indispensable to industry, medicine and science. Thus, quicksilver is a metal far greater in importance than the value of its annual production would indicate.

Now for a look at the production end of the game. Scientists, chemists and geologists—the so-called experts in the field of metallurgy—would have little to experiment with in the quicksilver industry were it not for the highly skilled hard-rock miners. First, the elusive mineral had to be located and then not only wrenched from the ground but separated from its parent rock. The specialists in the cinnabar mines were the surface discoverer or prospector; the explosive expert or powderman; the underground discoverer or tunnel man; and the furnace tender or retort man. Often in the Ochoco mining district, two or three men served in all capacities and each, with the exception of surface discovery, had its own specific hazards.

The recovery of quicksilver is a major problem. When heated, cinnabar breaks up into sulfur and quicksilver vapor. Sulfur combines with oxygen to form sulfur dioxide gas and the quicksilver vapor passes through condensers and turns liquid upon cooling. The boiling point of quicksilver is 674° F. Heated to 570° F, there is little danger of being poisoned by the vapor but in an effort to speed up production, furnaces were designed to heat the cinnabar to over 1076° F as fast as possible to release the vapor immediately into condensers where it is rapidly cooled to liquid; and therein lies the danger.

In vapor form, quicksilver can escape through the most minute crack, posing a serious health hazard to those who inhale the fumes. Miners who worked the reduction process were in constant danger of being "salivated" as they called it. This was a suitable name as one of the effects of mercury poisoning was an abnormal increase in the flow of saliva followed by loss of hair and teeth. Cleo Gray, tending the retort at Horse Heaven, pulled a charge too fast which temporarily ended his mining career. Roy Matson took a shot of mercury fumes at the Champion mine leaving him a semi-invalid. Slim Davis inhaled his share at the Byram-Oscar mine. Mercury poisoning would take its grim toll at Blue Ridge, the Independent, Mother Lode. . . no mine was exempt.

In 1901—some two hundred years after the Spanish strike on Camp Creek—the Oregon King quicksilver mine was discovered some thirty-five miles north of Prineville. Actually, quicksilver had been discovered 17 years before but its importance had gone unrecognized. In 1884, Telford Wood was digging a well when he discovered the rich Oregon Queen quicksilver mine which led to the discovery of the Oregon King, both located near Ashwood in what is now Jefferson County.[3] Soon thereafter, a young prospector named Art Champion located high-grade cinnabar near the 6,000 foot level on the north slope of Lookout Mountain. He had discovered the glory hole of the Mother Lode mine. First development at the Mother Lode was done by the American Almaden company based at Howard, Oregon. In 1906, company records would note the production of three flasks of quicksilver and the Ochoco Mining District was born.

At its peak, the Mother Lode encompassed 280 acres. The initial focus was on copper and gold but later shifted to quicksilver. Opened in 1899, the Mother Lode yielded the most quicksilver of any of the Ochoco's 22 operating mines. Nearly 100 years later, it was the first to be targeted by the Ochoco National Forest for a massive clean-up effort. Between 1900 and 1962, when cinnabar was last mined, the Mother Lode produced 503 flasks of mercury. In the late 1980s the mine's tunnel and main shaft were dynamited closed and by 1997 the open ore pits—up to one acre in size—revealed abnormally high levels of extremely toxic mercury. The wood in the buildings, the mining equipment and everything in the processing plant was contaminated. Fish tested in nearby Canyon Creek also had dangerously high levels of mercury. This caused the Forest Service to go into panic and place the Mother Lode off limits to visitors in the area.

As one old hard-rock miner, who holds two 20 acre Mother Lode claims would question, "What's all the hubbub about? There's no threat

3 This is the same Whitfield Telford Wood who, in 1854, had been offered 60 lots of land on the barren Nebraska prairie for the Kentucky thoroughbred he was riding. Not being slow of wit, Wood refused the offer. One year later, a government land office was opened on the spot and today the lots Wood turned down are located in the heart of Omaha City, Nebraska. After three decades, his luck still hadn't improved. Like everyone else in the country, Wood didn't recognize the value of cinnabar.

whatsoever. The Forest Service is just making a big issue out of it."[4] From a common sense standpoint, he was right. It is too bad that concerned government mineral inspectors couldn't have visited the quicksilver production plants when they were really in operation. Then they would have had something to worry about.

The discovery of quicksilver would send the *Pacific Monthly* into fits of ecstasy. In an article entitled "On the Ochoco," a reporter would cry out: "Such mines as the Red Boy, Badger, Oregon King and others have a combined annual output in the millions of dollars!" This must have been a deliberate attempt to interest investors as the true figure was more in the thousands. The article would also reveal that the strike area was located in a region of heavy faulting due to the ground sinking. "The greatest area of extreme depression being in the upper Ochoco Valley and here is where the mineral bearing veins originate as the underground tracers can attest." Then caught in the throes of rapture, he continues: "Yet, as always, men are blind—blind when the very grass they tread, the charred hulks of fallen forest giants have written upon them in letters so large and plain that they almost shout aloud. 'Opportunity! Opportunity!' This land is pregnant with hidden resources, possibilities that almost stagger the imagination, opportunities!! A thousand million tongues are shouting 'Awake! Awake!! Awake!!!'"[5] And awake, they did.

Within the next thirty years all of the Ochoco quicksilver strikes were made. Besides the surface discoveries made by Champion, Staley and Westerling, chance finds were made by cattlemen and sheepherders, particularly the latter, who traversed much country on foot. Ontko and other bona fide tunnel men made the underground discoveries.

In the strike area, the ground was severely faulted, composed of John Day sediments overlain by Columbia lava flows. Plagued by water and cave-ins, development was dangerous, especially considering that the initial underground exploration in all the mines was done by one or two men. Although by necessity vertical shafts had to be driven deep into the ground, if at all possible, the miners avoided it for two reasons. One man could drive a tunnel and reap the full reward of his endeavors while it took two or more men to sink a shaft and thus the profits decreased.

4 "Old Mercury Mine Probed," *The Bulletin,* Bend, Oregon, August 3, 1997.

5 *The Pacific Monthly*, February 1904, pp. 134, 138.

Also, shafting usually meant that they would hit a vein of water which had to be bailed or pumped out before further progress could be made.

After several hundred feet of drift, the Blue Ridge Mercury Company—originally owned by a Japanese firm—had to sink an eight-foot by sixteen-foot shaft a hundred feet deep to continue working the cinnabar vein. The wet and sticky high-grade ore from this vein was not well-suited for retort treatment as was the case in many of the Ochoco mines. Also, tracing of mineralized veins brought on the specialists—men like Andy Ontko who could follow the disappearance of fractured veins in the underground maze of vertical walls, folded uplifts and broken fissures with unerring skill. These expert tunnel men would work the various mines wherever their talent was needed.

In 1942 the Champion mine sunk an inclined shaft to the depth of three hundred feet in an attempt to locate the main body of ore. At this depth, even in the dead of winter, it was like working in a steam bath. Ontko was running a drift at the 300 foot level when one evening near the end of a shift, he hit the mother lode—a pure vein of high-grade cinnabar five feet wide and God alone knows how thick. He had also tapped an underground river. With water increasing by the minute, Ontko retreated up the main shaft. Overnight, the water rose to the 190 foot level in the shaft making it 110 feet deep. Bailing operations with a 100 gallon ore bucket began immediately with no success. Finally a high-volume pump was brought in from Seattle and after days of 24-hour pumping, the water was drawn down to the 300 foot drift level but the tunnel, loosened by the water, was dangerous to enter. The moment the pump ceased operation the flow of water increased. With World War II hampering operations, the mine owners (Johnston Brothers) finally gave up and abandoned the mine.[6]

A half mile north of the Mother Lode, Champion found native quick in the grass roots and the Independent Mining Company was formed. Other strikes were being made in the Ochoco Valley: the Byram-Oscar mine on Camp Branch Creek developed by a shaft and four levels of tunnels; the Blevens mine opposite the mouth of Wolf Creek consisting of a main tunnel and several side drifts; the Staley-Barney mine better

6 The author, Andy Ontko's son, did the assessment work on the Champion mine for many years.

known as the Jimmie Ann on the south slope of Koch Butte; the Ontko mine; the Champion mine; and the Whiting mine which was located only 50 feet in elevation above the Ochoco River and was in constant threat of flooding. However, the Whiting mine did produce some 250 flasks before water took over the main body of ore.

Less than a half mile east of the Whiting mine a three-foot wide vein of high-grade cinnabar was found at the surface while excavating a basement for a government housing project. This vein was quickly hidden behind a cement wall and was dutifully unrecorded.

The Bear Group of mines were located on the head of Marks Creek while Johnson Creek, draining into Big Summit Prairie held the Westerling mine; the Johnson Creek mine; the Round Mountain mine (all discovered by Bill Westerling); Blue Ridge; and the Greenback. Strikes were also being made to the south and to the west. Clinging to the north face of the Maury Mountains were Towner's Sundown Mine and Planter and Dunham's Bear Creek Mine while within sight of Prineville, the Barnes Butte Mine was operating full bore.

During this flurry, Champion who was more interested in discovery than development, rounded up a partner—Grover Keeton—and headed for the Stephenson Mountain country mainly to check the area around the Oregon King mine. First known as the Silver King, it was located on the east side of Trout Creek about a mile north of Ashwood. Discovered in 1898 by Jim Wilson from Walla Walla, Wilson soon formed a mining company composed of John Kirby, Thron Thronson, J.T. and John Hubbard and John Knight. After sinking a shaft to the depth of 100 feet, they sold their claims—twelve in number—to the Oregon King Mining Company organized by P.J. Inealy of Krummerer, Wyoming and J.G. Edwards and C.M. Cartwright of the Hay Creek Ranch. Suspecting that there were more strikes to be made in the Trout Creek area, Champion began prospecting. On the north slope of an old Clarno cinder cone called Horse Heaven Mountain, he struck pay dirt in the head of White Rock Gulch. Much to his partner's disgust, Champion sold their interest in the strike for $500 cash to Charley Hayes and Ray Whiting.

By this time, Champion was gaining a reputation as the locator of high-grade cinnabar strikes. His penchant for discovery is best described by *Mining World*, a publication which adorned its front cover with his picture in 1940. It would state: "The photographic study of an intent prospector appearing on the cover of this issue shows Art J. Champion, manager of the Champion Mining Co., examining a piece of cinnabar ore. Miner though he is, Mr. Champion is essentially a prospector, and his name is associated with many of the properties in the Ochoco quicksilver district of central Oregon where he has been discovering and developing deposits of the red mineral for many years."[7] Art was also locating mines in Nevada and California with his bosom buddy, Death Valley Scotty. In fact when the old prospector finally married, he and his bride honeymooned at the Furnace Creek Inn—better known as Scotty's Castle.

While Champion played, Hayes and Whiting formed the Crystal Syndicate financed in part by Capt. E.W. Kelley, a retired British army officer who already had an interest in the Maury Mountain mines. Production began in late 1934 and the Horse Heaven mine became the third largest Oregon producer of quicksilver for that year. Within the next three years it produced over 4,500 flasks of mercury selling for $450,000 on the world market.

World War I with its demand for explosives had sparked renewed vigor in the Ochoco quicksilver industry. During the Depression when men were fortunate if they could make $100 a year, the two and three men mining operations were making anywhere from $500 to $1,000 per man annually. By 1930, the United States was second only to Spain in the world production of quicksilver and Oregon with Horse Heaven, Blue Ridge and the Independent in full swing was the top producer in the U.S., beating out California's New Almaden mine which had been in production since the early 1800's with a total production of 1 million flasks to date. For the next two years, the big three central Oregon mines would average $275,000 annually and between 1934 and 1941 over 3.8 million dollars was made.

The Ochoco mines were learning how to operate on the "cut and run" basis that was necessary for survival in the United States due to lack of protection from the dumping of foreign quicksilver on the domestic market. Although the local miners proved their inherent soundness by the manner in which they weathered the 1930s depression, they didn't have a chance against low-cost foreign competition. Spain's Almaden,

7 *Mining World*, August 1940, Vol. 2, No. 8, p. 1.

Austria's Idria and California's New Almaden could afford to cut operating costs where the little operations couldn't and the big companies would break them.

It was during the Depression that the international mining companies began to take notice of the Ochoco quicksilver operations. Two of the first to sell out were the Mother Lode and Independent. Backed by English capital, the Quicksilver Consolidated and the Independent Mining companies were formed with Col. John Mallory—another retired British army officer—in charge of operations. The Mother Lode, troubled with cave-ins, had only one tunnel open by 1937. Producing only 100 flasks that year, the Mother Lode had to close down. The Independent was faring little better.

Although native quick and 8-pound ore was found in the grass roots, the main ore body escaped detection. In 1937, Mallory started diamond drilling operations. In a period spanning four years, holes were sunk down to 180 feet hitting only low grade ore. Then in 1941, the drill hit pay dirt. Called the Ontko Vein, it produced $28,000 in two months time. Then, because the New Almaden mine of California engaged in a price war to eliminate all competition, the Independent stopped production.

During this period Horse Heaven—averaging 1,500 flasks a year—was taken over by the Sun Oil Company, a subsidiary of Shell (a Dutch controlled company). Johnson Creek, operating under the International Mercury Company, was controlled by Russians. With four tunnels, they were producing 250 flasks annually. Blue Ridge and The Greenback, also plagued by water, were owned by a Japanese firm and managed by mining engineer Takihashi. In 1942, Blue Ridge and The Greenback were confiscated by the U.S. government and shut down. The Japanese owners, including Takihashi, were placed in prisoner of war camps on the West Coast.

Due to a lack of manpower, the Jimmie Ann mine producing 253 flasks annually closed down. The Whiting mine with a production of 250 flasks was forced out of business by rising water. The Byram-Oscar mine operating on a shoestring with only 100-flask production couldn't make ends meet. The Sundown, Lost Cinnabar, Maury and Bear Creek mines followed the same fate. The big consumer of mercury, the U.S. government, had stock-piled before the war and was importing from Spain at one-tenth the cost it took to produce domestically. Spain had cornered the world market and by 1950 was producing 34,000 metric tons of mercury annually. The Ochoco mines were dead. . . priced out of the market.

Miners, merchants, cattlemen, sheepmen, loggers, homesteaders. . . all would share roles in the approaching drama of survival. As the 19th century slid into darkness, the actors hovered backstage awaiting their curtain call for Vigilantes, Act I. And the juniper trees would bear fruit.

EPILOGUE

HORSEMEN OF THE HIGH PLATEAU

Man prefers to believe what he prefers to be true.

—Francis Bacon
English Essayist

Since the beginning of the European conquest of western America, the Shoshoni had kept eastern Oregon in a stage of siege. Now, let's see who these tough mountain cossacks really were. Perhaps, in so doing, a long-standing fallacy can be put to rest.

Like a moth drawn to an open flame, I'm writing my own death certificate. Years ago I made a vow to never get into this subject but it begs for clarification. . . especially for the people involved. Quoting the old Nevada news reporter Mark Twain, I must admit that I have never let my schooling interfere with my education. So here goes the debate. Paying heed to the advice of Corbin Harney—the present spiritual leader of the Western Shoshoni Nation—it is time to come out from behind the bush and tell it like it is. Unless the reader thrives on controversy my suggestion is to skip this discussion. As for the hardy souls who are determined to ride this out, keep in mind it has been long overdue that the quibbling about the identity of Northern Paiutes and Western Shoshoni in eastern Oregon be laid to rest. Both groups are of Shoshonean stock and its only a matter of lifestyle as to who was who at any given time.

Any attempt to identify the people who did, in fact, inhabit the greater portion of eastern Oregon prior to the late 1800s is like trying to convince an evolutionist that there is a Creator. . . short of divine enlightenment, it can't be done. Sadly some modern descendants of the once powerful Western Shoshoni war tribes—whose ancestors were forcibly separated from their families and placed on alien government reservations—honestly believe that they are Northern Paiutes. And why shouldn't they? They are taught that the principal leaders of the Northern Paiute were Weahwewa (Wolf Dog), Ocheo (Has No Horse), Paulina (War Spirit), Howlock (Big Man), Chocktoot (Black Buffalo), Winnemucca (Bad Face), Egan (Pony Blanket), Oytes (Left Hand), Paddy Cap (Yellow Jacket) and Moshenkosket (Moses Brown), all of whom—with the possible exception of Moses Brown—were Western Shoshoni war chiefs.

There are several reasons for this misrepresentation, not the least of which is the testimony of Sarah Winnemucca, a well-intentioned Native American who got caught up in the prejudices of the times. Described as "fierce and warlike," the Western Shoshoni—who ranged across eastern Oregon, northern Nevada and western Idaho—were feared by other Pacific Northwest tribes (including Sarah Winnemucca) and thoroughly detested by the advancing white settlers; so it's not likely that anything beneficial to their character would get into print. Some of the latest contributions to the concept that the Western Shoshoni horsemen of the Ochoco were Northern Paiute are appearing in recent scholarly publications.

This is due in part to theories advanced by ethnologists, anthropologists, and archaeologists who have little firsthand knowledge as to what they are talking about. In the beginning it was pretty much guesswork as to the native population of eastern Oregon and the misconceptions made then have been perpetuated and expanded upon to this day. Without exception, the eastern Oregon Shoshoni are classified as Northern Paiutes. However, even the experts in humanistic studies admit that the term Paiute, in itself, is of uncertain origin.[1]

A literal translation of the word Paiute would mean that these people were true Utes, another Shoshoni tribe. By the same line of reasoning they could have been called Paishoshoni, indicating that they were true Shoshoni. Major John Wesley Powell, the foremost authority on Shoshonean tribes covering the period of 1860-1902, has this to say:

1 *The Handbook of North American Indians North of Mexico* published in 1907, flatly states that Paiute is a term involved in great confusion. In common usage it has been applied at one time or another to most of the Shoshoni tribes of eastern Oregon, southern Idaho, western Utah, Nevada, and southern California, pp. 186-87.

"The name Paiute properly belongs exclusively to the Corn Creek tribe of southwestern Utah but has been extended to include many other tribes. In the present case the term is employed as a convenient divisional name for tribes occupying southwestern Utah and southwestern Nevada."[2] And Paviotso is not a Shoshoni tribal division but of much greater importance—it is the name of the Western Shoshoni or Snake war alliance. . . the Paviotso Confederacy.

The area held and controlled by the Shoshoni—the third largest linguistic group on the North American continent—was exceeded only by the Algonquins and Athapaskan speaking people. The inhabitants of the Shoshoni nation could be divided into three distinct classes. First there were the aristocrats, rich in horses and big game hunters, who formed the governing body. Next in succession came those with fewer horses who depended more on fishing and gathering for subsistence. These middle-class citizens seldom participated in the nomadic lifestyle of the far ranging, horse-owning hierarchy.

And finally, as in any society, there was a poorer class who did not own horses and—at least temporarily—traveled on foot. Known to the Shoshoni as Walking People (Shoshoko), they could not hunt large game and were often dependent on the generosity of their more fortunate clansmen for subsistence, which they augmented by consuming seeds, rodents, and insects. They were called "Digger" by the American intruders because of their tendency to dig for edible roots. Apparently the sophisticated arrivals from the Atlantic side of the continent had forgotten—or chose to ignore—that they too grubbed in the earth for potatoes, carrots, turnips, and onions to supplement their food supply.

Modern scribes will tell you with no basis in fact that the twenty-one Northern Paiute bands are identified as "eaters" of something such as fish, seeds, birds, etc., which is meaningless. The Numa, or People as the Northern Paiute called themselves, could be any one of these designations dependent upon where they were and what they were doing at

---

2 Powell and Ingalls, Bureau of Indian Affairs Report 1873. Powell, who rose to the rank of major in the Union Army during the Civil War, was a trained scientist. He was instrumental in establishing the U.S. Geological Survey and in 1879 organized the Bureau of Ethnology for the Smithsonian Institution and was appointed the first director. He resigned from the Geological Survey in 1894 to devote himself exclusively to the Bureau of Ethnology, particularly the study of Native Americans. His books include *Instruction to the Study of Indian Languages,* published in 1880.

the time. If asked who they were when camped on a stream catching trout, they would reply, "We are fish eaters"; if gathering camas, they would say, "We are root eaters." In short, a family group could be rabbit eaters one day and grasshopper eaters the next day. Therefore, the name "eater" to classify a tribal unit is not only inaccurate but hints that little effort was made to grasp the true character of these people's infrastructure regarding tribal identity.[3] The Western Shoshoni eventually called the Northern Paiutes Rush Arrow People (Hogapagani).

Some Northern Paiute family groups did wander as far north as Harney Valley in southeastern Oregon and as far west as the lower Crooked River basin in central Oregon. Here, they lived peacefully with their more affluent kinsmen until the outbreak of the Shoshoni War. A friendly people who never harmed anyone, these timid wanderers were suddenly slaughtered by United States army personnel and their non-Shoshoni allies. Those who weren't murdered in their sagebrush wickiups were herded onto government reserves as prisoners of war, to be treated like slaves. There was no distinction made between dependent seed gatherers and the highly dangerous Snake dog soldiers insofar as killing was concerned.

In futile efforts to spare their lives, these horseless victims would plead that they were not of the warrior class. . . pleas which would fall on deaf ears. To this day, a Northern Paiute gets disturbed if called a Snake—a title which was persistently applied to the Shoshoni of eastern Oregon. Incidentally, never call a group of Western Shoshoni a "band." They are divided into clans and as one Shoshoni citizen told me, "A band sounds like we are nothing more than a herd of sheep." A Shoshoni who experienced the bitter central Oregon range war at the turn of the 20th Century holds no more use for a bleating sheep than a cattleman does. To be called a band is a grave insult to a Western Shoshoni.

Although the Shoshoni of eastern Oregon were related to the Aztecs—one of North America's most advanced native civilizations—you would tend to believe, after reading what is written about them, that they were intellectually handicapped. The early settlers—determined to claim the Ochoco as their god-given right—would describe

3 Information given to the author in interviews with members of both the Northern Paiute and Western Shoshoni tribes. For the academic point of view, see *A Guide to the Indian Tribes of the Pacific Northwest,* pp. 156-57.

the Shoshoni property owners as being "wretched, degraded and despicable. . . the meanest Indian in existence." The Shoshoni's side of the story is quite different. In the most recent publication on Native North Americans, rehashing the misjudgments of the past, it appears that nothing charitable can be said about either the Shoshoni or the Paiutes. Following are a few examples of this character assassination:[4]

"The traditional Paiute lifestyle [described as a simple organization] collapsed due to the culture shock of going directly from the Stone Age to the machine age." It just may have broken down due to mass murder. As for the Western Shoshoni: "Their hunting was done with clubs rather than bows and arrows or spears, and usually involved small game such as jack rabbits." Interesting. Just recently a Western Shoshoni told me how his ancestors hunted and killed buffalo and it wasn't with a stick. Another historian laments that "the Shoshoni survived with less in the way of worldly goods than many other Native Americans. . . they took what the land provided." The advancing white settlers did the same thing but that was considered progress.

"The Northern Paiutes" as some scholars suggest, "were sometimes designated as Snakes because they painted snakes on sticks to frighten their foes." This is a guess made by those who have followed the path of least resistance when it comes to recognition of Shoshonean traits. It is not to say that they are wrong. Perhaps the people now commonly called Northern Paiutes practiced such subterfuge but it doesn't correspond with Shoshonean tradition. I imagine that an oriflamme—the eight-foot long Shoshoni battle lance decorated with eagle feathers and sporting a 12 to 18 inch obsidian spearhead—inspired more terror than a snake painted on a stick.

Some would have you believe that the name "Snake" was applied to these people because they lived along the Snake River in Oregon, Idaho, and Wyoming. In reality the river was named for them and rightfully should have been called the Shoshoni River. In all probability the term "Snake" evolved in 1744 when one of the far-ranging Verendrye brothers—French explorers—blundered into a Shoshoni hunting camp on the Powder River in what is now eastern Wyoming. This camp was a

4 Excerpts taken from *The Encyclopedia of North American Indian Tribes,* pp. 123, 155; *The Smithsonian Book of North American Indians,* pp. 62, 190; A Guide to the Indian Tribes of the Pacific Northwest, pp. 155 - 156; and *The Native Americans,* p. 14.

detachment of the Big Lodge (Tuziyammo) clan whose intertwined furniture and huge willow-woven lodges were the envy of the Shoshoni nation. Through a misinterpretation of the Indian sign language—a graceful movement of arms and hands weaving imaginary willow lodges—Verendrye decided these natives must be "Gens de Serpents. . . the Snakes." From that day forward, Europeans referred to the Shoshoni (a name they, themselves, did not use) as Snakes.

Now, let's tackle the thorny issue of the Western Shoshoni now classified as Bannocks. These citizens were originally Walking People (Shoshoko), who by whatever means came in handy, again became horse-borne and under the now accepted definition became Mounted Paiutes. The aristocrats of the Western Shoshoni Nation for obvious reasons, called these horse rustlers "Banattees" meaning Robbers. As an in group in the Shoshoni ranks, the Robbers called themselves "Pannakwate" or Hair Tossed Over the Head People from their habit of wearing their hair in a pompadour over their forehead. The Mounted Paiutes called their Shoshoni compatriots "Wikin-nakwate" or The Ones on the Iron Side, thereby acknowledging the cultural superiority of the Snakes. By 1812, the Robbers had made contact with early fur traders who soon rendered Banattee and Pannakwate into a variety of forms which ultimately became "Bannock." Dr. Sven Liljeblad in his research of the *Idaho Indians in Transition 1805-1960* would stress that nowhere was there a Bannock society separated culturally or politically from the Western Shoshoni society.[5] You can't put it any stronger than that.

In 1852, at the height of westward migration, the powerful Shoshoni nation—the ruling class torn by internal strife over how to deal with the advancing Americans—split into two separate governing bodies. In a political conflict between the hawks and the doves, the militant followers of Wolf Dog (Weahwewa)—occupying eastern Oregon, northern Nevada and southern Idaho—would become the Western Shoshoni Nation. The peace followers of Gourd Rattler (Washakie)—moving into eastern Idaho, northern Utah and western Wyoming—became the Eastern Shoshoni Nation. Many of the noncombatants now classified as

5 The field work conducted by such men as Dr. Liljeblad, professor of history; James Teit, anthropologist; Dr. Berry Fell, linguist; Joel Berreman, anthropologist; and Brigham Madsen, author/historian, all of whom did extensive research of Shoshonean culture, has been generally ignored and in the discoveries of Teit and Berreman, even ridiculed.

Northern Paiutes, had they been mobile, would have joined the eastern camp. At the onset of the Shoshoni war, the United States government decided that it would be wise to endorse the eastern faction as being Shoshoni while officially branding the Western Shoshoni as renegade Snakes. No doubt the federal government was hoping that the Shoshoni rebellion would fade away. . . which it still wishes would happen some 145 years later.

Yes, the Native Americans inhabiting eastern Oregon in the latter half of the 19th Century. . . the fearless Paviotso dog soldiers who held the United States Army at bay for a decade were Western Shoshoni. Seven years after the close of the first Shoshoni war and three years before the second violent outbreak occurred, an official government Indian census was taken in 1875. Among the Indians held on the Klamath Reserve in Oregon, the Yakima Reserve in Washington Territory and the Round Valley Reserve in California, 589 of the captives were Western Shoshoni. Another 2,100 free roaming hostiles in Oregon were also Western Shoshoni. Nine hundred of these freedom fighters were specifically identified as Has No Horse's (Ochecholes) White Knife dog soldiers (Renegades). Equally important, in regard to the Indians known as Paiutes, none resided nor were any confined on reservations in Oregon.[6]

This statement, taken from the official report of the commissioner of Indian affairs, further added to the confusion of identity of the Shoshoni occupying eastern Oregon. In essence, the commissioner was attempting to convey that only those Snakes (Western Shoshoni) who were non-combatant were confined on a reservation—not as wards of the nation—but as prisoners of war. The War Department knew there were no Paiutes in eastern Oregon but the Interior Department, eager to make a showing, quickly accepted the starving Western Shoshoni's claim of being Paiute in an effort to protect their families and listed them as reservation Paiutes. They were, but only by the fact that they were prisoners of war. No Western Shoshoni tribe has signed a treaty with the United States government to gain reservation status.

This was at a time when the Malheur Reserve, in what is now Harney and Malheur counties, Oregon, was in full operation and being

6 *Table of Indians, Census of Tribes Living in the United States of America Omitting Those Living in Alaska,* compiled and tabulated from the Latest Official Reports of the Commissioner of Indian Affairs 1875 by Ado Hummis.

publicized as "The Great Paiute Reservation." It appears that a dedicated effort was being made by the U.S. Department of Interior's Bureau of Indian Affairs to suppress any reference to the Western Shoshoni at that time.

In 1873, five years before the second Shoshoni outbreak in eastern Oregon, Otis T. Mason—an ethnologist—began to prepare a list of all North American Indian tribes by linguistic classification. Meanwhile, James Mooney—author of *The Ghost Dance*—was engaged in preparing a similar list. This work continued for twelve years before either man or members of the Bureau of American Ethnology knew of the labors of each other in this field. The result of their endeavors was not very impressive. Sometimes individual clans within a single tribe were given distinctive tribal names which tended to confuse the issue even more. Henry Henshaw—a member of the Bureau of Ethnology—was assigned the Pacific states in an effort to come to terms with this misconception. He devoted his abilities to California and the Pacific Coast north of Oregon. Obviously Henshaw didn't think it was prudent to enter Oregon with the eastern two-thirds of the state over populated—by white standards—with hostile Shoshoni Indians.

Finally, Dr. W.J. Hoffman, under the personal direction of Major Powell, was to devote his energies to the Shoshoni. Apparently Dr. Hoffman never ventured into interior Oregon. Consequently, "various specialists" (namely college students) not directly connected with the Bureau of Ethnology were sent into the field to do the leg-work.[7] Since it would be much easier and safer to interview and study reservation Indians, the best information these investigators would obtain from hereditary enemies of the Shoshoni was based on hatred, guesswork and rumor. Because of this, Dr. Hoffman's examiners found out very little about Western Shoshoni character other than they were mean, shiftless and impoverished, just as they are described in the scholarly journals of today. If those who have the capability to right this wrong remain silent it will stay that way.

The Snakes (Western Shoshoni) were proud and highly capable freedom fighters in every sense of the word. To take them as stone-age seed-gatherers is to extend a terrible disservice to their very existence.

7 Hodge, *Handbook of North American Indians North of Mexico,* Part I, p. VIII.

Wolf Dog, Has No Horse and Paulina can stand shoulder to shoulder with Crazy Horse, Geronimo and Joseph and pass the test of time and honor.

Appendices

LIST OF SHOSHONI NAMES

BIBLIOGRAPHY

INDEX

LIST OF SHOSHONI NAMES

The following is a list of the known Shoshoni who fought to protect the Ochoco from American invasion

TRANSLATION	NAME	OTHER INFORMATION
Always Ready		Signed Bruneau Treaty 1866.
Annette Tallman	Odukeoi	Daughter of Tall Man, resident of Prineville, born 1859; mother killed by Warm Springs scouts along the John Day River in 1859.
Arrow	Ouray	Head chief Northern Utes 1859. Part Apache.
Bad Face	Wobitsawahkah; Winnemucca the Younger; Mubetawaka, Poito	Son-in-law to old Winnemucca (One Moccasin); wife Tuboitonie; surrendered June 1868; poisoned 1882.
Beads		War chief Bannock War; shot 1878.
Bear Claw	Honaunamp	Hung at The Dalles 1855.
Bear Hunter	Honauka	Chief; shot 1863.
Bear Skin		Medicine chief killed by the Arapaho in 1824. Father of Little Bearskin Dick.
Big Man	Oapiche; Oulux; Oualuck; Youluk; Howlock; Howlark; Nampa; Bigfoot; Chickocclox; Starr Wilkerson	Married Running Deer 1864; married Rainbow Woman 1867; shot 16 times in 1868 and survived; disappeared in 1869.
Big Porcupine	Muinyan	Red Wolf's war chief.
Big Rumbling Belly	Kwohitsauq	Medicine chief; father of White Man; grandfather of Wovoka (The Cutter).
Big Water	Pahwuko; Yahuskin (Water Belly)	Head chief; died in 1816.
Biting Bear	Haune Shastook; Annoyed Bear; Irritated Bear	Signed 1865 treaty; shot 1868; Always Ready's war chief.
Black Beard	Toomontso	Man Lost's war chief.
Black Buffalo	Chocktote; Chewhatney; Chatchatchuck; Chewhatne; Chokkosi; Sahtootoowe; Chocktoot; Tchaktot; Chowwatnanee; Chacchackchuck; Tchatchaktchaksn	War chief during the Sheepeater War of 1879; father of Dave Chocktote.
Black Coal	Tovuveh	Twisted Hand's war chief.

TRANSLATION	NAME	OTHER INFORMATION
Black Eagle	Wahweveh; Weahshau; Kwahu (Eagle Eye)	Often confused with Weahwewa (Wolf Dog) his half brother; brother to Paulina, Bright Eyes and Cactus Fruit. Head war chief in Sheepeater War of 1879.
Black Gun	Cameahwait; Tooitecoon	Brother to Sacajawea; died of smallpox 1847.
Black Spirit	Tamanmo; War Jack	Spiritual leader in Sheepeater War of 1879; killed by firing squad 1879.
Bloody Antler	Alatuvu	Married Mourning Dove; son-in-law to Has No Horse; daughter Rose married Dave Chocktote; shot in 1898.
Blue Bird	Chosro	Wife of Weasel Lungs; mother of Little Striped Squirrel; died of typhoid in 1838.
Boy	Natchez	Son of Bad Face; brother to Sarah Winnemucca.
Bright Eyes		Sister to Paulina and Black Eagle; married Lake Hunter; died in 1867.
Broken Knife	Shenkah; Shezhe; Shaka	Brother to Tall Man and Running Deer. Brother-in-law to Has No Horse and Pony Blanket. Married to Half Moon. Shot in 1866. Signed treaties of 1855 and 1865.
Buffalo Horn	Kotsotiala	War chief; shot in 1878.
Buffalo Meat	Ahtootoowe; Amaroko; Buffalo Meat Under the Shoulder	Signed 1865 treaty; shot in 1867.
Buffalo Tail	Peter Pahnina	Paulina's son; taken captive by Oregon Volunteers 1865; served as Warm Springs scout during Modoc War in 1873.
Burning Ember	Kooyahtovu	Wife of Old Deer Running; grandmother of Has No Horse; died of cholera 1832.
Burning Wagon	Enkaltoik; Enkaltoak; Tovucoona	Brother-in-law to Paulina, Black Eagle and Wolf Dog; shot in 1864.
Butterfly	Buli	Wife of Lost His Arrow; mother of Dawn Mist and Evening Star.
Buzzard Man	Urie-wishi	Has No Horse's medicine man. Picture in *Handbook of American Indians*, p. 556.
Cactus Fruit	Puna	Sister to Paulina, Black Eagle, and Bright Eyes; married Burning Wagon.
Cold Wind	Kinauni; Kinauney	Has No Horse's son; married Snow Bunting; killed in 1868; 17 years old at the time of death.

TRANSLATION	NAME	OTHER INFORMATION
Cougar Tail	Tahretoonah; Tonouh	War chief; shot 1867.
Cow Lick	Nowweepacowick; Nowhoopacowick	Warrior; signed 1865 treaty; shot in 1868.
Coyote Hair	Ishauya	Warrior; signed treaty of 1855 (No. 88).
Crooked Leg	Paseego	Married Lost Woman; Washakie's father; killed by Blackfeet in 1824.
Cut Hair	Wiskin	Medicine chief; succeeded by White Cloud (a white man named James Kimball).
Dancer	Genega Taniwah; Tauwadah; Tanwahda; Tanwah	Spiritual leader; shot in 1878.
Dawn Mist		Daughter of Lost Arrow; wife of Has No Horse; mother of Mourning Dove, Mountain Breeze, Red Willow, Cold Wind and Spotted Fawn; shot in 1866.
Dead Deer	Masiduedeeheah; Mike Daggett; Shoshoni Mike	Shot by the Nevada State Police in 1911.
Death Rattle	Tamowins	Paulina's medicine man; shot in 1864.
Deer Fly	Mohwoomkah; Mouche De Daim (Fly of the Deer)	Son of Old Deer Running; brother to The Horse and Iron Wristbands; shot in 1856.
Elk Calf	Chaizralelio	War chief; married to Summer Hair; shot in 1865.
Elk Tongue		War chief; shot in 1787.
Evening Star	Ashohu	Sister to Dawn Mist; married to Pony Blanket; shot in 1878.
Falling Star	Shohu	Wife of Paulina; spiritual leader; sometimes called Wild Wind.
Fish Man	Numaga	Minor Paiute head man who signed the 1863 Ruby Valley Treaty.
Four Crows	Watsequeorda	Clan chief; face branded in 1845 by members of Lost Wagon Train; shot as a prisoner of war in Oct. 1867.
Fox	Wahi	Surger, son-in-law to Left Hand; married Willow Girl; shot in 1878.
Funny Bug	Leliotu	Sister of Lame Dog; wife of Black Eagle; sister-in-law to Paulina.
Good Man	Teyuwit, Tasowitz	Clan chief.

TRANSLATION	NAME	OTHER INFORMATION
Gourd Rattler	Washakie; Washaki; Washano; Washekeek; The Rattler; Pinaquanah (Smells of Sugar); Rawhide Rattle; Shoots Straight; Sure Shot; Shoots-On-The-Fly; Shoots Buffalo Running; Gambler's Gourd; Buffalo Killer	Son of Crooked Leg and Lost Woman; head chief eastern Shoshoni nation; died February 23, 1900 of old age.
Grass Woman	Boinaiv; Porivo; Sacajawea	Sister to Black Gun; died December 20, 1812 at Fort Manuel.
Gray Head	Tosarke	Spiritual leader; shot in 1866.
Great Rogue	Tasokwainberakt; Le Grand Coquin	Weighed 275 pounds; head chief.
Ground Owl	Tecolote	War chief; shot in 1866.
Hairy Man	Poemacheoh	Clan chief; shot in 1864.
Half Horse	Peeyeam	War chief; shot in 1879.
Half Moon		Sister to Has No Horse; wife of Broken Knife; mother of Mattie Shenkah; prophet; murdered in April 1864.
Has No Horse	Cho-cho-co; Chocho-co-i; Shosho-ko; Chok-ko-si; Ochoco; Ocheko; Ocheo; Otsehoe; Ochoho; Ochiko; The Man Who Has No Horse; Albert Ochiho	Son of The Horse and Little Striped Squirrel; grandson of Old Deer Running; married Dawn Mist; children: Red Willow, Cold Wind, Mourning Dove, Mountain Breeze and Spotted Fawn; granddaughter Agnes Banning Philips; grandsons Tom, Dick, and Harry Ochiho; great grandson Burdette Ochiho. Signed 1869 treaty; shot in 1898 but survived. He was serving a two year prison sentence in Reno, Nevada when he died in 1914.
Hawk	Walkara (Hawk of the Mountains)	Head chief of the southern Utes.
High Head	Kälama; Kalim	Clan chief; signed treaty of 1855.
Honey Bear	Penointi	Sister to Pony Blanket; married Pipe; shot, 1878.
Horn	Ala; Mopeah	Sometimes called Horned Chief or Horn of Hair on Forehead; war chief in Bannock War; shot in 1878.
Horse Trap	Hadsapoke	War chief; shot in 1867.
Iron Crow		Gourd Rattler's war chief.
Iron Wristbands	Pahdasherwahundah Hiding Bear	Brother to The Horse and Deer Fly; Has No Horse's uncle; succeeded Yellow Hand in 1842; died in 1842 of natural causes.

TRANSLATION	NAME	OTHER INFORMATION
Jerk Meat		Married Grass Woman's (Sacajawea) imposter; had five children; warrior with Gourd Rattler's eastern Shoshoni.
Lake Hunter	Pagorits; Lapakugit	Warrior; imprisoned at Fort Klamath in 1866; killed in 1867.
Lame Dog	Shirriitze; Sheapchis; Shezhe	Brother to Funny Bug; brother-in-law to Black Eagle; executed in 1867.
Laughing Hawk	Tambiago; Laughing Jack	War chief; hung in 1878.
Lean Man	Torepe	Warrior; married Sorrowful Woman; shot in 1864.
Left Hand	Otiz; Owitze; Oete; Oits; Awiteitse; Owits; Oytes; Oitis; Oites; Puhiawatse	Prophet; grandson of Twisted Hand; father of Willow Girl; father-in-law to Fox.
Leggins	Cheegibah	Son of Natchez; grandson of Bad Face; associated with Yellow Jacket.
Little Bearskin Dick	Honalelo	Medicine chief; shot under a flag of truce in 1878. Son of Bear Skin.
Little Cloud	Okuwa	Married Red Willow.
Little Foot	Walsac	Associated with Big Man.
Little Lizard	Nana; Nawi; Nuni; Nooey	Signed 1865 treaty at Fort Klamath.
Little Rattlesnake	Sieta; Chihiki	Pit River war chief; surrendered in 1868; shot in 1878.
Little Shadow	Siwiin	Wife of Tall Man and mother of Annette Tallman; shot in 1866.
Little Striped Squirel	Nanawu	Daughter of Weasel Lungs; wife of The Horse; mother of Has No Horse (Ochoco).
Lost Arrow	Paiakoni	Father of Dawn Mist and Evening Star; married Butterfly; father-in-law to Has No Horse; clan chief.
Lost Woman		Daughter of Weasel Lungs and Blue Bird; wife of Crooked Leg; Gourd Rattler's mother.
Magpie Man	Uriposiwu	Sheep Killer chief; shot in 1864.
Man Lost	Pocatello; Pikatello; Pocatellah; Bokatellah; Paughatello; Man-Who-Strayed-From-The-Trail	Head chief; sons were Tom and John Pocatello.
Mattie Shenkah		Daughter of Broken Knife and Half Moon; died on death march to Fort Simcoe, Washington Territory, in 1879.

TRANSLATION	NAME	OTHER INFORMATION
Moses Brown	Motcunkasket; Moshunkoskkit; Moshenkosket; Moskosket; Moskosket; Moghenkaskit; (Modoc name: Pomoaks)	Head chief; listed in historical records as a Yahooskin Snake, but there was no such tribe.
Mountain Breeze		Has No Horse's daughter; married Wolf Jaws; shot in 1868.
Mountain Fog	Pogonip	Deer Fly's son; cousin to Has No Horse; shot in 1868.
Mountain Lamb	Umentucken	Red Wolf's daughter; married Joe Meek; killed by a Banattee arrow in 1836.
Mourning Dove	Huwitubic	Has No Horse's daughter; married Bloody Antler.
No Ribs	Kewatsana; Kepoweetka	Sub-chief; signed 1865 treaty; shot in 1867.
Old Bull	Teverewera	Warrior in Bannock War; escaped to Canada in 1878.
Old Deer Running		Father of The Horse, Iron Wristbands, and Deer Fly; married Burning Ember; died of cholera in 1836.
Old Woman	Lamneya	Taken prisoner on Lookout Mountain, June 1864.
One Eye	Giltewa	Warrior blind in one eye; prisoner at Fort Klamath in 1866.
One Moccasin	Wunamuca; Winnemucca; Onennemucca; Captain Truckee; The Giver of Spiritual Gifts	Medicine chief; prophet; father-in-law of Bad Face; died in 1859 of natural causes.
Otter Bear	Pansookamotse; Pahagiveto; Otter Beard	Clan chief; killed in May 1864 during a raid on Fort Maury.
Pigeon Hawk	Kela; Kele	War chief; first Shoshoni to sign 1855 treaty; beheaded in 1860.
Pipe	Chongyo (Charlie)	Medicine man; war chief; brother-in-law to Pony Blanket; shot in 1878.
Pit Viper	Chukai; Chumi; Chua (Mud Lizzard)	Warrior in the Bannock War.
Pony Blanket	Egan; Eegan;. Ehe-gant; Ezichquegah; E.E. Gantt; Weegant; Enkaltoik	Son-in-law to Lost Arrow; married Evening Star; Has No Horse's brother-in-law; succeeded Buffalo Horn as war chief in Bannock War; beheaded in 1878.
Prairie Flower	Olsombunwas	Sister to Turkey Buzzard; threatened to kill Kit Carson; married Snake Hawk.

TRANSLATION	NAME	OTHER INFORMATION
Race Horse	Pohave; Parvekee; Pahvissign	War chief in 1878.
Rainbow Woman	Tahaka	Second wife of Big Man; taken captive in 1868.
Red Sand	Tuwa; Tabby; Taiwe; Tabbi; also known as White Eye	War chief; ally to Has No Horse; signed treaty March 2, 1868.
Red Willow	Ochiho	Son of Has No Horse and Dawn Mist; married Little Cloud; natural death.
Red Wolf	Gotia; Roux Loup; Rougeatre Loup	Head chief Shoshoni nation; often confused with Twisted Hand; father of Mountain Lamb; father-in-law to Milton Sublette and Joe Meek; died of cholera in 1852.
Rippling Voice		Daughter of Sits-Under-The-Pine; married Wolf Tail.
Rock Way	Oraibi	Sub-chief; shot in 1845.
Running Deer		Sister to Broken Knife; called "Little Dear Legs" by soldiers; married Big Man; killed in 1866.
Runs Behind		Warrior in Bannock War; friend of Laughing Hawk.
Setting Sun	Tawasi; Tawash	Wolf Dog's son; Paulina's nephew; signed treaty of 1855 at age 17.
Shell Flower	Tocmetone; Sarah Winnemucca; Sally	Daughter of Bad Face; Paiute activist; U.S. Army scout and interpreter.
Six Feathers		Warrior; leader of Snake scouts; killed by Gourd Rattler in 1867.
Snake Hawk	Wakachau	War chief; married Prairie Flower; signed 1865 treaty; shot in 1865.
Snow Bunting	Chisro	Daughter-in-law to Has No Horse; married Cold Wind; killed in April 1868.
Snow Spider	Kokyou	War chief; shot in 1868.
Sorrowful Woman		Wasco slave found in 1859; married Lean Man.
Speaking Spring	Chakpahu	Medicine chief; died in 1854.
Spotted Elk	Chaizra; Boss; Medicine John	Spiritual leader; shot in 1878.
Spotted Fawn	Sowinwalelio	Has No Horse's daughter; married Woman Helper; shot in 1868.
Spotted Rabbit	Sowiette	Sometime friend of Gourd Rattler; peaceful chief 1840-1860; Snakes wanted his scalp for being a traitor.

TRANSLATION	NAME	OTHER INFORMATION
Starving Dog	Goship	Clan chief; bullet removed all of his teeth.
Stiff Finger	Taghee	War chief; died in 1871; signed the Treaty of Peace and Friendship in 1863.
Storm Cloud	Gshaneepatki; Shaw-nee	War chief; shot in 1878.
Summer Hair		Sister to Turkey Buzzard; married Elk Calf; their daughter, Rosa Summer Hair, was placed on the Umatilla Reservation where her picture was taken by Major Lee Moorehouse.
Sun Hunter	Tebechya; Tebachne	Warrior; member of treaty council of 1868.
Swamp Man	Pahragodsohd	Warrior; shot in 1866 on Dry Creek.
Sweet Root	Tashego; Jageon; Pasego; Passequah; Pashego; Petego; Pasheco	Snake prophet who caused much religious unrest among the Pacific Northwest tribes in the 1860s and 70s.
Swooping Eagle	Tobe	Guide for Lewis and Clark; died of typhoid in 1838.
Tall Man	Odukeo; Tokio; Injun Charley	Father of Annette Tallman; warrior; brother to Broken Knife; shot in 1866.
The Climber	Tendoy	Chief of the Lemhi Snakes; defector.
The Cutter	Wovoka; Jack Wilson	Son of White Man; founder of the Ghost Dance religion; died September 20, 1932.
The Horse		Father of Has No Horse; son of Old Deer Running; brother of Iron Wristbands (Hiding Bear) and Deer Fly; shot by the Blackfeet in 1833.
Three Coyotes	Ponce; Shoshoni Jack; Bannock Jack; Snake John; Big John; Paiute John; Ishaui; Big Bill; Bannock Bill	With the Mormon John D. Lee in the Mt. Meadow massacre in southwest Utah September 11, 1857. Mother was Apache; tracked down Cochise for the army.
Tiny Ant	Leliotu	Married Sun Hunter; captured and imprisoned at Fort Vancouver in 1864.
Tobacco Root	Kooyah; Chemma; Cheonma	Warrior; signed 1865 treaty.

TRANSLATION	NAME	OTHER INFORMATION
Turkey Buzzard	Wishoko; Wiskaka	Brother to Prairie Flower and Summer Hair; brother-in-law to Snake Hawk and Elk Calf; doctor who treated Lt. Fremont; signed treaty of 1855; shot in 1868.
Twisted Hair		Clan chief; shot in 1838.
Twisted Hand	Owitze; Bad Left Hand; Mauvais Gauche	Took control of Shoshoni nation in 1785; grandfather of Left Hand; shot in 1837.
Walking Rock	Oderie; Omrshee	Chief of Nevada Snakes; ally to Has No Horse.
War Hoop	Weerahoop	Warrior.
War Spirit	Paulina; Paluna; Pushican; Paninee; Panaina; Poloni; Paulini; Paunina; Pichkan; Pelinis; Pannina; Purchican; The Brutal Devastator;	Has No Horse's number one war chief; had a scar on his forehead from Gourd Rattler's war axe; signed treaty of 1855; married Falling Star; brother to Black Eagle, Bright Eyes, and Cactus Fruit; half-brother to Wolf Dog; father of Buffalo Tail shot in May 1867.
Water Lizard	Momobic; Monoa	Medicine man; at Council Ruby Valley, Nevada, October 1, 1863.
White Cloud	James P. Kimball	Succeeded Cut Hair as Wolf Dog's medicine chief; a native American born in New York state in 1829; taken captive by Bear Killer Snakes in 1848; escaped in 1859.
White Man	Tavibo; Taviwunshear; Taysoba	Married into Walking Rock's band; father of Wovoka (The Cutter); spiritual leader; died 1870.
Willow Girl	Ohoctume	Daughter of Left Hand; married to Fox; shot in 1867.
Winter Frost	Oyike	Prophet.
Wolf Dog	Weahwewa; Weahweah; Kwewa; Wasenwas; Wewawewa; Weyouwewa; Yewhowewa	Succeeded Red Wolf as head chief of the Western Shoshoni Nation; half-brother to Paulina, Black Eagle, Bright Eyes and Cactus Fruit; signed treaty of 1855; shot in 1878.
Wolf Jaws	Kwewu	Son-in-law to Has No Horse; married Mountain Breeze; in 1880s was Has No Horse's medicine man. Shot by IZ sheep shooters, 1898.
Wolf Tail	Kwewatia	War chief.
Woman Helper	Tonnat; Tonoyiet	Head game driver, son-in-law to Has No Horse; married Spotted Fawn; shot in 1868.

TRANSLATION	NAME	OTHER INFORMATION
Yellow Badger	Sikamonani; Skytiattitk	War chief; shot in 1865.
Yellow Hand	Ohamagwaya; Amaquiem; Yellow Wrist	Commanche prophet; often confused with Twisted Hand; associated with Shoshoni by 1820; succeeded by Iron Wristbands (Hiding Bear) in 1842; died natural death, 1841.
Yellow Jacket	Potoptuah; Paddy Cap; Paddy; Whitka; Padé Kape	Head chief; army scout; served as a double agent; signed treaty of 1855; placed on the Duck Valley reservation on the Oregon-Nevada border in 1878; listed as a "mounted Paiute."

Note:
All historical documents and newspaper articles refer to Big Man as Oulux, which in Chinook Jargon means The Snake.

THE SNAKE WAR TRIBES
Which Comprised the Paviotso Confederacy

ENGLISH TRANSLATION	SHOSHONI TRIBE
Antelope Hunter	Togwingani, Pit River
Bear Killer	Hunipui, Hoonebooey
Big Lodge	Tuziyammo
Big Nose	Motsai, Gwinidba
Bird People	Kuyuidika, Giditika, Gidutikadu
Buffalo Killer	Saidyuka
Dog Ribs	Shirrydika
Juniper People	Lohim
Mountain People	Walpapi (a minor offshoot of the Hunipui)
Pony Stealer	Wahtatkin, Wadihtchi
Robber	Banattee, Bannock
Rye Grass People	Waradicka, Wadatika
Sheep Killer	Tukaricka, Tukuarika, Tukaduka
Sun Hunter	Tebeckya
White Knife	Tussawehee, Tosawi
Wild Sage People	Pohoi, Pohogwe

The northern Utes were also involved in the Confederacy.

NOTE: Such terms as "Kutshundika" (Buffalo Eaters) or "Agoitika" (Salmon Eaters), etc. were not tribal names. The same people could call themselves both depending on what they were hunting or eating at the time. Dr. Sven Liljeblad who did extensive research on the Shoshoni and their culture has this to say: "To interpret them as tribes as has frequently been done in literature is utterly wrong." Anyone who has interviewed the old-time Shoshoni will find this to be a true statement.

BIBLIOGRAPHY

Books and Articles

- Angel, Myron. *History of Nevada with Illustrations and Biographical Sketches of Its Prominent Men and Pioneers*. Oakland, 1881.
- Amundson, Carroll. *History of the Willamette Valley and Cascade Mountain Military Road Company*. University of Oregon thesis Series #17, 1928.
- Armstrong, David A. *Bullets and Bureaucrats: The Machine Guns and the United States Army 1861-1916*. Westport, New York, 1982.
- Bailey, Paul. *Walkara, Hawk of the Mountains*. Los Angeles, 1956.
- Ballantine, Betty and Ian Ballantine (Eds.). The Native Americans, Atlanta, 1993.
- Bancroft, H.H. *History of Oregon*, Vol. II, 2 vols. San Francisco, 1888.
- ———. "Scrapbooks." Vol. 93. Bancroft Library, Berkeley, California, N.D.
- Bourke, Captain John, G. *On the Border with Crook.* New York, 1891.
- Brady, Cyrus Townsend. *Northwest Fights and Fighters*. New York, 1907.
- Breckous, Joseph. *Washakie, Chief of the Shoshoni*. New York, 1927.
- Brimlow, George Francis. *Bannock War of 1878.* Caldwell, Idaho, 1938.
- Brimlow, George Francis. *Harney County and Its Range Land.* Burns, Oregon, 1980.
- Canfield, Gae Whitney. *Sarah Winnemucca of the Northern Paiutes*. Norman, Oklahoma, 1983.
- Corles, Hank. *The Weiser Indians: Shoshoni Peacemakers.* Salt Lake City, 1990.
- Corning, Howard McKinley, (ed.). *Dictionary of Oregon History*. Portland, 1956.
- DuPont, Henry A. *The Campaign of 1864 in the Valley of Virginia and the Expedition to Lynchburg*. New York, 1925.
- Fee, Chester Anders. *Chief Joseph, the Biography of a Great Indian*. New York, 1936.
- Forsyth, George A. *The Story of a Soldier*. New York, 1905.
- Freidel, Frank. *The Presidents of the United States of America*. Washington, D.C., 1981.
- Ganoe, Col. William, A. *The History of the United States Army*. A private publication by Eric Lundberg, 1964.
- Garcia, Andrew. *A Tough Trip Through Paradise 1878-1879*. New York, 1967.
- Glassley, Ray Hoard. *Pacific Northwest Indian Wars*. Portland, 1953.
- Haines, Francis. *Nez Perce and Shoshoni Influence*. Great American Series. Berkeley, California, 1945.

- Hamersley, T.H.S. *Complete Army and Navy Register of the United States of America*. N.D.
- Hanley, Mike. *Owyhee Trails: The West's Forgotten Corner*. Caldwell, Idaho, 1974.
- Harney, Corbin. *The Way It Is,* Nevada City, California, 1995.
- Harris, Jack. "The White Knife Shoshoni of Nevada." *Accumulation in Seven American Indian Tribes*. New York, 1940.
- Hasley, John. *The History of Idaho*. Boise, 1910.
- Hawthorne, Julian. *The History of the United States: 1846-1912*, Vol. III. 3 vols, New York, 1912.
- Hayes, Rutherford B. *Diary and Letters of Rutherford B. Hayes*. 5 vols. Columbus, Ohio, 1922-1926.
- Hebard, Grace R. *Washakie: An Account of Indian Resistance of the Covered Wagons and Union Pacific Railroad Invasion of Their Territory*. Cleveland, Ohio, 1930.
- Heline, Theodore. *The American Indian*. Los Angeles, 1952.
- Hodge, Fredrick Webb, (ed.). *Handbook of North American Indians North of Mexico*. 2 vols., Bureau of American Ethnology, Smithsonian Institution Bulletin 30. Washington, D.C., 1907.
- Holbrook, Stewart. *Burning an Empire*. New York, 1943.
- Hooper, Albon W. *Indian Affairs and Their Administration, 1849-1860*. University of Pennsylvania Thesis, N.D.
- Hopkins, Sarah Winnemucca. *Life Among the Piutes: Their Wrongs and Claims*. Privately printed, 1883.
- Howard, Gen. O.O. *Autobiography*. 2 vols., New York, 1907.
- ———. *Famous Indian Chiefs I Have Known*. New York, 1908.
- ———. *My Life and Personal Experiences Among Our Hostile Indians*. Hartford, 1907.
- ———. *Nez Perce Joseph*. Boston, 1881.
- Hunter, George. *Reminiscences of an Old Timer: The Bannock War*. San Francisco, 1887.
- Jackson, Helen Hunt. *A Century of Dishonor*. Boston, 1901.
- Jackson, Royal and, Jennifer Lee. *Harney County, an Historical Inventory*. Burns, Oregon, 1978.
- Josephy, Alvin M., (ed.). *The Great West*. New York, 1965.
- Karolevitz, Robert F. *Newspapering in the Old West*. New York, 1965.
- Knight, Oliver. *Following the Indian Wars: The Story of the Newspaper Correspondents Among the Indian Campaigners*. Norma, Oklahoma, 1960.
- Klapthor, Margaret Brown. *The First Ladies*. Washington, D.C., 1981.

- Kimerlin, H.B. *History and Geologist's Report of the Mayflower Group of Mines*. Berkeley, California, 1926.
- Kopper, Philip. *The Smithsonian Book of North American Indians*. Washington, D.C., 1986.
- Lefarge, Thomas H. *Memoirs of a White Crow Indian*. New York, 1928.
- Liljeblad, Sven. *The Idaho Indians in Transition,* 1805-1960. Pocatello, Idaho, 1972.
- Longstreet, Stephen. *War Cries on Horseback*. Garden City, New York, 1970.
- Landrum, Francis S. *Guardhouse, Gallows and Graves,* Klamath Falls, Oregon, 1988.
- Lyon, Juana Fraser. "Archie McIntosh, the Scottish Scout." *Journal on Arizona History* Vol. VIII, (1966).
- Madsen, Brigham D. *The Northern Shoshoni.* Caldwell, Idaho, 1986.
- McArthur, Lewis A. *Oregon Geographic Names*. Portland, 1952.
- McCoy, Keith. *Melodic Whistles in the Columbia River Gorge*. White Salmon, Washington, 1995.
- McLoughlin, Denis. *Wild and Wooly: An Encyclopedia of the Old West.* New York, 1975.
- McNeal, William H. *History of Wasco County*. The Dalles, Oregon, 1953.
- Meacham, A.B. *Wigwam and Warpath: Or the Royal Chief in Chains*. Boston, 1875.
- Miller, Joaquin. *Shadow of Shasta: The Modoc War*. Chicago, 1881.
- Monaghan, Jay (ed.). *The Book of the American West*. New York, 1963.
- Mooney, James. *The Ghost-Dance Religion and the Sioux Outbreak of 1890*. Washington, D.C.: Bureau of American Ethnology, 14th Annual Report, 1896.
- Moorhouse, Major Lee. *Souvenir Album of Noted Indian Photographs*. Pendleton, Oregon, 1906.
- Morgan, Thomas. *My Story of the Last Indian War in the Northwest.* Portland, Oregon, 1953.
- Payne, Doris Palmer. *Captain Jack-Modoc Renegade*. Portland, 1938.
- Riddle, Jefferson C. *The Indian History of the Modoc War and the Causes That Led to it.* San Francisco, 1914.
- Rothchild, Samuel. *Reminiscences of Oregon Pioneers: The Indian War of 1878*. San Francisco, N.D.
- Ruby, Robert H. and John A. Brown. *A Guide to the Indian Tribes of the Pacific Northwest.* Norman, Oklahoma, 1986.
- Schmitt, Martin F. (ed.) *General Crook: His Autobiography.* Norman, Oklahoma, 1946.
- Schmitt, Martin F. and Dee Brown. *Fighting Indians of the West.* New York, 1968.

- Scott, Harvey W. *History of Oregon Country*. 6 vols., Cambridge, Massachusetts, 1924.
- Shaver, Fred (ed.). *The Illustrated History of Central Oregon*. Spokane, 1905.
- Slattery, Charles Lewis. *Felix Reville Brunot 1820-1898*. New York, 1901.
- Sprague, Marshall. *Massacre: The Tragedy at White River*. Boston, 1957.
- Stenberg, Millie P. *The Peyote Cult Among Wyoming Indians*. Laramie, Wyoming, 1946.
- Stewart, Patricia. *Sara Winnemucca*. Nevada Historical Society Quarterly 14, No. 4, 1971.
- Swift, Ernest. *The Glory Trail: The Great American Migration and Its Impact on Natural Resources*. Washington, D.C.: The National Wildlife Federation, 1958.
- Talbot, Ethelbert. *My People of the Plains*. New York, 1906.
- Thompson, Erwin N. *Modoc War: Its Military History and Topography*. Sacramento, 1971.
- Thompson, Col. William. *Reminiscences of a Pioneer*. San Francisco, 1912.
- Trenholm, Virginia Cole, & Maurine Corley. *The Shoshoni: Sentinels of the Rockies*. Norman, Oklahoma, 1964.
- Vestal, Stanley. *Sitting Bull*. Boston, 1936.
- Voegelin, Erminie Wheeler. *The Northern Paiute of Central Oregon: A Chapter in Treaty Making*. Indiana University: Ethnohistory No. 2, Spring, 1955.
- Wallace, Robert. *The Miners*. Alexandria, Virginia: Time-Life Books, 1976.
- Webb, Todd. *The Gold Rush Trail and the Road to Oregon*. Garden City, New York, 1963.
- Yenne, Bill. *The Encyclopedia of North American Indian Tribes,* Greenwich, Connecticut, 1986.
- Ziegler, W.H. *Wyoming Indians*. A private publication by the Episcopal Church of Laramie, Wyoming, N.D.

Government Documents, Legislative Reports and Other Official Records

- Adjutant General of Oregon. *Annual Reports,* 1869-1880.
- Bureau of American Ethnology. *Annual Reports,* 1869-1880.
- Bureau of Indian Affairs. *Annual Reports,* 1869-1880.
- Commission of Public Docks Reports. 1867-1880.
- General Laws of Oregon. 1866-1880.
- *Historical Highlights of Public Land Management 1498-1962*. Washington, D.C.: United States Department of Interior, 1962.

- Letter, Commanding General, Military Division of the Missouri to Commanding General, Military Department of the Platte, March 16, 1877. (Concerns over a Snake uprising in eastern Oregon.)
- Modoc War Official Correspondence. Bancroft Library, Berkeley, California.
- Office of Indian Affairs. *General Files, Oregon, Idaho and Nevada*, 1869-1880.
- O.I.A. *Special Files, Oregon, Idaho and Nevada,* 1869-1880.
- O.I.A. *Oregon Superintendency, Letters Sent and Received,* 1869-1880.
- O.I.A. *Idaho Superintendency, Letters Sent and Received,* 1869-1878.
- O.I.A. *Nevada Superintendency, Letters Sent and Received,* 1869-1878.
- Oregon House of Representatives Journal. 1870-1880.
- Oregon Supreme Court Library. *McKay Verses Campbell Case No. 8839 and 8840, District Court D, Oregon, September 26, 1870; November 7, 1871.*
- Records, Department of Medicine. Willamette University, Salem, Oregon.
- Schuette, C.N. *Quicksilver in Oregon.* State Department of Geology and Mineral Industries, Bulletin No. 4. Salem, 1938.
- U.S. Adjutant General Office. *General Orders, Special Orders and Circulars*, 1869-1880.
- U.S. Army Department of the Columbia. *Commands and Annual Reports*, 1869-1879.
- U.S. Army Division of the Pacific. *General Orders, General Court Martial Orders, Special Orders and Circulars*, 1869-1879.
- U.S. Army Department of the Platte. *Military Correspondence*, 1876-1878.
- U.S. Department of the Interior. *Bureau of Indian Affairs Report,* 1873.
- U.S. Department of the Interior. *General Files, Oregon*, 1869-1880.
- U.S. Land Office Documents. *The Dalles City, Oregon*. Series No. 2896.
- U.S. National Archives Records. *Office of Indian Affairs*, 1869-1880.
- U.S. Secretary of the Interior. *Annual Reports to Congress*, 1869-1880.
- U.S. Secretary of War. *Annual Reports to Congress*, 1869-1880.
- U.S. House of Representatives. *Executive Documents*, 1869-1880.
- U.S. Senate. *Committee Reports and Executive Documents*, 1869-1880.
- U.S. Senate. *Bill 695.*

Miscellaneous Publications, Magazine Articles and Letters

- *Army and Navy Journal*, Vols. XII-XV. June 1875-June 1878.
- Brimlow, George F. "The Life of Sarah Winnemucca." *Oregon Historical Quarterly.* June, 1952.
- Burdette Ochiho to Gale Ontko, letter dated Klamath Falls, Oregon. August 4, 1956.

- Chinn, Lt. Col. George M. *The Machine Gun*, Vols. I and IV, Navy Bureau of Ordinance.
- Collier, A.J. *A Geologist With the Oregon Bureau of Mines and Geology*. Salem, Oregon, 1914.
- *Corrine Idaho Record*, Vol. 13, No. 1. August 25, 1877.
- Crook County Mining Register. *Ochoco Mining District Records*, 3 vols. Prineville, Oregon.
- *Dictionary of American Biology*, Vols. VIII and XIV.
- *Dictionary of the Chinook Jargon.* J.K. Gill & Co. Portland, Oregon, 1889.
- Clark, Keith and Donna (eds.). *Daring Donald McKay: Or the Last Trail of the Modocs*, Oregon Historical Society. Portland, Oregon, 1971.
- *How to Kill a Nation: U.S. Policy in Western Shoshone Country Since 1863.* Western Shoshoni National Council, P.O. Box 210, Indian Springs, Nevada, 89018.
- McKay, William C. *McKay Papers*. Umatilla County Library, Pendleton, Oregon.
- Matthew Cullen to Gale Ontko, letter dated Portland, February 5, 1971. *Oregon Historical Society List of Warm Springs Scouts Serving in the Snake and Modoc Wars.*
- National Archives Publication No. 2598, Military Department of the Platte, July 3, 1878 (concerning the Bannock War).
- O'Callaghan, Jerry A. *The Disposition of the Public Domain in Oregon*. Washington, D.C. 1960.
- Oregon Historical Society. *Oregon Historical Quarterly*, Vols. III, IX, X, XI, L, LXVIII, LXXIX.
- *City Directory*. Portland, Oregon, 1875.
- Reid, ______. *Progress of Portland for the Year Ending 1877-1878*, a pamphlet published in 1879 by the Secretary of the Portland Board of Trade.
- Rinehart, W.V. *Unpublished Manuscript.* Bancroft Library, Berkeley, California, N.D.
- Rinehart, W.V. "War in the Great Northwest." *Washington Historical Quarterly.* April, 1931.
- Rock Creek Mining District. *Articles of Operation*, filed in Grant County Records, Canyon City, Oregon.
- Santee, J.F. "Egan of the Paiutes." *Washington Historical Society Quarterly.* January 1935.
- Schaefer, _____. "President Grant Plays Samaritan When Wild West Show Goes Broke." *WPA Oregon Historical Records Survey for Umatilla County, Oregon.* State Archives, Salem, Oregon.
- Southworth, Jack (ed.). *Grant County in the Beginning.* John Day, Oregon, 1990.

- Steward, Julian H. "Basin-Plateau Aboriginal Sociopolitical Groups." *Bulletin 120*, Bureau of American Ethnology. Washington Printing Office, 1938.
- Steward, Julian H. "Changes in Shoshoni Culture." *Scientific Monthly*, Vol. XLIX. Washington D.C., American Association for the Advancement of Science, 1939.
- Steward, Julian H. and Wheeler-Voegelin, Erminie. *Paiute Indians,* Vol. 3. New York, 1974.
- Throckmorton, Major. "Shoshoni Must Die." *East Oregonian.* Pendleton, Oregon, July 27, 1878.
- Turby, J. David. "Hailstorm of Death." *VFW Magazine*. February 1972.
- Veazie, A.L. *Address to the Dedication of a Monument to the Pioneers of Crook County*. Prineville, Oregon, August 7, 1939.
- Western Shoshone Defense Project, Vols. 3-4. 1995-1996.

Newspapers

- Ashland Tidings (Oregon)
- Blue Mountain Eagle (John Day, Oregon)
- Carson City News (Nevada)
- Corinne Reporter (Utah)
- Daily Alta (San Francisco, California)
- Daily Bulletin (Portland, Oregon)
- Desert News (Salt Lake City, Utah)
- East Oregonian (Pendleton, Oregon)
- Elko Independent (Nevada)
- Evening Gazette (Reno, Nevada)
- Evening Post (San Francisco, California)
- Evening Press (Asbury, New Jersey)
- Humboldt Register (Winnemucca, Nevada)
- Humboldt Star (Winnemucca, Nevada)
- Idaho Enterprise (Boise)
- Idaho Statesman (Boise)
- Jacksonville Reporter (Oregon)
- Nevada State Journal (Carson City)
- New York Times (New York)
- Omaha Herald (Nebraska)
- Oroville News (California)
- Oregon Journal (Portland)
- Oregonian (Portland)

- Owyhee Avalanche (Silver City, Idaho)
- Owyhee News (Owyhee, Nevada)
- Pocatello Tribune (Idaho)
- Reese River Revielle (Austin, Nevada)
- The Bulletin (Bend, Oregon)
- The Chronicle (San Francisco, California)
- The Dalles Mountaineer (Oregon)
- The Dalles Optimist (Oregon)
- The Dalles Times (Oregon)
- The Silver State (Winnemucca, Nevada)
- The Tribune (Salt Lake City, Utah)
- Twin Falls Times (Idaho)
- Virginia City Union (Nevada)
- Washington Chronicle (Washington, D.C.)
- Wells Herald (Elko, Nevada)

INDEX

THUNDER
OVER THE OCHOCO

VOLUME I: *The Gathering Storm*

Covering hundreds of years from pre-Columbian times to the collapse of the world fur trade in 1840, Volume I meets the Shoshoni Indians before the arrival of the Europeans and tracks their rise from peaceful eastern Oregon agriculturists to the aggressive Snake war tribes, rulers of the Pacific Northwest. By 1812, they had clashed with every major world power in their jealous guardianship of a land they called Oyerungun. Their undisputed hunting grounds beyond the setting sun would soon become coveted by white foreigners searching first for precious metals and later for valuable fur-bearing animals. The gathering storms of hatred would hover ominously on the distant horizons. Volume I chronicles the events which inevitably would lead to war.

VOLUME II: *Distant Thunder*

The twenty-year period between 1840 and 1860 would see overland migration across the land known to the Shoshoni as the Ochoco—Land of the Red Willow. The Americans would call it eastern Oregon. Never on friendly terms with the white invaders, the Shoshoni tolerated passage across their ancestral hunting grounds only so long as the American homesteaders stayed strictly on the dusty thoroughfare called the Oregon Trail. When they transgressed, the distant thunder of gunfire reverberated across interior Oregon like the tolling of a death knell. Volume II narrates the suffering, heartache and death of those unfortunate souls who dared to venture into the Ochoco; and it covers the first brutal Indian wars fought west of the Mississippi River.

VOLUME III: *Lightning Strikes!*

Between 1860 and 1869 rich deposits of gold were discovered in eastern Oregon, and the citizens of the Willamette Valley were out to claim their share at any cost. Shoshoni dog soldiers were equally determined that they keep to their side of the Cascade barrier. War was officially declared. The opposing forces went for each other's throats locked in a death struggle that seemed endless. The crashing crescendo of thunder was accompanied by lightning strikes of destruction which ricocheted into four western states—and the military campaign they thought would last but a few weeks stretched into years. In flashing raids, Shoshoni dog soldiers humiliated the Oregon Cavalry, taking a deadly toll on mining settlements, homesteads, stagecoaches and wagon trains. It would take a battle-hardened army baptized in the carnage of the Civil War four years to bring the Shoshoni to their knees: an aggressor with unlimited resources pitted against a foe that was undermanned, undernourished and outgunned—but desperately fighting for survival. Volume III is the story of the first violent Shoshoni outbreak, which would again erupt in the 1870s.

VOLUME IV: *Rain of Tears*

The thirteen year interval between 1866 and 1879 would witness monumental changes in the Ochoco. With the surrender of Has No Horse's battered army, western Oregon had free rein to exploit the Ochoco as it saw fit. In a blind daze, the Shoshoni would witness frontier towns springing up where their lodges had once stood. As thousands upon thousands of bawling cattle and sheep trampled their ancestral hunting grounds to dust, the proud warriors of a by-gone year again rebelled. And, for a fleeting moment, shook the state of Oregon to its very foundations. Then it was over. Stripped even of reservation rights, the few survivors drifted between the four winds on their final journey into the bitter rain of tears.

VOLUME V: *And the Juniper Trees Bore Fruit*

Between 1880 and 1916, the birth of industry would give vent to new bloodshed in the Ochoco. Six-shooters roared in the night, ranchers disappeared never to be seen again. . . and the juniper trees bore fruit: the dangling bullet-ridden bodies of men whose only crime was to oppose the land barons who ruled old Crook County with a Winchester rifle and a rawhide rope. As the 19th century staggered to a close, a Shoshoni visionary born in the Ochoco foretold the rebirth of Indian supremacy. His wondrous dream was buried in a common grave at Wounded Knee, South Dakota. By the time the 20th century blundered onto the scene, saddle-blanket blazes hacked into the Ochoco pines marked the deadlines between sheep and cattle range and woe unto him who crossed these barriers. Rifle shots echoed the length and breadth of the Deschutes canyon as the Hill-Harriman railroad giants battled to link central Oregon to the outside world. Ironically, the last Indian war fought in the United States would explode on the Oregon-Nevada border in 1911 when a Shoshoni chief led his followers, armed only with bows and arrows, in a suicidal charge against a group of stockmen. Thus ended the *Thunder Over the Ochoco*. Would the new owners do a better job of managing the land they had wrenched from the Shoshoni? I leave that to other writers to decide.